About Island Press

Island Press is the only nonprofit organization in the United States whose principal purpose is the publication of books on environmental issues and natural resource management. We provide solutions-oriented information to professionals, public officials, business and community leaders, and concerned citizens who are shaping responses to environmental problems.

In 1999, Island Press celebrates its fifteenth anniversary as the leading provider of timely and practical books that take a multidisciplinary approach to critical environmental concerns. Our growing list of titles reflects our commitment to bringing the best of an expanding body of literature to the environmental community throughout North America and the world.

Support for Island Press is provided by The Jenifer Altman Foundation, The Bullitt Foundation, The Mary Flagler Cary Charitable Trust, The Nathan Cummings Foundation, The Geraldine R. Dodge Foundation, The Charles Engelhard Foundation, The Ford Foundation, The Vira I. Heinz Endowment, The W. Alton Jones Foundation, The John D. and Catherine T. MacArthur Foundation, The Andrew W. Mellon Foundation, The Charles Stewart Mott Foundation, The Curtis and Edith Munson Foundation, The National Fish and Wildlife Foundation, The National Science Foundation, The New-Land Foundation, The David and Lucile Packard Foundation, The Pew Charitable Trusts, The Surdna Foundation, The Winslow Foundation, and individual donors.

When City and Country Collide

When City and Country Collide

Managing Growth in the Metropolitan Fringe

Tom Daniels

ISLAND PRESS
Washington, D.C. • Covelo, California

Library of Congress Cataloging-in-Publication Data
Daniels, Tom.
When city and country collide : managing growth in the metropolitan fringe / Tom Daniels.
p. cm.
Includes bibliographical references and index.
ISBN 1-55963-597-5 (paper)
1. Metropolitan areas—United States—Planning. 2. Regional planning—United States. 3. Land use—United States—Planning. I. Title.
HT334.U5D35 1999 98-42236
307.1'216'0973—dc21 CIP

Printed on recycled, acid-free paper 

Manufactured in the United States of America
10 9 8 7 6 5 4 3 2 1

To those who work to keep America a good place to live, now and for future generations.

Contents

List of Figures, Tables, and Photos

Figures

Tables

Photographs

Preface

Between the open countryside and the built-up cities and suburbs is a huge area where the landscape is growing and changing. To date, this area—which I call the metropolitan fringe or the rural-urban fringe—has been largely ignored in national policy debates. But population and economic growth pressures are vigorously pushing outward from the suburbs, causing the haphazard development of rural lands and drawing vitality from the inner cities. No longer can America afford to consider land use just a local town, city, or county issue. Rather, it is time to examine regional approaches to land use and growth management that reflect the interaction of the several counties, the core city, the many suburbs, the edge cities, and the expanding fringe that make up a metropolitan area. The implications for accommodating population and economic growth, as well as issues of environmental quality and competitiveness in the global economy, are profound.

The fringe is where America's struggles over population growth and the development of open space are most visible and bitter. New or improved growth management programs are needed to avoid development that wastes land, is expensive to service, and diverts private investment and public funds from existing cities and towns. Also, many federal, state, and local spending, taxation, and regulatory programs that encourage sprawling development need to be reformed.

In the 1970s and 1980s, local and national media were largely silent about the fringe. But in the 1990s, sprawling suburban housing subdivisions and shopping malls eating up remaining open space caught the attention of local media and led to some national coverage. Yet, while the media may lament the construction of houses on fields that had been farmed for centuries, there is usually a "progress is inevitable" spin to the stories.

The media, along with concerned citizens and several land-use experts, have ably described the painful consequences of sprawl: the conversion of farmland, the parceling of timberlands, soaring infrastructure and transportation costs, loss of wildlife habitat, increased air pollution from more vehicles traveling more miles, and water pollution from the widespread use of on-site septic systems. But formulating and implementing solutions to sprawl and managing growth in the fringe have seemed elusive. As the nation's population and economy expand, the challenges of managing growth in the fringe will become more heated and complex.

One purpose of this book is to illustrate and evaluate the nationwide struggles to manage such growth and development. Another purpose is to provide a wake-up call to schools of planning. Planning schools have traditionally focused on urban areas, even though for the past three decades most of the inner cities of the United States have been losing population, economic strength, and political clout to the suburbs. Planning jobs in the fringe will be a growth industry. The zoning counter in the big cities will not.

A third purpose of the book is to alert national policy makers in Washington, D.C., to the fact that federal spending programs are encouraging the development of the fringe to the detriment of older suburbs and inner cities. The outcome is expensive new roads, schools, and sewer and water facilities being built in fringe areas, while older infrastructure deteriorates.

Fourth, the book aims to show city dwellers and those who live in the fringe that they have a common interest in managing the growth of the fringe. If the cities continue to decline, more people will flood the fringe. And if the fringe simply opens the gates, which has been pretty much the case, then cities will be harder pressed to compete for state and federal grants for education, transportation, and sewer and water plants.

The rural-urban fringe is America's land-use battleground. Here, developers, long-term landowners, quick-buck land speculators, politicians, and realtors are matched against other long-term landowners, politicians, environmentalists, and newcomers who want to keep their new communities attractive and fiscally manageable. These different interests must learn to work together rather than fight pitched, and often protracted, battles over what land gets built on and with how many stores, offices, or homes. The current contentious system of land development versus land conservation serves neither end. Much of the development that is built relies on public subsidies for infrastructure; and many conservation projects are too small and isolated to protect a sustainable amount of wildlife, watersheds, farmland, and forestlands.

Growth management means striking a balance between economic and population growth on the one hand and land development and environmental quality on the other. In recent years, rising affluence and continued urban problems have made the rural-urban fringe more attractive. As a result, the challenge of growth management in the fringe has become more intense. Traditional farm and timber landowners are having greater difficulty making a living off the land,

and communities are struggling to accommodate increasing populations and the houses, businesses, and industry that result.

Inhabitants of dozens of fringe communities across the United States have recognized the threats of uncontrolled residential and commercial sprawl. In response, politicians with public support have implemented land-use and spending programs to manage growth. In a few cases, state governments have stepped in to require local governments to plan for both growth and the conservation of land and natural resources. This is not just an intellectual exercise. Business owners and managers have come to recognize that workers want a safe, attractive, affordable, and healthy place to live and work. Like businesses, people want communities where they can put down roots and invest with confidence. To make these desires a reality requires changes at the state, federal, and local levels of government. Tom Hylton, Pulitzer Prize–winning author of *Save Our Land, Save Our Towns,* believes that ultimately it will take a change in personal values: More people must be willing to live in the inner cities and older suburbs and forge good communities, rather than move to the fringe in search of the American Dream of a single-family, detached home with a large lawn and a big garage.

As the nation's population increases each year, the availability of sustainable places to live and work, with high environmental quality, will emerge as a national priority. This book describes and illustrates several ways to achieve more sustainable communities in the rural-urban fringe. The efforts must be long-term, vigorous, openly debated, publicly supported, carefully planned, and implemented by willing, committed politicians. A key ingredient to sustainable communities in the fringe will be to maintain rural industries that provide the open space and rural character that fringe residents cherish.

Chapter 1 describes the land-use struggles caused by the growth of the fringe, defines how the fringe differs from traditional suburbs, and explains the need for managing the growth of the fringe.

Chapter 2 explores the origins of the rural-urban fringe, what forces made the fringe happen and will continue to affect both the geographic growth of the fringe and the type and location of development within the fringe.

Chapter 3 takes a hard look at the obstacles to growth management in the fringe.

Chapter 4 presents the comprehensive planning process for fringe communities and counties as a way to decide where future growth should or shouldn't go. Communities then have a choice of pursuing a pro-growth strategy, balanced growth, or a no-growth or slow-growth future.

Chapter 5 illustrates several design principles for new development in the fringe and describes how new development can fit in with what is already there. Design standards can augment the effectiveness of the comprehensive plan by promoting attractive development that is sensitive to its surroundings. On a larger scale, the design of the entire community helps in the visioning element of a comprehensive plan when citizens can respond to the question, "What do you want your community to look like?"

Chapter 6 examines the impact of federal spending programs and regulations on the growth and development of the fringe. Many of these programs have subsidized development. On the other hand, environmental regulations have included standards to protect air and water quality, which are important ingredients in the overall quality of life in the fringe. This chapter suggests changes to federal spending and regulations that would improve the fairness and effectiveness of growth management in the fringe.

Day-to-day decisions affecting growth management are mainly under the control of state and local governments. Chapter 7 discusses state-level spending programs and regulations that affect the growth of the fringe.

Chapter 8 reviews the many growth management techniques that have been used in fringe areas.

Chapter 9 looks at regional planning efforts, including urban and village growth boundaries and regional governments.

Chapter 10 discusses ways to protect farmland, forestland, and natural areas to help control sprawl.

Counties and municipalities have applied a variety of programs to control both the size of the fringe and growth within the fringe. Chapter 11 evaluates the success of these efforts in a series of case studies.

Chapter 12 summarizes the search for managing growth in the fringe and discusses possible futures for fringe areas.

Citizens, elected officials, planners, landowners, and the development community should understand the issues behind growth management in the fringe and make informed choices about the future. The fringe is a finite area; successfully accommodating growth requires specific techniques and programs, and careful spending of public and private dollars. With this book, I hope to help communities form strategies to manage their growth and implement those strategies to achieve satisfying long-term results.

Tom Daniels

Acknowledgments

I wish to thank John Keller for many good suggestions and longstanding support. My wife, Katherine Daniels, read parts of the manuscript and corrected several errors. My father, Robert V. Daniels, fed me an endless stream of newspaper articles on sprawl and growth in the fringe. Deborah Bowers read an early draft and made several good suggestions. David Schuyler gave me valuable and generous advice. Mark Lapping supported my original proposal. In addition, my thanks go out to people with whom I discussed the book: John Bernstein, June Mengel, Kathleen Bridgehouse, Linda Conley, Jay Parrish, Amy Collett, Scott Standish, Jim Erkel, Lee Ronning, Phil Rainey, Jr., and my editor at Island Press, Heather Boyer.

Acknowledgments

[illegible]

CHAPTER 1

The Metropolitan Fringe: America's Premier Land-Use Battleground

It's a war. How else would you describe it?

—Til Hazel, Virginia developer

Short-term gains have been defining the character of the battlefield. The short-term gain of a few at the expense of the many—not to mention the inefficient, non-sustainable use of the land—is not right.

—Councilperson, Lorain County, Ohio

One Man's Struggle: A Cautionary Tale

Next to Clay Peterson's cattle farm, a developer has proposed building thirty-four houses on a 173-acre tract. Peterson's rolling farmland is about four miles from Interstate 83 and thirty miles northeast of Baltimore, Maryland. Peterson has owned his property for nearly twenty years, and in 1987 he sold his development rights to restrict the land to farmland and open space. He is worried that dozens of neighbors may threaten his livelihood and his way of life. Thirty-four homes could draw groundwater from the same aquifer, possibly lowering the water table and threatening his own water supply. Peterson expects to hear complaints about the smell of his cattle and is afraid his insurance rates could soar because of neighbors wandering onto his farm and possibly hurting themselves.

Clay Peterson has decided to fight the development in court, hoping either to reduce the number of houses or to force the developer to put them farther from his property line. It's too late to change the zoning next door, which allowed the houses to be clustered on one-acre lots as in a suburban subdivision. Sooner or later houses will be built next to Clay Peterson's farm.

"In two years, I'll see fifteen houses right out my front door," predicts Allen Moore, a neighbor to Peterson, adding, "this whole issue of development is a very heated one."[1]

Once the Peterson case is settled, Baltimore County planners have vowed to change the zoning to avoid future conflicts between farmers and nonfarm neighbors.

Clay Peterson's predicament encapsulates the political, legal, social, economic, and environmental struggles that are erupting all across America in the fringe countryside just beyond the suburbs. Politicians want to promote economic growth, yet they have to be sensitive to the wishes of the voters to control taxes, protect the environment, and maintain a good quality of life. Politicians, planners, and developers are trying to decide how much development should be put within cities and towns and how much in the countryside. Local governments are sensitive about imposing land-use controls that may stir up property-rights advocates or be ruled a taking of private property by the courts. For landowners, developers, and concerned citizens not satisfied with the planning process, the courts have become the forum of last resort.

Newcomers from the cities and suburbs can bring pronounced and rapid changes, and long-term rural residents, like Clay Peterson, can feel invaded. Newcomers alter the social mix, reduce the amount of open space in the landscape, and change the local political priorities. As the number of newcomers increases, owners of farmland, timberland, and open ground face rising property taxes to pay for more public services, especially schools. And lucrative offers from developers tempt rural landowners to sell.

Some observers may see the changes to the countryside as a form of "creative destruction," a term coined by economist Joseph Schumpeter to describe the process of economic growth. Silicon Valley, for example, emerged in the Santa Clara Valley on top of what was once highly productive orchard land. The contribution to economic growth made by the computer industry has far exceeded the value of growing fruit. Others, however, may claim the countryside is worth retaining as a haven from urban life or as a place to produce food and fiber.

Differing opinions about the countryside beyond the suburbs point to the fact that it has become a tremendous economic asset. The strong economy of the 1990s, along with the communications revolution of computers, modems, faxes, and e-mail, has meant that Americans have a greater choice about where to live. The highly concentrated heavy manufacturing economy of the first half of the twentieth century has given way to a global economy dominated by services and high-tech manufacturing. The owners, managers, and employees of these businesses want to live in quality environments. Christopher Leinberger, managing director of Robert Charles Lesser and Company, the nation's largest independent real estate consulting firm, explains, "In the new knowledge economy, an area's quality of life translates into economic growth. Yet the places with the highest quality of life are always at risk of being 'loved to death.'"[2]

Economists Peter Gordon and Harry Richardson point out that "most job growth, regardless of economic sector, is in the *outer* suburbs far away from downtowns and transit stations, even in the more transit-oriented metropolitan areas."[3]

A home in the country is often perceived as a better investment than one in the city or suburbs. And the rural environment may be more pleasant. There is less traffic and crime and more open space, fresh air, and privacy. But as more people move to the countryside, these amenities begin to disappear.

Much of the new housing and commercial developments in the countryside comes in one of two forms: (1) a wave of urban or suburban expansion that sweeps into the countryside; or (2) scattered housing, offices, and stores outside of established cities and towns. Both of these forms of development are called sprawl, and sprawl presents a complex and serious challenge to local, county, and regional governments seeking to manage their growth.

Growth Management

Growth management describes how people and their governments deal with change. The purpose of growth management is to provide greater certainty and predictability about where, when, and how much development will occur in a community, region, or entire state; how it will be serviced, and the type and style of development. Lack of predictability about the future growth and development of a community leads to costly struggles that may pit governments, developers, and concerned citizens against each other.

Growth management features:

- government land-use regulations, such as zoning;
- public infrastructure spending programs, such as for sewer and water facilities;
- tax policies, such as use-value taxation for farmland;
- incentives, such as a density bonus to allow a developer to build more houses on a site in return for a compact, pedestrian-oriented design.

Together these growth management techniques influence the location, amount, type, timing, appearance, quality, and cost of new private development. Growth management must encourage attractive, well-sited, and cost-effective development as much as discourage sprawling, rapid development that can be unsettling and costly to residents. The challenge to local governments is how to accommodate economic and population growth without sacrificing manageable local finances and a sense of place. The search for solutions to growth problems takes time, thoughtful debate, trial and error, and a long-term commitment of both public and private money and personnel.

Community, county, and regional land-use planning is essential for effective growth management. Planning involves the careful study and analysis of current land-use needs and the anticipation of future needs based on population projections. A comprehensive plan provides a sense of direction and goals and objectives to work toward. Planning helps create more predictable, efficient, and sustainable patterns of development.

But the more planned and predictable development becomes, the clearer it is that not every landowner is going to be able to cash in big from selling land for development. Also, some developers may want to build in the wrong place, and some communities within a region may have to accept more development than they want to.

Successful growth management programs have produced community consensus, political strength, creative development, manageable public finances, and effective land protection. Managing growth can soften the collision between urban and rural people and how they use the land. Moreover, protecting the environment while carefully placing new development is emerging as a wise and sustainable economic development strategy.

America: A Metropolitan Nation

Nearly four out of five Americans live within 273 metropolitan regions (see figure 1.1). These regions include a central city of at least fifty thousand people, suburbs around the central city, suburbs that have grown into "edge cities," and a fringe of countryside (see figure 1.2).

In the fringe, a vast war zone has erupted. The outer reaches of the metropolitan landscape still display much of the traditional pattern of small towns set amid woods, streams, mountains, and working farms or ranches. But new single-family homes, office complexes, and shopping malls are changing the rural and small town landscape to a patchwork of city, suburb, and open space. Housing subdivisions and commercial strips are sprouting along highways, at the edge of reluctant towns, and far from existing settlements in farm fields and forests.

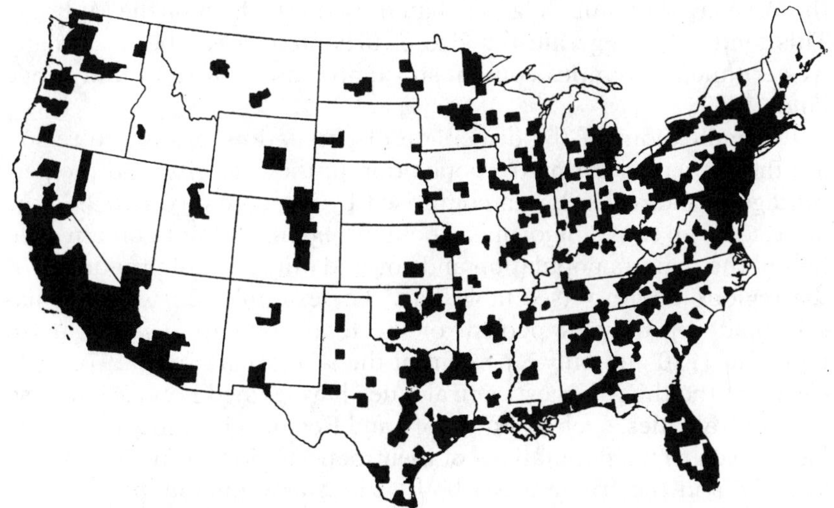

Figure 1.1 Metropolitan Counties of the United States, 1990.

In 1993, the United States Office of Budget and Management classified more than one-quarter of the nation's 3,041 counties (and similar government units) as belonging to metropolitan areas.[4] Counties included in metropolitan areas are eligible for certain federal programs that rural counties are not, and vice versa. Metropolitan areas are measured in part on the basis of commuting patterns between counties; so the more spread out the population, the greater the metro area tends to be. There is no standard geographic size for a metropolitan area. For example, the Los Angeles metro area is much larger than the Burlington, Vermont, metro area. Moreover, using a county as a unit of measurement can be misleading. Metropolitan counties in

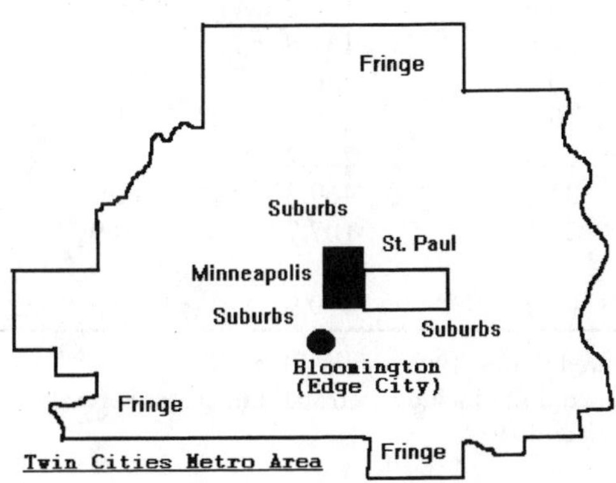

Figure 1.2 The Twin Cities Metropolitan Area.

the West are often much larger than those in the East or the Midwest. This tends to exaggerate the size of urbanized areas because many western metro counties contain substantial areas of rural and fringe land.

Two indications of the dispersion of population in a metro region are the percentage of metro population in the core city, and the percentage of metro land area comprised by the core city. In 1993, the largest city in most major metropolitan regions did not contain even half of the region's population and covered only a small proportion of the region's territory (see table 1.1).[5] For example, Boston's population made up only 14 percent of the total population in its metro region in 1990 and only 3 percent of the land area.[6] Since 1970, only eleven of the thirty largest central cities have gained population. Several central cities, such as Baltimore and Boston, continue to lose residents even as the populations of their metro regions grow. The newer suburbs and the fringe areas both attract new inhabitants, but the low-density settlement patterns in the fringe mean that the land area covered by the fringe increases dramatically and the amount of open space declines in tandem.

A prime example of metro fringe growth is the booming Greater Washington, D.C., area. The rate of population increase has been most rapid in the outlying metro counties of Virginia and Maryland, and the region is expected to lose over 300,000 acres of open land between 1990 and 2020, a rate of 28 acres a day.[7]

Table 1.1 Land Area and Population of Selected Cities and the Percentage of the Metropolitan Area and Population, 1992

City	*Population*	*Percentage of Metropolitan Region Population*	*City Land Area (square miles)*	*Percentage of Metropolitan Region Land Area**
Albuquerque	398,000	64.6	132.2	55.5
Atlanta	395,000	12.6	131.8	14.4
Baltimore	725,000	30.2	80.2	3
Boston	552,000	10.1	48.4	3
Chicago	2,768,000	32.9	227.2	6
Los Angeles	3,490,000	23.1	469.3	11
Minneapolis–	363,000	24.1	107.7	10.9
St. Paul	268,000			
Phoenix	1,012,000	43.4	419.9	50.5

Source: Statistical Abstract of the United States, 1995, tables 43, 46.
*Based on the 1980 census; the census did not include metropolitan areas. Several metro areas grew in size between 1980 and 1982.

Within many metropolitan regions, particularly in western states, there are large areas of farms, ranches, forests, or open space. Greater Phoenix, Arizona, is well known for its spread-out development pattern. Figures 1.3A and B show different views of the settlement pattern in Arizona—especially in the Phoenix metro area—obtained by using counties or census tracts as the unit of measurement. As mentioned previously metro counties have a core city of at least fifty thousand inhabitants. The census tracts cover a smaller area and are a more accurate measure of the location of population; they indicate a much larger fringe area (the striped area showing at least 2 percent of the residents commuting to the urban core) than urban core or outlying suburbs.

Despite the expansion of metropolitan regions, Americans still live on a small fraction of the nation's land. According to the Bureau of the Census, more than half of all Americans reside in the fifty largest metropolitan areas. In 1994, metropolitan counties accounted for just under one-fifth of a percent of the nation's land base. But remove the 40 percent of the nation's land owned by all levels of government and those privately owned places that are too flat, wet, cold, or remote for most Americans' tastes, and the number of desirable locations rapidly shrinks.

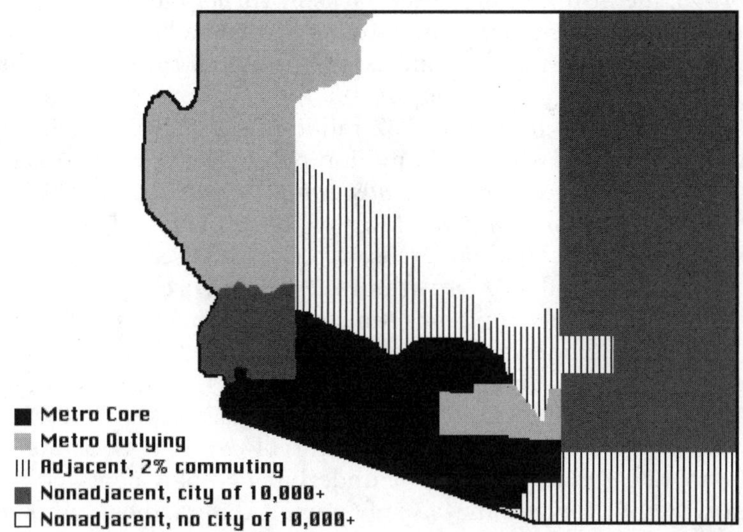

Figure 1.3A County-Based Rural-Urban Continuum, Arizona, 1990. *Source*: John Cromartie and Linda Swanson, *Defining Metropolitan Areas and the Rural-Urban Continuum*, U.S. Department of Agriculture, Economic Research Service, Staff Paper 9603, 1996.

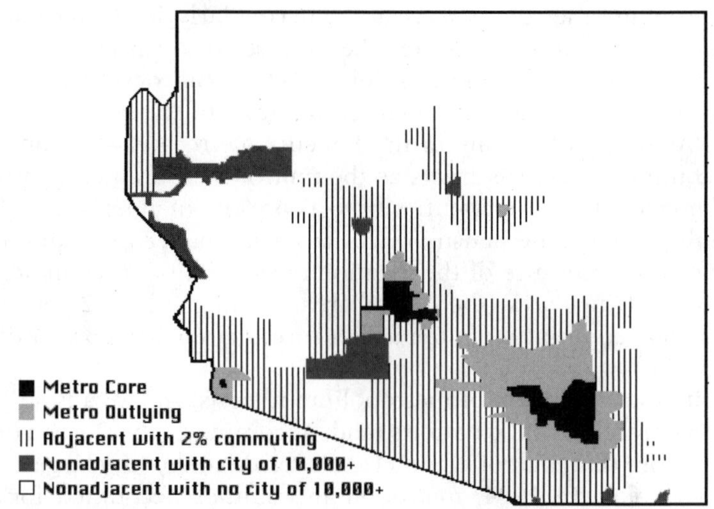

Figure 1.3B Census Tract–Based Rural-Urban Continuum, Arizona, 1990. *Source*: John Cromartie and Linda Swanson, *Defining Metropolitan Areas and the Rural-Urban Continuum*, U.S. Department of Agriculture, Economic Research Service, Staff Paper 9603, 1996.

In 1893, the historian Frederick Jackson Turner announced the end of the American frontier, meaning that America had reached the limit of its geographic expansion and population growth would result in less available space per person. By 1995, the nation's population had risen by nearly 200 million to 262 million. The Census Bureau estimates that America will add 34 million people between 1996 and the year 2010.[8] *This is equivalent to absorbing the population of another California in just fourteen years.* Most of this growth will occur in the outer fringes of metropolitan areas, as Americans search for space to live. While the population growth of the urban core lags behind that of the rest of the metro region, Americans moving to the fringe are using up more land per person than urban dwellers by purchasing large residential lots and working in campus-style office and industrial parks. Real estate consultant Christopher Leinberger predicts that "geometric increases in urbanized land will continue at a rate of at least 8 to 12 times faster than the underlying employment and population growth."[9] He cites the case of Greater Atlanta, the nation's most sprawled-out metro region, which grew from spanning 65 miles north to south to 110 miles in 1998. [10]

This continued sprawling development has a powerful impact on the cost of the necessary public services. According to a 1991 study by the Urban Land Institute, "Studies conducted over the last 30 years

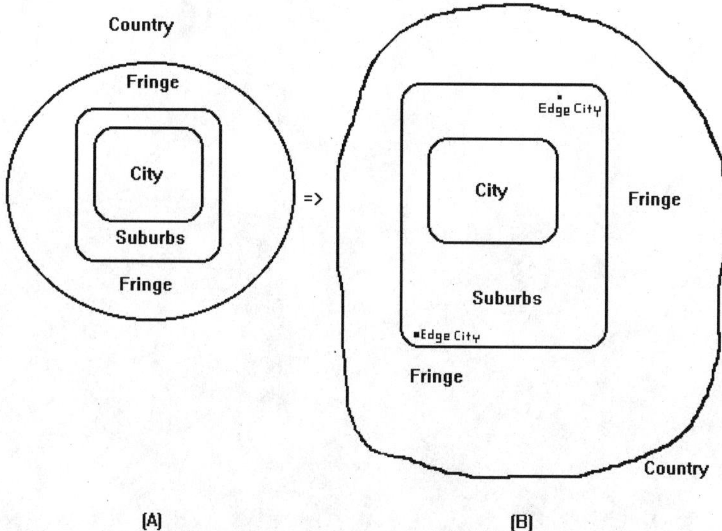

Figure 1.4 The Growth of Fringe in a Metropolitan Setting, from Panel (A) to Panel (B).

have concluded that when development is spread out at low densities, the per-unit cost of constructing and maintaining public facilities increases. The reason for this is that low-density development requires more miles of roads, curbs, sewers, and water lines; and municipal services must be delivered over a greater geographic area"[11] (see figure 1.4).

Defining the Rural-Urban Fringe

The semirural area beyond suburbia yet within its shadow has been given several names: the countrified city (Doherty), the ex-urbs (Spectorsky), semisuburbs (Louv), technoburbs (Fishman), the galactic city (Lewis), postsuburbs (Garreau), the urban fringe, and the rural-urban interface. I prefer to describe this region as *the metropolitan fringe* or *the rural-urban fringe*, a hybrid region no longer remote and yet with a lower density of population and development than a city or suburb.

Like a fringe, strips of urban and suburban "fabric" have extended into the countryside, creating a ragged settlement pattern of "subdivisions, single-family housing on five- to 10-acre lots, shopping centers, retail strips, schools, and churches all separated by farms, forests, or other open spaces."[12] Towns and villages of under ten thousand residents are adding homes and commercial buildings, especially along main roads leading in or out of the community. These

Photo 1.1 A farm and new housing developments compete for space in the metropolitan fringe.

decentralized patterns blur the distinction between rural, urban, and suburban.

Some people may see the fringe as the suburbs of the suburbs and an area for future suburban growth. Others may see the need to oppose the forces of suburbanization that threaten to turn a community into "Anywhere U.S.A." The juxtaposition of opposite ideas in the term rural-urban fringe also suggests the social, economic, and political tensions that accompany change or the threat of change.

The rural-urban fringe is best thought of not just as a geographic area within a metropolitan region, but also as a step in the development hierarchy between rural areas and a central city. The fringe is a region of middle ground between wide-open rural lands that are beyond commuting distance to a metro area, and expanding suburban residential and commercial development. America's fringe areas have emerged on the edge of cities since the early 1800s. As fringe areas gained population and economic activity, they became suburbs. As the suburbs expanded, even more rural lands became accessible, within the orbit of the metro fringe. And in the 1980s, some fringe areas at ten to thirty miles from the core city actually bypassed the suburb stage and burgeoned into edge cities with major office and retail complexes.

The obvious question arises: When does a fringe area become a suburb or edge city, and when is it just a fringe area? The answer is not clear-cut but depends on the amount of open land (more open land means more rural character), population per square mile, and the make-up of the local economy, especially the relative importance of the traditional rural industries of farming, ranching, forestry, or mining.

It is not easy to say exactly where the suburbs end and the fringe begins, partly because many sections of fringe are in the process of turning into suburbs. The landscape is being fragmented into residential and commercial lots, and more and more of the people who live there make a long commute to jobs in the suburbs or the central city. But from GIS (geographic information system) parcel maps and aerial photos, it is possible to identify where smaller, suburban-type parcels give way to the larger tracts of fringe.

The fringe includes the less developed regions of metropolitan counties and sections of many nonmetropolitan counties that border metro counties. Population density in the fringe is less than one thousand people per square mile and often less than five hundred per square mile. Fringe areas vary in size, extending from a few miles beyond small cities to forty miles or more outside of major urban centers. Agriculture is found in most fringe areas and perhaps some forestry and mineral extraction, but these land uses and industries are yielding to housing subdivisions, office complexes, and retail development, along with employment in the growing service economy. In fact, the new high-tech information economy means that businesses and workers can settle in just about anywhere they please. For instance, as of 1998, there may be as many as 10 million telecommuters, loosely defined as someone who works at home rather than in the office at least one day a week. The number of telecommuters is sure to increase, and when they look for a place to live, the amenities of the fringe—open space, slower pace, and a sense of safety—are a great draw.

How the Fringe Differs from the Suburbs

Metropolitan fringe areas differ from suburbs in their greater distance from a central city, less economic and political clout, newness, lower population density, scattered developments amid open space, the more noticeable impact of newcomers, less sophisticated land-use planning, and greater growth management challenges.

The growth of the fringe marks America's third major population shift in the twentieth century. The first migration began around 1900, when people started to leave the farms to work in the cities. In 1900, about one-third of all Americans lived on farms. Today, fewer than 5 million Americans, less than 2 percent of the population, live on farms. The call to arms in World War II, the availability of good-paying factory jobs, and the mechanization of agriculture accelerated this move to urban areas. Then after the war, people began leaving the central cities for the suburbs. Cheap land, easy credit, and abundant home financing, and the combination of roads and cars fueled the exodus. This inner ring of postwar suburbs took shape between 1947 and 1970. And soon the jobs followed. The employment and shopping opportunities gave rise to an outer ring of suburbs, many of which are still growing. Today, most Americans and over half of the nation's offices are located in suburbs.[13]

The third migration from the cities and suburbs to the fringe began in the 1970s, and affects a far larger area than the population shift from the cities to nearby suburbs. For example, in 1961 the New York metropolitan region consisted of twenty-two counties and fourteen hundred units of local government spread over a 40-mile sweep. By 1996, 20 million people lived in a Greater New York that included thirty-one counties and two thousand governments within a hundred-mile reach.[14] A 1997 report from the Bureau of the Census found that metropolitan areas lost about 250,000 people between March 1995 and March 1996.[15] The most popular place to settle was in nonmetro adjacent counties—an indication of growing fringe areas.

The term *fringe* implies something out of the mainstream. The suburbs, central cities, and edge cities are where America's economic and political clout is concentrated. But increasingly, the people who wield the power are choosing to live in fringe areas.

As America's population continues to grow, much, if not most of the growth will occur in the fringe. According to journalist John Herbers, "Because development or expansion of communities in the outer reaches is a more radical step than the opening of the suburbs a generation ago, its potential for further change may also be greater."[16]

The development in the fringe is consuming more land per person than the suburbs. Tom Hylton sadly describes the evolution of suburban sprawl into fringe sprawl: "In every decade it gets worse. In the 1950s, when people first started leaving the cities, if you lived on a quarter-acre lot, that was really something. Then, in the '60s, you wanted a half-acre lot. Now, for every house we build, we're using up an acre or two acres. For every shopping center or corporate center, we're using more land than ever before. It's an incredible waste."[17]

Experience bears out Hylton's description. From 1970 to 1990, metropolitan Chicago expanded to cover 46 percent more land, while the population grew by only 4 percent. Similarly, the population of metropolitan New York rose by just 5 percent between 1965 and 1990, but the amount of developed land soared by 61 percent, consuming one-fourth of the region's farmland, forests, and open space.[18]

The rural-urban fringe does not have the vast stretches of single-family houses that characterize suburbia. The fringe does have open land and scattered, low-density settlement patterns, with housing on 1- to 10-acre lots at a distance well removed from the city limits.

These features make the fringe different from the bedroom-community, commuter suburb of 1950s fame. The fifties suburbs featured small homes on small lots typified by the Levittowns on Long Island and just north of Philadelphia. These densely packed suburbs arose close to a major city at a time when most workers commuted from their suburban homes to jobs inside the city limits. By contrast, today's fringe dwellers often work not in a central city, but in a suburb or edge city.

Older suburbs and fringe areas face very different growth management challenges. Many older suburbs need to become more urban by acquiring a sense of identity, such as a definable downtown and public meeting places. The challenge to the fringe communities is how to retain their semirural atmosphere while absorbing more population and development.

The fringe is also different from the newer suburbs, where local zoning laws often require a half acre or more to build a house. The new suburbs are essentially for commuters, many of whom drive to work in another suburb. Most new suburban development depends on municipal sewer systems. But many if not most fringe-area developments use on-site sewage disposal systems, particularly for single-family houses. The on-site systems enable scattered development to occur anywhere the soil will perc. However, the widespread use of on-site septic systems and wells for drinking water can lead to water-quality problems and health hazards.

The fringe differs considerably from the edge cities that gained prominence in the 1980s. Edge cities are new urban centers usually found on the outer reaches of the newer suburban ring, several miles away from an urban core and, according to author Joel Garreau, they have five distinctive features:[19]

- Over 5 million square feet (125 acres) of office space
- 600,000 square feet (14 acres) or more of leasable retail space (i.e., shopping malls)
- More jobs than bedrooms
- A mix of jobs, shopping, and entertainment
- Growth from next to nothing into cities within a thirty-year stretch between 1960 and 1990

Box 1.1 How to Tell if You Live in the Rural-Urban Fringe

1. You live 10 to 50 miles from a major urban center of at least 500,000 people. Or, you live 5-30 miles from a city of at least 50,000 people.
2. Your commute to work takes 25 minutes or more each way.
3. You have an on-site septic system and your own well.
4. The population density in your community is less than 500 people per square mile.
5. Your community has a mix of long-term residents and those who moved in within the last 10 years.
6. Your elected officials and your neighbors talk a lot about population growth, property taxes, and the rising cost of public services.
7. You drive over 15,000 miles a year.
8. Agriculture and forestry are declining industries in your community.

A final observation is that edge cities are connected to interstate-type highways, which makes them readily accessible both from the suburbs and from the fringe. As a result, it is common for residents of the fringe to work in edge cities. In fact, if it weren't for edge cities, the rural-urban fringe would cover much less territory and contain considerably fewer people.

Suburban and Fringe Residents

Suburban areas attract residents largely because of good schools and a sense of safety compared to cities. The lifestyles of suburban dwellers, whether newcomers or long-time residents, are fairly similar; most commute to work in an office and live on a single-family lot or in an apartment.

Newcomers to the fringe are often searching for a lifestyle that offers the best of both city and country living. There is the promise of peace and quiet, a closeness with nature, a feeling of space, and a slower pace of life (at least on the weekends). At the same time, the central city, with its cultural amenities and hustle and bustle, is accessible. Some newcomers, however, are simply trying to escape from the city or suburbs and bring with them an "enclave" mentality. They post "No Trespassing" signs on traditional hunting and fishing lands. They want to live on their large lots with a minimum of government regulation, taxation, and contact with others.

Journalist John Herbers summed up the newcomers in the fringe as "made up of a prosperous, adventurous middle class superimposed over small towns and countryside in a way suburbs never were."[20] James Brown and colleagues were not quite so sanguine about newcomers in their 1981 study of urban fringe land markets. They reported that the spread of suburban-style development and newcomers "has been likened to an ecological succession, whereby an existing population is progressively replaced by another more complex, invading community."[21]

The friction and resentment between newcomers and long-term residents reaches a boiling point over new development. Many newcomers left the cities and older suburbs to avoid crime, grime, traffic congestion, inadequate schools, and rising property taxes. Ironically, as John Herbers pointed out in *The New American Heartland*, many newcomers want the good public services of the suburbs but are not willing to pay the taxes to have those services.

The long-term residents find themselves in two camps; some deplore the growth that has already occurred and want no more, and others see the growth as an economic opportunity. Long-term residents normally have a greater percentage of their wealth tied up in real estate. The value of land for development is almost always higher than for farming or forestry. Especially for older landowners whose land is their retirement account, the sale of land at a high price can mean financial well-being after a life of hard work.

The battles between those who want to pull up the drawbridge and close the door to new development (known as "the last one in" syndrome) and those who see profits from growth can be extremely bitter. A community's appearance and quality of life may be at stake if a large housing subdivision or major discount chain store is built. Or because one neighbor may stand to gain from the sale of land, other neighbors may have to become accustomed to looking at houses instead of cornfields out their windows.

Land-Use Planning in the Suburbs and in the Fringe

Two important differences between fringe communities and the suburbs are the settings for land-use planning and the extent of planning experience. The suburbs and edge cities are primarily built environments. Typically, development projects are placed next to other developments. Properties are redeveloped, and some land is developed for the first time. Moreover, the local governments generally have professional planning staffs. This is not to say that there is no opposition to development in suburbs or edge cities, but more often than not, residents in those places expect development to occur.

In the fringe, most new developments are built on green fields outside of incorporated municipalities on land under county or township jurisdiction. These sites may or may not be near other developments.

Planning the growth of fringe communities has become more contentious. One reason is that planning was largely a foreign concept to many fringe communities until the last twenty years. Even today, many fringe places lack a full-time planning staff, and the community or county comprehensive plan and zoning ordinance may be more than ten years old. Appointed citizen planning commissions have had to shoulder a rising workload of development proposals, often without perceiving how the different building projects fit together in a cumulative impact on the community.

Added to the fringe planning challenges is a sense of urgency, a feeling that time is running out because changes are happening fast. Many newer suburban communities look and function very differently from the rural places they were only ten or twenty years ago. And many fringe communities do not want to become suburbs or lose their rural character. At the same time, fringe inhabitants recognize that change is not easily reversed, and the decisions about development have long-term, lasting consequences.

Edge cities, as Joel Garreau points out, are not limited by political boundaries, and the same is true of the fringe. It typically spreads across more than one county and encompasses several towns and villages and a wide swath of countryside. Local governments have traditionally shown a reluctance, if not downright hostility, toward working together. Planning should increase local control over the destiny of the community. Given the large territory of fringe areas, however, localities can no longer stand alone. Their futures are linked to the entire fringe region, the suburbs, and urban centers.

Planning for metropolitan regions has a limited track record in America because of the tradition of small local governments. Nonetheless, regional coordination and cooperation by local governments on issues of housing, transportation, sewage, water, property taxation, education, and economic development hold the best hope for combatting sprawl and encouraging developers to build the right projects in the right locations.

The Importance of Managing Growth in the Fringe

The risks of too much growth in the fringe are threefold. First, as more people and development locate in the fringe, the territory of the fringe also increases, adding to a more dispersed settlement pattern. This is a short-sighted and expensive way to accommodate the housing, shopping, and employment needs of a growing population. Low-density housing consumes more acreage than necessary, and energy demands are high. Residents and businesses alike are heavily dependent on cars, trucks, and roads to travel and transport goods and services. And busing children to and from school is expensive. New infrastructure in the form of roads, schools, and sewer and water, fire, and police facilities must be built, at an enormous cost to taxpayers—both business owners and homeowners. For example, utility companies must extend electrical, gas, and phone lines to service a rather small number of customers; and urban and suburban customers actually end up subsidizing the extensions.

Second, the impacts on the environment are not light. Scattered development has been made possible through a proliferation of on-site septic systems for sewage disposal and wells for drinking water. These systems are often not properly maintained, threatening groundwater quality and supplies over the long term. Wildlife habitat shrinks as the countryside is parcelled out. Longer commutes to work and shopping mean more gasoline is burned and more air pollution generated.

Third, the development of the fringe is siphoning much needed public and private capital away from the inner cities and older suburbs. But the growth of the fringe also increases the separation of a largely white middle and upper-middle class from lower-income and mostly minority inner-city inhabitants. This separation pulls apart the social and economic fabric of the metropolitan area. Do Americans care if the inner cities deteriorate to the point of abandonment? And can a metropolitan region thrive if its core city is unraveling?

Take, for example, the city of Detroit and neighboring Oakland County. Each jurisdiction has about 1 million inhabitants. But in 1996, Detroit issued only eighty-six new residential building permits while Oakland County issued a whopping 7,197. The median household income in Detroit was slightly more than $21,000 a year. The median Oakland household earned over $47,000 a year.[22] These figures suggest a widening gap between the economic well-being of the inner city and the suburbs. How long can this trend continue?

Several fringe communities are creating buffers against haphazard and chaotic suburban sprawl (see chapter 11). Americans are discovering that sprawl defeats community and diminishes the sense of place, providing no central gathering place other than the malls.[23] Dispersed, single-use development increases reliance on the automobile to get to work and shopping, which isolates people from each other. Sprawl is also unsightly and wasteful of space. Open space disappears as new homes and shopping centers replace farms and forests; and there is a loss of character and identity as a once small town is transformed with strip commercial development and acres of tract homes. A sense of history and personal roots fades. There is no feeling of permanence or enduring purpose to many of these places.

The choice in the fringe is not so much between growth or no-growth, but between sustainable and unmanageable growth. The fringe is absorbing a significant amount of America's population growth, and this trend seems likely to continue for many years. The impacts of growth on the appearance and functioning of many fringe areas will be significant. In a 1997 report, the Bureau of the Census estimated that there will be 393 million Americans by the year 2050, up from 262 million in 1995.[24] Elected officials are making crucial choices about growth and development that have long-term consequences for the future livability of their communities. Growth management strategies promoted by governments should establish clear rules for development so that businesses and developers know where to build and individual landowners have some assurance of what kind of development is allowed in the vicinity. Land-use planning isn't perfect, but it does offer a way, in our democratic society, to balance the rights of individuals with the interests of the community.

A Guiding Vision for Fringe Areas

A vision for the rural-urban fringe has yet to be developed. Visions provide direction for action. There is little disagreement that the fringe should offer a healthy living environment, but there is certain to be controversy over *at what amount of growth does a fringe area become a suburb*? Similarly, there will be debate over *carrying capacity*—how many people the fringe can support before the quality of life declines. The challenge for fringe communities is to accommodate development without sacrificing the environmental qualities that attract development.

Ideally, a mix of farms, forests, natural areas, houses, stores, offices, and factories could result in some working rural landscapes together with some urban-type employment opportunities and quality, affordable housing. But to achieve this balance, urban uses will have to be largely confined to existing town and village areas, leaving the countryside mostly open.

There is a clear need for communities of a manageable size, regional planning, and control by citizens over their neighborhoods. Americans have already shown a strong desire for clean air and water, and Congress responded with a string of laws protecting air and water quality. However, the efficient and attractive settlement of the landscape has not yet been made a centerpiece of any national political agenda. In order to take control of the political agenda, citizens first must understand and reform the land-use planning process that has brought about the chaotic patterns of residential and commercial development.

CHAPTER 2

How the Fringe Came to Be

> The future city will be spread out, it will be regional, it will be the natural product of the automobile, the good road, electricity, the telephone, and the radio, combined with the growing desire to live in a more natural, biological life under pleasanter and more natural conditions.
>
> —*Planner John Nolen in the 1930s*

The fringe pattern of houses and businesses spread out among farms, ranches, and forestlands did not happen overnight. The struggle for the countryside has been going on for more than a century. In the 1800s, fringe areas were limited in size, sparsely settled, and adjacent to cities that were small by today's standards. As cities grew, people began to move outward to develop the fringe into residential suburbs. Once a suburban community was established, rural land outside the suburb came under its influence. In this pattern of growth, rural land near cities and suburbs first became part of the rural-urban fringe. As population and development increased in the fringe, the fringe was eventually absorbed by urban and suburban expansion. At the same time, new fringe areas were created as additional rural land came within the sphere of influence of the suburbs.

Today's rural-urban fringe took shape in the latter half of the twentieth century, with the dramatic growth of suburbs and the advent of dispersed metropolitan regions. According to growth management expert Douglas Porter, between 1977 and 1997, while the large cities of the thirty-nine most populous metropolitan areas gained fewer than 1 million residents, the suburban population increased by 30 million.[1] In addition, the modern version of the rural-urban fringe was created by the 20 million people living in the more than seven hundred counties added to metropolitan areas since the 1950s.[2]

As the suburbs expanded, more rural land came under development pressure. Thus, the history of the suburbs and the conversion of rural land is key to understanding where the fringe came from and where many fringe areas are headed.

The First Suburbs

To Americans of the early 1800s, a rural estate was something to admire and even aspire to own. The nation knew well of George Washington's Mount Vernon and Jefferson's Monticello. English peers and landed gentry and those of continental Europe had long lived in stately houses, chateaux, and castles. The countryside was quiet, green, and spacious. By comparison, cities were notorious for their crime, filth, and plagues. Poverty led to thievery, burglary, and begging. Public sanitation was sorely lacking. Crowded, dirty living conditions gave rise to tuberculosis. Polluted drinking water supplies brought on raging epidemics of cholera and typhus. Dolly Madison, wife of the fourth president, lost her first husband to a yellow fever epidemic in Philadelphia in the 1790s.

At the beginning of the nineteenth century, in the walking and horse-drawn era, there was a clear line where cities ended and the countryside began. The city or village center was the traditional hub of commerce and administration, with markets, courts, and shops mixed with houses. These settlements were densely built, partly for defensive reasons, and often they ended abruptly at an edge of farm fields and woods. Land outside the city or village was sparsely settled, and beyond the farms was wilderness.

The trick was being able to afford the transportation out of the city to a country residence yet hold a job in the city. But horseback was not rapid transit. So a person both lived and worked in a city, a village, or the country.

The first suburbs were largely independent villages near the small but growing cities of the Eastern Seaboard. For instance, between 1820 and 1850, Cambridge, Massachusetts, across the Charles River from Boston, boasted its own economy of farms, manufacturing, and Harvard College. Few residents of Cambridge commuted to work in Boston.

The railroad brought about the first real suburbs, by providing a cost-effective and reasonably swift link between the city and the countryside. In the late 1850s, the first American railroad suburb arose in Llewellyn Park, New Jersey, some thirteen miles from New York City. Like many subsequent suburbs, Llewellyn Park was designed for the well-to-do. Winding roads, two- to eight-acre lots, a ban on industrial uses, and a fifty-acre park were *planned* to create a quiet, bucolic place to live. Large, expensive houses were built for single families. In short, suburbs have an elitist origin, which excluded the poor and manufacturing establishments.

After the Civil War, other suburbs, such as Frederick Law Olmsted's Riverside outside of Chicago, soon followed. The emphasis on greenery and large residential lots in a parklike setting was common. Historian Robert Fishman describes the Philadelphia railroad suburb of Chestnut Hill as the archetypal suburb, with "tree-shaded streets, broad open lawns, substantial houses set back from the sidewalks."[3] From the lawns arose lawn sports such as croquet, tennis, badminton, archery, and horseshoes. The sense of the suburb as a place of refuge from the city grew even as the economic link between the suburbs and the city increased. Commuters rode the trains into the city to earn their livelihoods and bring back their pay to their bucolic homes.

The streetcar enabled a boom in suburban construction to occur from the 1870s to 1920. During that time, the magnates of the Industrial Age drew together human labor, raw materials, and machines into factories to mass-produce goods. Cities expanded rapidly, fueled in part by immigrants. The streetcars were the first real mode of mass transit on a daily basis. They covered more extensive routes than the trains and carried more passengers.

Streetcars enabled many more people to live in a less crowded setting yet continue to commute to a job downtown. The streetcar suburbs were noteworthy because they were fundamentally middle-class, not elite, enclaves. Houses were commonly built on uniform long and narrow lots. But more important, the streetcar suburbs truly underscored the separation of where people lived from where they shopped and worked.

In 1912, Los Angeles enacted the nation's first zoning ordinance. But New York's 1916 ordinance was far more influential in promoting the separation of large areas for specific land uses. The purpose of the ordinance was to stabilize property values and, as every planning student learns: "to promote the public health, safety, welfare, and morals." Zoning would, for example, prevent a smoke-belching factory from being located in the heart of a residential neighborhood and thus reducing both air quality and the value of the homes. In 1926, the U.S. Supreme Court upheld the legality of zoning in *Euclid v. Ambler Realty* and set the stage for zoning to become the primary land-use control in America.

The Standard Zoning Enabling Act of 1928, fashioned by the U.S. Department of Commerce, brought the practice of zoning to every state. Counties, municipalities, and townships then received the power to zone from their state legislatures. Suburbs soon drafted zoning ordinances, often tailored to keep out "undesirable" development such as low-income apartments or factories. Even though sanitary conditions had improved in the cities and the Great Depression dampened new home construction, the suburbs continued to gain in status. Suburbs became increasingly successful in resisting annexation by the central cities. This firm proclamation of political independence set the stage for the social, economic, and demographic dominance of the suburbs after World War II.

The Automobile Takes Command

Historian Kenneth T. Jackson points out that expensive roads, cars, and the consumption of enormous quantities of gasoline have made possible America's sprawling settlement patterns.[4] No other technological advance has so changed the metropolitan landscape. The automobile has meant greater personal freedom and more options of where to live in relation to work and shopping.

The automobile became popular after World War I, thanks largely to the mass-production techniques that enabled Henry Ford to deliver cars that many Americans could afford. The car, in turn, generated a huge demand for roads, and for the next seventy years the majority of American public works programs were devoted to building and maintaining the most extensive road network the world has ever seen. Roads, cars, and trucks enabled Americans to project suburbs over a much wider landscape and allowed more dispersed settlement patterns at a lower density than the trains or streetcars had (see photo 2.1).

Photo 2.1 A typical suburban residential street with big houses on large lots.

In the 1920s, new suburbs were shooting up on the edges of every major city.[5] By 1925, there were more than 17 million cars and 2.5 million trucks registered in the nation, and two years later there was one motor vehicle for every five Americans.[6] Cars and trucks helped give birth to suburban shopping centers, the first of which was the County Club Plaza outside Kansas City, designed in the 1920s by the J.C. Nichols Company. The cars brought the people while the trucks moved the necessary merchandise to stores outside of the old downtowns.

Local governments made the decision to pay for local roads out of general property taxes under the assumption that roads benefited everyone and road access would raise property values. The federal government began its tradition of subsidizing road construction in 1916 with the Federal Road Act, which made grants to states with highway departments. The Federal Road Act of 1921 offered states a 50 percent federal match for the paving of certain major roads.

While new home and commercial construction slowed dramatically during the Great Depression, the road building tradition continued in the 1930s. Parkways and beltways, especially around New York and Los Angeles, opened up more countryside to urban influence.

After World War II, the increase in roads and automobile ownership changed the way most Americans live. Because of the greater mobility they provided, cars became the preferred mode of transportation. Meanwhile, as cars rose in popularity, streetcars declined. Thus began the anti–mass-transit bias that has plagued transportation planning ever since.

Lewis Mumford once made the hopeful comment that suburbs were "a collective effort to live a private life."[7] But the suburban growth process was ruthlessly gobbling up land. John Herbers describes the voracious appetite of sprawling suburbs: "With rare exceptions, all of the little towns and residential roads in their path were either destroyed or changed so drastically they cannot be recognized today for what they were."[8]

The 1950s suburbs were almost exclusively residential. Suburbanites typically commuted from bedroom communities to work and shopping in the central city. Between 1956 and the early 1970s, 42,500 miles of high-speed, interstate highways were paved. Beltways and "ring roads" around cities made escaping to the hinterlands affordable and attractive, and country roads were upgraded. This elaborate network of roads accelerated the pace of surburban growth. Commercial, convenience, strip development popped up near interstate interchanges and along arterial highways. Suburban shopping malls replaced urban Main Streets as the new downtowns. Subdivisions of tract homes filled in between the arterial highways. Often parcels of farmland and open space became trapped between the subdivisions and commercial strips as builders and developers leapfrogged around large landowners who were not yet willing to sell for development. Critics rightly charged that the scattered development patterns were expensive to furnish with public services of sewer and water lines, roads, and schools.

A further contributor to auto dependence was the surge in the number of working women, especially two-income families, beginning in the 1970s. The two-car family became the norm, and total vehicle miles traveled increased.

The necessity of having a car in the suburbs made Americans more dependent on imported oil for gasoline supplies. Despite two oil-price-and-supply shocks in 1973 and 1979, Americans continued to move father into the rural-urban fringe and put up with longer commutes. Yet, because of increased foreign supplies and despite greater dependence on imported oil, in 1998 the price of gasoline, adjusted for inflation, was lower than the price in 1973.

How long gasoline supplies will remain plentiful and prices fairly low, no one can say. Short of some cataclysm, the price of oil is not likely to rise again soon to $40 a barrel, a level it touched during the panic buying just before the Gulf War in 1991. Saudi Arabia, the world's largest producer, has been running budget and trade deficits for several consecutive years. The Saudis need to maintain a steady flow of oil in order to pay off their debts, caused by providing a generous welfare state and a modern military force. Kuwait, Iran, and Iraq—all major OPEC producers—are hungry for oil revenues and are likely to remain so for several years.

What this means for suburban and fringe-dwelling Americans is that they should continue to be able to afford to drive to and from work, shopping, school, and recreation areas. Estimates that there may be only fifty years remaining of proven oil reserves at current rates of consumption do not seem to be discouraging settlement outside of cities. Our economy and way of life rely heavily on oil. Roughly one in six American jobs is related to the automobile. Our food is grown with petrochemically based fertilizers, and diesel tractors do the planting and harvesting.

Nonetheless, America imports about 44 percent of the oil it consumes, which contributes about $50 billion a year to our trade deficit. How much longer can we afford such extravagance? This is but one indication that the dispersed settlement pattern in the rural-urban fringe has caused America to live close to the edge of, if not beyond, its means.

But the convenience of the automobile is gradually being thwarted as commuting times and distances increase for fringe dwellers. More congestion on the roads is a foregone conclusion. New road construction is exceeding $1 million a mile, and maintaining existing roads is becoming a higher priority. From 1987 to 1997, miles of new road in the United States increased by only 1 percent. But the number of cars grew by 27 percent, and vehicle miles traveled grew by 35 percent.[9]

The Fringe Becomes Popular

The growth of suburbs and the construction of the interstate highways made tens of thousands of acres of rural land accessible for commuters to urban and suburban employment centers. In the 1960s, the rural-urban fringe gained popularity among people who were appalled and frightened by racial unrest and rising urban crime. Cities were seen as dangerous and dirty. Racial strife in major urban centers such as Los Angeles, Newark, and Detroit drove many, mostly middle-class, whites to the suburbs and beyond. The expression "white flight" was coined to describe the sometimes hectic outmigration of middle-class and wealthier people to the suburbs and fringe areas.

The economic ties between the cities and their suburbs loosened as the economic and social conditions continued to unravel in many central cities. The suburbs added thousands of offices, factories, and stores, providing job opportunities for those who could live beyond the suburbs. Jane Holtz Kay reports that "from 1963 to 1987, nearly three of every five jobs created were located in the once rural countryside."[10] To critics, the suburbs had already become boring privatized pods of housing with little sense of community or civic culture. Most suburbs lacked an identifiable downtown or public meeting place. Functions that had been filled by a town center were increasingly fulfilled by the shopping malls.

The 1970s became known as the era of the "rural renaissance" when, for the first time since the early 1800s, the populations of nonmetropolitan counties grew at a faster pace than metropolitan counties. A strong agricultural economy, the location of industrial branch plants, and the hippie-driven back-to-the-land movement all fueled rural growth. But a sizable portion of this growth occurred in counties that were adjacent to metro areas, helped in part by newcomers to the fringe who commuted to jobs in the metro regions.

Awareness of environmental conditions burst upon the nation's consciousness in the seventies. In response to the first Earth Day, April 22, 1970, President Nixon created the Environmental Protection Agency. The environmental movement made substantial legislative gains, such as the Clean Air Act Amendments of 1970, the Federal

Water Pollution Control Act of 1972, and the Coastal Zone Management Act of 1972, the Endangered Species Act of 1973, and the Safe Drinking Water Act of 1976. The fringe beckoned with clean air and water, as well as safety from rioting and rising urban crime.

Like suburbia, the fringe is a largely middle-class invention that embodies the ideal of the house in the garden, or, as James Kunstler calls it, "the little house in the woods." But as Robert Fishman and Joel Garreau point out, by the 1970s, many suburbs had grown into cities, and the element of nature had been subdued. In this light, the fringe came to represent both a rejection of the density and sterility of suburbia and a continuation of a long-held American sentiment against cities.

Although the fringe has not pushed steadily outward since the 1960s, its growth has been remarkably resilient. The energy crisis of 1973–74 curtailed gasoline supplies and sent prices soaring, pushing up the cost of commuting. A sharp recession in 1974–75 put a crimp in new home construction. The upward spike in energy prices in 1979 kindled double-digit inflation. In response, the Federal Reserve drove up interest rates to historically high levels in an attempt to wring inflation out of the economy. The ensuing recession of 1980–82 cut sharply into housing construction and the growth of the fringe. Population growth in nonmetro adjacent counties slowed. The Tax Reform Act of 1986 and another recession at the end of 1989 slowed the construction of new office space in edge cities. But the metropolitan suburbs gained enough residents that by 1990, America had become a suburban society. For the first time, more Americans resided in the suburbs than in central cities or rural areas. For census purposes, many residents of the fringe were included as suburbanites.

Visionary Architects or Designers from Hell?

Architects bear a special portion of the responsibility for the rise of the suburb. What began as good intentions to create livable cities resulted in a wholesale urban environmental disaster and flight to the suburbs from which some of the nation's older major cities have yet to recover. The City Beautiful Movement, initiated in the aftermath of the "White City" of the 1893 Chicago Exposition, was primarily aimed at creating impressive public buildings and spaces. Architect Daniel Burnham, the driving force behind the Exposition, made the famous statement, "Make no small plans," which gave hope that cities could be transformed into efficient and aesthetically pleasing places to work and visit. But private housing was notoriously absent from the White City, suggesting even then that its future lay outside the city center.

Perhaps the most revolutionary vision of the city came from the designs of the Swiss-born architect, Le Corbusier. His Radiant City almost completely separated the built environment from nature and featured monolithic skyscrapers rising above green space and multilane highways. American designers followed Le Corbusier's lead, and office blocks of concrete and steel with windows that do not open became fashionable from the 1950s to the 1970s.

In the fifties, the federal government embarked on a nationwide attempt to remove slums from the older central cities and rejuvenate downtowns. The slums would be replaced with public housing in the form of high-rise apartments, and private investors would replace older commercial buildings with shiny, new high-rise office space. Le Corbusier's Radiant City would become a reality.

Things did not work out as planned. Urban Renewal often went beyond slum clearance. Hundreds of older and sometimes historic buildings were leveled as America became infatuated with the Modern. Many of the older buildings were replaced with parking lots. Often, the poor whose homes were leveled had nowhere to go. Those who moved into the high-rise apartments found them sterile and soon crime-ridden. The often-cited example of the failure of urban renewal is the Pruitt-Igoe high-rise apartment building in St. Louis, which won an urban design award and was torn down ten years later as unfit for human habitation. Commercial projects were often slow to develop and soon could not compete with the auto-oriented shopping centers in the suburbs. Street life, which made city living vibrant, declined. Crime escalated. As downtowns all across America were being dug up and reshaped, the flight to the suburbs intensified.

The suburb had long suggested "an unspoiled synthesis of city and country."[11] While America's central cities were struggling with schemes for urban renewal, the rapid and vast growth of the suburbs reflected in part the vision of the great American architect Frank Lloyd Wright. He recognized that the old centralized cities would eventually give way to a new form of city. In the 1920s, he produced Broadacre City as the guide to the future for urban America. Broadacre City did not include suburbs (see the discussion of Albuquerque in chapter 11). Instead, Broadacre City was suburbia triumphant: four square miles of low-density buildings, open space, single-family homes on more than one acre. And everyone had a car. Wright gushingly foresaw a "family freed from the corruption of the city, restored to harmony with nature, endowed with wealth and independence yet protected by a close-knit, stable community."[12]

Instead of the Shining City on a Hill envisioned by Puritan John Winthrop, Wright foresaw a slumless and scumless city spreading across the plains. "The present city," he wrote in 1932, "is yet only about one-tenth the motor city it will be."[13]

As the Radiant City was imposed on the inner city as the flawed model for urban renewal, the spread-out Broadacre City became the model for suburban America of the 1950s and 1960s. However, the cookie-cutter lots and identical houses of Levittown and other suburbs were a perversion of Wright's original idea, which had offered a diversity of spaces and houses.

Robert Fishman aptly summarizes the combination of demographic and economic decline of the inner cities and the rise of the suburbs:

> Between 1950 and 1970 American central cities grew by 10 million people, their suburbs by 85 million. Suburbs, moreover, accounted for at least three-fourths of all new manufacturing and retail jobs. . . . The 1970s central cities experienced a net out-migration of 13 million people.[14]

By the 1970s, there seemed to be no way to reverse the trend of urban population moving to the suburbs. In fact, urbanites who moved to the suburbs were seen to be bettering themselves.

A vision for accommodating metropolitan growth that differed from Frank Lloyd Wright's was put forth by Lewis Mumford and his cohorts. In 1921, they founded the Regional Planning Association of America in part to promote regional planning as a solution to the nation's expanding cities. Mumford agreed with Frank Lloyd Wright that the major American cities had grown too big, too congested, and too polluted for healthy habitation. Mumford also recognized that populations and economic activity were overflowing from the cities into the countryside.[15] But unlike Wright, Mumford wanted to manage the decentralization, and, borrowing from the work of Englishman Ebenezer Howard, he saw garden cities of ten thousand to thirty thousand people as a sort of dam, holding back the rush of people from overwhelming the natural environment. In emphasizing a regional approach to planning, Mumford believed that "each region has . . . a natural balance of population and resources and manufactures, as well as of vegetation and animal life."[16] Mumford felt a balance could be struck between economic growth and the natural landscape if development would "respect limits and diversity."[17]

Mumford's model city was based on the New England village, where cooperation and a democratic spirit were in harmony with the human scale of buildings and green spaces, and there was an absence of commercial strip development along highways. Radburn, New Jersey, was an attempt by Mumford and others associated with the Regional Planning Association to design and build a garden city that combined modern technology with a sense of human scale and community.

Good design, it was hoped, would bring about social reform and harmony.

The Radburn site plan featured large blocks with housing clustered along cul-de-sacs and interior parks and a separation of auto and pedestrian areas. But Radburn had four flaws. First, it lacked a surrounding greenbelt; second, there was no low-income housing; third, businesses and industry stayed away; and fourth, it could not achieve the goals of a network of satellite garden cities all by itself. Instead of a largely self-sufficient settlement, Radburn soon became an upper-middle-class bedroom community, not functionally different from other suburbs.

Although Radburn was not a commercial success, it did raise some awareness of the possibilities of garden cities. Rexford Tugwell, of Franklin Roosevelt's New Deal brain trust, wanted to resettle urban slum dwellers in garden cities and then raze the slums for urban parks. Although three greenbelt towns were built in the 1930s, a strong government role in real estate development was unpopular with Congress. Without government help, it seemed unlikely that private developers could build more than a few large, planned communities.

William Levitt's Levittowns of the 1940s and 1950s featured thousands of identical homes in standardized-lot suburbs that seemingly had no other purpose than to provide affordable starter homes for newlyweds. While developments on the scale of Levittown were an exception, the cumulative impact of thousands of residential subdivisions and commercial shopping centers added up to urban sprawl.

By 1956, Lewis Mumford had become alarmed by the urban growth that was "fast absorbing the rural hinterland and threatening to wipe out many of the natural elements favorable to life which in earlier stages balanced off against the depletions of the urban environment."[18]

Two years later, William H. Whyte, Jr., in his classic essay entitled "Urban Sprawl," unleashed a blistering indictment of sprawl as wasteful, costly, and an aesthetic disaster.[19]

Single-use, single-family, residential zoning was a major culprit. Suburban municipal governments saddled developers with rigid design requirements. Large house lots and the setback of houses from streets and property lines produced a predictable uniformity of design and huge amounts of land devoted to lawns. The cost of roads and sewer and water lines rose to service the less compact housing. Developers introduced cul-de-sacs and curving streets in an attempt to reduce the monotony of design, but to little avail. Cul-de-sacs were intended to reduce traffic and provide privacy but more often increased isolation and automobile dependence. Many subdivisions were built without sidewalks, allegedly to create a more rural atmosphere, but in reality this reduced social interaction and the developers' costs. New homes were built with garages attached to the house and facing the street. Patios at the back of the house replaced front porches as privacy replaced community interaction.

Beginning in the 1970s, corporate America joined the exodus to the suburbs to be closer to where its executives lived. The rubberband theory of locating corporate headquarters was based on sticking pins in a map showing where the top executives lived, placing a rubberband around the pins, and identifying the most central site for the executives to reach by commuting. At the same time, suburban land was less expensive and corporate offices and industrial parks were less heavily taxed in suburbia than in the inner cities.

According to landscape expert J.B. Jackson, Americans have a love of the horizontal. The Radiant City on which urban renewal was modeled was strictly vertical. In moving to the suburbs, many businesses built horizontal, "campus-style" office complexes surrounded by acres of parking and at least some green space.

The 1970s also saw the growing popularity of that particularly horizontal American emporium known as the regional shopping mall.[20] The first shopping centers sprung up in the suburbs as far back as the 1920s, but the first enclosed mall opened in Edina, Minnesota, in 1956.[21] Suburban malls offered acres of free parking, private security, a roof against the elements, and a wide selection of merchandise within a radius of a few hundred feet. Downtowns could not compete with the convenience and the variety of malls, which typically contained dozens of specialty stores built between at least two "anchors"—brand-name department stores. In the 1980s, more than sixteen thousand malls were built.[22]

A variation of the mall, the discount chain, grew rapidly, and by the early 1990s, Wal-Mart had burgeoned into the world's number one retailer with more than two thousand stores, $60 billion a year in sales, and a stock market capitalization greater than the venerable Coca-Cola Company. Add the crime and congestion of the city, the length of commuting to downtown, and it is no wonder that the Saturday shopping chores were done in the burbs closer to home.

The masses of new corporate office complexes, industrial parks, and shopping malls constituted a new settlement pattern, dubbed edge cities by author Joel Garreau. These cities, which have sprung up in the outer reaches of the suburbs several miles from the metro urban core, tend to have more jobs than residents. They are essentially in the mold of the Radiant City, featuring large buildings (though more horizontal than vertical) and acres of wasted space. Nature has been conquered, and the buildings are often nothing short of surreal.

Photo 2.2 The campus-style office development.

Photo 2.3 Suburban shopping centers such as this one have proliferated in metropolitan areas.

The pedestrian can walk only to and from the car to shop or to work; a leisurely stroll in an edge city does not seem possible. It is a difficult landscape to enjoy.

According to Joel Garreau, edge cities have definite commercial advantages over central cities. First, large amounts of land are easier to assemble for malls, shopping centers, and offices. Second, transportation networks in the form of roads are better for auto-dependent commuters and shoppers. Third, most Americans now live in suburbs with fairly good access to edge cities.

Settlement Patterns: Yesterday, Today, and Tomorrow

In 1826, the German economist Johann Heinrich von Thünen published *The Isolated State* (*Der isolierte Staat*), which attempted to explain the location of agricultural development. Using a village center and rings of land around the center, von Thünen theorized that in an ideal world, more perishable and heavy-to-transport farm products would be raised closer to the city center, and easier-to-carry products would be raised farther out (assuming equal land quality).

Von Thünen drew concentric circles to represent the intensity of land use for farming (see figure 2.1). The closer land was to the village center, the more valuable it was. This orderly arrangement made sense for its horse-drawn day. Von Thünen could have noted that when a city or village expanded, houses rarely leapfrogged over fields at the edge. Expansion occurred more like a slowly inflating tire. Suburbs did not truly exist. It was safe to say that a property was either rural or urban.

In the early 1920s, economist Ernest W. Burgess adapted von Thünen's model of concentric circles in an attempt to show that land values and the intensity of development would decrease in a steady, orderly fashion the farther land was from the urban core. But the railroad, streetcar, and automobile enabled the rush to the suburbs and eventually to the fringe, dispersing different income groups and nodes of commercial activity throughout the metro area. Distance from the city center alone no longer accurately predicted real estate values or the intensity of development. For example, there is land in the inner cities and even older suburbs that isn't worth a third of equal-sized land in the more distant suburbs. The land market is no longer a set of well-defined rings: urban core, residential-suburban, and farmland. The market is fragmented more by the wealth status of a particular suburb or street, or the quality of a particular neighborhood. The fragmented land market means that the amount and quality of development is also spotty, based on the three main tenets of real estate development: location, location, location. Today's fragmented market is

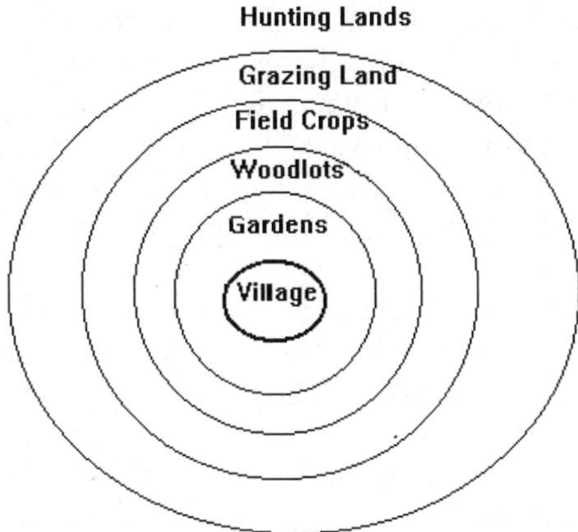

Figure 2.1 Von Thünen's Model of Location and Land Use.

often an excuse for segregation by income class if not race. (One wag has remarked that the rule of thumb in real estate is location, caucasian, location.)

A more realistic depiction of settlement patterns is the star-radial or web model. The center of the web is the main city, and arterial highways radiate out to the end points of the web or star. Areas of suburban development fill in the spaces between the arterial roads. Some tips of the web may grow into edge cities and begin to generate new webs, pushing development farther into the countryside.

Another relevant model is the sector theory developed by Homer Hoyt in the 1930s. Hoyt, who identified high- and low-income city neighborhoods and commercial and industrial districts, pointed out that high-income neighborhoods are more likely to expand into suburbs. Similarly, high-income suburbs are more likely to expand into the fringe.

People in the fringe are tied economically to a region, not the inner city alone; and, as Joel Garreau observes, the inner city is becoming less relevant to fringe dwellers. Moreover, since the late 1970s, the federal government has reduced financial programs aimed at the central cities. And the tax laws favor building anew rather than replacing or repairing old buildings and infrastructure. The result has been fractured metropolitan regions of cities, suburbs, edge cities, and fringe areas that are rather loosely connected in any social, environmental, or land-use sense.

The fringe model of development has eluded geographers and planners because it is, in John Herbers's words, "neither urban, suburban, rural, nor small town."[23] For instance, distance rings of value lose explanatory power for residences; privacy and access to natural features such as streams, hills, and forests often generate more value than proximity to a village. Clusters of houses spring up in the countryside without connection to farming neighbors. Businesses string out along highways but not with the dense mix of gas stations and fast-food franchises made famous in the suburban miracle mile. The fringe exhibits a spread-out, low-density, and seemingly random pattern of development. In turn, the location, size, and type of new development has become less predictable. Just ask people who moved to the fringe only to have major roads, shopping centers, or even a few annoying houses crowd in on their pastoral ideal.

What will the new settlement model be? Herbers contends that "we can't go back to clearly defined cities, suburbs, towns, and rural countryside."[24] Yet a number of counties are using growth management techniques in the fringe with the hope of separating suburbs and cities from the countryside and retaining the identity of small towns. The alternative is continued sprawl. The missing link is revitalizing the inner cities and older suburbs so that fewer people flee to the fringe.

Housing the Newcomers

Housing is big business in America. It provides millions of jobs for home builders, lenders, and makers of appliances and home furnishings. Economists point to new home construction and the sale of existing homes as key barometers of the nation's well-being. In 1992, construction began on 1.2 million new dwelling units, enough space to house over three and a half million Americans, or about 1.3 percent of the nation's population.[25] By 1998, the annual rate of housing construction exceeded 1.5 million new dwelling units.[26]

Before the Great Depression, banks required a large down payment and offered short terms, usually seven years, for a home mortgage. Even with these conservative lending requirements, thousands of homeowners defaulted on their mortgages in the 1930s, and banks failed. By 1932, about half of the mortgages in America were technically in default. To stimulate employment, encourage homeownership, and minimize the impact of mortgage defaults, Franklin Roosevelt's brain trusters devised the Federal Housing Administration (FHA). The FHA provided government guarantees to private mortgage lenders and at the same time relaxed lending standards by lowering the minimum down payment to 10 percent and lengthening the repayment period to twenty or thirty years. The FHA, however, also contributed to suburban development by favoring loans for new, single-family detached houses: just the kind that were more likely to be found in the suburbs. Historian Kenneth Jackson, writing in 1985, summed up the role of the FHA: "No agency of the United States has had a more pervasive and powerful impact on the American people over the past half-century. . . ."[27]

The Home Owners Loan Corporation (HOLC), which was formed in 1933 to refinance private mortgages, began the practice of "redlining" to identify city neighborhoods that were risky for home and business loans. Although the HOLC made loans in those neighborhoods, private lenders soon adopted redlining as a way to avoid risky areas. Often, redlining occurred in racial and ethnic minority neighborhoods. As a result, central cities soon faced a shortage of private capital for economic development. Lenders instead focused on the growing suburbs, where loans were perceived as safer.

But it was after World War II that the suburban housing market boomed. On the one hand, financing was easy. In addition to the FHA guarantees, the Veterans' Administration offered low-interest mortgages with *no down payment,* and mortgage interest payments became tax deductible—a whopping subsidy (see box 6.1 in chapter 6). On the other hand, home builders adopted mass-production techniques. Prior to World War II, few builders erected more than one hundred homes in a year. Banks were skeptical about property loans.

The renowned pioneer in suburban housing was William Levitt, who built sixteen thousand homes in Levittown on Long Island beginning in the 1940s and developed Levittowns in New Jersey and Pennsylvania in the 1950s. Those communities were settled almost exclusively by whites. In fact, residents were discouraged from renting or selling to people of color.[28] By the 1960s, most homes were built by companies that constructed more than one hundred houses a year. The Great Suburban build-out was in full swing. But the new mass-produced suburban homes did not quite meet the standards of the American Dream. Uniform, monotonous houses on similar-sized lots with wide streets and no sidewalks were usually cut off from shopping, the workplace, and schools. One new housing development often looked like the next, and in driving through a subdivision or along a strip arterial, a driver was at a loss to tell where one suburb ended and another began.

But the diffusion of houses and businesses into the countryside was not without cost. The 1974 study *The Costs of Sprawl* reported that as much as 62 percent of private development costs could be saved by moving from the normal, low-density, fringe development pattern to mixed-housing, clustered communities.[29] Public operating costs could be reduced by 73 percent. But the report did little to change the uncreative zoning and pro-growth land-use policies of most local governments. Even while the federal government tried to pump money

Photo 2.4 Suburban housing sprawl covers the landscape.

into the cities in the 1960s through the Model Cities and housing programs, the exodus from the cities continued, especially in the East and the Midwest. Writing in 1997, Kenneth Jackson pointed out that "since 1950, the population of Chicago proper has dropped 25 percent, Baltimore 28 percent, Philadelphia 29 percent, Washington 32 percent, Cleveland 43 percent, Pittsburgh 45 percent, Detroit 46 percent, and St. Louis 54 percent."[30]

These people didn't simply disappear. They moved to the suburbs and beyond into the fringe, and they took property tax bases and economic vitality with them.

The Debt and Real Estate Link

In 1998, the average price of a single-family house in the United States was $120,000. Between 1977 and 1987, debt in America—government, corporate, and household debt—tripled. At a time when real interest rates (adjusted for inflation) were at historically high levels, the Reagan administration deregulated banks and savings and loan associations.

The savings and loans could trace their roots to the early nineteenth century, and they began to be relied upon during the Depression to finance home ownership. They served a useful role in the boom times of the fifties and sixties, but in the 1970s they ran into trouble. In the mid- to late-1970s, the rate of inflation often exceeded the rate of interest. That meant that real interest rates were *negative*: people were crazy not to borrow money, because they would have to pay back loans in the future with dollars that were worth a lot less. S&Ls loaned out money for mortgages at fixed rates of interest for up to thirty years. Inflation made those mortgage payments worth less and less. At the same time, the federal government regulations restricted the level of interest S&Ls could pay on deposit accounts. In the early 1980s, money market funds, which had no interest rate restrictions, became popular, and the S&Ls lost billions in deposits. In short, the S&Ls were squeezed from two directions: inflation was eating into earnings, and depositors were taking their money out.

The wizards of Washington tried to make life easier for the S&Ls by allowing them to make commercial real estate loans and invest in risky high-yielding "junk" bonds. The federal government insured deposits up to $100,000 per account so the S&Ls couldn't lose by risking depositors' money on shaky real estate loans and junk bonds. The outcome of this freewheeling financial gambit has been a $500 billion bill placed on the American taxpayers.

The *carte blanche* to make commercial real estate loans was a big impetus to the creation of the edge cities described by Joel Garreau, though Garreau did not foresee that the frenzied construction of offices and stores would soon lead to vacancy rates approaching 20 percent, a rash of foreclosures, and an oversupply of office space that was not absorbed until the late 1990s.

The Public Revenue Rat Race

Much of the post–World War II suburban development has been subsidized by taxpayers and utility rate payers. America offers the most generous income tax deduction for mortgage interest payments of any industrialized country. This helps to facilitate purchasing one's own house and thus achieving the American Dream. The interstate highways provide easy access between the center city and the surrounding countryside. Municipal bonding for roads, water, and sewer systems; property tax breaks and industrial parks to attract new manufacturing plants; and cheap rates for utility extensions have all combined to encourage the spread of single-family residences, commercial development, and industrial plants outside of urban areas.

And local property taxes, the source of the majority of local government revenues, just seem to keep going up.

The purpose of the suburbs in the fifties and sixties was simply to grow in population and economic activity. The conventional wisdom of the day held that development—residential, commercial, and industrial—paid for itself. Population growth translated into more buildings, and buildings meant a greater property tax base, as well as jobs in construction and retail furnishings. Economic activity surged as money was spent over and over again in the community, a wonderful result known as the multiplier effect. Growth was perceived as a win-win situation. To be antigrowth was un-American.

But along with real estate development, demands for public services—schools, roads, water, and sewers—and the government projects and personnel to provide those services grew. As the population of a community increased, there were more children to educate, and education typically accounts for two-thirds to three-quarters of local government budgets. To raise revenue, local governments searched for "ratables," shopping centers, offices, and industrial plants that would generate more in tax revenues than they would demand in services. Some communities successfully implemented such plans because the people who worked in the commercial and industrial spaces lived in homes in neighboring communities that saw their school costs skyrocket. This beggar-thy-neighbor type of competition was clearly unfair, but revenue sharing across local political boundaries has never been popular in America. More often though, a community would attract new enterprises only to attract new residential development as well. Then the rat race sped along at full tilt: Local governments needed more property tax revenue so they encouraged commercial and industrial development, which attracted residential development, which drove up the cost of public services, especially schools.

The Growth of the Fringe in the Nineties

Writing in 1986, John Herbers characterized the growth of the fringe as "scattered development that leaves many farms, forests, villages, and old buildings intact."[31] But the strong economy of the 1990s has brought a new wave of growth and development pressure to fringe areas. The ongoing telecommunications revolution has reinforced the trend of dispersed fringe settlement by enabling a growing number of people to work at least some of the time at home and telecommute to an urban or suburban office. More farms and forests are disappearing as the open spaces between villages become filled in with strip malls, offices, and housing tracts. In the words of Philip Langdon, many fringe areas have been transformed from boondocks to "boomdocks." Public opinion polls consistently show that most Americans would prefer not to live in big cities.[32] The fringe also displays the American love of independence. For example, both long-term residents and newcomers to the fringe seem to want their own on-site septic systems for sewage disposal and wells for water. They also do not wish to tax themselves to build public sewer and water systems. And both groups want elbow room, a comfortable distance from neighbors.

To those moving to the fringe to escape the suburbs and for many long-term residents of the fringe, suburban sprawl has become the bogeyman. Yet the growth of the fringe is an example of the American culture of consumption. There is open land in the fringe to be consumed for housing, shopping malls, office complexes, and factories. The shopping malls have evolved to include entertainment, particularly movie theaters and health clubs, and have added upscale stores that once were found only in the central cities. Gourmet restaurants and night spots have sprouted up in the nearby suburbs. Sports facilities rise up outside of core cities—Auburn Hills, Michigan; Foxboro, Massachusetts; and the New Jersey Meadowlands—to name only a few. The out-migration of these urban amenities has diminished the cultural allure of the central city.

In the fringe, a car is a necessity and a way of life. One could consider a metropolitan region as a new sort of supercity where the shops, offices, and recreation areas are simply more spread out. Many newcomers to the fringe have made a Faustian bargain to escape the urban-suburban morass. They still have to work there and penetrate the traffic gridlock, unless they can join the ranks of telecommuters or be self-employed at home. Saturday shopping is usually done in the suburbs, too. The new fringe residents are, in the words of author Jane Holtz Kay, "trading time behind the wheel for space in the exurbs." These "work-bound Americans travel from before daybreak to after dark to ever more sprawling homes."[33]

Interest rates in the 1990s have been favorable for borrowers—from real estate developers to home buyers—and except for a brief jolt in oil prices during the Persian Gulf War, energy supplies generally have been plentiful and prices tame. Long-distance commuting to work of forty-five minutes or more each way is not uncommon. The two-wage-earner family has often meant the selection of a location that is in the fringe and roughly equidistant between both spouses' jobs. And the income from two workers makes the move to the fringe financially feasible. It is no mere coincidence that the growth of the fringe has taken off along with the greater participation of married women in the workforce since 1970.

Meanwhile, the American economy has continued to add jobs in the service sector and in information technologies. Some of these jobs do not require workers to commute by car or train to work every day. They can live farther out in the countryside and visit the main office two or three days a week. Simply put, the computer, modem, fax, copier, and printer, along with e-mail and the Internet, have made it easy to set up an office just about anywhere in the fringe. A corresponding boom in mail-order shopping has also enabled people to live farther from stores. Federal Express, UPS, and the postal service can find even the most secluded residences and businesses.

As a result, people who live in the metropolitan fringe are far less dependent on the central cities for jobs, shopping, and culture than the post–World War II suburbanites.

The cost advantages of living in the fringe are often cited as lower property taxes and less expensive housing, compared to the suburbs and the central city. Lower car insurance rates are another bonus. Commuting costs for gasoline and wear and tear on cars are generally offset by the savings on property taxes and housing costs. There may be little difference in utility rates but there are opportunities to save on heating costs by burning wood as opposed to oil, natural gas, or electric heat.

The rising affluence of many Americans really drives the development of the fringe, because as income increases, the choices of what to spend money on expand as well. Personal tastes play a powerful role in today's consumer society, and the choice of where to live can be seen as another consumer decision, albeit a more important, enduring, and expensive one. Many people like to own not just a house but land as well. They feel more secure and more in control than in an apartment or in a house in a suburban residential neighborhood. For some people, a healthy and enjoyable lifestyle is more important than earning the maximum possible income. The fringe offers amenities that the suburbs and central cities do not have or possess in short supply, such as open space, the chance to keep a horse, clean air, and clean water.

Summary

The rural-urban fringe is a new and expanding phenomenon on the American landscape. The fringe covers more land area than central cities, suburbs, and edge cities combined. While many suburbs have in essence grown into cities, the fringe areas are the new semirural, middle landscape between the suburbs and the countryside.

Like the suburbs, the rural-urban fringe has evolved through land speculation, transportation access, technology, personal tastes, affluence, and national population growth. Federal tax depreciation laws, lower property taxes, and fewer regulations in the suburbs and fringe communities have made building on open land cheaper than renovating older buildings in the cities.

America's suburbs began as bedroom communities from which residents commuted to work in a central city. Transportation advances through trains, streetcars, and the automobile made suburbs not only possible but boomtowns. The migration of offices and stores to the suburbs has resulted in the partial abandonment of central cities and the creation of edge cities. These new suburban cities support more jobs than inhabitants, enabling thousands to live farther out in the fringe. The high-tech economy also allows many workers to telecommute, so that immediate access to the main office is not as important as a nice, semirural place to live. The rural-urban fringe appears poised to grow well into the future. Difficult choices over growth management will increasingly dominate public debate and public policy, as well as the concerns of private businesses and citizens. The major choice will be whether a fringe community should grow into a suburb or edge city or try to retain a human scale and a rural, small town atmosphere.

CHAPTER 3

Obstacles to Managing Growth in the Fringe

> We are left with the task of directing growth in a way that would preserve the amenities of the land and the natural environment and avoid the soul-searing ugliness of the development we have spread over our most populated areas.
>
> —*John Herbers,* The New Heartland

> Maximizing our individual independence is diminishing our collective independence.
>
> —*Robert D. Yaro and Tony Hiss,* A Region at Risk

The history of how and why suburbs arose and evolved provides insight for avoiding the mistakes of the suburban form of development, and for creating a vision of how the rural-urban fringe can look and function far into the twenty-first century. Visions, like personal goals, offer a sense of the possible and a direction in which to strive. Some people believe that if past trends of a growing and highly mobile population continue, America will become a set of huge metropolitan areas from which suburban rings stretch out for a hundred miles or more. Already the high cost of housing in the San Francisco Bay Area has pushed commuters far to the east into the San Joaquin Valley, the nation's leading fruit- and vegetable-producing region (see box 10.1 in chapter 10). The tri-state metro region of New York, New Jersey, and Connecticut stretches outside of New York City for over fifty miles and has even brought parts of Pennsylvania within its influence. Most planners would like to see towns, villages, cities, and the countryside retain those qualities that make them distinct, even as they experience growth. Still, some residents of the fringe would like to have no change at all and are hoping that growth will go somewhere else.

Unlike residents of built-up suburbs, most fringe dwellers still have time to make choices about where development should or should not happen. But for many fringe places, growth pressures are mounting and time is running out. County commissioners and town councils are spending more time and money on land-use issues than ever before. And they are struggling to balance the rights of landowners and developers with the rights of citizens, wildlife, and the environment. At the same time, concerned citizens in dozens of fringe counties and communities have begun to organize in the search for a common vision of sustainable, manageable development and to forge workable programs to make that vision a reality.

Three rallying points are the rising property taxes, seriously crowded schools, and traffic congestion that sprawl typically brings. According to Douglas Porter, president of the Growth Management Institute in Chevy Chase, Maryland, "Schools are now very much a flashpoint for unrest and dissatisfaction with the pace of growth."[1] Argues Tim Powers, who founded the Loudoun County (Virginia) Taxpayers Alliance, "People on a massive scale are now understanding that development equals tax increases. To them it's a pocketbook issue and a quality of life issue."[2] In 1995, Loudoun County officials estimated that a new home would have to sell for at least $400,000 to generate enough property taxes to cover the cost of the county services it would use.[3] Linda Budreika, a homemaker and mother of four in Prince William County, Virginia, adds, "The only way we can get accountability is to hold [officials'] feet to the fire and say, 'Enough of this sprawl. We aren't going to pay for it any more.'"[4] In the fall of 1997, Georgia Public Television aired a program "Appalled by the Sprawl," which highlighted the traffic impacts of sprawl in Greater Atlanta. The program called traffic "Atlanta's most hated pastime" and presented the results of a survey of 731 commuters: 29 percent drove at least forty-five minutes *one way*, 31 percent drove an hour or more to get to work.[5] This survey does not include time spent driving to shop and chauffer children around. In short, auto-dependent sprawl takes up a lot of time to get anywhere.

Identifying the problems caused by sprawl is rather easy. The real work and hard choices arise in the search for fair and effective solutions to managing growth.

Eight Obstacles to Planning and Growth Management in the Fringe

Forming a vision of how the community, county, or region should look and function is the first step in the planning and growth management process. But a vision must be realistic, not a wish list for a perfect community. It is important to understand the obstacles to managing growth because they will influence the relevance of the vision for and the planning potential of a community, county, or metropolitan region.

At least eight obstacles hinder coordinated, long-term, and effective growth management in the metro fringe:

1. Fragmented and overlapping governments, authorities, and special districts
2. The large size of fringe areas
3. Lack of a community, county, or regional vision
4. Lack of a sense of place and identity
5. Newcomers, social conflicts, and rapid population growth
6. The spread of scattered new development
7. Too few planning resources
8. Outdated planning and zoning techniques

These obstacles are often interrelated, which makes them more complex and difficult to overcome.

Perhaps the greatest barrier to managing fringe growth is the many overlapping local governments, regional authorities, special districts, state agencies, and even federal agencies that make separate decisions about growth and development in fringe areas (see box 3.1). At one extreme, metropolitan Pittsburgh has 2.3 million people divided among "330 local governments—five counties, 184 municipalities, and 141 townships,"[6] not to mention the sewer and water authorities and dozens of school districts. At the other extreme, city-county consolidation between Indianapolis and Marion County, Indiana, has

Box 3.1 The Authorities That Influence Development in the Fringe

- State agencies, especially departments of transportation, health, environment and natural resources, planning, and commerce (economic development)
- Regional agencies with powers to coordinate transportation planning and facilities, and river basin water use
- Special authorities and districts for airports, sewer and water, and other services that are beyond the political control of

(continues)

Box 3.1 (*continued*)

voters and whose boundaries often do not coincide with municipal or county boundaries

- School districts, which often have budgets and boundaries separate from those of the city, town, and county
- County governments vary in their functions. Counties, excluding those in the Northeast and parts of the Midwest, have control over land-use planning and zoning and the expansion of city limits, known as annexation. Nearly all counties are responsible for administering the courts and processing legal documents. Most also deliver road and bridge construction and maintenance, and social welfare programs. The majority of counties are governed by an elected board of three to seven members. These board members may be called commissioners, judges, or other names. The elected board enacts legislation through resolutions and spending programs, sets policy, and administers the day-to-day business of running county government
- There are two kinds of individual townships. Counties in the Midwest and West are made up of townships of 36 square miles. In a number of midwestern and western states, townships have control over local roads and most other infrastructure, as well as special districts (such as for sewer and water), and sometimes zoning. Counties in New England and New Jersey, New York, and Pennsylvania are also made up of a dozen or more townships that typically cover 15-20,000 acres each. These eastern townships have control over township roads and over planning and zoning (known as "home rule")
- Municipalities, or incorporated areas—villages, towns, cities, and boroughs—often ranked by population size (class of municipality), which denotes the powers they may exercise, typically control of land-use planning and zoning within their boundaries
- Unincorporated settlements ranging from about fifty to three hundred inhabitants, which have no formal power but must be given consideration because of their claims over local control
- Federal agencies, which administer some lands that fall within the metro fringe, particularly in the West. (These lands may include national forests under the U.S. Forest Service, grazing lands under the Bureau of Land Management, and national recreation areas under the National Park Service. In addition, the Bureau of Reclamation has control over water allocation in parts of western states. The Bureau of Indian Affairs technically holds in trust 50 million acres of tribal land, some of which is within the metro fringe, especially in the western states.)

reduced the number of local governments in Greater Indianapolis to seven counties and a couple of dozen municipalities.

A consolidation of some units of government, special districts, and regional authorities is long overdue. Greater efficiency and better coordination in planning land use and infrastructure are likely to benefit taxpayers and improve the growth management process in the fringe. A very real problem is that governments and other entities often work at cross purposes in planning and supplying the resources for developing the fringe. This lack of coordination contributes to the sprawling patterns of residential and commercial development. Sewer and water authorities, for example, are often beyond political control. The expansion plans of these authorities frequently are not in sync with county or township comprehensive plans.

A typical example is a local water district that is in the business of selling water but also plays a major role in shaping the pattern of development. Water districts are initially funded by state and federal grants but are maintained by customer installation and user fees. The more customers the water district has, the more revenue it earns. With more cash on hand, the district can build more water storage towers and distribution lines, which encourages the conversion of open land to suburban uses. In this way, the goals of the water district may run counter to the county comprehensive plan goals of compact development and the protection of farmland and open space.

School districts in fringe areas that have been closing small schools in towns and villages and replacing them with regional consolidated schools in the countryside provide another example of growth promotion. These new, larger schools, in turn, act as growth magnets, spurring nearby residential and commercial development outside of established settlements.

Local governments are notorious for "fiscal zoning" or "zoning for dollars" in trying to attract commercial, industrial, and high-end single-family homes to broaden the property tax base. As local governments compete with each other over property tax ratables, they encourage highway strip commercial and large residential lots in the countryside that generate more property taxes than they demand in public services. But these commercial and residential developments draw economic and social activity away from downtowns. The result is more sprawl and not necessarily lower property taxes in the long run.

The conflicting goals of governments, authorities, and special districts have two main negative effects. First, the perception of bloated bureaucracies and wasted taxpayer dollars breeds distrust and contempt for government among ordinary citizens. If governments are going to take the lead in growth management, they have to earn the faith and support of their constituents. Growth management efforts will succeed only if voters are willing to support spending and regulatory programs. Second, local governments are often confused by their dual role as both land-use regulator and development promoter. As a result, they tend to water down their comprehensive plans into policy plans, which provide little direction for the day-to-day planning decisions about how and where to grow. The policy plans are usually wish lists of vague goals in which the hopeful word "should" appears repeatedly. The weak policy plans then wind up on a shelf. Zoning, which is based on the comprehensive plan, is likely to be weak and overly permissive, allowing development just about anywhere. The weak plans discourage communities and counties from undertaking new and better plans because the local governments argue that they already have a plan.

A second obstacle to managing growth in the fringe is the large size of the fringe area compared to the planning resources. For example, in their book on the third regional plan for Greater New York, Robert Yaro and Tony Hiss shy away from calling for the creation of a regional government. They conclude that the enormous size and diversity of the region, containing parts of three states and 20 million people, is simply too big for a single government. David Rusk reaches a similar rejection of a regional government for the six counties of metropolitan Baltimore.[7]

In the absence of a regional metropolitan government, the responsibility for growth management falls on individual counties and communities, some of which have little land-use planning capability. Fringe development usually occurs over a substantial portion of a county, covering three hundred to five hundred square miles (or more). The county must inventory, evaluate, map, plan for, and then monitor those lands outside of municipalities. A typical semi-rural county has a handful of planners and others involved in mapping and zoning enforcement. To cope, planners and other policy makers must select development sectors or "highway corridors" to focus their efforts. Also, where there is weak county planning and zoning, or where townships exercise planning and zoning powers, conflicting land uses, such as landfills and industrial sites, often occur along municipal boundaries. This creates bad feelings among municipalities and works against regional cooperation for managing growth.

Private planning firms are willing to help draft county comprehensive plans, but it is increasingly difficult to convince a county government to spend $50,000 to $150,000 for a plan in these tax revolt times when it already has a local planning staff.

The third obstacle is a lack of vision at the community, county, or regional level. A vision provides direction for where and how to grow and develop in the future. Vision requires a definable community with a sense of identity and place. It is difficult to decide how and where to grow when development is leapfrogging beyond villages, along interstate highways, and across the countryside. Traditional planning works fairly well for neighborhoods, employment centers, and city or town centers, but fringe growth is not cohesive: commercial strips occupy country crossroads, housing encroaches on farm fields, and workplaces are often small industrial parks outside of town.

In the late 1990s, a number of fringe communities and counties drafted new comprehensive plans with a title of "Vision 2020" or "2020 Vision." The comprehensive plan, also known as the master plan or the general plan, summarizes the current condition of a community or county, projects future needs, and spells out policy goals and objectives for development and conservation. The comprehensive plan provides a legal basis for zoning and subdivision ordinances and is helpful in drafting capital improvements programs. These two ordinances and the capital improvements plan, along with the day-to-day decisions on development proposals, enable planners and elected officials to put the comprehensive plan into action and work toward realizing the community's vision of the future.

One vision might be distinct towns, villages, and small cities that are separated by open spaces. Another vision might be the growth of small cities into regional centers. But without a vision, many fringe areas will share the same fate as those suburbs that became *name places* but failed to maintain clearly defined boundaries, an identifiable center, or a sense of community.

Two key factors in creating a vision and a growth management system are political will on the part of elected officials and the involvement of a diversity of concerned citizens. Politicians can serve as true leaders in moving the community to examine itself and shape a vision for the future. But most politicians are short-sighted in part because they rarely hold office long enough to see a vision become a reality. Politicians must also be willing to commit funds to hire trained and capable staff to draft and implement an effective growth management system.

Visions, of course, can change. Population growth and development cause residents, planners, and politicians to support new visions. A new vision can set in motion any of the following responses from a local government:

- A new or updated comprehensive plan to serve as an overall guide for future development
- A revised zoning ordinance to put the goals, objectives, and

Box 3.2 A Comparison of Political Will in Two Fringe Counties

Fauquier and Loudoun are Virginia counties that lie on the edge of the Washington, D.C., metro region. Fauquier County is about fifty miles southwest of the nation's capital and has a population of fifty-two thousand. It is also home to many of the wealthiest residents of Virginia, who have little need or inclination to develop their land. Over thirty years ago, the county decided to limit major developments to nine towns and villages, which take up only 5 percent of the county's land area. But between 1980 and 1990 the county population increased by about one-third. In the early 1990s, the county adopted a tight rural-cluster development ordinance that requires 85 percent of a parcel to remain as open space. Between 1990 and 1996, the county population grew at a rate of about 1 percent a year.[8] One resident summed up the results of the county's slow-growth efforts: "Fauquier County is about as pretty a piece of property as this country owns. And it's not by accident."[9]

Loudoun County, thirty miles west of the White House, is the fastest-growing county in the D.C. metro area. Between 1982 and 1997, the county population doubled to 123,000, and it is expected to double again in the next fifteen years.[10] County supervisors have approved over fifty-two thousand new houses—in addition to the current forty thousand dwellings—and a whopping 170 million square feet of commercial and industrial projects, more than ten times the current amount of commercial and industrial space.[11] Clearly, Loudoun County is headed toward becoming another edge city of Greater Washington. Meanwhile, between 1990 and 2020, the county is expected to lose nearly sixty thousand acres of open space—a loss of five and a half acres a day.[12]

According to Fauquier County resident Hope Porter, "Loudoun used to be [the] best-planned and best-protected county on the East Coast. And then it got some bad supervisors, and it went down the drain."[13]

But politicians change. In late 1997, the Loudoun County supervisors denied a proposed development of thirty-five hundred houses—the first such decision in a decade.[14] Part of the credit goes to greater citizen involvement. As County Supervisor David G. McWatters noted, "There are a lot more people paying attention."[15]

vision of the comprehensive plan into action and to encourage development in some areas but not in others

- Updated subdivision regulations to ensure safe, quality development
- Capital facilities planning to service new development with

roads, schools, police, fire protection, and public sewerage and water

- Other, more sophisticated and costly growth management techniques (see chapter 8)

Public involvement is essential for successful planning. If many people representing a variety of interests become active in the planning process, a consensus on the vision for the community will reflect broad support. Planners have long complained about the apathy of the public during visioning exercises, drafting the comprehensive plan, and forging the zoning ordinance. A common problem is that later community residents will protest when development is proposed that they don't like. The planners will then ask, "Where were you when we were drafting the comprehensive plan and zoning ordinance that allowed this type of development in this location." By then, it is usually too late. The only avenue open to the citizens is to file an expensive legal challenge to try to defeat the development.

A fourth barrier to managing growth in the fringe is the disappearing sense of place. Effective growth management comes from people who care about the place they live. A vision of the future applies to a definable place, and any vision will include characteristics of a place that should be retained along with desired changes. Similarly, a comprehensive plan needs to refer to a specific community or geographic area. But it is difficult to form a vision for a community or identify a planning area when commercial highway strips and scattered houses in the countryside are pulling economic and social vitality away from cities, towns, and villages. When government buildings like post offices and town halls move out of downtown to the highway, there

Box 3.3 The Vision of Fremont County, Idaho

- Assure that future development will be economically and environmentally sound.
- Discourage leapfrog development in rural areas. Such development can be costly to taxpayers.
- Direct new development to compatible areas.
- Do not permit industrial land uses that have the potential to adversely affect the environment.
- Protect the county's farmland and natural resources.
- Require developers to pay the cost of new infrastructure (roads, sewers, and law enforcement).

are fewer reasons for residents to identify downtown as the center of the community.

Many fringe communities are simply becoming bedroom communities for residents who work and shop in the suburbs and edge cities. Newcomers to the fringe tend to work far away from where they live, and they exhibit "a shop-around behavior, making stops for groceries in one town, patronizing a movie or a restaurant in another, and worshipping in a third."[16]

In short, fringe communities have become dispersed over a wider area and, not surprisingly, have become less socially and economically cohesive. Moreover, when development spills over from a neighboring city or town, it becomes difficult to determine where one community ends and another begins.

Fifth, the fringe is becoming more populated and more socially contentious. Rapid population growth is the bane of planners. The essential piece of a county or community comprehensive plan is the projection of population growth and the land-use and infrastructure needs based on the expected increase in residents. Rapid-growth areas not only make comprehensive plans obsolete within a few years, they also render zoning ordinances ineffective in managing growth; breed sprawling development patterns; and severely strain public services for schools, roads, and sewer and water.

Take, for example, metropolitan Atlanta. A newspaper editorial in 1997 observed that urban Atlanta is spreading like Kudzu, a notoriously noxious weed,[17] and the numbers support that view. According to the Atlanta Regional Commission, between 1990 and 1995 the population of the ten-county metro area increased by 324,000. Between 1995 and 2020, another 1.29 million people are expected. "The danger is," says Jeff Humphreys of the University of Georgia's School of Business, "we may outgrow our infrastructure."[18]

At one time, membership in a community followed years of residency, service, and contribution. But now, newcomers see themselves as settled as soon as the new home is carpeted and long before the lawn has grown in. This pioneer spirit of instant citizenship inspires newcomers to jealously guard their space, reflected in the adage, "I was here first and want none to follow." In public hearings for development permissions, the constant cry from new residents is that more change will ruin the rural character of the community. These sentiments have crystalized into two famous acronyms: NIMBY (Not in My Back Yard) and BANANA (Build Absolutely Nothing Anywhere Near at All).

Over twenty years ago, John J. Tarrant observed: "The confirmed exurbanite wants his own house and a piece of ground and he will continue to fight to maintain the 'character of the town,' meaning to keep out those who are different in background, occupation, ethnicity, size of income, and general outlook on life."[19]

Little has changed since Tarrant wrote *The End of Exurbia*. Most newcomers are escaping higher-density living environments in search of a more bucolic setting. But Tarrant was describing an elitist attitude ("you're okay if you're my type"), whereas today the prevailing attitude of newcomers in many fringe communities can be outright misanthropic and antidevelopment. Many have a fervent conviction not to let where they live become just another suburb.

Newcomers can afford to oppose growth because their wealth comes primarily from good jobs elsewhere. But the wealth of many long-term residents is in their land, and they want the freedom to develop it if the need arises. The irony is that newcomers bring with them the development and rising property taxes that they want to avoid. Long-term residents of the fringe resent the rising property tax burdens and fees needed to support the new development. And these taxes and fees are higher than necessary because of a sprawling rather than compact development pattern. Newer residents are equally adamant to hold the line on property taxes and keep public services to a minimum. But such fiscal austerity may be unrealistic, especially when new schools must be built to educate increasing numbers of children or public water facilities are needed to replace on-site wells that have become polluted.

The inability of local governments to keep pace with infrastructure needs may actually spur fringe growth. Glenn Knoblauch, planning director of Berks County, Pennsylvania, explains, "When there's limited infrastructure—you don't expand the roads, you don't expand the sewer and water lines—then you give people no choice but to develop farther out."[20] Developers may be drawn to areas farther out where local governments have minimal requirements for them to provide roads and septic and water facilities, and land costs are lower, too. Residents may be attracted to more distant areas because of lower house prices and property taxes. But development farther out relies on on-site septic systems and wells, which in some cases means sewage being deposited under one part of a building lot and water being drawn from under another part. Septic systems polluting wells is a nationwide problem.[21]

But usually only after several septic and well systems have failed do local governments or other authorities make proposals and draft preliminary plans for central sewer and water facilities. Long-term residents, many of whom may be forced to hook onto sewers and public water, may object to funding services for newcomers. Ironically, newcomers may also object because of what they see as "sunk costs" in their new wells and septic systems.

In many fringe communities, the influx of newcomers has a "threshold effect" on public services. That is, the amount and capacity of services must increase dramatically, and so does the cost of providing those services. For example, new schools must be built, water and sewage treatment plants constructed, and full-time police hired; and the number of government employees rises to manage these expanded services.

Many newcomers to the fringe come from urban and suburban communities with higher levels of public services, and they expect those same services in the fringe. In response, rapidly growing Larimer County, Colorado, adopted a "Code of the West" to give fair warning to new fringe residents that they would receive the same level of services as long-term residents (see appendix 1). Geneo Knight, a county commissioner from Teton County, Idaho, an area coping with a 10 percent annual population growth rate, summarized the problem of newcomers and public services as follows: "They [new residents] say, 'We're coming here because it is so beautiful. We just love it.' But in reality, they want to make it just the way things were where they came from."[22]

Sixth, a strong economy, rising affluence, and low gasoline prices in the 1990s have spurred the demand for housing and commercial sites in the rural-urban fringe. These three factors are beyond local control, and yet they have profound and lasting impacts. In a fairly typical example, the town of Standish, Maine, issued a total of ninety building permits between 1990 and 1992, but from 1993 to 1996, it issued 264 building permits.[23]

According to architect-planner Jonathan Barnett, "Corporate headquarters and research installations are beginning to move to rural sites beyond the new [edge] city. Land is easier to find, development approvals are faster, and the journey to work from the new city out to a rural area avoids most of the places where traffic gridlock takes place now."[24] Barnett goes on to cite the migration of Sears from downtown Chicago to Hoffman Estates, thirty-seven miles northwest of the city, which was made possible in part through $186 million in public subsidies.[25]

The pattern of fringe development in the 1990s has been noticeably different from that in previous decades. During the 1960s and 1970s, professional developers in the fringe sought to build at strategic locations such as interstate highway exits and interchanges, along paved roads, in good school districts, and beside lakes and waterways. In the 1990s, strategic locations appear far less important, and professional developers are often supplemented by small-time operators in the quest for profits from land sales. Large tracts are seldom bought and left to ripen in value over several years. Instead, small construction firms and individual investors are buying small parcels of ten to fifteen acres and within a year or so subdividing them into three- to five-acre lots. This practice spreads new growth throughout the fringe countryside with little or no thought of what it will cost to extend services or maintain old infrastructure. Planners must divide their efforts in supplying new services to relatively remote areas while at the same

Box 3.4 Developer Goals and Practices

Developers, like any businesspeople, prefer to have as much predictability and certainty as possible for their projects. Real estate development runs on borrowed money. Developers bear the risk of building a project that can't be sold, losing money if their projects are denied or delayed, or selling a project at a loss if the economy turns sour. In short, the sooner a development is built and sold, the sooner the developer can pay off real estate loans and turn a profit. Also, if the developer will retain ownership of the project, communities with relatively low property taxes are attractive.

Small-scale developments of a few houses here and a highway store there have a better chance of passing the scrutiny of local planning commissions. Often, local governments treat the creation of three or fewer lots as a minor subdivision, subject to minimal standards for road access and sewerage and water. But if a developer proposes a large and complicated project, the complexity of the review process and the element of risk can increase enormously. On the other hand, large-scale developers have the clout to negotiate property tax abatements and infrastructure subsidies from local and state governments. For example, the Walt Disney Company lined up a $160 million package of subsidies for its proposed American history theme park in Prince William County, Virginia, on the fringe of Greater Washington, D.C. (see box 4.1)

A developer prefers to build on land that: (1) is zoned to permit the proposed project, which avoids potentially long and costly rezoning fights; (2) is in the right location, with good highway access (reducing the need for traffic improvements) and scenic views and open land adjacent; and (3) has access to public services such as schools, sewer, and water, reducing the cost of perc and water tests, as well as land dedication, and making the development more attractive to buyers.

In sum, what developers want from the community is a consensus on where development is appropriate. Many developers like to have the public help pay for infrastructure and like to receive property tax inducements that make their projects more profitable.

time maintaining the level of services for the concentrated growth at the previously developed locations.

In their important 1981 study of fringe land markets, James Brown and his colleagues estimated that 70 percent of fringe land was held by residents, farmers, and businesspeople; another 18 percent was held by investors and speculators, and only 2 percent was held by developers.[26] Brown and his colleagues described the land development process as the sale of land to an investor or speculator who would hold the land until it increased in value, but without making improvements to the property. A developer would then purchase the land and, within a few years, make improvements and erect buildings for sale.

Brown's model of the development process was probably accurate at the time. But since then, the fringe has grown substantially in size and population. Developers have become larger and better financed and tend to hold more land in the pipeline. Also, landowners themselves have become more active in subdividing lots to meet the demand for large home sites. The cumulative impact of this "nickel and dime" housing on scattered lots can have long-lasting negative effects on the cost of public services, wildlife habitat, and farming and forestry activities. The most significant factor in predicting when a landowner will sell is the extent of nearby development. Encroaching development puts upward pressure on land prices and often leads to the sale of raw land within ten years.

A seventh constraint on growth management in the fringe is that planners have little time for drafting and updating long-range comprehensive plans. If the comprehensive plan is weak or out of date, then the land-use regulations will probably be ineffective in guiding growth. A comprehensive plan must anticipate change and land-use needs. Frequently, communities undertake a planning effort after a population and building boom has begun to overwhelm them. Then planning simply becomes crisis management. As population growth outstrips the capacity of public facilities and services, the financing of new and upgraded roads, schools, and sewer and water service takes precedence over long-range planning.

A good comprehensive plan requires time, effort, and creative thought. Planners in the fringe are consumed with current planning tasks of zoning, subdivision, and review of land development proposals. Although current planning should follow an up-to-date long-range master plan for the area, the evaluation of development proposals for planning commissions and politicians has a higher priority and can be very time consuming. Even simple proposals can take a week or more for staff to review and evaluate in a written report. Larger, more complex proposals may require months to investigate site conditions, available infrastructure, and potential area-wide impacts. The monthly or bimonthly cycle of planning commission hearings demands that planners devote the majority of their time to preparing reviews for these hearings. Moreover, many local governments have small planning staffs, and in some places the planning tasks are left to the planning commission.

The main function of a planner is to help bring order, efficiency, and safety to the future of local development. To paraphrase the well-worn definition by management guru Peter F. Drucker, what the planner does is to recognize the futurity of present decisions. That perspective is essential in overcoming the obstacles to managing growth in the metro fringe. At the same time, it helps if there is community momentum for planning. Politicians need to be willing to risk political capital for planning, and citizens need to turn out at meetings to debate and support planning efforts.

A final obstacle to managing growth in the fringe is the reluctance of fringe politicians to reform outdated zoning and adopt a coordinated package of growth management techniques. Some communities avoid growth management techniques that have been used elsewhere and are not "homegrown." Others borrow zoning ordinances from dissimilar communities rather than spend the time and money to draft an ordinance that meets local needs. But all too often, local zoning ordinances allow far more residential, commercial, and industrial development than the community wants or needs. When development in a fringe community meant a few houses and a couple of new stores each year, the existing zoning and subdivision regulations seemed adequate. But one- and two-acre-lot zoning in the countryside can lead to major changes when a developer buys a two-hundred-acre farm and proposes to build the one hundred to two hundred houses that the zoning allows.

Even more shocking to small fringe communities is when a large developer purchases commercially zoned ground and presents a plan for a huge regional shopping mall or a multibuilding office park. The old zoning envisioned a mom-and-pop convenience store or gas station, not a commercial behemoth. If the community tries to use delaying tactics or negotiate from a position of weakness, the developer's battery of lawyers may pummel the community in court.

Zoning is a potentially good tool that has been poorly implemented. First, the local government must regard its comprehensive plan as a binding policy document to give the zoning ordinance a sound legal footing. Next, the comprehensive plan must identify where development is and is not appropriate. Then the zoning ordinance can be crafted to accommodate development in some areas and tightly control it in others. But if the comprehensive plan does not specifically identify places for growth and conservation, the zoning ordinance will probably be inadequate, too. The result will often be haphazard development patterns that unnecessarily raise the cost of public services and threaten water resources, farms and forestland, and natural areas.

Landowners who intend to develop at least some of their land fear zoning will restrict their development plans. There is a concern that zoning is "set in stone" and will handcuff the community, driving out business and tax base. In reality, zoning can be a flexible tool. Special exceptions, conditional uses and variances, and rezonings are ways that zoning regulations can respond to unique situations. Zoning is subject to change by elected officials. In some cases, however, zoning has been overly flexible, such as when rezonings, variances, and spot zonings are readily granted, which invites the cynicism of those distrustful of government or opposed to change. Fair, balanced, and justifiable zoning is an essential part of successful growth management.

When a community proposes to adopt new, stiffer zoning regulations or other growth management techniques, three responses may occur. In the short run, some landowners and developers may race to file development plans. After adoption, some developers may move on to communities with fewer restrictions and better development prospects. But other developers, businesses, and new residents will be attracted to the better-managed community.

The leaders of many fringe communities see themselves as part of the last frontier, with newcomers pouring in, bringing growth and prosperity. Long-term residents have a chance to sell their land for handsome sums to finance a comfortable retirement. Attempts to zone the countryside for very low development densities may be met with hostility by landowners who want to keep their options open.

An effective exercise in planning and zoning battles is the mapping of a build-out scenario. A build-out scenario simply shows how much development would occur if the community were completely developed according to the existing zoning ordinance. Local governments rarely have made any link between the amount of land *designated* for future development and the amount of land *needed* for future development. Many fringe communities still think of themselves as rural. Yet they have chosen zoning ordinances that would allow the community to build several times the current number of houses and an overabundance of industrial and commercial projects along the highways. Such communities are asking to become a suburb or an edge city.

In 1997, East Amwell Township, New Jersey, created a build-out scenario for its agricultural area, which was zoned for three-acre lots (see figure 3.1). After reviewing the build-out scenario, the planning

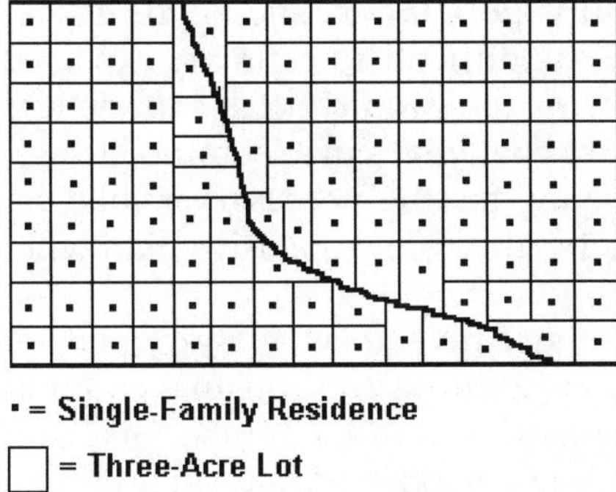

Figure 3.1 Build-out Scenario Based on East Amwell Township, New Jersey.

commission determined that the current zoning would not protect farmland and recommended a zoning density of one dwelling per sixteen acres.

The community or county planning commission can take the zoning map, overlay it with a grid of boxes representing the lot sizes allowed and make a dot on the map for each building permitted. The number of new dwellings, stores, and factories can be added up. Local residents will probably be amazed. That's not what we want, they may say. That's not realistic. But what you zone for is what you can get.

The Comprehensive Plan: Setting the Vision for Growth Strategies

The place to start in planning for growth is the community or county comprehensive plan. The comprehensive plan is a statement of policy and direction: where the community or county should grow and where what type of development should go. It is a guide for developers, landowners, concerned citizens, planning commissions, and elected officials as they make decisions about land. The plan is based on citizen input and careful studies of the planning area, which merge into a broad consensus on land use and the location of development. That is, the comprehensive plan sets forth a realistic vision for how the community or county should grow and develop (see box 3.2). The planning process should include a wide range of participants: landowners, developers, realtors, concerned citizens, bankers, businesspeople, a politician or two, and planners.

The crucial ingredient in the plan is an estimate of population growth over the next ten to twenty years. The population projections will influence the vision for the community or county and the goals and objectives. Population projections suggest the amount of land needed for future development to support the increased population.

Estimates of future population should be as realistic as possible, although it is always difficult to estimate expected in-migration over a decade or two. A community that experiences rapid population growth faces severe challenges in accommodating where development will go and in paying for the necessary public services. In a rapidly growing community, the comprehensive plan will need to be updated every few years.

Next, the plan must inventory, analyze, and identify existing and future needs and capabilities for housing, commercial and industrial development, transportation, schools, historic resources, water resources and utilities, parks and natural areas, and farm and forest-lands. Then for each of these areas there must be goals and objectives to work toward. Maps of current and future desired land uses are drafted and form the basis of the zoning ordinance.

Finally comes the challenging task of choosing taxation and spending programs, as well as regulations that can help make the vision into a reality. The comprehensive plan establishes a legal basis for zoning and subdivision regulations, which, along with capital improvements programs, serve to put the comprehensive plan into action. That is, zoning and subdivision regulations and spending on infrastructure should be aimed at achieving the goals and objectives of the comprehensive plan.

Community planning efforts in the United States have traditionally emphasized planning for development and the protection of residential property values. Zoning and subdivision regulations were devised to separate potentially conflicting land uses and to make development orderly and efficient. But population and economic growth in the fringe have created enormous challenges to the goal of orderly, sustainable development.

The comprehensive plan should help to *reform* development patterns; that is, to keep what is good and to promote new housing and commercial operations in places where they can be efficiently served with roads, schools, parks, sewers, water, fire, and police.

A comprehensive plan must be realistic and timely. Says Berks County, Pennsylvania, planning director Glenn Knoblauch, "Unfortunately, officials in most municipalities think about comprehensive planning after the problems arise."[27] The fundamental planning and growth questions facing fringe communities are: How much development is desired? What type of development should it be? and Where should it go? Most fringe communities want at least some economic growth and development. They believe they need growth to: (1) broaden the property tax base to pay for public services; (2) provide jobs for residents; and (3) protect property, business, and infrastructure investments in the community.

Box 3.5 Benchmarking: A Planning Technique for All Growth Strategies

Every community or county, regardless of its attitude toward growth, can benefit from keeping alive the vision in its comprehensive plan. Sadly, towns and counties throughout the nation have spent millions of dollars and countless hours involving the public in drafting plans that wind up on the shelf. Certainly, a planning commission should refer to the plan when making recommendations to elected officials on rezonings and proposed developments. The elected officials should consult the plan when drawing up budgets. But once a year a community or county can review the progress in putting the plan into action. An annual report on what measurable targets have and have not been achieved keeps the plan in front of the public and local government. Benchmarking also helps to keep a long-range planning perspective by measuring progress toward long-term goals.

Says Scott Standish, head of advanced planning for Lancaster County, Pennsylvania, "It's not enough to develop goals and objectives in a plan. You have to take the next important step and implement the plan. One way to ensure that the plan remains a living document is through an annual action plan process. It measures how successful we are in implementing the plan. It makes people accountable."[28]

Since 1992, Standish has worked with other county departments, private nonprofits, and townships to produce an action plan that summarizes the prior year's accomplishments and the next year's objectives. The objectives serve as benchmarks toward achieving the general goals in the comprehensive plan. Benchmarks might include: housing affordability, air and water quality, loss of farm or forestland, economic growth, unemployment, taxes, and so on.

For example, the Parks Department might have a goal of acquiring an additional one hundred acres of parkland in 1999. This would be consistent with the goal of the comprehensive plan to provide more parkland for the county residents. In the 2000 action plan, the Parks Department would report whether the hundred-acre benchmark was met, not met, or exceeded. The benchmarking process can help identify successes, problem areas, and needed adjustments in policy and spending priorities.

To help with benchmarking, the local government can use a geographic information system to track development in the community and region by matching subdivision and building approvals with specific parcels. The GIS maps can show where development is occurring, changes from previous years, and predictions of what will happen under current zoning. The GIS maps can help a community anticipate infrastructure needs, identify loss of open space, and monitor the protection of resource lands.

At the same time, many residents do not want growth to be the sole purpose of the community. Protecting farmland and open space is important to the quality of life. Affordable housing is a valid issue. And maintaining a sense of place and a sense of cohesion is an increasingly popular goal. A poll of one thousand parents in the April 1997 edition of *Reader's Digest* found that close-knit, drug-free communities, safe streets, good schools, and top-quality health care were the leading priorities. A clean environment, a growing economy, and an affordable cost of living were also important.

Overcoming the Obstacles

The land-use decisions of one community or even a single county can affect neighboring communities and counties. This is especially the case in metropolitan regions that are experiencing steady economic and population growth. Regions are expanding their influence to include a wider sweep of fringe areas, which underscores the need for metropolitan-area comprehensive plans.

Local control of land use has limited value in dealing with developments that have a regional impact. For example, a mega-mall built in one community can damage the retail base of several other communities. Also, natural resource protection for watersheds, forests, and farmland is effective only if done on a regional scale.

A regional comprehensive plan, however, requires regional political support. Until there are regional, multicounty governments, regional comprehensive plans will lack the necessary political force. In the absence of regional government, state governments can promote and fund regional planning efforts. In its Act 200 the state of Vermont has required regional plans that serve two purposes. First, state agencies are required to adopt spending plans that are consistent with regional plans. Second, local governments are encouraged to adopt comprehensive plans that are consistent with regional plans. In addition, through Vermont's Act 250, proposed developments of regional impact must go through a permit-review process.

The weak link in regional planning is that there is rarely any regional zoning ordinance or regional capital improvements program to implement the regional plan. Instead, a patchwork of local ordinances and spending programs implements local plans that do not incorporate a regional scope. Until metropolitan residents can think and plan regionally, the fragmented decisions of many local governments will continue to produce haphazard, uncoordinated growth.

For a discussion of regional planning efforts that have shown some success, see chapter 9.

Summary

Planners who take up the challenge to fight the growth management wars in the metro fringe should understand the obstacles they face. Perhaps the single greatest challenge is the fragmented control over development among dozens of local governments, special districts, and authorities. At the same time, planning resources have not been adequate to handle increasingly dispersed development patterns. A thoughtful comprehensive plan, based on public input and careful studies of the current community situation and likely trends, provides an essential foundation for community action. How the community puts the comprehensive plan into action will depend on the growth management strategy the community wants to pursue. But regional planning will be necessary to respond to developments of regional impact and to coordinate growth and protection of natural resources in the fringe and across the entire metro area.

CHAPTER 4

Growth Management Strategies and the Law of the Fringe

In the right context, with certain policies in place and good quality planning, sprawl can be good.

—Wayne A. Lemmon, Maryland real estate economist

We recognize this place is going to grow. We just have to figure out how we can preserve the ambience.

—Vince Parmesano, mayor of Sheperdstown, West Virginia, 60 miles west of the nation's capital.

If the Twin Cities population continues to grow, but nearby communities such as Mendota Heights and Lake Elmo resist growth, where are new households to go?

—Lynda McDonnell, staff writer, St. Paul Pioneer Press

Attitudes toward population growth and new construction do not follow strict political lines. There are liberals who favor economic growth and land development as a way to provide jobs and increase incomes, and there are conservatives who want nothing to change. Some liberals deplore the spread of development and want to use the power of government to control growth. Some conservatives think landowners should be able to do as they please with their property.

Residents of fringe communities have three basic choices about growth. Each choice is valid but should be recognized and understood by the residents of the community. The resulting planning policies and land-use regulations are very different, as are the consequences for the local landscape, economy, and social mix.

1. *The Pro-Growth Strategy*: Allow a suburban style and amount of development to turn the fringe community into another suburb

or even an edge city. The fringe is essentially a holding area for future urban and suburban expansion.

2. *The Balanced-Growth Strategy*: Target some areas of the community for growth and protect other areas. That is, the choice isn't between growth and saving the environment, but how to manage growth so that the environment remains attractive and an economic asset.
3. *The No-Growth or Very-Slow Growth Strategy:* Turn the community into a fortress. Make development difficult and expensive. Keep change to a minimum.

The settings for these choices vary among fringe communities according to the present population, how much open land exists, the distance from suburbs and edge cities, the composition of the local economy, and the attitude of elected officials. For example, a pro-growth strategy might be attractive in a county or community with:

- a rather small population;
- a large amount of open land;
- good access to suburbs and edge cities;
- a high rate of unemployment; and
- politicians who seek change.

After experiencing substantial development and population increases, a pro-growth community might want to adopt a balanced-growth approach or even a slow-growth strategy. In any of the three cases, the implementation depends mainly on political will and local financial resources. In addition, no community or county stands alone. Its ability to manage growth as it sees fit will be influenced by the land-use choices made by neighboring communities and counties.

The Pro-Growth Strategy

The essence of the pro-growth strategy comes from four beliefs:

- Growth is good. For example, according to the National Association of Home Builders, building one thousand single-family houses produces 2,448 jobs, $75 million in wages, and about $37 million in state, local, and federal taxes and fees.[1]
- Private property rights if allowed to be exercised will result in development that is in the public interest.

- Market forces of supply, demand, and price should be allowed to decide the location of development and the use of land.
- Government regulations should be kept to a minimum.

In the pro-growth scenario, progress equates to more people and jobs and the construction of houses, offices, factories, malls, and commercial strips. Larger size means greater importance. The increased cost of more and better roads, schools, and sewer and water facilities will be shared by more people and supported by a broader property tax base. And from a regional perspective, the growth of the fringe will relieve the congestion of suburbs and inner cities.

The comprehensive plan of a pro-growth community usually anticipates a significant increase in population over the next twenty years. To meet the needs of a growing population, the comprehensive plan emphasizes more housing; better transportation, such as highway access; and economic development in the form of new commercial and industrial areas.

Sustainable development, in an economic sense, means that there will be jobs for local residents to make a good living in the future. The Information Age, built on computers, software, and telecommunications, is the driving force in today's global economy. Competition in the global economy is intense because high-tech firms can locate virtually anywhere. A community's ability to attract high-tech plants, offices, and the workers employed in them bodes well for the economic future of the community.

Pro-growth supporters do not emphasize amenities much, but take it on faith that, just as in the suburbs, office parks will provide open space and malls will be cultural centers as long as they have movie theaters. Historic buildings and sites are useful for a tourist industry but cannot be expected to stand in the way of progress if owners propose better uses for those locations.

Planning the Pro-Growth Community

Government and the private sector usually work smoothly together in pro-growth communities. The common goal of building up the community translates into planning, zoning, and public investment in infrastructure that permit and encourage private investment. Community leaders believe that broadening the property tax base by bringing in commercial and industrial development is the solution. The separation of residential, commercial, and industrial sectors reflects a need for safety and health. But it is not unusual to see the comprehensive plan of a pro-growth community with the word "vacant" written across farmland and open space, as if that land were idle and waiting to be developed.

Residential areas with sewer and water typically are zoned for 10,000- to 20,000-square-foot minimum lots. In the countryside, one- to three-acre lots that use on-site septic systems and wells are common. These lot sizes make the sale of open land for development an attractive proposition. Highway frontage is often zoned for commercial or industrial uses. But on the positive side, pro-growth communities are often the most open to affordable, low-income housing. If a pro-growth community were strictly elitist, it probably wouldn't grow very much.

In sum, pro-growth fringe communities have embraced a destiny of growth. Within a decade, these communities will become suburbs or even nascent edge cities. Pro-growth communities believe they can grow their way out of problems. However, the race between broadening the property tax base and providing more public services will probably result in higher property taxes. Several studies have shown that residential development usually demands more in government services than it generates in taxes. Also, not all commercial and industrial developments produce a fiscal surplus because of property tax

Box 4.1 A Pro-Growth County Faces the Consequences

Prince William County, Virginia, is located thirty miles southwest of the nation's capital and is part of the burgeoning Washington, D.C., metro area. The county had 144,703 people in 1980 and had surged to 250,000 residents by 1998. While county supervisors lamented the financial strain that thousands of new homes were placing on county roads, schools, police, and fire protection, the same supervisors approved nine out of ten rezoning requests for more development from 1990 to 1995.[2]

In most cases, farmland was rezoned for residential development, and in all, the supervisors okayed roughly 17,700 new houses or 150 percent more than the existing number of dwellings in the county.[3]

In 1991 the county adopted a new five-year comprehensive plan, which designated much of the county for residential growth. The supervisors were often afraid of lawsuits from developers if they did not approve the rezonings. As supervisor Michele McQuigg explained, "If it's in the comprehensive plan for residential, then we really don't have too much of a choice."[4] The county failed in its bid to attract a Disney theme park.[5]

The pursuit of a broader tax base has not kept Prince William from experiencing the highest real estate tax rate in Virginia, as well as badly crowded schools.

inducements and wear and tear on public roads and sewer and water facilities. The aesthetic and environmental quality of a pro-growth community will eventually differ considerably from a semirural fringe community. There will be less open space, more people and traffic, and greater pressure on air and water quality.

The Balanced-Growth Strategy

Who can reasonably oppose balanced growth? The promise of attractive development in the right places with ample open spaces and reasonable taxes sounds ideal. Like the pro-growth strategy, proponents of balanced growth recognize and accept the fact that change in the form of more buildings and more people is going to happen. And like the no-growth or very-slow-growth supporters, those who favor balanced growth can point to the fiscal problems, infrastructure shortcomings, and environmental harms of rapid and poorly planned development.

Key to the balanced-growth approach is a concern for environmental quality. The protection of water supplies and resistance to regional landfills and other large-scale projects rate as priorities (see box 4.2). But in some communities, a balanced-growth strategy may be nothing more than a way to buy time. That is, as more land is developed, more pressure comes to bear on the remaining undeveloped land. Population continues to increase along with the need for more developed land. A population growth rate of 3 percent a year means that the number of community residents will double in twenty-three years. A 6 percent annual growth rate produces double the population in twelve years. The question for the balanced-growth community is: How long can growth go on before the balance is lost and the quality of life declines?

Planning the Balanced-Growth Community

Landowners, politicians, developers, and concerned citizens can work together in pursuit of balanced growth. Compromises must be made, but areas of agreement can be reached. Each of the four groups of players has interests to protect. Balanced growth most often means designating some undeveloped land for building sites and limiting development on other land. In the ideal balanced-growth scenario, everyone wins. The landowners enjoy rising property values as the demand for land and housing remains firm. Politicians have the satisfaction of brokering a compromise between development and the environment and maintaining public support. Developers continue to build houses and commercial space and make a reasonable profit.

Box 4.2 Citizens Working to Achieve Balanced Growth

McHenry County, Illinois, lies forty miles to the northwest of Chicago and along the Wisconsin border. Citizens there have long been active in the effort to achieve balanced growth. The McHenry County Defenders originated in 1969 from a fight against the construction of a freeway. The Defenders are primarily an environmental group, involved in recycling efforts and the protection of wetlands and rivers. By necessity, their activities take them into land-use and growth management issues. The Defenders emphasize educational outreach, such as explaining how to challenge a rezoning proposal, and have won several awards for their efforts.

But is this enough? In 1960, McHenry County was a sleepy farming area of 64,000 people. By 1990, the population had nearly tripled to 187,000. In 1979, the county enacted one of the stiffest agricultural zoning ordinances in the Midwest. The ordinance allowed only one dwelling on 160 acres and withstood a legal challenge in 1981. Even so, from 1987 to 1992, McHenry County lost over sixteen thousand acres of farmland. Betweeen 1990 and 1992, it was the fastest-growing county in Illinois, and the price of farmland doubled.[7] McHenry County farmer Allan Hamilton succinctly described the impending squeeze on his farm, "They are building 2,800 homes on 900 acres to the south. It is only a matter of time until someone decides they don't like having my farm and feedlot for a neighbor.[8]

In 1995, the county commissioners relaxed the agricultural zoning to allow one dwelling per forty acres. McHenry County has become caught up in the path of the expanding Chicago suburbs. The county is expected to have 230,000 residents by the year 2010. The Defenders and county farmers have their hands full.

Concerned citizens are generally pleased with the location of new development (i.e., not near them). And low- and middle-income people can find affordable housing.

But how does a community know when it is losing its balance? If the population growth falls below 1 percent a year for several years and the unemployment rate stays above the national average, politicians, developers, and concerned citizens might feel that growth is happening too slowly. They might explore more vigorous economic development efforts.

On the excess growth side, the imbalance first pinches on activities that require large amounts of land: farming, forestry, and wildlife. The per-acre market value of farms, forests, and natural areas is almost always below the market value of that land if it could be converted to home sites, office complexes, factories, or stores. As population growth drives up the value of land in a community, the community budget increases to pay for new schools, police, and fire services. Property taxes also rise—even for owners of farmland and forests who receive preferential use-value assessment. The greater property tax burden and high land values compel some landowners to sell their land, usually for development.

When nearby or neighboring properties become parcelled out and developed, owners of farms and forestland become convinced of the inevitability of selling their land for development. They cut back on investing in their farm or forestry operation as they wait for the value of their land to appreciate. This process, known as the impermanence syndrome, is a particular threat to the balanced-growth strategy. The reality of having hundreds of acres of farmland come on the market can lead to major housing or commercial projects in a short period of time (see box 4.3).

In short, balanced growth is usually a fragile balance. For farms, forestry, and wildlife to survive and thrive, a county or community must maintain a critical mass of available land. A critical mass is that amount needed to sustain farm or forestry support services: trucking, processing, feed mills, saw mills, veterinarians, and machinery dealers. Looked at another way, critical mass means the number of acres below which things will change. Dairy and grain farms will disappear. Smaller truck farms, horse farms, and horticultural greenhouses will emerge, but much of the farmland will be converted to suburbs. Wild animals will die out or leave, except for the rabbits, bats, skunks, raccoons, and occasional deer that can adapt to smaller habitats.

Fringe communities pursuing balanced growth are usually in good shape for the short run. Economic growth is not really a problem, so long as the national economy does not falter. Many, if not most, community residents earn their living outside the community. But in the long run, the quality of the environment and the social pressures of a growing and more diverse population are the main challenges that need to be addressed.

In the search for balanced growth, communities have spent millions of dollars on planning studies and advice on how to craft growth management systems. The thorny issues arise, however, when zoning techniques are proposed that would sharply restrict the use of private property, and when taxpayers realize that growth management may mean an increase in taxes to pay for new public programs, such as the purchase of development rights to keep land undeveloped.

Box 4.3 The Greig Farm of Red Hook, New York

Norman and Michele Greig operate one of the last remaining farms in the town of Red Hook, New York. The 550-acre farm is located in northern Dutchess County in the Hudson River Valley, less than a one-hour drive south of Albany and under two hours north of New York City. In the 1980s, the county lost farmland at a rate of eighteen hundred acres a year, thanks largely to the creation of new housing sites.

The Greig farm is the second biggest tourist attraction in Dutchess County, after Franklin D. Roosevelt's home at Hyde Park. About 100,000 visitors a year flock to the farm to pick their own berries, apples, and vegetables. The Greigs also milk a sixty-cow herd, more to make use of the land than to make money. "We asked children how they knew they were in the country, and they said the cows,[9] Norman said. The Greigs advertise in New York City to promote their niche market, and they put on special events, in part to educate city dwellers about farming.

Norman and Michele would prefer not to sell or develop any of their land. "I have a genetic inability to sell land," Norman joked.[10] But property taxes are seriously high. If the Greigs do decide to sell or develop, their land is already zoned for three-acre house lots. Legally, the Greigs could put more than 175 houses on their farmland. That would change the character of Red Hook in a hurry.

Michele Greig has been active in drafting a "Greenprint" for Red Hook that would offer incentives for developers to build in places where growth is desired. Farmers and other landowners would be able to sell development rights to a resource bank, and developers could purchase rights to increase densities. For a further discussion of this transferable development rights approach, see chapter 10.

The takings issue of the Fifth Amendment strikes fear into some balanced-growth communities. They worry that their land-use regulations will "go too far" in restricting the private use of land and landowners will mount a successful challenge in court.

Furthermore, the planning process favors developers with deep pockets. If a local government denies a developer's project, the developer can modify the proposal and resubmit it. The local government must then go through another costly review. Perhaps the second time through, the developer will threaten a lawsuit, and the local government must decide whether to defend its plan in court. Similarly, when a citizen group takes a developer to court to oppose a project, the citizen group had better have a good case, well-heeled backers, or both.

Developers without deep pockets are vulnerable to citizen opposition or a prolonged government review of the project. Legal challenges or delays mean money lost, and both situations can cause financial backers to pull out. But in a balanced-growth community, developers should be able to avoid most controversy if they build according to what and where the local zoning allows.

Finally, how balanced is balanced? Many communities have drafted comprehensive plans that include the following type of goals:

- Maintain the rural character of the community.
- Protect the community's agricultural land and agricultural heritage.
- Protect natural areas.

Box 4.4 Planning the Rural-Urban Fringe in New Jersey

The New Jersey State Plan identifies Fringe Planning Areas at the edge of the developing Suburban Planning Area. The Fringe Planning Areas have a density of less than one thousand people per square mile spread across a region of more than one square mile. A Fringe Planning Area does not have urban-level infrastructure, nor is it expected over the life of the plan. The Fringe Area is served primarily by on-site wastewater systems and wells for drinking water. The roads have two lanes. The Fringe Area landscape has scattered small communities and free-standing residential and commercial developments. Much of the Fringe Area is in farms, some fairly large-scale.

Without an effort to manage growth carefully in the Fringe Planning Area, development will most likely continue in a dispersed and inefficient pattern, making the future provision of public facilities and services very expensive. In addition, uncontrolled development will increase conflicts with agriculture and environmentally sensitive lands. More compact, deliberately designed communities can reduce land conflicts and encourage the preservation of rural character. A well-planned and managed Fringe Planning Area can be an effective buffer between more intensely developed urban and suburban areas and the agricultural and environmentally sensitive lands.

The New Jersey State Development and Redevelopment Plan proposes that development within the Fringe Planning Area be concentrated in or at the edges of existing communities or in well-planned, self-sufficient new communities, as centers for accommodating the area's population and employment growth. Outside of the centers, the land should remain open.[11]

- Manage a phased expansion of urban and suburban areas.
- Pursue the efficient use of public infrastructure, and avoid the unnecessary duplication of services.

Yet, when it comes to zoning land, the farmland will often be in an agricultural zone that allows the land to be cut up into two-acre or five-acre house lots. Such large house-lot zoning does little to protect a critical mass of farms and farmland and may actually hasten development. This sort of inconsistency tilts the balance in favor of development. In keeping the development of open lands to a minimum, a community with a balanced-growth strategy will need to employ the kind of strict zoning that is usually found in slow-growth communities.

The No-Growth or Very-Slow-Growth Strategy

Many fringe residents are very protective of their landscape, tax base, and quality of life. They see their community on a collision course with urban and suburban growth, and they are worried. "We don't want to become just another suburb" is a widespread sentiment. In extreme cases, residential developments have become gated communities as a way to exclude undesirables and thwart crime.[12] But inhabitants of a town, village, or county cannot simply throw up a wall and tell newcomers to go away. At the same time, residents believe they cannot drop their guard against the threat of out-of-control development. That is why no- or slow-growth communities have armed themselves with an arsenal of growth management techniques.

In the no-growth or slow-growth community, there is little love lost between concerned citizens and developers. Politicians, who depend on the support of concerned citizens, do not give developers much of a sympathetic ear. Some residents have become self-styled watchdogs, keeping an eye on development proposals that appear before the local planning commission. Although some concerned citizens earn the title of NIMBYs for their opposition to nearly all forms of development, these people are nonetheless exercising their political and legal rights in the community planning process. Citizen groups sometimes coalesce with the fervor of wartime camaraderie, united in their opposition to large-scale commercial, housing, or public projects (such as a landfill or highway). Their purpose is to wear down developers and sway politicians with their protests. The easiest way for a community to kill a project is to study it to death. A long, slow review is expensive for a developer who may have to present engineering studies, architect's drawings, a traffic impact analysis, an environmental impact study, and perhaps even a cost-benefit estimate of the net effect of the project on public service costs and property tax revenues. If a developer slogs through this paper swamp, the answer from the community may still be no. Then the developer must decide whether to drag the community into an expensive court battle with an uncertain outcome.

On occasion, developers have filed legal suits against citizen groups to silence their opposition. These so-called strategic lawsuits against public participation (SLAPP suits) are designed to hit citizen groups with large legal bills unless they back down.

The confrontation between the developer and the community is obviously a wasteful process. But the stakes are high. The community hopes that by discouraging a developer or two, word will spread to stay away. The developer who can pick a path through the planning-permit land mines not only might build a profitable project but stands to gain a reputation for doing projects that meet the high-quality standards of an exclusive community.

Several communities throughout the United States have attempted to reduce the rate of residential growth in order to better control local finances and to protect open space. Limits on the number of building permits issued in a year have been enacted in Petaluma, California, and Litchfield, New Hampshire. Ramapo, New York, will not build infrastructure until there is sufficient demand to pay for it. Many communities have from time to time imposed sewer moratoria, halting new hookups to sewer lines until new sewer capacity can be built. The state of Maryland's Smart Growth legislation of 1997 is targeting state housing and infrastructure funds to designated growth areas to discourage sprawl into the countryside and to promote more compact, cost-effective development.

Planning the No-Growth or Slow-Growth Community

Residents advocate for a no- or slow-growth community in part because they desire social stability and a manageable pace of change. The location, type, scale, and *timing* of development are key decisions in the planning process. Residents may have strong opinions of what the ideal size is for their community. The major differences between the balanced-growth and the no- or slow-growth strategies are the estimates of how much development the community can afford to accommodate and how much development the community is willing to absorb and how fast.

A no-growth or slow-growth community will employ an array of growth management techniques to ensure that the location, type, and scale of development fits in with what exists and the rate of new development and upgrade of public services will be manageable for tax-

Box 4.5 Boulder, Colorado: The Slow-Growth Success Story?

Boulder, Colorado, with a population of almost 100,000, is not a fringe community. As the home of the University of Colorado and several high-tech companies, Boulder enjoys a thriving urban economy. But in the words of journalist Neal Peirce, "The town has developed a portfolio of growth-management tools that citizens anywhere, given sufficient political will, could emulate.[13]

Boulder's growth management efforts have come together piece by piece over time. In 1959, the city enacted a "blue line" ordinance that banned any development above the 5,870-foot mark on the mountain overlooking the city. This growth boundary has remained in place, protecting spectacular mountain views.

In the 1970s, voters approved a limit on population growth of 2 percent a year and set a cap on the number of building permits issued each year, with preference for multifamily housing. New housing projects in the city must set aside 15 percent of the units for low- and moderate-income residents. The city drafted a comprehensive plan that carefully spelled out where development could or could not go. A formal growth boundary now exists between the city of Boulder and Boulder County. In 1995, Boulder County adopted a transfer-of-development-rights program to transfer development density from the countryside to growth areas, one of which is around the city of Boulder.

In the 1980s, Boulder voters passed a one-cent sales tax in part to raise funds for purchasing open space around the city. The city has also sold bonds to raise revenue to purchase open space. Nearly twenty thousand acres of preserved greenbelt now discourage sprawl and create a buffer between the city and the countryside. The city estimated that the cost to the public of servicing developed land was about $3,000 per acre per year, while the public expense to maintain open land was only $75 per acre per year.

Slow growth has brought some negative side effects for Boulder. Home prices are high, and Boulder's ability to manage its growth has probably pushed sprawling development into neighboring cities and counties. But to its credit, Boulder has a vibrant downtown and remains a highly desirable place to live and work. Boulder's real secret is that it has taken control of its own destiny.

payers. Growth management techniques might include: residential zoning that features large minimum lot sizes for single-family homes (which make homes expensive and discourage population growth); zoning for little (if any) multifamily housing; strict design standards; impact fees; and fiscal, traffic, and environmental impact studies for proposed developments. Also, in the countryside, zoning for farm and forest areas will be protective, such as forty-acre or more minimum lot sizes. For an extensive list of growth management techniques, see chapter 8, table 8.2.

A no- or slow-growth community must recognize that it does not stand alone. Land-use decisions in neighboring communities can spill over in the form of increased traffic, greater demand for housing and commercial development, and reduced air and water quality. Also, a no-growth strategy runs the risk of court challenges for exclusionary zoning, particularly if no apartments or low-income housing units are allowed. On a county level, a slow-growth strategy will emphasize containing growth where it already is. But even a single county is vulnerable to developments of regional impact in adjoining counties, such as mega-malls, major highways, and residential subdivisions with hundreds of homes.

While spending programs will vary according to tax base and growth priorities, each of the three growth strategies shares common ground in protecting public health and safety. Although members of the pro-growth approach may complain somewhat, the long-term health of the community is a powerful argument for keeping a community an attractive place to live and work. If a community develops environmental problems, such as groundwater pollution, the negative impact to property values and economic growth could be severe, and it could be difficult for the community to recover.[14] Concerns over design and the amount of development will continue to differ among communities. But water remains a fundamental ingredient for life.

The Law of the Fringe: Private Rights, Public Powers

Land-use law establishes the ground rules for both land development and growth management programs. The Fifth, Tenth, and Fourteenth Amendments to the U.S. Constitution form the basic legal framework for the management of growth in the United States. These three amendments are especially important in the rural-urban fringe, where counties and communities are using a variety of growth management techniques and examining others. Growth management programs that have a solid legal foundation and are operated fairly, openly, and with careful attention to proper procedure have the best chance of success.

The Fifth Amendment says, ". . . nor shall private property be taken for public use without just compensation." A government regulation goes too far and results in a "taking" of private property if it restricts the use of land so severely that no valid economic use of the property remains. In such a case, the courts may find the regulation unconstitutional and strike it. However, growth management expert Douglas Porter comments, "Regulations that merely reduce property values or dampen their potential increase are seldom held to be a taking of property."[15] For example, restrictions against building on wetlands, floodplains, or steep slopes are justifiable for protecting health and safety.

State courts differ about how far growth management techniques may go in restricting land use. For instance, agricultural zoning is limited to two- to five-acre minimum lot sizes in most New England states, but Wisconsin allows a thirty-five-acre minimum lot size. In addition, a state legislature must pass enabling legislation for local governments to use certain practices such as impact fees and purchasing or transferring development rights.

It is important to note that on the other side of the takings controversy is the "givings" reality. That is, public investments in roads, sewer and water lines, and schools enhance private land values. Landowners are often reluctant to recognize that the rise in the value of their property is caused primarily by public expenditures. Arguments have been made, most forcefully by nineteenth-century economist Henry George in his famous Single Tax proposal, to tax away part or all of the "unearned increment" in private land value brought about by public infrastructure. The state of Vermont in 1973 even enacted a special capital gains tax on land sold within six years of purchase in an attempt to curb land speculation and capture some unearned increment.

The Tenth Amendment allows the use of government "police power" to protect the public health, safety, welfare, and morals. The police power takes the form of nuisance ordinances to prohibit unsightly junkyards or noisy activities during certain hours of the day. The police power also takes effect as zoning and subdivision regulations over the use of privately held land. Zoning serves to separate potentially conflicting land uses, such as houses and factories. Subdivision regulations require that new developments meet standards in design, safety, and services. The landmark case of *Village of Euclid, Ohio v. Ambler Realty Co.*, 272 U.S. 365 (1926) remains the fundamental legal support for zoning as a valid exercise of government police power.

The Fourteenth Amendment says, "No State shall . . . deprive any person of life, liberty, or property, without due process of law; nor deny to any person within its jurisdiction the equal protection of the laws." The equal protection and due process concepts are designed to achieve fairness in how governments treat all citizens and a technical correctness in following procedures. Decisions by government officials may not be "arbitrary and capricious" but must be supported by the facts. In a land-use situation, a local government cannot discriminate between a zoning request from a newcomer and a similar request from a long-time resident of the community. Nor could the government in a similar case, pile requests for development impact studies on the newcomer while granting the long-time resident an approval after little review.

The Fourteenth Amendment also guarantees an individual's right to free travel. The right of free travel means that an American citizen may live anywhere in the United States. A state, county, town, or township cannot legally prevent a person from moving into that jurisdiction. The right of free travel is one of the fundamental liberties that Americans enjoy, especially in a society where, on average, people move every five years.

Private property rights are not well understood even by property owners. What a landowner owns is a bundle of rights to a property. These rights include: air rights, water rights, mineral rights, the right to sell the property or pass the property on to heirs, the right to use the property, and the right to develop the property. Any single right may be separated from the bundle and sold or given away. The rights to use and develop property are not unlimited. The landowner cannot use or develop the property in ways that would harm others. But the use of private property is an important liberty and a major source of wealth creation in America.

A property owner has the right to defend the property through legal means against trespass and nuisances occurring on neighboring properties. A property owner also has the right to challenge government regulations.

Just as a government regulation cannot take private property without triggering compensation, a government is also under no obligation to guarantee a landowner's capital gain. Owning a piece of property, just like owning stocks and bonds, carries an element of risk.

The tension between private property rights and government protection of the public health, safety, and welfare sometimes explodes into nasty fights. Many people move to the rural-urban fringe out of a desire for less government interference, especially in the use of their property. But no one is an island; everyone has neighbors. And as more people settle in the fringe, land-use regulations usually become more strict.

A competent realtor will tell a prospective buyer that the first thing to check when purchasing real estate is the underlying zoning. The zoning will tell a prospective buyer what he or she can reasonably expect to do with the property without going through a zoning change. Bitter struggles between landowners and local governments erupt when governments tighten the zoning restrictions to allow fewer houses or businesses to be built. The landowners cry foul because they have harbored expectations about what they could do with their land, and suddenly the rules have changed. Some landowners even claim that the government has reduced the value of their property without paying "just compensation." On the other hand, a landowner may suddenly learn that the local government is allowing a nearby property to be developed for a use that may threaten neighboring property values.

In the mid-1990s, eighteen states passed laws requiring governments to compensate landowners for regulations that reduce the value of a property below a certain percentage. Ironically, many of the complaints from landowners have come from federal government regulations on wetlands and endangered species (see chapter 6).

Land-Use Regulations

Municipal and county governments are creations of state government. Some states have granted local governments "home rule" powers that allow local governments the authority to adopt comprehensive plans and land-use regulations. For instance, in New York State, cities and townships (not counties) have authority over planning and zoning. In states without home rule, local governments must examine state laws for authority to implement specific land-use controls, or they must receive approval for specific actions from the state legislature. For example, the Virginia legislature denied Loudoun County's attempt to create a transfer-of-development-rights program in the 1980s.

Zoning is the most common land-use regulation in America. In addition to the takings test, zoning must also be reasonable and must be used to protect the public health, safety, and welfare. The reasonableness test is largely a matter of common sense, but there should be a clear link between the goals of the comprehensive plan and what the zoning ordinance allows. Local governments should use the future desired land-use map of the comprehensive plan as the basis for the zoning map.

Zoning can protect the public health by separating potentially conflicting land uses, such as requiring noisy and air-polluting factories to be located away from residential neighborhoods. Zoning setback requirements are aimed at providing air and light access as well as fire safety. The public welfare is broadly defined and can include zoning to protect farmland from development for aesthetic, fiscal, and local economic reasons.

There is no requirement that a local government must protect the public health, safety, and welfare through the use of zoning. Plenty of pro-growth fringe communities have loose, outdated zoning, and some have no zoning at all.

Balanced-growth communities are on fairly solid legal ground because they usually have zones that allow a variety of residential, commercial, and industrial developments as well as zones for agricultural or conservation uses.

No- and slow-growth communities may run the risk of being exclusionary and having their ordinances challenged in the courts. Also, the concept of a regional fair share of affordable housing has legally taken hold in Oregon and New Jersey.[16] Pennsylvania communities must use zoning to provide for every conceivable land use, which includes multifamily housing. A community that does not have a certain use is vulnerable to a "curative amendment" to allow that use.

The Property Rights Debate and Growth Management

Individual property rights have dominated the land-use debate in recent years. Some landowners, especially those aligned with the wise-use movement, argue that they should be able to do whatever they want to with their land. They see their land and house as their largest investment or retirement nest egg, which they will fight to protect. They cite the takings clause of the Fifth Amendment both in opposing any new government land-use regulations and in arguing for compensation for existing government regulations that reduce the value of their land.

Proponents of government land use and environmental regulations point to the Tenth Amendment, which allows the use of police power to further the public health, safety, and welfare. These proponents claim that government regulations are a reasonable means of controlling the use of private property.

Development in America occurs within a free land market based on private property rights and constrained by laws and regulations indicating the uses a piece of land can be put to and standards for how it should be developed.

Land-use regulations may come from the government or through private property agreements (covenants, homeowners' association rules, and restrictions). The need for safe and sanitary living conditions gave rise to government controls over the location, density, and uses of new buildings. Building codes set standards for plumbing, wiring, fire safety, and overall livability. Zoning ordinances have been used for decades to protect middle-class residential housing values from incompatible industrial, commercial, and low-income housing. Communities have enacted nuisance ordinances to try to limit conflicts between neighbors over the enjoyment of their property. Subdivision regulations spell out how land is to be divided into smaller lots and what infrastructure a developer must provide before lots can be sold. While not perfect, land-use controls and codes are aimed at safe, orderly development that fits into a community-wide or county-wide comprehensive plan.

The property rights debate has stolen the growth management spotlight in four Supreme Court rulings: *Nollan, Dolan, Lucas,* and *First English.*[17] *Nollan v. California Coastal Commission* and *Dolan v. City of Tigard* both involved dedication requirements in exchange for building permission when there was no clear link (rational nexus) between what the landowners proposed and what the public officials wanted the landowners to cede to the public: public beach access in return for permission to build a house in a coastal area in the *Nollan* case, and a public bike path in trade for permission to expand an existing business in the *Dolan* case. Also, the court felt that the required dedications to the public in *Nollan* and *Dolan* were out of proportion to the landowners' development proposals.

The issues in *Lucas* and *First English* revolved around the timing of the government restrictions and the fact that properties in both cases were rendered useless for building sites. (An economist could argue at length that a property that cannot be built upon retains an economic use so long as someone is willing to pay money to visit the property.) In *Lucas v. South Carolina Coastal Council,* the South Carolina coastal zone regulation went in place after Lucas had purchased the beachfront property, which at the time of purchase was zoned for residential use. Lucas claimed that the coastal zone regulation deprived him of any reasonable economic use of the property, and the Supreme Court agreed.

In *First English Evangelical Lutheran Church v. County of Los Angeles,* a camp for handicapped children had been wiped out in a flood and Los Angeles County enacted a temporary floodplain ordinance that prohibited rebuilding on the church's property until final floodplain development rules were passed. The church argued that California law does not compensate for a regulatory taking and that the only remedy available was an invalidation of the floodplain regulation. The U.S. Supreme Court found that invalidation was not sufficient when all or nearly all value and use had been stripped from the property.

The Court established a "temporary takings rule" that would require compensation from the time a regulation takes effect until, and if, it is ruled invalid for denying all reasonable use of the property. In this way, the *First Church* case has deterred local governments from using temporary regulations.

The U.S. Supreme Court did not address the taking issue in *First Church* and remanded the case to the California 2nd District Court of Appeals, which found that the county restrictions did not amount to a taking. The court noted that the church could pitch tents on the site when it was not submerged by floodwaters, and therefore no compensation was owed by the county.

The development community and individual property owners have taken heart from these four Supreme Court rulings, even though the fundamental uses of zoning—to separate conflicting land uses and to protect the public health, safety, and welfare—were not at issue. In essence, these four cases were squabbles over money. Furthermore, these cases and the property rights movement are masking the bigger question for growth management: Can local governments accommodate more people and development while maintaining a healthy environment?

The Right of Free Travel

While the nation's land-use debate has been side-tracked by property rights advocates, no-growth or slow-growth fringe communities may make decisions that conflict with the hallowed right of free travel. The right to free travel has been interpreted to mean that a community, county, or state cannot establish a population cap.[18] Nor can residents surround their city, town, or county with a barbed-wire fence and signs that say "keep out!"

One of the central concepts in environmental planning is *carrying capacity*, which describes the ability of an area to support development without experiencing a significant decline in air, water, and land quality. Carrying capacity indicates the limits to growth of the community or region: the maximum number of people that the area can accommodate.[19]

Carrying capacity can be measured in part through changes in air and water quality and linking these changes to population growth and new development in an area. Carrying capacity is not necessarily fixed. Air and water quality can improve even as population increases; or new development can reduce water quality, and more people driving to and from the fringe can worsen air quality. Keeping track of carrying capacity over time is important. New technologies should enable planners to make fairly accurate estimates of carrying capacity. Geographic information systems and computer models are powerful tools that can provide important information and simulations to anticipate the potential impacts of population growth and development on the environment.

Because most fringe communities will continue to grow, they run the risk of becoming unmanageable. Must a community, in order to uphold the right of free travel, accommodate more and more people until it exceeds its carrying capacity? At what point do the rights of newcomers surpass the rights of the longer-term residents to enjoy their property and lifestyle? If personal freedom of travel results in the degradation of the environment, was that freedom worth having in the first place? What kind of responsibility goes along with the right of free travel? The responsibility not to exceed the carrying capacity of a place?

In the long run, the right of free travel may prove to be the single largest and most recalcitrant obstacle to effective state and local efforts to manage population growth and land development.

If the right of free travel were modified to reflect environmental carrying capacity or fiscal capacity, state and local governments could produce plans for sustainable growth management but at a cost of less individual choice about where to live. For example, in 1994, a bill was introduced in the California legislature that would require cities and counties to identify the water supply they intend to use before allowing new suburban developments.[20] In the near future, water will be a limiting factor to development in parts of Florida, California, and the Southwest.[21]

Environmental concurrency—requiring adequate sewage capacity, water supplies, and air quality before development can occur—will become more widespread in years to come and will hinder both development and free travel. For example, air pollution in metropolitan regions presents a serious challenge to carrying capacity and local population growth. Vehicle miles traveled continue to increase, resulting in greater gasoline consumption despite the improved energy efficiency of cars and trucks. The federal government has threatened to withhold funds for highway projects that would increase air pollution levels above federal standards. Several metropolitan areas face the prospect of stifling themselves through a combination of air pollution and traffic congestion. The traffic congestion is made worse by the fact that people have been moving to homes and jobs in the fringe, away from the inner cities and suburbs, and increasing their reliance on the automobile.

Should the Right of Free Travel Be Limited?

If limits are placed on the right of free travel, what should those limits be? And who should determine what they are? Could the right of free travel be redefined to "visit but don't stay," as coined by Tom McCall, Oregon's governor in the 1970s, who pushed for the adoption of Oregon's pioneering land-use law? Are population caps realistic? Should limits be determined on the basis of a municipality, county, or state? Can economic growth occur without population growth, especially since homebuilding and construction are major industries?

In metro areas, some jurisdictions have attracted high-value residences to become elite suburbs; others have struggled to expand their tax bases. Meanwhile, most inner cities continue to lose people and tax base. But can America allow millions of people nationwide to keep pushing farther away from the inner cities in a land-consuming, auto-dependent style of development? Is this an abuse of the right of free travel, impinging on both human well-being and the health of the environment?

Limits on the right of free travel are especially threatening to the development community and the economically disadvantaged. Developers would generally prefer to build a $300,000 house in the suburbs rather than a $300,000 apartment or three $100,000 homes in the inner city. And if the economically disadvantaged were not allowed to move from the city to a fringe community because of a population cap in that community, wouldn't that limit opportunities for upward mobility?

Table 4.1 lists some of the arguments for and against limiting the right to free travel. The arguments in favor of limits are mostly environmental. Better control of public service costs is important, too. In short, the limits may allow for more manageable and sustainable communities. The arguments against limits are mostly social, in that limits run counter to the America traditions of opportunity, freedom to pursue happiness, and civil rights against racial and ethnic discrimination.

The danger of limiting free travel with population caps is that it could place jurisdictions on a slippery slope to authoritarianism and outright racial discrimination. On the other hand, a population cap might be imposed when there is a "clear and present danger" to the community, such as a water shortage. To be democratic, a cap could be voted on through a referendum. A similar process could be used with a target population in reference to measurable environmental and fiscal benchmarks. But with a mobile population settling in the fringe, carrying capacity can be assaulted in a relatively short period of time.

Table 4.1 The Pros and Cons of Limiting the Right of Free Travel

Pros	*Cons*
• Helps maintain air quality	• Is exclusionary, elitist, and potentially discriminatory
• Maintain Water Quality	• Will produce many legal challenges
• Ensures a more stable local tax base, more stable public service needs	• Reduces economic growth
• Helps maintain open space	• Creates fortress mentality among communities, unwillingness to cooperate
• Helps create long-term environmental sustainability	

Summary

Local governments in the fringe generally pursue one of three growth management strategies: pro-growth, balanced-growth, or no- or slow-growth. Each of these strategies will feature different goals in local comprehensive plans and different standards in local ordinances and growth management programs. Some local governments, however, seem to have no strategy at all and simply let development happen.

The takings issue and private property rights will dominate the national land-use debate in the near term. But over time, the right of free travel will increasingly become the focus of growth management efforts. Slow- or no-growth fringe communities may look to impose annual growth limits or population caps to protect the residents' enjoyment of a quality environment.

CHAPTER 5

Designing the Fringe: Joining Appearance and Performance

Low-density settlement is the overwhelming choice for residential living.

— *Peter Gordon and Harry W. Richardson, economists*

Americans are reacting to the ugliness that they see on the landscape and the speed with which places they love are being destroyed. They are saying, 'Is this what America has to look like?'

—*Constance Beaumont, National Trust for Historic Preservation*

The fringe landscape has six different kinds of settlements: farmsteads, dispersed housing and commercial strips, crossroads community, villages of a few hundred to a few thousand residents, towns of up to ten thousand inhabitants, and cities of less than fifty thousand people. How these settlements function, look, and interact with each other affect land-use patterns, transportation, environmental quality, economic activity, and social relations now and in the future.

The appearance of a community reflects feelings of pride and a collective attitude toward land use. In many growing fringe places, short-term profit has shaped both architectural styles and where people live, work, and shop. A community that is a jumble of houses and stores strewn along a highway or that has a deteriorated downtown touches off feelings of distaste and disconnection. Land uses that are isolated from each other serve to isolate people from one another and diminish the sense of community and place. Community design is about place making. The physical layout of the community can and should connect people with each other, with the community, and with the surrounding countryside.

Attractive buildings, a mix of different land uses, and a visually pleasing landscape contribute much to a fringe community's quality of life. Developers often say that they build what the market wants. In fact, developers also build what local government ordinances require. Reform of local zoning and subdivision ordinances to allow, encourage, and even require compact, mixed-use developments adjacent to existing cities and towns is long overdue. The fringe pattern of development not only scatters houses, stores, offices, and factories, it also lacks public spaces and buildings that hold together a community as an identifiable place. If the design and location of new developments are to promote a vibrant, livable community, then local ordinances must change along with the preferences of those who buy the homes and operate the businesses.

Community Design and Land-Use Planning

Should design drive the land-use planning process or vice versa? Design and land-use planning should complement each other in affecting the overall appearance and functioning of a community—how the many properties and land uses fit together into a whole system—and the use and design of specific sites. Design standards for different parts of the community should reflect the vision set forth in the comprehensive plan and future land-use map. Illustrations of desirable design in the community's zoning and subdivision regulations can help developers and landowners understand what the community wants in landscaping and the height, size, and style of buildings. While the regulation of aesthetics is tricky at best, other elements of design respond to site-specific concerns, such as traffic and water quality.

The cardinal rule of architecture and landscape design is: Form follows function. What then is the function of the rural-urban fringe? Specific answers may vary, but they usually include providing an alternative to the monotony and density of the suburbs and an escape from the congestion and grime of the central city. In short, the fringe should offer a good place to live, often referred to as the American Dream.

The American Dream is of a single-family, detached home with a lawn and a garage in a friendly, tree-lined neighborhood that is safe from crime. The residents enjoy fresh air and clean water. The neighborhood is located within easy access to work, shopping, and schools. Property taxes are low, the public schools are good, and public services are efficient. The town or city is a manageable size. There is a sense of community, of knowing one's neighbors, of shared aspirations and concerns, of belonging to an identifiable place.

The American Dream may be an illusion, but it might suggest a vision for a community to work toward. Many communities in the fringe seem to be constantly growing and changing, thwarting people's desire to put down roots. Residents fear that their neighborhood could be suddenly transformed by any of a number of mega-developments: a high-voltage power line, a freeway, a swarm of tract homes, or a "power center" mall. These changes could drive down property values, as well as create environmental hazards, make living in the neighborhood less safe, and thwart the achievement of the American Dream.

Since the early 1970s, Americans have increasingly regarded their homes as not just a place to live but as an investment vehicle as well. Except for a few brief periods, fringe real estate has appreciated steadily over the past twenty-five years. Homeowners have enjoyed federal income tax deductions for property taxes and mortgage interest, and beginning in 1997, generous capital gains tax treatment on the sale of homes (see chapter 6). These incentives mean that Americans have invested and will invest heavily in their homes. In the rural-urban fringe, it is common to find new homes in the $250,000-and-up price range. These homes, often set on an acre or more, are known as "McMansions" because of the gaudy style and emphasis on putting the garage up front, close to the road. There is something out of place about these homes. They isolate people from each other and defeat the sense of place and community. They are an attempt at creating rural estates, mini–Mount Vernons and Monticellos, except that neither Washington nor Jefferson made a daily commute of dozens of miles to and from work.

If neither the large-lot McMansion pattern nor the suburban sea of houses is desirable land-use planning, what then is a good development design for the fringe?

Fringe Design Principles

Planners, architects, and landscape architects should have a sense of how the world ought to look and work. They need to recognize the complex interaction of design elements—buildings, transportation networks, and open space—that make up the overall quality of the community and regional environment.

To counter the car-oriented landscape and lifestyle, a group of architects in the early 1990s formed the New Urbanism movement. New Urbanism advocates—like Lewis Mumford and the regional planners of the 1920s—hold the village as the model for development. The idea is that a village has a human scale; a fairly dense settlement pattern; and social, architectural, and economic cohesion. The village exhibits order and neatness and close-knit society conveys a sense of security.

New Urbanist architect Peter Calthorpe has set down four design principles that are applicable to fringe communities: scale, pace, pattern, and bounds (see table 5.1). For a community to function successfully as a place to live and work with a high quality of life, all four of those elements must blend harmoniously.

Scale. Small, human-scale developments can be made to blend in with the community. Such developments can connect with the community and enhance community identity instead of detracting from a sense of place. Large-scale developments are simply urban or suburban growth imposed on the landscape. The choice is between shops and superstores. One way to maintain a human scale is to limit the size of buildings in commercial zones to less than twenty thousand square feet. Another way to maintain scale is by preserving historic buildings through design ordinances and facade easements.

Pace. A slower, safer speed for traffic helps to connect drivers with their surroundings. Traffic-calming devices, such as speed bumps or narrow streets, can help. Sidewalks and walking streets encourage social interaction. Bike and pedestrian trails can link cities and towns to the countryside as well as reduce dependence on the automobile.

Pattern. The location of different land uses makes up the pattern of the community. A community can encourage mixed-use developments that blend commercial and residential uses. Also, small blocks and lot sizes make for a higher density. "As population density rises, people do less driving and more walking, says Seattle environmentalist Alan Durning.[1] The key, he adds, is better neighborhoods: walking neighborhoods with a comfortable pace and a human scale. Parks and public spaces enhance private developments. In-filling between developments can reduce leapfrog patterns that confuse.

Table 5.1 Good and Bad Design Features of Fringe Communities

Feature	*Good Design*	*Bad Design*
Scale	Human-scale buildings and settlements	Huge buildings and sprawling cities and towns
Pace	Slow to medium pace of traffic	Rapid pace of traffic
Pattern	Recognizable streets, roads, buildings, landmarks, and neighborhoods	Confusing jumble of buildings; no sense of place
Bounds	Distinct break between town and countryside, visual clarity	Sprawl along arterial roads for making separate communities grow into a blob

Box 5.1 The Ahwahnee Principles for Development Design

The Ahwahnee Principles were the outcome of an intensive seminar at the Ahwahnee Hotel in Yosemite National Park in 1991 that attracted many of the New Urbanists, including Peter Katz, Elizabeth Plater-Zyberk, Stefanos Polyzoides, Elizabeth Moule, Peter Calthorpe, and Michael Corbett.[2] The values stated in the Ahwahnee Principles are perhaps some of the most important area-wide planning concepts of this century. A selection of the principles related to community and regional planning shows that, although by no means new to the planning profession, they involve both a fine-grained approach and a return to the general plan as a controlling instrument.

Community Principles:

- All planning should be in the form of complete and integrated communities containing housing, shops, workplaces, schools, parks, and civic facilities essential to the daily life of the residents.
- Community size should be designed so that housing, jobs, daily needs, and other activities are within easy walking distance of each other.
- As many activities as possible should be located within easy walking distance of transit stops.
- A community should contain a diversity of housing types to enable citizens from a wide range of economic levels and age groups to live within its boundaries.
- The location and character of the community should be consistent with a larger transit network.
- The community should have a center focus that combines commercial, civic, cultural, and recreational uses.
- The community should contain an ample supply of specialized open space in the form of squares, greens, and parks whose frequent use is encouraged through placement and design.
- Each community or cluster of communities should have a well-defined edge, such as agricultural greenbelts or wildlife corridors, permanently protected from development.
- Streets, pedestrian paths, and bike paths should contribute to a system of fully connected, interesting routes to all destinations. Their design should encourage pedestrian and bicycle use by being small and spatially defined by buildings, trees, and lighting, and by discouraging high-speed traffic.
- The community design should help conserve resources and minimize waste.

(*continues*)

Box 5.1 (*continued*)

Regional Principles and Implementation Principles:

- The regional land-use planning structure should be integrated within a larger transportation network built around transit rather than freeways.
- Regions should be bounded by and provide a continuous system of greenbelt and wildlife corridors to be determined by natural conditions.
- Rather than allowing developer-initiated, piecemeal development, local governments should take charge of the planning process. General plans should designate where new growth, infill, or redevelopment will be allowed.
- Plans should be developed through an open process, and participants in the process should be provided visual models of all planning proposals.

Bounds. A distinct edge between developed areas and the countryside is both more pleasing to the eye and easier on the public purse than sprawl. Calthorpe is a strong proponent of growth boundaries as a way to separate built lands from open countryside. A definite boundary also lends a sense of cohesion to a community; it is not a limitless spread of houses and stores fanning out into the countryside.

If a village settlement pattern in the fringe is to succeed, people must become convinced of the advantages of living in a village rather than on a large lot in the countryside. A village offers a greater possibility for diversity of inhabitants and affordable housing than expensive, large-lot, residential developments. A village also has much greater potential for public transit.

Nearly every modern planning proposal for balanced metropolitan growth hinges on mass transit as the key transportation alternative. Mass transit is more environmentally benign and more energy efficient than the personal automobile.[3] Community design can promote the use of mass transit. The Transit-Oriented Design (TOD) approach, developed and popularized by Peter Calthorpe, combines a European-style transit system and the traditional American small town. In essence, he proposes a sophisticated version of the "streetcar suburb."[4]

Calthorpe created the TOD initially to meet conditions found in California, Oregon, and Washington State, where the TODs could make use of existing rail lines, many of which were abandoned after World

War II. These trunk lines serve as feeders to connect neighborhoods to dominant regional centers, such as a metropolitan downtown. In places without existing rail lines, buses could be used, or new light-rail lines could be built.

Calthorpe then designed compact, high-density "nodes" at intervals along the rail lines, with the transit stations serving as the center of town. The TODs include a core area of about a quarter-mile radius and a secondary area that extends outward for an additional quarter mile. Within this bounded area, development occurs at a full range of densities—houses, apartments, and commercial space within walking or biking distance of a transit line and an easily accessible town center at the transit hub. (See figure 5.1.) The compact design of the TOD helps keep the surrounding landscape open.

The Portland, Oregon, metro area has received considerable attention in the 1990s as a testing ground for New Urbanist ideas. The 2040 plan of the Metropolitan Council has identified thirty-five centers joined by main streets and transit corridors. These centers will occupy about one-fourth of the metro area and contain about half of the region's people. A light-rail system has served Portland and its eastern suburbs since 1986. A second line is proposed for the western suburbs. Transit-oriented developments are envisioned along the rail line to reduce dependence on the automobile and create pedestrian-friendly places.

Neotraditional design is the basis of the New Urbanism and emphasizes human-scale buildings more than pattern or public transportation. The village of Seaside, Florida, designed by husband and wife architects Andres Duany and Elizabeth Plater-Zyberk, has won widespread praise, as well as some criticism. Seaside covers eighty acres

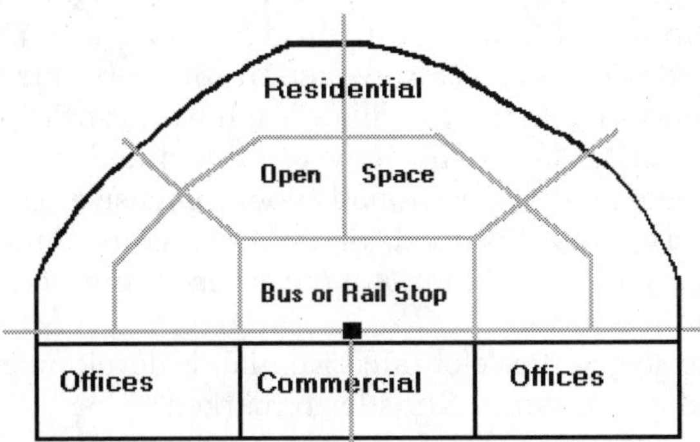

Figure 5.1 Transit-Oriented Development Design.
Source: Adapted from Calthorpe Associates, 1994, Berkeley, CA.

along the coast of the Florida panhandle. The buildings are low-rise and on a human scale; the streets are narrower to "calm" traffic; there are sidewalks; and the houses must have a front porch, a pitched roof, and a picket fence in front. While these features may sound like kitsch, the result is anything but. This is a refreshing place. It is also an upper-income community that is outside of the metro fringe.

The value of Seaside and the transit-oriented development is that they provide models of settlements that can function efficiently as well as visually and satisfy socially. But before the transit-oriented design and the neotraditional village become popular, two essential things have to happen. First, New Urbanism design harks back to older architectural styles and a pattern of mixed-land uses. Historic buildings and districts enforce a community's identity and sense of place. Many community zoning and subdivision ordinances need to be revised to allow the types of housing on small lots and mingled homes and shops within a district that make older villages attractive, compact, and pedestrian oriented. Also, codes must permit building designs with porches and zero lot lines on the front of the property to put a house or store right up to the sidewalk.

Second, these new development designs must translate into financially successful projects for developers to embrace them and for bankers to make loans for them. Bob Hankin is developing The Gardens, a small compact village of eighty-two houses on fifteen acres in Chester County, Pennsylvania, about twenty-five miles from Philadelphia. The houses sit on 6,000-square-foot lots and have porches and picket fences in front. The garages are detached, and there are sidewalks and back alleys.

"As the village streetscape takes form and sense of community increases, the appeal of The Gardens has grown, exceeding many of our conventional developments," Hankin remarks.[5] The Gardens will be joined by a paved trail to a larger development complex with a town square, shops, restaurants, a medical facility, and a YMCA.

If the perceived widespread dissatisfaction with suburbia is correct, there will be plenty of demand for villages and transit-oriented places. Even so, a valid criticism of the New Urbanism and neotraditional design is that they are not yet regionally comprehensive. The focus on a specific property, neighborhood, or even village is commendable, but a village set amid a sea of monotonous arterial commercial sprawl does not present a solution.

In response to seeing the celebrated Kentlands development in suburban Maryland, critic James Kunstler remarked:

> Kentlands lies embedded in one of the worst suburban crudscapes in America, like a Faberge egg in a county landfill. This

> is the so-called technology corridor between Rockville and Gaithersburg along I-270, one Radiant City office park after another, pod-upon-pod of income-targeted houseburgers, strip after numbing strip of chain stores, fry pits, and multiplexes. It's like Southern California, only arguably worse. . . . Except for a few tatters of remnant farmland, this is a tragic landscape of postwar zoning with all its predictable horrors.[6]

The village style of design implies the need to limit the size of the village in terms of both territory and population. Calthorpe favors growth boundaries, but Andres Duany is opposed to them. "There has never been a growth boundary that has held," Duany writes. "Not even Portland's. And the reason is simple: Such boundaries are arbitrary. . . . It is not organic."[7]

New Towns

Major renovations of suburban areas are unlikely to happen anytime soon, though retrofitting suburbs for transit-oriented development holds some promise. New villages and towns will usually have to be built from scratch on greenfields. Seaside, for instance, is a functioning new town, though critics question whether it has a viable town center.

New towns are a design concept rarely seen in America since the 1930s. The New Town movement began in England at the turn of the century. Sir Ebenezer Howard, in his book *Garden Cities of Tomorrow*, presented a vision of new towns that would be largely self-sufficient and planned and built from scratch. These small cities with a maximum of about thirty thousand people would be constructed in the countryside, beyond the suburban ring. Each city would contain all income classes and not serve as an exclusive suburban retreat from a major urban center. The garden cities would not have the congestion, crowding, or pollution of major cities. Factories and houses would be organized to allow people to walk to work and children to walk to school. There would also be ready access to garden plots, where people could grow at least some of their own food. Howard hoped that a network of these garden cities would be established with ample open and agricultural space between them.

Howard explained, "A town, like a flower or a tree, or an animal, should at each stage of its growth, possess unity, symmetry, completeness, and the effect of growth should never be to destroy that unity but to give it greater purpose."[8]

Howard's vision became something of a reality in Britain, where twenty-six "new towns" have been built since Letchworth in 1903 and

Welwyn Garden City in 1920. But in the British experience the new towns were either absorbed into part of a metropolitan area (such as Welwyn, now a London bedroom suburb, though still attractive) or built on a huge scale, such as Telford outside of Liverpool, which has more than 100,000 inhabitants.

In the United States, the New Town movement took root in 1933, when Congress appropriated $25 million to begin planning one hundred new communities, essentially suburban garden cities, to house both inner-city dwellers and homeless farm families. The head of the New Deal Resettlement Administration, Rexford G. Tugwell, developed working plans for twenty-five new towns, but the deepening depression and the mood of the Republican Congress against such "communist farms" limited actual construction to three communities: Greenbelt, Maryland, near Washington, D.C.; Greenhills, Ohio, near Cincinnati; and Greendale, Wisconsin, near Milwaukee. All three communities were constructed by 1938, but Tugwell's efforts to create dozens of such communities were by then politically dead.

Whereas Tugwell's efforts in the 1930s were bold, innovative, and visionary, the U.S. Department of Housing and Urban Development (HUD) administration of the New Towns program in the 1970s was cautious and reserved. The New Towns program—Section 701 of Title VII of the Urban Growth and New Community Development Act of 1970—began with a high degree of optimism. The goal of the act was to provide a national growth policy to "encourage the rational, orderly, efficient, and economic growth, development, and redevelopment of our States and metropolitan areas."[9]

HUD was not directly involved in the planning, acquisition, and policy direction for the new towns, although the secretary of HUD was authorized to provide technical assistance to developers. HUD also guaranteed bank loans to local communities and private development corporations for land acquisition costs, the development of infrastructure, and industrial development. Principal and interest payments on certain aspects of the loans could be deferred for up to fifteen years. In February of 1970, the first new town, Jonathan, Minnesota, was insured.

At the time of the New Towns legislation, federal planners estimated that ten new communities a year would be approved for assistance. By 1972 a total of twenty projects had completed the application process. The initial projected population of these new communities ranged from 110,000 in Park Forest South, Illinois to 25,000 in Pattonsburg, Missouri. Eventually, only about a dozen new communities under the HUD loan guarantee process achieved any real success. All of the federally assisted new communities were in precarious financial condition from the very beginning. Jonathan, the first federally assisted new community, defaulted on a $468,000 interest payment.[10]

While publicly funded new towns have lost luster, private new town developments, such as Columbia, Maryland, Radburn, New Jersey, and Reston, Virginia, are still discussed as one means of relieving the pressure on the urban fringe. But Radburn is a suburban community, and Reston and Columbia have been engulfed by the Greater Washington metro area.

If new towns had been envisioned as part of a coordinated federal, state, and local government development process, some success might have been achieved in directing infrastructure and services to satellite areas at the metropolitan fringe. Or, new towns could have accommodated the growth of selected, planned areas, such as within urban growth boundaries (see chapter 9). Perhaps the greatest fallacy of the New Towns program was that people would flock to these settlements because they wanted a planned environment. That way of thinking simply ignored the fact that fringe sprawl occurred because people wanted to go there. They preferred the semirural, centerless environment to an organized, patterned, and generally efficient type of settlement that runs counter to their expectations.

Interestingly, some New Urbanism planned communities appear successful, while many publicly funded new towns failed. One reason may be that the private-sector developers have aimed at creating communities with added design amenities and carefully crafted, more expensive homes. The higher-income residents are less likely to default on mortgages. By contrast, the public new towns did not favor any economic class.

Harvard planning professor William Alonso, writing about the creation of the second generation of new towns, offered the following opinion:

> There is much to be done to improve our cities, and perhaps some experiments with new towns would help. I say only that, even if new towns turned out to be wonderful places, they would still be almost powerless to affect our present urban problems; and I fear that, as sirens of utopia, they might distract us from our proper work.[11]

The likelihood of new towns becoming a major feature of the metro fringe is remote. The amount of money and time required to amass the land and erect the buildings would be daunting to any but the largest corporations. The one example of a new town, partially completed, is the Disney Corporation's Celebration, Florida, outside of Orlando. The architects hired by Disney have designed a neotraditional town with small lots, houses with front porches, and a downtown with a mix of commercial and residential spaces. Most residents live within a five-minute walk of the downtown. And most of the working residents commute to jobs in Greater Orlando. Celebration is being designed for a target population of about twenty thousand—a number slightly smaller than the optimal size identified by Ebenezer Howard a hundred years ago. Disney has no plans to embark on another new town.[12]

Box 5.2 Rural Village Strategy in Loudoun County, Virginia

Loudoun County, Virginia, is in the famous horse-and-hunt country some thirty-five miles west of Washington, D.C., and just east of the Blue Ridge Mountains. For over ten years, county planners and residents have wrestled with ways to keep the rural land in the western part of the county open and yet accommodate the development that is spreading from the northern Virginia suburbs. Most of the county is zoned for three-acre house lots, and as previously mentioned, a large amount of commercial and residential development has already been approved (see Box 3.2). This development is slated for the eastern side of the county.

To protect the western portion of the county, a new comprehensive plan, adopted in 1991, discourages the extension of sewer and water service into the countryside. Instead, the plan calls for a strategy of clustering development in hamlets of no more than twenty-five houses and villages of up to three hundred houses. In building a cluster, developers must keep 80 percent of the land in open space, and both the villages and hamlets require communal septic and water systems. While hamlets are limited to houses only, villages are planned for a variety of uses, including businesses, stores, and schools. The villages are an attempt to build new developments that resemble the historic crossroad villages in the county. According to County Planning Director Julie Pastor, "We are creating little communities."[13]

As of 1997, two villages had received approval but had yet to be built. The challenges to the village approach are the several years developers have to spend to get a village designed and approved and to arrange the financial means to build.

Steve DeLong, president of the Loudoun County chapter of the Northern Virginia Building Industry Association, expressed caution about hamlets and villages: "I think the jury is still out on whether builders like that sort of development. Lots of builders and homeowners like the 5- and 20-acre lots."[14]

Designing the Fringe Countryside

Good community and environmental design is not just a matter of making cities and towns prettier places so people will want to live there; the design of the countryside will also influence where people choose to live. The following design principles can promote visual quality, environmental protection, and the efficient use of rural land in the face of change:

Create and maintain edges, which help to organize land-use patterns and to maintain visual quality. Edges may be natural, such as ridges, hills, streams, rivers, and woods, or human-made in the form of roads, fences, and municipal boundaries. A clutter of houses and stores scattered through the countryside is both a waste of space and visually disorienting. Edges separate villages, suburbs, and cities from the countryside. This means limiting commercial strip development along the entrances to the city or village. Edges also define farm fields from woods and help to create buffers between farms and settlements.

Protect water quality and quantity. Development in the countryside should be sustainable and therefore sensitive to the carrying capacity of land. Design should conserve wetlands, forests, farmland, and water supplies.

Build to survive natural hazards. Buildings should be placed so as to avoid steep slopes, shallow and hydric soils, and high water tables. Buildings should also be kept out of floodplains and coastal areas and away from seismic fault lines.

Protect viewsheds. Viewsheds can be mapped and any proposed development evaluated according to its impact on scenic views. Development might be moved to a less intrusive site or trees or other vegetation used for camouflage.

Protect historic landscapes. Historic landscapes help make a community or region identifiable and distinct. Historic sites are worthy of preserving, but not all of a historic landscape needs to be maintained in “museum condition.” Still, what development is permitted should be designed and located in ways that do not detract from the historic landscape. These landscapes have economic as well as historic and aesthetic value. They are often important tourist attractions and may be actively farmed or logged.

Four Rural Design Models

There are four general schools of thought about how the fringe countryside should look and function (see figure 5.2 and table 5.2). The first school is closely allied with the pro-growth strategy. The central

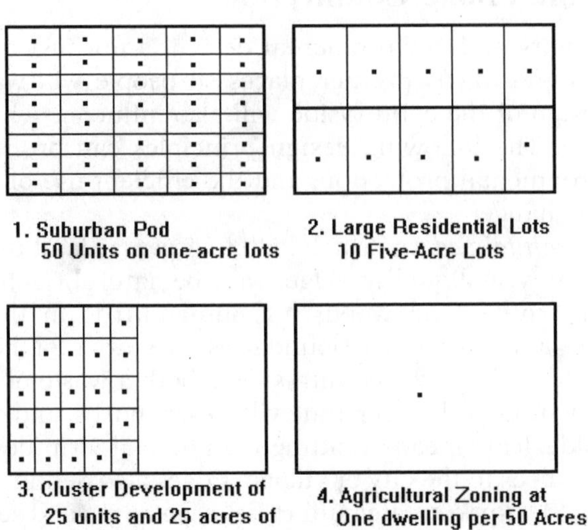

Figure 5.2 Four Development Options for the Fringe Countryside, on 50-Acre Sites.

idea is that the countryside is waiting to become developed into a new suburb. Large residential "pods" of several dozen to hundreds of houses are envisioned, separated by a scant amount of open space. The pods tend to have a uniform appearance, with houses set on quarter-acre to one-acre lots along curvilinear streets and in cul-de-sacs.

The second approach also reflects an attempt to be pro-growth but with an eye to protecting the public purse. Zoning the countryside for large residential lots of three- to five-acre minimum sizes allows for a proliferation of country estates, also known as hobby farms, farmettes, and ranchettes. These rural residences often generate enough property tax revenue to cover the cost of the government services they demand. But if there is a need to provide public sewer or water to dispersed houses, the cost will easily exceed the tax revenue.

The downside of the large-lot approach is that it scatters residential development, separating neighbors and making busing children to school expensive. Residential lots of two to ten acres eat up the landscape in large bites, creating parcels that are too big to mow and too small to plow. Planner-architect Jonathan Barnett dryly notes, "Out in two-acre-zoning country, old ideas of neighborhood and neighborliness are hard to sustain: borrowing a cup of sugar from the house next door might mean a five-minute walk."[15]

The large-lot strategy is often presented as a balanced-growth technique, or even a slow-growth technique. In a suburban setting, large

Table 5.2 Design Strategies for the Fringe Countryside

Strategy	*Pro*	*Con*
Suburban pod	Houses many people	Single-use, car-dependent
Large lots	Low public service costs	Uses a large amount of space for relatively few people
Cluster	Sensitive to environmental constraints; leaves significant open space; cheaper to build than a suburban pod	Risk of water pollution from on-site septic tanks put too close together; overuse can produce clustered sprawl
Working rural landscape	Keeps large amount of land open	Farm and forest operations may not be financially strong; may cause legal and political challenges from rural landowners

lots can be prohibitively expensive for all but an elite few. But farther out in the fringe, large lots are more affordable and cater to people who want their place in the country. Barnett points to large-lot zoning as a primary culprit in generating sprawl: "Large-lot zoning applied uniformly over the landscape, interspersed with strip commercial zones along highways, is the recipe for urban sprawl; and sprawl will continue as long as these regulations remain in force."[16]

Clearly, several large residential lots can consume much more space for a few people than can quarter-acre lots. But quarter-acre lots will not be developed with on-site septic systems and wells. They will require public systems and therefore will have to be located near existing development. Large-lot zoning is simply antithetical to compact development.

The third design technique is cluster development, or open-space zoning. The key issues are the density allowed and the amount of a site required to remain as open space. A relatively high density is essentially suburban oriented. For example, East Amwell Township in Hunterdon County, New Jersey, employed clustering in its agricultural zone, based on one dwelling per three acres. Within a few years, the township planning commission declared that clustering at that density would not protect farmland.[17]

In the Nashua River Watershed region of northeastern Massachusetts, eleven of fifteen towns allow cluster development by special permit. The open-space requirement varies from 20 percent to 50 percent of the site.

Clustering is best understood as a way to protect some open space, but probably not large blocks of contiguous acreage. It is precisely these large blocks, however, that are necessary for agricultural and forestry production and wildlife habitat.

Clustering has been used with some success in devising conservation subdivisions, also known as golf course design without the golf course. In looking at a tract of land, a developer first identifies the steep slopes, wetlands, and remote access that are not suitable for development. Next, house sites are located in places with adequate drainage and water supply that also provide good views or seclusion, leaving fields open. As planning professor Reid Ewing explains, "Permanent open spaces enhance the value of nearby residential properties and offer economies in site development."[18]

But some real estate developers have expressed reservations about the smaller house lots that are typical in cluster developments. They are concerned that the smaller lots will have less appeal and potential as an investment.

Clustering without public sewer and water facilities raises questions about sewage disposal and water supplies. Many people who move to the countryside want to have their own septic system and well. But if houses with these systems are placed close together, groundwater pollution problems can happen within a decade. An alternative is to have a community on-lot septic system, managed by a private homeowners' association. Or the developer could use a small, package sewage treatment plant, assuming a nearby body of water. The U.S. Environmental Protection Agency is beginning to frown on small, private water systems, however, because of unreliable maintenance; and a number of states discourage or forbid the use of package sewage treatment plants, partly out of a fear that they could proliferate throughout the countryside.

If the on-site septic systems in a cluster development fail, then there is a serious health problem. Rather than abandon the homes, public sewer and water will probably have to be extended to provide sewage disposal and safe drinking water. When these lines are installed, customers typically pay a charge based on average cost. This creates an incentive to have more people hook into the lines to reduce the average cost. Also, the new sewer and water lines running out to the cluster development will put pressure on nearby owners of open land to develop their properties.

Finally, if many cluster developments are built in the countryside, the result will be clustered sprawl, not much different from the residential pods of the pro-growth strategy. Jonathan Barnett adds a warning that rural cluster development "allows developers to skip more difficult infill sites that ought to be developed first."[19]

The fourth design model is the working rural landscape. Here, commercial farm, forest, and ranch operations dominate along with uninhabited open land. Rural residences are sparse. A few houses can be developed to put some cash in the landowner's pocket while the remaining land is used for open space or farming. Perhaps the best example of a consciously planned working rural landscape is found in the state of Oregon.

The Oregon Land Use Act of 1973 required all thirty-six counties to first inventory all lands needed for or committed to urban uses. All other rural land must be zoned for Exclusive Farm Use (a misnomer because some nonfarm residences are allowed), Timber Conservation, or Rural Residential.

The Exclusive Farm Use zones include NRCS Class I–IV lands in western Oregon and Class I–VI soils in the rangeland of eastern Oregon; to date, about 16 million acres have been placed in Exclusive Farm Use zones. The zones use a large minimum lot size of 80 acres in the Willamette Valley and up to 320 acres in Deschutes County east of the Cascades.

Timber Conservation zones range from 80- to 160-acre minimum lot sizes, depending on the timber productivity of the area.

Rural Residential zones are designated for lower-quality soils in places where houses will not interfere with commercial farm and forest operations. These zones feature 3- to 5-acre minimum lot sizes.

Oregon has been able to sustain the zoning for the working rural landscape because agriculture and forestry are the state's second and third leading industries. Also, the majority of new development has been accommodated within urban growth boundaries. This more compact style of development reduces sprawl in the fringe countryside.

Comparing the Countryside Design Models

Countryside design should attempt to protect the natural environment as much as possible. This includes protecting hillsides, implementing storm-water management and drainage to minimize runoff and flooding, and protecting groundwater and surface water from pollution. Development should be compact to consume as little land as possible.

The suburban pod design may consume relatively little land, but it is also the most likely to be imposed upon the landscape. Large-lot residential development may be more sensitive to environmental features, but it consumes substantial amounts of land for rather few people. The cluster approach is meant to be sensitive to environmental constraints; but unless the cluster is based on low-density zoning, the number of houses permitted will approach the density of the suburban housing pod, albeit with more open space set aside. The working rural landscape design features farms and commercial forests, which can help to limit rural residential development and suburban sprawl. However, farming and forestry are industries with the potential to cause water pollution from soil erosion, the use of chemicals, and manure, in the case of farming.

The first three design techniques are site specific, not community- or regionally oriented. There is little sense of how a pod, several large lots, or a cluster development owuld fit in with the surrounding community or region. The working rural landscape encompasses an overview of a wide area.

The first three design techniques also make a relatively few rural landowners well off by allowing them to sell their land for rather high-value residential development. The working rural landscape approach places on the rural landowners a heavy expectation and potentially a financial burden for keeping land open. Property tax breaks and purchase or transfer of development rights may be helpful in providing financial support for rural landowners (see chapter 10).

Perhaps the single biggest land-use regulation problem in the fringe countryside is difficulty in zoning large tracts for conservation and open space. This is especially the case in areas where farming, ranching, or forestry is rapidly disappearing and the land has considerable value as home sites. Conservation and open space offer no immediate economic use for the landowner, unless some development is allowed. In Pennsylvania, for example, the strictest allowable conservation zoning is one dwelling per ten acres, a variant of the large-lot approach. The subdividing of large tracts into housing lots and even commercial sites indicates a trend toward suburbanization.

Involving the Public in the Design Process

Aesthetics are subjective. What one person finds appealing, another judges uninspiring. But planners can use the current and potential appearance of the community to stimulate responses from residents. There are two techniques to get people involved. The first, made popular by Rutgers University professor Anton Nelessen's Visual Preference Survey, is a way to find out what people in the community want for development and where they want it. The second method is the charette, an activity of drawings, photos, and discussion that takes a few days of intense work.

Getting residents to think about their community and how it could look can start a review of the community's comprehensive plan, implementing ordinances, and overall growth management efforts. The design of a community is hard to hide. Making the connection between the community's appearance and the rules that govern development can compel community residents to become more involved in determining the future of the community.

Box 5.3 Computer-Aided Design and Visioning for the Public

Local governments and citizens have an interest in knowing how proposed developments will fit into the landscape or streetscape if they are built. Through new and improving software technologies developers can show in living color the visual impacts of their projects. Given that fringe residents are often wary of change, the computer images can serve much as sketch plans do in the subdivision process.

A developer could submit drawings and blueprints, supplemented with computer-derived landscape images. The local planning commission and design review board could then review the images and suggest changes before official approval and eventual construction. If the local government has a design review committee, the images should help to speed and improve the project.

The Land Information Access Association, based in Traverse City, Michigan, has pioneered the use of a "kiosk" with easy-to-operate computer-imaging data. The idea is to put a kiosk in a public place where citizens could simply touch the screen to look at a variety of maps, photos, and development scenarios for their neighborhood or community. A zoom feature would let people concentrate on specific properties, neighborhoods, zoning districts, wells, wetlands, sewers, and other land and development elements. Such kiosks could bring about a better understanding of the community and region and encourage more citizen interest and involvement in the planning process. The overall goal is to build a better sense of place.

Summary

Suburban-style housing subdivisions and commercial strips pose serious threats to the fringe landscape. New design principles for settlements and the countryside are emerging, however, and how they are applied will influence not only the appearance but also the functioning of fringe communities. The village design can enhance a sense of community. One approach features a series of transit villages connected by public transportation networks to suburbs, edge cities, and the core city. But the success of the village model will depend in part on how much development is allowed to scatter throughout the countryside. The design of the fringe countryside should emphasize protection of the environment, compact settlements, and maintaining open lands.

CHAPTER 6

Changing Federal Programs That Promote Sprawl in the Fringe

> Suburbanization was not an historical inevitability created by geography, technology, and culture, but rather the product of government policies.
>
> —*Kenneth T. Jackson,* Crabgrass Frontier

> We subsidize continuously at the fringe.
>
> —*Robert Freilich, noted land-use attorney*

Some people may find it comforting to think that sprawl just happens as a matter of time and circumstance. "It was destined to happen," and "You can't stop progress," are comments we all have heard at one time or another. But, in fact, sprawl results from millions of individual private decisions that are influenced by government tax policies, spending programs, and land-use regulations.

Economic and population growth does result in more open land being developed, unless all the growth is absorbed within high-rise buildings. But growth does not need to occur in a sprawling pattern of commercial strips along highways or residential pods plopped at random throughout the countryside. Compact growth at the edge of established cities and towns uses less land and energy, requires fewer extensions of public services, and is less expensive both to businesses and to taxpaying homeowners in the long run. Therefore, if private individuals and businesses are to make sprawl-minimizing decisions, governments must come up with the right incentives as well as regulations to encourage compact development.

It is hard to cite examples of federally sponsored programs geared toward restraining sprawl at the metropolitan fringe. In fact, a number of federal spending programs and taxation policies continue to fuel fringe growth and promote the separation of metropolitan Americans by income group. Over the past fifty years, highway construction has helped to drain core cities of wealthier people, economic activity, and tax base. Spending on infrastructure for sewer, water, and schools has favored the newer suburbs, while much of the older infrastructure in the core cities has been allowed to decay. Only recently has the federal government undertaken to clean up hazardous waste and brownfield sites inside cities.

The federal government must make a policy decision as to whether it is in the national interest for Americans to continue to sprawl out in all directions. So far, the federal government has appeared to leave the individual, day-to-day land-use decisions up to landowners, businesses, and state and local governments. But this hands-off approach to authority masks the federal tax, spending, and regulatory programs that have a profound impact on local government and private-sector land-use decisions. The federal aversion to addressing local land use also has threatened national economic and environmental goals. For instance, most new jobs are being created in the suburbs, while the poverty rate in the inner cities has risen from 14 percent of the population in 1970 to 21 percent in 1995.[1] Meanwhile, spread-out development patterns continue to produce increases in vehicle miles traveled and auto-generated air pollution.

A community or county should understand how federal government actions affect local growth management efforts. Moreover, state and local governments should identify and propose changes to those policies and programs that currently hinder sustainable communities in the rural-urban fringe.

The Federal Vision for the Fringe

The federal government has yet to articulate anything close to a clear vision of how rural-urban fringe areas should grow or how they should relate to suburbs and inner cities. Fragments of a vision, like pieces of broken glass, exist within different federal departments and agencies. But no expressed policy exists to guide federal investment. In 1974, Senator Henry "Scoop" Jackson of Washington State introduced a bill to create a national land-use act. This bill would have required state and local comprehensive plans that met national standards. The bill came remarkably close to passing but then faded quickly from the congressional agenda.

Rather than such a sweeping approach to guiding land use, individual federal departments and agencies operate their separate programs under separate policies. Often these programs and policies conflict, in part because of the "pork barrel" practice of funding pet congressional spending programs—a highway here, a federal office building there—but largely because there is no federal land use policy. As a result, no one in Washington seems to be evaluating the costs and benefits to the public of various spending, tax, and regulatory programs.

But equally distressing to taxpayers is that the individual federal departments do not draft coordinated capital improvements programs. These programs would examine alternative projects and maintenance costs over a five- to ten-year period. If local governments can draw up capital improvements programs for public investment and maintenance, then so should states and the federal government. The lack of coordination among levels of government for investment in such powerful projects as roads, sewage treatment, and water facilities not only boggles the mind but also results in poor planning on the ground.

The main federal departments that affect land use in the fringe are the Department of Housing and Urban Development, the Federal Highway Administration, the Department of Agriculture, the Interior Department, and the Environmental Protection Agency. The programs and policies of these departments together with federal tax policies can best be analyzed in six areas: housing, economic development, transportation, agriculture, federal lands, and the environment.

Tax Policies and Homeownership

Individual ownership of a single-family home is the cornerstone of (unwritten) federal housing policy in the fringe. Public multifamily units and federally subsidized single-family dwellings do not make up more than a small fraction of the fringe housing stock.

The key federal tax policies to encourage single-family housing feature deductions from taxable income for: (1) "points" paid to banks or mortgage companies on home mortgage loans; (2) annual interest paid on a mortgage; and (3) property taxes. The size of the resulting income tax savings can be substantial (see box 6.1).

The sum total of the federal mortgage interest deduction is worth tens of billions of dollars nationwide each year. Only the deduction for retirement accounts is worth more. But more important, according to the Congressional Budget Office, American households with incomes over $75,000 capture more than half of the tax savings from the interest deduction.[2] And most of these high-income households are located in the suburbs or, increasingly, in the fringe. Ironically, the more a wealthy household borrows for a house, the more it can deduct against income, up to $1 million in interest payments from the purchase of a home and up to $100,000 on a home equity loan.

Box 6.1 Estimating the Value of Federal Tax Breaks for the Buyer of a $150,000 House with a $120,000, 30-Year Mortgage at 8 Percent

Homeowner Gross Income = $60,000
Year 1: Owner Buys the House, Deducts the Cost of:
    a) Points: 2% × $120,000 = $2,400
    b) Mortgage interest = $9,563 (assuming a January 1 purchase date)
    c) Property taxes = $2,100
    Total Deduction = $14,063

Taxable Income = $45,937
Net federal tax saving in 28% bracket: $14,063 × .28 = $3,937

In years 2 through 30, the amount of mortgage interest will decline as more of the monthly payment goes to pay off the loan principal. Even so, the amount of the mortgage interest deduction over this time will add up to just over $201,000! Property taxes will rise along with inflation and community growth, at an average of about 3 percent a year, coming in at just under $100,000.

The total income deduction over 30 years is about $300,000. If the homeowner is in the 28 percent bracket, this would mean a tax savings of $84,000.[3]

Reporting on research by Professor Thomas Bier of Cleveland State University, David Rusk writes:

> Most new housing starts are in upperend subdivisions that are increasingly farther out on the metropolitan periphery. . . . The newest high-end housing always sells, prompting successive waves of homeowners to "move up" (in price) but also "move out" (of inner cities and older, blue-collar suburbs). The net surplus of housing over demand causes the economic abandonment of otherwise sound housing in the urban core.[4]

A further benefit for homeowners is the ability to shelter profits from the sale of a home by purchasing another home of greater value, known as "trading up." But the federal 1997 Balanced Budget agreement gave homeowners a whopping capital gains tax exemption of up to $500,000 on the sale of a house.

The federal tax code allows owners of commercial and rental properties to depreciate the value of those properties over thirty-one and a half years. This situation creates an incentive to "write off" buildings once they have been depreciated down to zero. There is little reason to refurbish them. Furthermore, local property taxes discourage reinvestment in property and general upkeep. It is usually easier and more financially advantageous to keep moving farther out into the suburbs and fringe and build new buildings, selling off or abandoning older ones in the cities.

Infrastructure Development

The U.S. Department of Housing and Urban Development makes grants to cities and counties for infrastructure development, especially sewer and water lines. The location of these lines has powerful implications for future growth. A typical problem in the fringe is the failure of on-site septic systems, resulting in groundwater pollution and health hazards from leaking sewage. To remedy the problem, sewer and water lines must be extended from suburbs or villages. But land between the village or suburb and the problem area comes under development pressure once the sewer and water lines are put in. Because sewer and water costs are apportioned on an average-cost basis, there is an incentive for the public sewer and water operators to encourage additional hookups. Thus, it is common for "arms" of development to stretch out into the countryside along with the sewer and water lines.

Communities and counties should first be careful in allowing the siting and operation of on-site septic systems. See chapter 7 for a discussion of regulations that counties and municipalities can use to ensure more efficient use of on-site septic systems.

Transportation

Americans enjoy remarkable freedoms. One of the most cherished is the ability to get in one's car and drive. Road building has been a national priority, and mobility is the essence of the American lifestyle. Car and truck drivers have enjoyed tremendous subsidies through public road construction and gasoline prices that do not reflect the air and water pollution costs generated by driving. According to the U.S. Department of Transportation, gasoline taxes and user fees cover only about 70 percent of the cost of building and maintaining the nation's roads.[5]

No other society in history has moved around like Americans in the last half of the twentieth century. An estimated 86 percent of America's workforce (about 85 million people) commute to work by car.[6] And trucks haul some 80 percent of all consumer goods.[7] Ironically though, many Americans are angry and frustrated with the struggle of getting from place to place. They spend long, nightmarish hours in traffic trying to get to and from work, to and from shopping, and to and from recreation areas (soccer moms and dads, in particular). This dependence on cars and trucks is not new, but it is becoming self-defeating as the number of vehicles increases and highways become more clogged. To compensate, many drivers have bought cell phones to make their cars an extension of their homes and offices.

The spread-out settlement patterns in the metro fringe mean more travel time and less time to shop. It is no coincidence that there has been a boom in mail-order business and just in time manufacturing (assembling and shipping goods as they are needed), causing trucks to deliver more goods to more dispersed homes and stores. The cost of busing children to and from school rises as children must be carried more miles through the fringe. For example, journalist Neal Peirce estimated that the state of Maryland would save $100 million if kids could walk to school.[8] Land-use patterns, transportation costs, and modes of transport are closely linked. The dispersed fringe residential and commercial development creates a reliance on motor vehicle transport that is costly to homeowners and businesses and produces more wear and tear on road networks and more air pollution than compact, mixed-use development.

As described in chapter 2, before the construction of the 42,500-mile National Defense Highway System (better known as interstate highways) began in 1956, suburbs extended only a few miles outside of central cities. The alleged purpose of the interstates was to facilitate the evacuation of the central cities in the event of nuclear attack. And so these high-speed, limited-access highways plunged into the heart of downtowns, razing working-class neighborhoods, and then stretched out into the hinterlands, siphoning off population and economic vitality from the cities. The interstates were hardly the regional "townless roads" envisioned by Lewis Mumford. Rather, the interstates greatly expanded the range of places that commuters could live and still reach jobs in the central city or, eventually, in the suburbs. Soon, shopping centers, office parks, industrial plants, and secondary roads sprouted near interstate interchanges. The highways had enabled the jobs to follow the workers out to the suburbs. The interstates lowered the cost of transporting goods and provided safe, convenient access for customers and employees. The interstates were built with 90 percent federal money and 10 percent state dollars, but the federal government offered much lower funding for interstate maintenance and comparatively little for investing in other modes of transportation, such as mass transit.[9] By the 1980s, the maintenance bill for interstates was placing a heavy burden on state transportation departments.

The interstate highways spurred the economic and population growth of the fringe. Both the long commute and the search for affordable housing in the sprawling growth beyond the suburbs was made possible by fast, accessible transportation links. From 1969 to 1989, the population of the United States increased by 22.5 percent, and the number of miles driven (vehicles miles traveled or VMT) increased by 98.4 percent.[10] From 1983 to 1987, the population of the United States increased by 9.2 million people while the number of cars and trucks jumped by 20.1 million.[11] Given the growth in fringe development, it can be deduced that many of the new vehicles purchased were used for commuting inward from the fringe and reverse commuting from suburbs to the new service industries in the outer-metro fringe counties. In the larger metropolitan areas, the amount of vehicle miles traveled appears to be increasing eight times faster than the population.[12]

While the number of registered vehicles and vehicle miles traveled continue to increase, the heyday of federally financed highway construction has passed. This reality portends greater congestion on existing highways. Between 1983 and 1993, America's road mileage increased by only 1 percent to 3.9 million miles.[13] The 1997 federal budget called for highway spending to drop from $19.6 billion in 1996 to $19.1 billion in 2002, not allowing for inflation. This proposed reduction in federal highway funding comes at a time when the federal Highway Trust Fund is taking in more money from motor fuel taxes and showing a substantial surplus.

Some new roads and highway bridges are still being built, but they are expensive. Limited-access highways typically cost over a million dollars a mile. This does not include the cost of maintaining existing roads and bridges, especially in the interstate system, which has fallen heavily on the states. While the miles of new road construction have fallen dramatically, the number of cars and vehicle miles traveled have steadily increased. As the pace of traffic slows and travel times lengthen, cars spew more air-polluting exhaust. Building new roads alone will not solve the traffic jams, air pollution, or transportation bottlenecks. One possible solution, mass transit, suffers from less than adequate federal spending of $2.5 billion a year.[14]

The federal government has recently influenced the growth of the fringe by keeping the federal gasoline tax the lowest among industrialized nations. As of 1997, federal gasoline taxes were ten cents a liter (about thirty-eight cents a gallon) compared to twenty-two cents a liter in Canada, eighty cents a liter in Britain, and ninety-three cents a liter in oil-rich Norway.[15]

At the start of 1997, the United States had only enough proven oil reserves to last for ten years at present rates of consumption.[16] Greater dependency on imported oil portends economic vulnerability as well as political blackmail, as happened in the 1973–74 Arab oil embargo and the sharp, OPEC-induced rise in the price of oil in 1979 that helped to touch off double-digit inflation and a painful economic recession.

The Intermodal Surface Transportation Efficiency Act of 1991 (Public Law 102-240), more refreshingly referred to as ISTEA (pronounced "ice tea"), authorized $155 billion over six years for the creation of a national intermodal transportation system.

In 1998, Congress reauthorized ISTEA with a whopping $204 billion over six years. A large majority of the funds have been targeted for highway construction and maintenance, and new roads will open up more fringe land for commercial and residential development. The intermodal concept in ISTEA encourages metro areas to link different transportation networks, such as buses and trains or cars and trains, so that people and goods move more smoothly. ISTEA funds have been spent on mass transit, congestion pricing and mitigation, and air quality improvement. The Transportation Enhancements portion included limited but important funding for designating scenic or historic highways and sites, highway beautification and the removal of billboards, and the reduction of highway runoff that causes water pollution.

In terms of changing the planning of metropolitan areas, ISTEA may be the most important piece of federal legislation in thirty years. Certainly, it is a watershed event in federal transportation policy. Prior to ISTEA, federal transportation programs featured a top-down, one-size-fits-all approach with a strong element of congressional pork barrel projects. While the pork barrel projects may not disappear anytime soon, the thrust of ISTEA to make transportation more responsive to local and regional needs is a major change.

In addition to highway construction, the emphasis of ISTEA is on maintaining existing transportation systems, ensuring the efficient operation of those networks, improving intermodal integration, and, most important, increasing state and local control over investment decisions. Local decisions are made by granting responsibility and authority to metropolitan planning organizations (MPOs). MPOs were originally established in the early 1960s. Under ISTEA, they are designated to receive broad public input and draft long-range transportation improvement plans with land-use and air quality issues and impacts in mind. These plans must include transportation alternatives to the automobile, pedestrian- and bicycle-oriented communities, and the protection of wetlands, wildlife habitat, and open space. Currently, there are some 350 MPOs, ranging from small metro efforts to multistate authorities.

ISTEA thus is more than a funding package and a return to local decision making. It could indeed foster innovative thinking about how we create and arrange settlements on both a local and a regional scale. The "E" in ISTEA—efficiency—should focus new and serious efforts on in-fill development rather than continued sprawl. ISTEA has already compelled planners to begin to address the most neglected means of transportation—walking and bike riding—in those fringe communities totally dominated by motor vehicle travel. The new attitude in many of those communities is to fix local transportation first before designing faster transportation links to speed commuters home to where they are forced into automobiles to obtain the basic necessities of home life and leisure.

ISTEA also focuses on both large- and small-scale mass transit as alternatives to private vehicle travel. Nearly every modern planning theory for bringing balance to metropolitan growth hinges to a greater or lesser degree on mass transit as a key transportation alternative. Mass transit is, inherently, more environmentally benign and more energy efficient than systems based on the use of personal automobiles. Tying into mass transit is the Transit-Oriented Design approach, developed and promoted by architect Peter Calthorpe (see figure 5.1).

Finally, if Americans are to live in decentralized, low-density settlements on the fringe, the federal government might require stricter fuel-efficiency standards as a long-range energy conservation measure. For example, sport utility vehicles, the leading type of vehicles sold in the late 1990s, average less than twenty miles per gallon. By comparison, midsize cars average over twenty-five miles per gallon.

Airports and Sprawl

Tied to sprawling road construction is the location of airports in the metropolitan fringe. In the late 1960s and 1970s, major airports located within or very near core urban areas were posing environmental problems of noise, air pollution, and traffic congestion. A number of large-scale airports were subsequently planned for rural sites within thirty miles of downtown. The thinking was that a more rural location would overcome the problems of air and noise pollution, as well as significantly relieving traffic congestion and increasing safety by avoiding dense urban development.

No one pointed out the two major flaws in this otherwise rational solution to airport congestion. First, the attractiveness of the airport itself as a major employer, as a multipurpose economic development location, and as a magnet for service and entertainment industries was vastly underestimated. Most major air terminals, thought at the time to be too removed from the central cities to attract significant growth, have proven to be a potent economic stimulus and an additional cause of leapfrogging development in the outer suburbs and the fringe counties.

The Kansas City, Missouri/Kansas, International Airport is a good example. Located about twelve miles (a sixty-minute metro bus ride) north of the inner-city core, it serves the Kansas City metroplex of 1.7 million people, plus a regional area of approximately 150 miles in diameter. The airport is one of the nation's largest in terms of area, 9,500 acres, and there are plans to increase it to 10,500 acres. Combined with major road links, it has exerted a phenomenal influence on the sprawling, centerless growth patterns in what was once primarily a farming and resource-extraction portion of northern Missouri. Thanks in part to the airport's location, Greater Kansas City is the second most spread-out metropolitan region in the nation.

Agriculture: More Land Preservation but Less Reliance on Crop Subsidies

For more than sixty years, the federal government has subsidized farmers through direct payments for certain crops, milk price supports, and low-interest loan programs. But these are changing times for farmers. In the 1996 Farm Bill, Congress decided to end most "deficiency" payments for crops, so that beginning in 2002, nearly all farmers will receive a price for their crops determined by the supply-and-demand forces of the marketplace. Milk price supports will also be removed, so the federal government will no longer buy up surplus milk to keep prices higher. The result will probably be downward pressure on milk prices, at least in the short run.

These changes come at a difficult time for many fringe farmers. The number of nonfarm neighbors is increasing as more people move out to the fringe. Many of these newcomers do not understand farming or appreciate the sound of machinery early in the morning or late at night. Add in the smell of manure, clouds of dust, chemical sprays, and slow-moving farm machinery, and a newcomer's ideal of country living comes crashing to earth.

The confrontations can be bitter and expensive. Even though every state has a right-to-farm law that protects farmers from nuisance suits for normal farming practices, those laws do not prevent neighbors from bombarding the farmer with complaints.

And the more neighbors, the higher the farmer's property taxes are likely to rise to help pay for more public services and more children to educate. The combination of rising taxes, more neighbors, and the lure of substantial dollars to sell land for development put pressure on fringe farmers to cash in and move out.

The U.S. Department of Agriculture has contradicted itself on occasion as to whether the loss of farmland to sprawl merits national concern. Some USDA reports have concluded that there is no problem.[17] And, in fairness, the price and availability of food in America are the envy of the world. Yet, besides soil conservation programs, the USDA administers two programs that are aimed at protecting the farmland base.

The 1981 Farmland Protection Policy Act called for the U.S. Department of Agriculture to review proposed federal projects that could result in the conversion of prime farmland. Other departments are required to send notices of such projects to the USDA. To date, most of the federal projects have involved highways. A weakness of the act is that it does not give private citizens any authority to oppose the federal projects. Few, if any, projects have been denied because of the act.

In the 1996 Farm Bill, Congress authorized the USDA to make $35 million in grants to state and local governments for the purchase of conservation easements (development rights) to farmland (see chapter 10). Because most of the state and local farmland preservation programs have grown up in fringe areas, that is where the majority of federal funds are being directed.

In 1997, Congress passed the Taxpayer Relief Act, a major overhaul of the federal tax code that included some very favorable estate tax provisions for working farms and ranches. Although the tax benefits will be phased in over time, the new law should eliminate estate taxes on most commercial farms and ranches. In the 1980s and early 1990s, the rising real estate values of farms and ranches, especially in the metro fringe, forced some heirs to sell the land for development to pay estate taxes.

The Taxpayer Relief Act includes five provisions to reduce estate taxes:

- The act increases the Unified Credit—the amount of a person's estate that is exempt from estate taxes—from $600,000 to $1,000,000 by 2006.
- The act adds a special $300,000 exemption for small business-

es, including farms and ranches that will remain in operation for ten years after the inheritance.

- The American Farm and Ranch Protection Act[18] portion of the act allows heirs to deduct 40 percent of the value of farm or ranch land (not buildings) subject to a donated permanent conservation easement when figuring a taxable estate. Beginning in 1998, up to $100,000 can be deducted per estate, rising to $500,000 by 2002.[19] For example, if the market value of farmland is appraised at $600,000 and the value under a conservation easement is $400,000, then the deduction from the taxable estate would be 40 percent of $400,000, or $160,000. Assuming a 50 percent tax bracket, this would mean an estate tax saving of $80,000.[20]

  In addition, the conservation easement has reduced the taxable value of the land by $200,000 for an estate tax saving of $100,000. The total estate tax savings from donating the easement are $180,000.

  There is one key restriction to this section of the tax code that makes it especially relevant for fringe landowners: *The estate exemption applies to land inside a metropolitan statistical area (MSA) and within twenty-five miles of an MSA, national parks, or national wilderness areas*. There are 273 MSAs defined by the Office of Management and Budget, which include over 800 counties.

- As long as the farm or ranch stays in the family and continues as a commercial operation, subsequent heirs may also take advantage of the conservation easement estate deduction.

- The executor of an estate may donate a permanent conservation easement on the farm or ranch land after the death of the owner.

These changes in tax policy create strong incentives for farmers and ranchers in fringe areas to donate conservation easements as part of their estate planning. Passing the land to the next generation will become more feasible, and the increase in preserved farmland could have far-reaching benefits for growth management by placing large amounts of land off limits to development.

Federal Lands

Roughly 40 percent of the land in America is held in public ownership. The federal government is the largest single landowner, with 32 percent of the nation's land, or about 750 million acres. Much of the federal domain is administered through the Department of the Interior (National Park Service, Bureau of Land Management, and Bureau of Reclamation) and the U.S. Forest Service within the Department of Agriculture. The Defense Department is also a major landowner. The primary significance of federal landownership in the fringe areas is that many western cities are adjacent to public lands, which limit the amount of territory for urban, suburban, and fringe area expansion. These limits in turn heighten the competition for remaining privately held land.

On the other hand, federally owned land can fit with local growth management planning. Perhaps the best example of this is in Marin County, California, across the Golden Gate Bridge from San Francisco. There the Golden Gate National Recreation Area and the Point Reyes National Seashore—both under the Interior Department—act as a buffer to the adjacent agriculturally zoned grazing lands where there are over twenty-five thousand acres of farmland preserved through conservation easements.

Since 1965, the federal Land and Water Conservation Fund has been used to purchase and reclaim land for outdoor recreation and open space. In over thirty years, the fund has helped protect 8 million acres of land and has provided matching funds to local governments and private land trusts for thirty-seven thousand recreation projects throughout the nation. Congress can authorize up to $900 million a year for the fund, but in the 1990s, it has given the fund only a few hundred million dollars each year. Some of the projects have occurred and will continue to occur in metro fringe areas.

Federal water subsidies that benefit western farmers actually serve to put something of a brake on the growth of the fringe. Farmers get very low-cost water and hence have little incentive to conserve it as they irrigate crops. But the availability of low-cost water helps keep the farmers in business. Agriculture in California, the nation's leading farm state, consumed an estimated 77 percent of all water used in the state in 1990.[21]

Still, the competition for water is becoming more intense as California's population increases and natural environments are pressured. For instance, the Central Valley Improvement Act of 1982 required the U.S. Bureau of Reclamation to allocate 800,000 acre feet of water a year for fish and wildlife habitat protection. Some farmers are beginning to feel a squeeze on their water supplies. Water reliability has emerged as a major issue in farmland protection. If farmers cannot get a reliable water supply, selling their land for development looks all the more attractive. Water policy expert Marc Reisner has even proposed offering farmers twenty- to forty-year water supply contracts if they agree not to develop their land over that time period.[22]

Development Impact on the Environment

The federal government has taken the lead in passing laws and enacting regulations that are aimed at protecting the environment. The U.S. Environmental Protection Agency, founded in 1971, has primary responsibility for enforcing clean air and water laws and toxic waste identification and clean up.

Humans and the environment are on a collision course in the rural-urban fringe. The cumulative impact of individual developments not only changes the aesthetics of the landscape, but also results in reduced air and water quality and the loss of wildlife habitat. In addition, as suburbs continue to move outward, fringe residents will become concerned that cities are exporting their problems to the fringe. One problem is the disposal of solid waste. The location of regional landfills in the fringe is one hotly debated issue, and another is the practice of urban sewer operators to pay fringe farmers to accept sewage sludge to spread on their land as fertilizer.

Several major environmental issues could change the way the fringe grows and develops. The first is air quality. If the federal government tightens clean air standards to protect public health, then the construction of roads into fringe areas could cause a metro region to violate air quality standards; hence, federal funds for new road construction could be withheld. Second, small, private water systems are coming under greater scrutiny. Jay Rutherford, Vermont's drinking water manager, notes that "it's very difficult for smaller systems to stay in compliance just with operating aspects, to say nothing about construction."[23]

Violations of federal safe drinking water standards are public knowledge, available through the Freedom of Information Act and through groups such as the Environmental Working Group (see "Contacts" in the back of the book). In the near future, private systems that serve over twenty-five people could be required to link up with regional public water systems.

Environmental quality is one of the most critical issues in the fringe. For example, many fringe communities rely on groundwater for drinking water supplies, and people living outside of towns typically get their water from wells. Once groundwater is polluted, it is very difficult to clean up and poses a serious threat to human health. Finally, the argument of a trade-off between economic growth and environmental quality rings especially hollow in the fringe. There, people are still primarily commuters to suburbs and cities. The high environmental quality of the fringe has attracted new residences and businesses, but if the environment deteriorates, people will move away.

Air Quality

Under the Clean Air Act Amendment of 1970, the EPA sets national primary standards to protect human health and secondary standards for visibility, building erosion, and plant and animal life. These standards apply to six pollutants: lead, sulfur oxides, ozone, particulates, nitrogen dioxide, and carbon monoxide (see table 6.1). In the mid-1990s, roughly one-fifth of all Americans were living in counties that did not meet at least one of these national air quality standards.[24]

Congress identified eighty-four hazardous air pollutants as part of the 1990 Clean Air Amendments. The EPA has the responsibility for setting standards for those pollutants and reducing emissions. The EPA also requires states to submit air quality management plans to meet and maintain the federal standards. EPA monitors air quality regions for compliance with and nonattainment of standards. An important provision for fringe areas is that states may prevent the construction of a project, such as a major highway, if it would cause air quality to fall below attainment levels.

The EPA reported decreases in the six major air pollutants from 1986 to 1995, yet in 1995, 80 million Americans lived in counties that exceeded the national air quality levels.[25] In 1997, the EPA proposed tightening the air quality standards for ozone (smog) to .08 parts per million over eight hours from .08 ppm over one hour, and for fine particle pollution to 15 micrograms per cubic meter from 60 micrograms-annual geometric mean (i.e., based on an average of measurements throughout the year). The EPA also proposed regulations on particles of less than 2.5 microns, which can lodge in lungs and damage lung tissue. But the stricter standards could limit the redevelopment of urban areas, which are important for taking pressure off the fringe. According to Donald R. Schregardus, director of the Ohio Environmental Protection Agency, "If [the] U.S. EPA changes the air quality standards for ozone and particulates, every urban area in Ohio will violate the standards, and businesses will be forced to look elsewhere to expand or locate new facilities. The more stringent air standards would hamper brownfield clean-up in urban areas and promote urban sprawl."[26]

In the period 1970–95, nitrous oxide pollution, generated primarily by cars, trucks, and buses, increased by 6 percent. Over the same time, the nation's population grew by 28 percent, and vehicle miles traveled soared by 116 percent.[27] As automobile dependence grows in tandem with the growth of the fringe, more air pollution emissions are likely, unless fringe dwellers begin to convert to electric-powered cars or successful mass transit systems are developed.

Table 6.1 National Primary and Secondary Ambient Air Quality Standards

Pollutant	*Primary Standard*	*Secondary Standard*
Lead	1.5 micrograms per cubic meter averaged over 3 months, not to be exceeded more than once a year.	Same as the primary standard.
Particulates	50 micrograms per cubic meter, annual geometric mean. 150 micrograms per cubic meter, maximum 24-hour concentration, not to be exceeded more than once a year. 15 micrograms per cubic meter, annual. 65 micrograms per cubic meter, 24-hour concentration, not to be exceeded more than once a year.	50 micrograms per cubic meter, annual geometric mean. 150 micrograms per cubic meter, maximum 24-hour concentration, not to be exceeded, more than once a year.
Carbon monoxide	10 milligrams per cubic meter (9 parts per million), maximum 8-hour concentration. 40 milligrams per cubic meter (35 parts per million), maximum 1-hour concentration, not to be exceeded more than once a year.	No secondary standard.
Ozone	160 micrograms per cubic meter (.08 ppm), maximum 3-year concentration, not to be exceeded more than once a year.	Same as the primary standard.
Nitrogen dioxide	100 micrograms per cubic meter (.053 ppm), annual arithmetic mean.	Same as the primary standard.
Sulfur oxides	80 micrograms per cubic meter (.03 ppm), annual arithmetic mean. 365 micrograms per cubic meter (.14 ppm), maximum 24-hour concentration, not to be exceeded more than once a year.	1,300 micrograms per cubic meter (.5 ppm), maximum 3-hour concentration, not to be exceeded more than once a year.

Source: U.S. Environmental Protection Agency, 40 C.F.R. Sections 50.4–50.11.
Note: All measurements of air quality are corrected to a reference temperature of 25 degrees Celsius and to a reference pressure of 760 millimeters of mercury (1,013.2 millibars).

Water Quality

Under the Federal Water Pollution Control Act Amendments of 1972, the EPA has given billions of dollars in wastewater treatment grants to states and localities. Section 208 of the act requires states to conduct sewage facilities planning, which can be a powerful tool in managing the location of urban-density development. Also, states must establish area-wide nonpoint-pollution treatment programs and water quality management plans. Furthermore, any pollution discharge permit under Section 402 of the act must be consistent with the Section 208 plans.

Congress passed the Safe Drinking Water Act of 1974 (SDWA) to reduce contaminants in public drinking water supplies.[28] Public water systems include: community water systems that serve at least fifteen connections or regularly serve at least twenty-five year-round residents; noncommunity water systems that serve at least twenty-five people for six months a year, such as in workplaces and hospitals; and all other water systems, such as in gas stations and campgrounds. The act enabled the EPA to set national drinking water quality standards for maximum contaminant levels, wellhead protection and sole-source aquifers, water quality monitoring, and water treatment. The act also was aimed at preventing underground injections of contaminated fluids. A ban on the underground injection of hazardous wastes was added in 1988.

The SDWA established mandatory maximum contaminant levels and nonenforceable (at the federal level) health goals, known as maximum-contaminant-level goals for each contaminant; these are the primary standards to protect human health. The EPA also set secondary standards to provide aesthetically acceptable water. Under the primary standards, for example, the EPA has set a standard for drinking water of no more than ten parts per million of nitrate. So far, only the state of Pennsylvania has employed this standard in regulating the use of on-site septic systems. That is, if a person wants to build a house in the countryside, that person must first have the groundwater tested. If the groundwater has more than ten parts per million of nitrate, then that person cannot use an on-site septic system. This standard has reduced home construction, particularly in fringe areas with nitrate loadings from the manure of hog, dairy, and chicken farms and large acreages of corn, which typically take ammonium nitrate fertilizer.

The states have primary enforcement authority for the Safe Drinking Water Act, but the EPA has the power to enforce the act if a state does not do a proper job. The states may on a case-by-case basis grant exemptions or variances from the federal regulations.

The reauthorization of the Safe Drinking Water Act in 1996 included $9.6 billion to fund state and local grants and low-interest loan programs for drinking water plant improvements. The SDWA amendments also mandated that state and local governments map water sources and draft plans for protecting adjacent lands. This protection may include the purchase of land or conservation easements and the implementation of wellhead protection ordinances to severely limit development near water supplies.

Tighter federal water quality standards and regulations appear likely, given outbreaks of cryptosporidium and continued violations of federal standards. The next major issue could be increased testing and regulation of private water supplies. The linkages between land-use controls and water supply protection will increase. Federal guidance and funding will continue to be important, but states and localities will continue to bear responsibility for implementing and enforcing tighter water quality standards and regulations (see chapter 8).

The U.S. Fish and Wildlife Service and the Endangered Species Act

Through the Endangered Species Act of 1973, the federal government has attempted to protect animal species that face a high probability of extinction. The parts of the act that most affect the fringe state that:

- It is illegal to harm, harass, hunt, shoot, trap, capture, or collect an endangered animal.
- A federal project may not jeopardize the continued existence of an endangered species.

The U.S. Fish and Wildlife Service administers the act and receives detailed petitions nominating a species as endangered. The service can take up to a year to evaluate a petition. As of 1997, over one thousand plant and animals species were listed as threatened or endangered. Endangered species merit a higher level of protection than threatened species, because of a greater likelihood of extinction. But in either case, the service can designate any critical habitat that must be protected if a species is to survive.

Wild animal populations are difficult to sustain in fringe areas. As the land base is split into more parcels and more houses are built, large animals such as bear, moose, and elk disappear. But even smaller animals can lose enough habitat that they decline sharply in numbers. Endangered plant species may also disappear as newcomers introduce exotic plants that compete with native species. The kudzu vine, for example, is a vigorous and rapidly growing plant that was introduced in the southern United States in the 1940s and since then has run rampant. Moreover, as fringe areas expand, they will eat into more endangered species habitats, threaten meaningful pieces of ecosystems, and set the stage for acrimonious battles over human property rights and the rights of wildlife.

Environmentalists complain that the Endangered Species Act has been hampered by a lack of funding and an "emergency room" approach to try to save species that have been allowed to decline to the brink of extinction. Also, the emphasis of the act has been on protecting individual species rather than entire ecosystems. Environmentalists would like to see the act maintain biodiversity through the regulation of land use.

On the other side are loggers, ranchers, farmers, and hunters who fear that the Endangered Species Act can and will be used by governments to steal their livelihoods. Some landowners have destroyed endangered species on their land because they fear the government could use the act to severely restrict what they can do with their land. Moreover, some landowners worry that the government would not pay them compensation as long as the endangered species are on their land. Even the possibility of government compensation through eminent domain does not appeal to many of these landowners. They simply want to use their land as part of a business or for recreational activities as they choose. Meanwhile, the penalties for violators of the act can be stiff, with fines of up to $100,000 and a year in prison.

Developers frequently accuse environmentalists of using the Endangered Species Act as a way to block development. The landmark example was that of the endangered snail darter that brought to an end the construction of the half-finished Tellico Dam on the Little Tennessee River.

In an effort to balance development and protection of endangered species, Habitat Conservation Plans were added to the Endangered Species Act in 1982. The Habitat Conservation Plans permit development when it is offset by conservation measures such as habitat restoration and the relocation of endangered plants and animals. But the plans also identify critical ecosystem habitats that are vital to endangered species and are off limits to development. By 1997, about 350 Habitat Conservation Plans were in place covering 16 million acres, including one-tenth of the commercial forestland in the Pacific Northwest.[29] An added strength of the Habitat Conservation Plans is the assistance of state and local governments in the planning and funding of habitat areas (see box 6.2).

Box 6.2 The Coastal California Gnatcatcher and the Habitat Conservation Plan

The metropolitan regions of Orange County and San Diego County, California, cover about 2.5 million acres, of which only some 400,000 acres are remaining natural areas. Over the next twenty-five years, the population of San Diego County is expected to increase by 50 percent and that of Orange County by 29 percent.

The Coastal California gnatcatcher, a bird indigenous to Southern California, had been declared endangered and had the potential to block development in the high-value property market between Los Angeles and San Diego. A court ruling compelled the Fish and Wildlife Service to designate a critical habitat for the gnatcatcher. Secretary of the Interior Bruce Babbitt listed the gnatcatcher as threatened to allow controlled development of the area under a series of Habitat Conservation Plans that cover 380,000 acres. San Diego County put in place a Multiple-Species Conservation Program through which the county reserved 82,000 acres of state and federal land. Then the state of California and local governments in San Diego County purchased an additional 27,000 acres of habitat for $300 million. Development companies agreed to set aside 63,000 acres of sage shrub habitat to promote the recovery and future survival of the gnatcatcher. The developers can now build on remaining lands without fear of violating the Endangered Species Act. This case is likely to set a precedent for future efforts to protect endangered species, especially in fringe areas. By coincidence, California has more federally listed threatened and endangered species than any other state.[30]

National Environmental Policy Act: A Missed Opportunity?

The National Environmental Policy Act of 1969 (NEPA) contained great potential for tempering America's appetite for fringe development. The NEPA legislation, an awakening of sustainable development consciousness, was adopted to "foster and promote the general welfare, to create and maintain conditions under which man and nature can exist in productive harmony, and to fulfill the social, economic, and other requirements of present and future generations of Americans"[31] (NEPA, 42 U.S.C. Section 4331, Title 1). Its stated responsibilities were to:

- ensure that each generation acts as trustees of the environment for succeeding generations;

- assure for all Americans safe, healthful, productive, and aesthetically and culturally pleasing surroundings;
- attain the widest range of beneficial use of the environment without degradation, risk to health or safety, or other undesirable or unintended consequences;
- preserve important historic, cultural, and natural aspects of our national heritage, and maintain, wherever possible, an environment that supports diversity and a variety of individual choices;
- achieve a balance between population and resource use that permits high standards of living and a wide sharing of life's amenities.

NEPA required all federal agencies to review their present statutory authority, administrative regulations, and current policies to determine what measures would be necessary to come into compliance with the act. The centerpiece of NEPA was the environmental impact statement (EIS), a comprehensive study of the social, economic, and environmental impacts of proposed significant federal actions. NEPA held out real promise for dealing with many, if not most, aspects of uncontrolled growth, especially near the nation's major metropolitan areas. NEPA has been applied piecemeal, rather than as a broad legal framework for federal development policy. Ideally, NEPA would have denied federal projects that would have resulted in an irreversible commitment of natural resources. Also, NEPA reviews could have resulted in the use of alternative sites or project modifications to encourage more compact, energy-efficient, and cheaper-to-service development patterns.

Such missed opportunities have haunted many of the significant federal actions that made fringe growth possible. The federal government was the major player in supplying planning, transfer dollars, and direct support to both the interstate highways and the federal aid road system, what could be considered the exit roads from the city to exurbia. The scale of leapfrog growth we are now experiencing would not have been possible without deep subsidy loans through both the Department of Housing and Urban Development and the Farmers Home Administration, nor would the sheer volume of development have been possible without federal assistance to local governments to lay rural water pipe throughout the countryside or improve and extend local wastewater treatment. Nor has the federal aid to states for building an immense system of water storage and recreation lakes, a magnet for fringe development, ever seriously been questioned under NEPA as a major contributor to sprawl.

How the Federal Government Can Help Manage Growth in the Fringe

The Congress, the president, and the federal agencies should recognize their roles in promoting development and protecting the environment in the metropolitan fringe. Probably not until individual states, major corporations, environmental groups, and thousands of private citizens make growth management in the fringe a leading item on their agendas will adequate pressure be put on the federal government. While the reform of many federal policies and programs is needed, those policies and programs that have encouraged urban redevelopment and discouraged the growth of the fringe could be expanded.

Increase the Cost of Living in the Fringe

One way to manage growth and limit development within the fringe is to make travel by car much more expensive. The higher cost of travel would create an incentive for people to live closer to work, school, and shopping. This, in turn, would foster a greater sense of community and social cohesion.

As of 1998, the price of gasoline was less than the cost of bottled water. The federal gasoline tax at $.38 a gallon was far lower than national gas taxes throughout Europe. A rise in the gas tax would tend to reduce vehicle miles traveled, reduce air pollution, and raise federal revenues to help reduce the national debt. Planning professor Reid Ewing estimates that the gasoline tax would have to be as high as $6.60 a gallon to reflect the true costs of driving to the economy and the environment.[32] On the downside, an increase in the federal gas tax would apply to all Americans, not just residents of the fringe. Moreover, many fringe commuters are well-to-do and would not be greatly affected by higher commuting costs.

Then should supply be restricted? If gasoline were rationed to, say, twenty gallons a week, how many households in the fringe would stay, and how many might move back to inner suburbs or within city limits?

While a large hike in the federal gas tax is unlikely and supply restrictions are even more remote, gasoline taxes and supply availability are conscious policy choices made by Congress and the executive branch in Washington. According to figures from the British Petroleum Corporation, *America has enough proven oil reserves to last for only ten years at current rates of production.*[33] A cheap energy policy may not be a problem in the short term, but unless cost-effective alternative energy sources are developed, America risks a tremendous dependence on imported oil. Higher energy costs would influence the selection of where to live and work and make fringe areas less attractive.

By the mid-1990s, minivans and sport utility vehicles had become the transportation choice of millions of suburban and fringe residents. The spacious interior, four-wheel drive, rustic feel, and greater safety of a large vehicle have contributed to their popularity. But there has also been a not-so-hidden government subsidy of these vehicles. The federal government has classified minivans and sport utility vehicles as trucks. This means they avoid the federal fuel economy and pollution standards that cars must meet. These vehicles may legally generate almost twice the nitrous oxide emissions of a car and need to achieve only 20.7 miles per gallon compared to 27.5 miles per gallon for cars.[34] Remarkably, minivans and sport utility vehicles are not subject to the gas-guzzler taxes that apply to fuel-inefficient cars or the luxury taxes that fall on cars costing over $36,000.[35] Redefining minivans and sport utility vehicles simply as large family cars would go far in requiring more energy-efficient and less-polluting vehicles.

Another effective policy could be a levy on cars and trucks entering congested areas. This tax would tend to reduce the amount of traffic and help pay for road maintenance. A third possibility is the construction of private toll roads to provide limited-access highways for those who want to avoid traffic jams. A private toll road is already in use connecting the suburbs of northern Virginia and the western fringe.

The metro fringe is a region of relative affluence. The federal government could:

- raise income taxes on those earning over $100,000 (who have been the main beneficiaries of tax cuts since 1981); and
- eliminate the mortgage interest deduction on second homes and limit the deduction on primary residences to $15,000 a year. This would reduce the demand for housing of $150,000 and up.

On the other hand, the construction, home appliance, furnishing, and landscaping industries are important components of local economies. Less home construction would translate into slower economic growth, at least in the short to medium term. Because the president and Congress hold office for the short to medium term, they are unlikely to support measures to control growth that would also slow down economic growth and hence jeopardize their chances for reelection.

Increase State and Local Control of Transportation Planning

ISTEA set up a good framework for metropolitan planning organizations to have input into how federal transportation dollars are spent. The MPOs need to have more control and more freedom to spend federal money on a variety of transportation projects. For example, the purchase of conservation easements along scenic and historic highways would protect valuable views and sites as well as channel development elsewhere. The funding of transit-oriented development in suburbs would reduce dependence on the automobile, encourage mass transit, reduce energy use, and reduce air pollution.

Increase Funding to Preserve Natural Resource Lands

The federal government could greatly help the efforts to preserve resource lands in fringe areas. One place to start is an expansion of the 1996 Farm Bill grants to states and local governments to purchase development rights to farmland. The 1996 Farm Bill authorized $35 million over seven years, an average of only $5 million a year. By contrast, a $50 million-a-year program would go far toward providing seed money to start up new state and local purchase-of development-rights programs as well as supplement active programs. Because most of the federal farm subsidy programs will be phased out in the year 2002, more than enough federal money will be freed up to fund a long-term purchase-of-development-rights program. The result would be greater protection of farmland in the metro fringe and better growth management.

At the same time, the 1981 Farmland Protection Policy Act needs to be strengthened. Amazingly, the current act does not allow citizen groups to cite it in opposing federally financed development projects that would result in the conversion of prime farmland.

Federal purchases of land through the Land and Water Conservation Fund can also help protect valuable natural lands in the fringe. Full annual funding of this program is needed. Two other federal programs—the Wetlands Reserve Program and the Conservation Reserve Program—assist with land conservation. An increase in funding for both programs could be joined with a targeting of funds toward fringe areas where soil erosion threatens to do the most damage to drinking water supplies.

Increase the Cost of Developing the Fringe

A national farmland conversion tax modeled after the state of Maryland's would help discourage development in the fringe and could raise revenues for farmland preservation.

Federal infrastructure grants could be linked to developer contributions for infrastructure such as sewer, water, roads, and schools. This would place a greater burden for the cost of new development on the developers.

The downside of increasing the cost of developing the fringe is that the cost of housing would rise, making fringe areas all the more elite. Local affordable housing programs would be necessary to mitigate the impacts of increased development costs.

Direct Federal Spending to the Central Cities and Older Suburbs

In June of 1997, President Clinton offered a three-part plan to revive the nation's central cities. The Department of Housing and Urban Development would give police officers a 50 percent discount on homes they purchase from the department in neighborhoods they patrol. About one thousand police officers would qualify. Next, the Federal Housing Administration would reduce the points it charges from 1.75 percent to 1.5 percent for first-time home buyers in the inner cities. The total saving for home buyers is projected at $4 million. Third, a federal government pilot project would let two thousand families use federal rent subsidies toward buying their own homes.

Although these new efforts recognize the importance of fighting crime and the need for greater homeownership in the inner cities, they are pathetic gestures by the world's wealthiest nation. These programs are simply not commensurate with the magnitude of the problems.

The ghost of urban renewal has long deterred the federal government from attempting large and bold programs to revitalize the nation's central cities and older suburbs. But lavish federal spending and tax policies have enabled the suburbs and the fringe to flourish. Estimates are that roughly 20 percent of urban areas consist of open land and available building lots.

Federal spending can be directed to central cities by targeting federal infrastructure dollars to existing communities. The federal government would do well to study the Smart Growth initiative underway in Maryland (see box 9.3). The state of Maryland is having counties designate growth areas that will receive priority for infrastructure funds. This will discourage sprawl and help to sustain areas that are already developed.

Focusing on brownfields recovery, especially the cleanup of hazardous waste sites, holds real promise for reviving industrial and commercial activity. As of 1997, the EPA had selected and sponsored sixty-four national and fifty-one regional brownfields pilot cleanup and redevelopment projects. But, according to Paul Helmke, mayor of Fort Wayne, Indiana, and chairman of the U.S. Conference of Mayors, there may be as many as 500,000 brownfield sites spread across America. Mayors in thirty-three cities reckoned the lost tax revenues of brownfield sites in their cities at $200 million a year. Mayor Helmke argues about the urgency of cleaning up and reusing brownfields: "The real menace of brownfields is not what they do to America's center cities, it's what they don't do: they don't encourage expansion, investment, or jobs."[36]

In August of 1997, the federal government proposed letting the states guide the cleanup of abandoned industrial sites and the recovery of cleanup costs. Included would be relief from liability under the Superfund law to companies and investors who redevelop lightly polluted properties.

Expanding the tax credits for individuals and companies that invest in poor neighborhoods is a step in the right direction. Currently, for each dollar investors put into such federal empowerment zones, they receive eighty-nine cents in tax credits, spread out over ten years. New and refurbished housing and commercial properties are prime needs. Already this program has shown it can revitalize housing in New York City.[37]

Expanding the tax credits for the rehabilitation of historic buildings for commercial use can also help. In 1976, Congress granted tax credits for the restoration and remodeling of historic buildings for income-producing commercial uses. These credits created a powerful incentive for reinvestment in urban centers and older suburbs. In 1986, Congress passed a tax reform package that included a reduction and a complication of the historic tax credits. The twelve years since then have shown a sharp decline in the rehabilitation of historic buildings from the 1976–86 period. Developers generally claim that it is cheaper to build a new building than remodel an old one, partly because of modern building and fire codes. The historic tax credits help to level the development playing field and even tilt the advantage in favor of rehabilitation. A further attraction of the historic tax credits is that they tend to promote pleasing urban design (such as Laclede's Landing in St. Louis) and places that are refreshingly different from the glitz and plastic of the malls.

A Historic Homeowner Assistance Act, introduced in Congress in 1997, would make homeowners eligible for income tax credits for rehabilitating historic homes. Older urban neighborhoods would be prime beneficiaries.

The main obstacles to revitalizing the nation's central cities are political. Central cities no longer contain the majority of the nation's population. The suburbanites have the political power in Washington, and, in state capitals, a coalition of rural and suburban politicians is often aligned against urban interests.

The federal government is notorious for spending little time on monitoring and assessing the impacts of its programs. This has been especially true of growth management. The federal government could charge the Council on Environmental Quality with performing periodic assessments of the impact of federal programs on growth management. Alternatively, private, nonprofit groups could make similar assessments. These assessments would help identify problems and perhaps lead to corrective legislation.

Summary

The federal government has no overall vision for the future of the rural-urban fringe. Some federal programs encourage development of the fringe, and few discourage it. Federal tax policy creates incentives for new home construction, commercial office and retail outlets, and industrial plants on greenfields. Highway construction grants have helped to make a huge area of land accessible to expanding metropolitan regions. As a result, the population of the fringe and the geographic size of the fringe have steadily expanded.

Agricultural programs have not yet begun to fully address the loss of fringe farmland. The revised estate tax laws will help many farmers pass along the farm to the next generation, but much more federal funding for purchasing development rights and more careful review of federally funded road and infrastructure projects are needed.

The Environmental Protection Agency, through the enforcement of Clean Air Act standards and Safe Drinking Water standards, holds the power and potential to limit the growth of the fringe. Federal transportation grants are already being linked to local and regional compliance with air quality standards. Limiting the spread of small private water systems could help rein in sprawl.

Major changes to federal spending and tax policies are needed to revitalize central cities into desirable places for many, if not most, Americans to live. These changes would help to take some of the growth pressures off the fringe.

The primary need and preferred role of the federal government today is to provide incentives for states and local areas to get back to the basic task of providing quality, sustainable communities and regions. The metropolitan planning organizations formed under ISTEA legislation are a tremendous step in the right direction. They are, quite frankly, the only organizations close enough to local programs, yet broad enough to have a long-range, wide-angle view of the many problems that beset metropolitan regions. In the spirit of the ISTEA legislation, the federal government must come to realize that one size does not fit all and that local metropolitan planning organizations will differ in their approach to regional challenges.

If the federal government is to become truly effective in shaping and balancing growth in the twenty-first century, it must take a lesson from the landmark efforts of states such as Oregon, Washington, and Maryland and promote compact development by tying the urban growth boundary concept to area-wide metropolitan planning organizations with at least enough power to override the disastrous land-use decisions of local governments in the outer fringe counties (see chapter 9).

CHAPTER 7

Divided We Sprawl: The Role of State and Local Governments

Township, county, and state programs need to work together to achieve a balance in planned land use to meet all goals and provide a future for the next generation.

—*Citizen, Cuyahoga County, Ohio*

Unchecked sprawl has shifted from an engine of California's growth to a force that now threatens to inhibit growth and degrade the quality of life.

—*Beyond Sprawl: New Patterns of Growth to Fit the New California (1995)*

Suburban sprawl fans out from every major American city, and, in most places, it will continue to eat into fringe areas. At the same time, scattered low-density residential and commercial sprawl will consume bits and pieces of the outer-fringe countryside. Sprawl does not further the national goals of racial integration, energy efficiency, affordable housing, environmental quality, or economic competitiveness. Yet the federal government has given state and local governments little direction about how to control sprawl. Instead, federal tax policies, regulations, and spending programs have been powerful contributors to sprawl.

Decisions about land use are made mainly by municipal and county governments. These local governments need to understand how their comprehensive plans, property tax policies, zoning regulations, and spending programs induce sprawl. But as Henry Diamond and Patrick Noonan point out, "Many communities continue to rely on a legislative framework that was created for a very different pre–World War II America. As a result, the planning and growth management mechanisms in force in most states in the 1990s are woefully out-of-step with the times."[1]

Box 7.1 A Survey of Opinions About Land-Use Planning in New York State

New York is a home-rule state, which means that the 1,530 local governments can enact comprehensive plans and adopt zoning, subdivision, and site-plan regulations for private property within their borders.

In 1993, Pace University Law School asked the consulting firm of Kinsey and Company to conduct a survey of opinions about land-use planning in New York.[2] Over two thousand local officials, planners, and developers responded to the survey. Over half (57 percent) said the current land-use planning system was unacceptable, and only 16 percent rated it acceptable.

The main complaints concerned poor use of infrastructure dollars, poor location of business activity, lack of affordable housing, weak protection of agricultural land, and loss of community character.

Respondents reached a general consensus on the following ways to improve land-use planning:

- Tie local plans with county or regional plans.
- Land-use planning needs to precede regulations.
- Integrate land-use planning and infrastructure planning.
- Coordinate state and local infrastructure budgets.
- Make land-use planning more orderly and logical.

Meanwhile, state agency spending programs play a powerful role in influencing the location and intensity of development. State infrastructure projects, such as sewer and water facilities and roads, promote economic growth and often encourage sprawl. On the other hand, state and federal environmental regulations can restrain growth while protecting air and water quality and natural resources. But state agency plans and programs are rarely coordinated with each other or with local comprehensive plans.

Comprehensive plans are meant to be the foundation of a community or county growth management system, but many state planning and zoning enabling laws do not clearly spell out that a comprehensive plan should be the basis of the zoning ordinance and other growth management techniques, or that the plan and the implementing ordinances and infrastructure spending programs should be consistent. Nor is there a requirement that the comprehensive plan and zoning ordinance be kept up to date.

Reform of state planning and zoning enabling laws is long overdue. Local governments need to make sure their comprehensive plans and land-use ordinances are timely and can produce compact, cost-effective, and sustainable development. An added benefit in reforming and updating growth management statutes and ordinances is that state and local governments can work to offset the federal influences that encourage and even reward sprawl.

State and Local Government Actions That Contribute to Sprawl

The following examples of poor growth management are meant not to place blame but rather to serve as a warning of the results of ineffective planning, counterproductive tax policies, and short-sighted spending programs by state and local governments. Identifying the problems with government growth management is the first step toward devising and implementing solutions.

Lack of Coordination among Local Governments

Planners can easily become frustrated as they attempt to devise a comprehensive land development and land protection program in a fringe community or county. Chapter 3 discussed the major barriers to effective, coordinated, long-term development and land conservation strategies. The biggest problem is perhaps the most intractable: the overlapping jurisdiction of different governments, authorities, and regulatory agencies making piecemeal and often redundant claims over policy making and development permissions in the fringe. Although the structure of local, regional, and state governments varies considerably, it is not uncommon to have several separate entities, each with its own agenda, active within a single township, municipality, or county.

Many problems in the fringe are regional. Landfills, water supplies, agricultural land protection, highway networks, and large developments of regional impact almost always require the cooperation of two or more local governments to implement solutions. Most states have missed opportunities to bring local governments together to undertake regional efforts for economic development, infrastructure, and environmental protection.

Sloppy Planning

Anyone who drives down a miracle mile of franchise outlets amid a sea of parking lots and a forest of signs, or who passes a subdivision of houses that face in awkward directions, might ask why they should have any faith in public planners or private developers.

In his book *A Better Place to Live*, Philip Langdon pulls no punches about weak planning efforts by local governments. He cites three widespread examples of why poor planning occurs:

1. *Planning failures have lowered the ambitions of planners.* Planners work for politicians, who are usually cautious and reluctant to "plan big." Because planning is a political process, politicians often feel the need to have sufficient "political capital" in the form of public opinion polls, petitions, or coalitions of interest groups behind them before they push for strong growth management measures. Usually, it takes a crisis or several years of organizing to amass sufficient political capital. But if these growth management efforts fail, planners and politicians get the blame and risk losing their jobs. Failure breeds reluctance to take bold planning measures, even when they are needed.

2. *Planners can be heavily influenced by commercial and business interests.* Economic development is a main goal of many local politicians. For instance, the strip commercial development that results from local government planning and zoning appears not much different from what the private market would produce without government planning. So why have government land-use planning?

3. *Planners tend to focus on the planning process rather than on how their plans and regulations can shape specific projects and overall land-use patterns.* Planners have become, in Langdon's words, "application-accepters" and "permit-dispensers."[3] They spend little time assessing the cumulative impact of the recent and proposed development projects on community services and land-use patterns.

Why then should anyone expect things to be different any time soon? Many local and state governments are remarkably parochial. If an idea does not originate in their state, county, or municipality, it is suspect. When a new planning technique from the outside is discussed, locals tend to say, " That may work for you, but we could never do that here." This kind of defeatist attitude, identified by Philip Langdon, has retarded planning efforts in many communities, as well as attempts at regional planning. In addition, county and municipal attorneys have often obstructed the adoption of new planning techniques by warning about legal challenges that could cost the local government. And in some states, a basic problem is outdated planning laws. For example, in Pennsylvania, a local zoning ordinance does not have to be consistent with the comprehensive plan. This means that the zoning can defeat the purpose of a carefully drafted plan that reflects thoughtful studies and citizen input. The comprehensive plan might include goals for enhancing existing village centers and protecting open space, but the zoning ordinance might allow sprawling residential lots and commercial highway-strip development throughout the countryside.

Because elected local officials normally make the final decision about development proposals, planning is a political process. Yet America is facing a political crisis of leadership, not only in Washington, but also at the state and local levels. Distrust of government runs high. Many elected and appointed officials have noted a reduction in the civility of public debate, and some of the rancor and distrust is well deserved.

A valid charge against local planning is that it is frequently so flexible as to appear incompetent, reckless, and downright corrupt. Decisions of planning commissions and elected officials can mean windfalls to some property owners and a wipeout of property value to others. When local planning commissions and elected officials routinely approve special exceptions, variances, and rezonings, they weaken the planning process, and citizens lose faith in the local government's commitment to managing growth. After successfully pushing for uniform local zoning codes in Rhode Island, homebuilder Robert Cioe explained, "We wanted to make it difficult for the zoning boards to make political decisions for their friends."[4]

In describing the planning and development struggles in Saratoga Springs, New York, James Howard Kunstler refers to the pro-growth advocates as "an efficient local land development machine made up of lawyers, bankers, realtors, and speculators, dedicated to maximizing their short-term profits at the expense of the town's future."[5] Implied here is a lack of *community vision*, and without a vision, planning efforts really have no direction.

Ineffective and Separatist Zoning

All too often, the planning process is, in the words of Rutherford Platt, "reactive, negative, and supplementary."[6] Developers present projects and wait for a response from the planners and elected officials. The zoning regulations that govern development mostly emphasize inflexible, negative rules, rather than encourage creativity. The developer has pretty much decided what to do with the property—have the planning process and zoning ordinance provided good direction?

The comprehensive plan, which should guide development, all too often sits on the shelf. Zoning ordinances are permissive about density yet rigid on permitted uses and development design. The frequent result is similarly sited houses on cookie-cutter lots. Many American towns built in the nineteenth century could not be built today. They would violate their own zoning ordinances. This is a major problem that New Urbanists face when proposing mixed-use developments.

Local zoning practices separate rather than connect people. One zoning district is for single-family residential, another for commercial, another for multifamily. To get a loaf of bread, people have to get in their cars and drive to a store. To find recreation, they have to drive to a park. And residential neighborhoods often lack public places to meet. Allowing a mix of residential and commercial uses, buildings close to sidewalks, or an absence of bulk coverage requirements are but a few examples of how zoning ordinances could change to encourage more flexible and pedestrian-oriented design. Large-lot residential zoning in the fringe countryside separates neighbors from each other, uses up more land than necessary, and defeats the goal of fostering compact, mixed-use development.

But what you zone for is what you get. Americans have been willing to live and work in sprawled-out housing and commercial developments. There has been a long debate as to whether developers mold buyers' tastes and preferences or respond to the demands of housing and commercial-space consumers. In fairness, developers continue to build tract subdivisions and commercial strips because that is what the auto-inspired zoning regulations ask for, what banks will lend for, and what turns a profit. Alternative, more attractive, and better functioning places to live and work, as described in chapter 5, need a wider audience among developers, consumers, business operators, and local planners and elected officials.

Fiscal Zoning: Wedding Taxation to Local Zoning

Local governments depend on property taxes to pay for schools and most other public services. This puts pressure on local governments to compete for development that will broaden the tax base. As a result, local governments join their tax needs with short-sighted land-use planning to become prime contributors to sprawl in the fringe.

Fiscal zoning occurs when local governments zone land to encourage developments that will generate more in property taxes than they demand in services. The competition among communities and counties for stores, offices, gas stations, restaurants, factories, and high-value residential property tax "ratables" drives much of the struggle over land in the fringe. Property taxes commonly are lower on county or township land outside of incorporated cities and towns, because there are fewer public services to pay for. This is especially true if new commercial and residential development can use private on-site septic and water systems, which holds down the need to develop expensive public sewer and water systems and keeps property taxes low. Finally, land costs are lower and the appreciation potential of real estate is often greater than in core cities and older suburbs. Thus, both businesses and households have strong incentives to locate in the metro-fringe countryside. Commercial and residential developments outside of existing settlements add to sprawl, sap economic and social vitality from cities and towns, and defeat efforts to create compact communities.

Education is the largest single item in the cost of local government, despite the fact that the local government often has no control over the budget of the school district. Nonetheless, politicians know that the most effective way to keep voters happy is to keep property taxes under control.

Take, for example, a forty-acre tract of open land at the edge of a town. If the local government zones the land for two-acre lots and $250,000 houses are built on them, those twenty homes probably will generate sufficient property taxes to pay for the public services they require.[7] But if the local government zones those forty acres for quarter-acre lots, 160 homes could be built and the average value of those homes might be in, say, the $125,000 range. If we assume an average of two children per house, that's over three hundred children to educate, not to mention new streets and public sewer and water facilities.

Thus, just as housing consumers have a financial incentive to buy as much house as possible (including the large lot) to take advantage of the federal mortgage interest deduction, the local government has a financial incentive to zone land for low-density sprawl to minimize public service costs. One of the ironies is that farmland and open space tend to generate more in property taxes than they demand in services. So as the local government allows single-family homes to consume more farmland and open space, a public financial gain is wasted.

In some places, notably Wisconsin, it is not uncommon for the local government to approve the subdivision of lots and then not tax them at development value until they are sold for building lots. This practice both subsidizes the holding costs of the subdivider and encourages landowners to keep lots available for development. In fairness, a legally subdivided three-acre lot should be taxed as a residential building site, not as open space or agricultural land.

Fiscal zoning can have other negative impacts on the community:

- Single-family residential zones do not allow apartments (called "multifamily housing"), which could house more people in a much smaller area.
- Highway frontage is zoned for commercial strips and developed. In these "combat zones," approvals are readily granted, usually with little traffic planning, site design, or landscaping.
- Industrial development may not prove a net gain in local finances. Often, property tax breaks are needed to induce factories to locate in the community.
- An increase in commercial, residential, and industrial development means more jobs and attracts more people to live in the community, driving up land prices and property taxes. The vicious circle of searching for property tax revenue and continued land development and population growth suggests a dog chasing its tail.
- The favored 25 percent of the suburbs, identified by Myron Orfield as the new and growing suburbs, capture not only most of the new property tax revenues but also most of the state and federal infrastructure grants.[8] In short, the wealthier suburbs are being subsidized. A state program of infrastructure grants could easily include a "means testing" of communities so that wealthier communities would be required to make a larger local contribution for infrastructure projects than poorer communities.

Until there is a way to pay for public services and education from a regional source and have it based more on income than real estate, the competition for development among communites and counties threatens to defeat rational land-use planning. (For a discussion of regional tax sharing, see the discussion of the Twin Cities in chapter 9 under "Regional Government and Planning Efforts.")

In 1997, the Vermont Supreme Court declared it illegal for cities and towns to use the local property tax to fund education. Because education costs normally have made up two-thirds or more of these local governments' budgets, the search for greater property tax revenues has created a bias for growth, especially short-term strip development that may not be sustainable. The Vermont legislature responded to the court's decision by passing Act 60 to provide state-level funding of education. The act also includes a provision that allows a municipality to offer long-term school tax breaks to lure prospective businesses only with the approval of the legislature.

While the impact of Act 60 will take years to unfold, John Ewing, former chairman of the Vermont Environmental Board, predicts that "towns will plan for their growth on the basis of more rational factors than chasing tax dollars. They will no longer have to promote development at any cost to ensure a tax base."[9]

Nonetheless, better land-use planning will come about only if taxpayers and elected officials can be shown that it will save money compared to separatist and fiscal zoning. One way to do this is a cost-of-community-services study. Recent studies have shown that residential development, on average, is a net drain on local government budgets, costing between $1.15 to $1.50 in services for each dollar paid in taxes. Commercial and industrial properties produce a surplus by using only 35 to 65 cents in services for every dollar of local taxes paid. Similarly, farmland and open space require 30 to 50 cents in services for every dollar of tax.[10] The residential ratio of taxes paid to services demanded will change the higher the value of residential real estate. For example, five-acre minimum lot size agricultural or residential zoning without sewers will usually result in a surplus of tax revenues over services required. But this zoning will do little to protect agricultural land. It is fiscal zoning aimed at excluding multifam-

Box 7.2 Measurable Indicators of Sprawl That Portend Impacts on Public Finances

- Increase in the number of commercial and residential subdivisions approved
- Increase in the total number of lots approved
- Increase in the acreage approved for development
- Increase in building permits
- Increased number of on-site septic systems
- Increased traffic counts
- Increase in population
- Rising per capita property taxes
- Loss of acres of agricultural land

ily housing. Some communities have even calculated the "break even" home value for their community. Typically, this home value is quite a bit higher than the average existing home value in the community.

Another way to measure the fiscal impacts of growth is to compare the community's population growth rate with the change in per capita local government spending. For communities growing at 1 to 2 percent a year, per capita costs usually do not increase much. But in communities with annual population increases above 3 percent, per capita spending rises rapidly. Part of the reason is that new capacity must be built. This can be dramatic, as in the case of having to spend tens of millions of dollars to build a new high school.

Subsidizing Mobility

It seems that no one pays the true cost of mobility. Public transit relies in part on direct public subsidies in order to keep moving. Although gas taxes go for road construction and repair, car drivers are the beneficiaries of lavish government subsidies. Trucks generate freight taxes as well, but trucks do the most damage to roads.

State departments of transportation (DOTs) are the states' equivalent of the Defense Department on the national level. About 20 percent of state budgets go to the car.[11] As with any large bureaucracy, the power of a state DOT depends on its ability to expand its staff and clout and to deliver projects to the districts of many elected representatives. Highway projects, like the defense industry, mean jobs. And jobs help politicians get reelected.

Roads are powerful growth inducers in the fringe. A commuter railroad usually has no more than a dozen stations along its route. A bus line faces a limited and concentrated ridership. Roads provide access to a broad area, and, as any realtor knows, access is value.

In the metro fringe, mass transit is generally not feasible because of the scattered development patterns. Instead, fringe dwellers contribute to the statistic that more than eight out of ten Americans drive to and from work. As more people move out to fringe areas, older country roads become clogged with traffic. Also, safe driving at high speeds becomes a serious issue. The solution most often touted is to spend millions of dollars on building and widening roads. New highway construction emphasizes bypasses and ring roads around cities and towns, and widening roads from two to four lanes. But as more roads are built and improved, the more they are used to add to the dispersed housing and commercial developments they were first attempting to service.

The cost of building major new roads can be staggering. For instance, the cost of Atlanta's proposed 211-mile outer-perimeter interstate has been estimated at $5 *billion*.[12] This outer beltway would circle the core city at a distance of thirty-five miles, pushing suburban development and the rural-urban fringe farther out into the countryside. Houston and Washington, D.C., are also considering the construction of such second-tier ring roads.

Ultimately, highway funds are limited. Suburban and fringe road projects divert highway funds from urban and rural projects. From the state perspective, maintenance of the interstate system has a major priority. But, in the meantime, many secondary roads and thousands of bridges are not receiving needed attention.

While speaking out against major new road projects, Vermont Transportation Secretary Glenn Gershaneck warned, "The idea that we can build our way out of severe congestion flies in the face of available land, money, people, or will."[13]

The choice then appears to be between greater traffic congestion and raising the cost of driving to more accurately reflect the air pollution, road maintenance, and construction costs imposed on society. But over time, new and rehabilitated development might reduce people's dependence on the car.

In 1994, the City of Portland, Oregon, released a groundbreaking study entitled "Land Use, Transportation, Air Quality Connection" (LUTRAQ). The study showed that building more highways around Portland would lead to more auto-dependent sprawl and increased air pollution. This conclusion helped to stop a proposal for a major highway along the west side of Portland. As an alternative, the study proposed the compact transit-oriented developments described in chapter 5.

Annexation

Annexation occurs when one local government expands its territory by taking land from another local government. Typically, a city will annex land from a county or township. A city generally cannot annex land from another city. The land to be annexed must usually be contiguous to the annexing city. Forty-four states allow annexations. Hawaii and the New England states, except Massachusetts, do not. Although annexation laws vary from state to state, in twelve states property owners outside the city must start the annexation process. Annexation may or may not require the approval of a majority of the residents who are to be annexed.

According to David Rusk, "During the 1980s, 398 central cities added a total of 2,625 square miles through annexation."[14] Most annexations occurred in the Sun Belt, with the South the leader and the West not far behind. The Midwest had some, while the Northeast had almost no annexations. Early in the twentieth century, several Boston suburbs refused to become part of the city of Boston and so started a trend of stopping the expansion of East Coast cities. Since World War II, annexation has rarely occurred in the Northeast. Boston, for instance, covers a mere 3 percent of its metro region, and its percentage of the metropolitan population has steadily declined.

Descriptions of battles over the annexation of county land by cities could fill several books. On the positive side, annexation can help a city control how quickly and where growth occurs. Ted McCormack, an official with Virginia's Commission on Local Government, explains, "Towns are looking at annexations because they're seeing development coming, and they want to have some say in it."[15] Local governments may have a stronger bargaining position with developers over contributions for necessary public services. By annexing, a city or town can avoid the duplication of public services and the fragmenting of services between municipality and county. Also, annexation can help to keep development next to existing cities and towns and minimize sprawl throughout the countryside.

Annexation can also reduce the creation of elite suburbs whose residents work in the nearby core city but contribute little or nothing in city taxes. In essence, the city becomes a regional government, a regional economy, and a regional society. This is the argument former Albuquerque Mayor David Rusk makes in his book, *Cities Without Suburbs* (see the Albuquerque case study in chapter 11). Rusk contends that "the greater the fragmentation of governments, the greater the fragmentation of society by race and economic class."[16]

On the negative side, annexation, like fiscal zoning, is a way that one jurisdiction competes with another over economic growth and tax base. In the rush for economic growth, a city might annex a large amount of open land and allow it to be developed in a sprawling pattern, without an infrastructure and development plan for the area. Commissioner Ruth Bracket of San Luis Obispo County, California, keeps an eye out for excessive annexations: "What we look for is to prevent long fingers of development that encourage wasteful low-density infill. We require that the urban area remain compact and have the ability to provide all foreseeable services."[17]

Annexation can lead to bad feelings on the part of those who are annexed. For example, in 1997, the city of Hiawatha, Iowa, annexed 4,500 acres (or seven square miles) of Linn County, Iowa, into its city limits. This was an "involuntary" annexation, meaning that the people who lived in that part of Linn County were not necessarily in favor of becoming residents of Hiawatha.

If Linn County and Hiawatha had made an agreement about how, where, and how fast the city would grow, a nasty fight and bad feelings could have been avoided. Hiawatha did not have an immediate need for such a large additional acreage. And now the threat of future annexations has struck fear into the landowners within a mile or two of the new city limits. For one thing, city taxes are higher; for another, much of the open land swallowed by the city will probably be developed over time.

The Township Board of Trustees in Bath, Ohio, summed up the danger of annexation run rampant:

> Perhaps the worst effect of annexation is what it does to carefully prepared zoning goals and careful land use development that results from good land use planning. Today, annexation is used extensively to subvert zoning. Lands planned to remain in agricultural or in forested open space preserves become part of urban sprawl by a mere signature on an annexation petition.[18]

But annexation alone may not guarantee success in controlling sprawl. David Rusk noted that "Kansas City, Kansas, and Kansas City, Missouri, annexed more [increasing their land area by over 300 percent] and got less from it than any other region of the country."[19] And annexation laws can change. By a mysterious quirk, legislation passed in Tennessee in 1997 put a stop to all annexations.

Public Infrastructure and Service Costs

It is no accident that the costs of local government are rising along with the increase of sprawl. A 1989 review of development patterns reported that taxpayers made subsidies of $35,000 to $48,000 per dwelling unit in a sprawl pattern, compared with less than $18,000 per dwelling in a more compact pattern.[20] The lack of coordination of infrastructure between communities means that economies of scale may be lost, and hence the infrastructure may be more expensive than necessary. For example, in the early 1990s, a developer proposed to build a six-hundred-unit retirement home in Earl Township, Lancaster County, Pennsylvania, just outside of the borough of New Holland. The logical source of sewer service was from the borough, but the borough refused. The developer then worked with the township for the construction of a new sewage treatment plant. The new plant was built within a mile of the borough's plant, and new sewer lines had to be laid over two miles to reach the retirement home.

Population growth often produces "threshold effects" for the provision of public services. That is, above a certain number of residents, new schools, sewer and water, police, and fire personnel are needed, often at a much greater cost. For example, Gordon County, Georgia, lies in a growth corridor between the metro areas of Chattanooga, forty-five miles to the north, and Atlanta, sixty miles to the south. In the early 1990s, Calhoun, the county seat, spent $5 million to expand its sewage treatment plant. Five years later, because of population growth, Calhoun needs to expand its plant again at a cost of $10 million.[21]

Some communities have been careless in the expansion and uncentered location of infrastructure. Siting consolidated public schools in the countryside rather than in a town is a prime example. Placing government offices out along highways is another. In many cases, no lines have been drawn between where the infrastructure (especially public sewer and water) will end and the areas that will remain unserviced. This lack of predictability gives rise to land speculation as speculators buy up land in anticipation of where infrastructure expansions will occur. Some speculators will guess correctly, and some will not. Or speculators and other landowners will lobby politicians for service extensions to their properties.

Most towns of below ten thousand inhabitants do not draft a formal five-year capital improvements program showing the proposed expansion, upgrading, maintenance, and financing of infrastructure projects. Also, sewer and water authorities may not coordinate their expansion plans with local towns and counties. This lack of infrastructure planning has often put communities in the position of playing catch-up to provide adequate public facilities. An adequate public facilities ordinance can require developers to wait until the community can provide the necessary infrastructure to make the developments safe, accessible, and in compliance with health standards.

It is becoming increasingly common for communities to ask developers to help pay for the new or expanded services that will be necessary to support new development. For decades after World War II, developers were able to build their subdivisions and commercial projects and pretty much leave the tab for schools, roads, and sewer and water facilities to the taxpayers. Impact fees, mandatory dedication of open space, and road upgrades are some of the ways that many communities are requiring developers to share the burden for services. In 1995, Prince Georges County, Maryland, even passed an ordinance that requires developers of new housing to demonstrate that the anticipated number of students from a subdivision will not push the area's schools above their capacity.[22] Developers must pay $5,000 for each student expected to exceed the capacity.

In the long run, the best way for a community to manage public service costs is to promote compact, mixed-use development. This land-use pattern avoids unnecessary extensions of sewer and water lines and premature hiring of additional police and fire personnel. In short, compact development is cheaper to service. It also tends to rely on already existing infrastructure and supports existing businesses. Writing about downtown Burlington, Vermont, and the construction of suburban shopping malls, journalist Sam Hemingway lamented: "For 20 years, the writing has been on the wall: If you build too much retail space too far from the region's center, you undermine the public infrastructure in place and the future vitality of a downtown on which everything depends."[23]

Because it is illegal to place population limits on a community, there may be no way to restrict growth other than through zoning ordinances that require large lot sizes for new houses or temporary sewer or building moratoria. But such practices are increasingly likely to be viewed as "exclusionary" by the courts and hence overturned. In fact, in the planning profession today it is often said that communities must accept their "regional fair share" of new residential development.

The Loss of Open Space and Development Conflicts with Farmers

Open space—farm fields, rolling hills, forests, and scenic vistas—is an important amenity and economic asset for metro-fringe communities. Yet many fringe communities are witnessing significant losses of open space. For instance, rapidly growing Greater Atlanta loses an estimated five hundred acres of open space to development each week.[24] The disappearing open space makes more distant and rural parts of metro areas that are much more attractive to households. This out-migration to the countryside simply produces more dispersed, auto-dependent settlement patterns. And as more people move to the fringe countryside, they come into contact with long-standing commercial farming, ranching, and forestry operations.

Local and county governments in the fringe have generally done a poor job of alerting prospective newcomers to the discomforts and dangers of living in the countryside. A few places have placed nuisance disclaimers in their zoning ordinances to warn about inconveniences that might occur when living near farm and ranch operations. As mentioned earlier, Larimer County, Colorado, has produced a wonderful common sense document called "The Code of the West," which spells out the potential hardships and hidden costs of living in the countryside (see appendix 1).

While living in the countryside can be financially and emotionally rewarding, newcomers often do not think about basic services such as water, roads, and trash removal before purchasing their homes or building lots. Nor do they anticipate the development of neighboring properties, which can change the appearance and their enjoyment of the area.

The look-before-you-leap warning is often most appropriate when newcomers settle near farm and ranch operations in the rural-urban fringe. A farm or ranch is first and foremost a business, part of a local and regional agricultural industry. The conversion of farmland to a residential, commercial, or industrial site can have a sharply negative impact on the local farm economy. As the number of farms and farm acres dwindle, farm support businesses—the feed mills, machinery dealers, processing, and transportation companies—also fade. This puts heightened cost pressure on the remaining farmers, who must travel farther for supplies and services.

Nonfarmers in the fringe often perceive farmland and ranch land as valuable only for its scenic views and open space amenities. In fact, many farmland protection efforts in fringe areas are aimed at preserving open space rather than maintaining agriculture as an economically viable industry. This strategy misses the simple point that there can be no farms without farmers. The need for integrated farmland and agricultural policies is especially evident in the fringe because land-use restrictions alone do not guarantee the financial success of a farm, and the value of farmland is usually much higher for home sites, a mall, or an office park.

As more people move to the fringe, they bid up the price of land, isolate tracts of farmland through leapfrog development, and hasten the decline of local farming. Farmers and ranchers in fringe areas have been discouraged by vandalism to crops, livestock, and machinery. But nuisance ordinances enacted by local governments to restrict farming practices, such as hauling manure or operating machinery late at night or early in the morning, have especially frustrated farmers and ranchers. Newcomers to the fringe like to settle near farms but often do not want to tolerate the noise, dust, odors, chemical sprays, and slow-moving machinery associated with farming activities. These conflicts between farmers and newcomers have given rise to "right-to-farm" laws, which nearly every state uses to protect farmers from nuisance suits if they employ standard farming practices that do not violate state and federal laws. Right-to-farm laws vary from state to state. For example, some states do not protect a farmer from nuisance suits if the farmer significantly changes the farm operation, such as from a dairy farm to a hog farm.

Right-to-farm laws do not have much of a track record in the courts. But this is likely to change as more people move to the fringe, and as newcomers file suits based on trespass rather than nuisance doctrine. That is, a plaintiff may claim that noise, dust, and odors are leaving the farm and entering his or her nonfarm property and reducing enjoyment of that property.

Even with the existence of a right-to-farm law, a plaintiff may choose to file a nuisance suit against a farmer. Although the plaintiff has little chance of winning, the cost and aggravation to the farmer can be daunting as well as harmful to the farm operation. Michigan's right-to-farm law requires the plaintiff to pay the farmer's legal fees in an unsuccessful nuisance suit.

When farmers and ranchers see land in their vicinity being subdivided into house lots and commercial outlets, they tend to reduce the level of reinvestment in their farms and ranches, as they begin to anticipate selling their land for development in the near future. This process, known as the impermanence syndrome, describes how farmers and ranchers lose their commitment to agriculture in the face of persistent development pressures.

Every state offers preferential property tax assessment of farmland. This is intended to keep the burden of property taxes from driving farmers out of business. The preferential assessment is based on the use-value of the farmland rather than the land's highest and best use for development. But preferential assessment does not affect the property tax rate. As new development brings demands for new public services, especially schools, property tax rates can rise and drive up farm property tax bills.

Some states, mainly in the South, do not impose a penalty to recapture lost property taxes if the farmland is converted to a nonfarm use. This sets up a situation in which developers and speculators can buy farmland, receive preferential farm taxation, and then sell the land for development. In this way, preferential taxation can actually subsidize sprawl.

Weak agricultural zoning has also encouraged sprawl. Agricultural zoning is supposed to separate conflicting farm and nonfarm land uses and prevent the fragmentation of the farmland base. Many fringe communities and counties, however, view agricultural zoning as a means of protecting open space, rather than a means of helping maintain a viable agricultural industry in the local economy. This is especially true where minimum lot sizes are under twenty acres. It is not uncommon to find agricultural zones with two-acre, five-acre, or ten-acre minimum lot sizes that lead to the proliferation of nonfarm "estates" and hobby farms. These rural residences compete with commercial farmers over the land base. Only where minimum lot sizes are large enough to discourage intrusions by low-density residential development can commercial agriculture be protected from the parcellation of the land base and land prices that far exceed the agricultural value. Five- and ten-acre lot sizes also may result in more land being taken up by residences than necessary. A better means of conserving farmland is area-based allocation zoning that would allow a maximum two-acre house lot for every twenty-five acres of the farm. This would discourage the creation of large-lot hobby farms (see also the section on agricultural zoning in chapter 10).

Lack of Concern for Environmental Quality

Environmental quality is one of the main advantages that fringe areas have over cities and suburbs. Air and water quality are usually fairly good, and scenic vistas and the presence of wildlife are important attractions. But population growth and buildings bring stress on the natural environment. Local and state governments must recognize that the environmental assets of the fringe have significant value in economic development. Although environmental regulations bring additional costs of compliance, governments, the private sector, and the general public should see the safeguarding of environmental quality as a long-term investment in the quality of life. Quite simply, people want to live and work in pleasant, healthy surroundings.

Metropolitan Air Quality

Federal air quality standards are starting to impinge upon heavily auto-dependent metro areas that have tried to ignore their deteriorating air quality. One such place is Greater Atlanta. Business leaders are worried that economic growth will be stifled if the federal government withholds highway funds from metro Atlanta because it fails to meet the air quality standards of the Clean Air Act (see chapter 6). Said Sam A. Williams, president of the Atlanta Chamber of Commerce, "The number one threat to economic development is air quality."[25] He added that companies looking to locate in metro Atlanta will be forced to go elsewhere because they won't be able to obtain the needed environmental permits. Wayne Hill, chairman of the Gwinnett County Commissioners, warned that air quality standards could encourage more sprawl by causing companies to move to a more rural county at the metro fringe. With nearly half a million people in 1996, Gwinnett County is located about eighteen miles northeast of downtown Atlanta. Half of the county's workers commute to jobs in other counties or in Atlanta. According to Gregg T. Logan of the real estate consulting firm of Robert Charles Lesser, Inc., the average commuter driving time for Gwinnett County workers was thirty-four minutes in 1996, and he predicted that by the year 2020, it will increase to eighty minutes.[26] The longer time in traffic translates into more air pollution.

Water Quality and Quantity

State governments have contributed billions of dollars to help local governments build wastewater treatment systems. These systems have serviced existing communities and facilitated sprawl where sewer lines have been extended.

On-site septic systems have been an essential, and often abused, technology in enabling the growth and development of the metro fringe. Because much of the new development in the fringe has been outside of established settlements, many new houses in the fringe have been built with on-site septic systems and wells for drinking water. For homeowners, the feeling of not facing monthly or quarterly sewer and water bills is liberating. Yet several problems may develop, as outlined in the following paragraphs:

- Some homes are built fairly close together on lots of less than one acre. These lots are usually too small to absorb sewage effluent and keep it from entering the groundwater. Wells become polluted and a health crisis looms. In many cases, sewer and/or water lines must be extended from the nearest city or village. These sewer and water lines spur additional development in the countryside. A rule of thumb is that a single-family residence with an on-site septic system needs about two acres. This provides enough space for a backup leach field over the life of the house and is more likely to protect wells from pollution. Another rule of thumb is to require a test of the groundwater before a subdivision is approved or a building permit issued.

- Attempts to develop poor percolating soils or areas with poor-quality groundwater should be quashed. Lots above a certain size should not be exempt from percolation tests or required septic system technology. For many years, the state of Vermont allowed owners of lots of greater than ten acres to be exempt from such tests and rules; these exemptions created an incentive for buyers of building lots to purchase ten- to twenty-acre plots, which resulted in the needless loss of farm and forestlands.[27] Another insidious example—from Pennsylvania—is the "plume easement," which allows the area beneath neighboring land to be designated for receiving leachate from someone else's septic system.

- Some residents do not take proper care of their septic systems. A county or municipal ordinance that requires regular maintenance of septic systems is good health policy and can help the community avoid the expensive and growth-inducing extension of sewer and water lines into the countryside. In the metropolitan area of the Twin Cities, the Met Council has estimated that 90 percent of the lakes have water quality problems from onsite septic systems that do not meet minimum treatment standards.[28] For an example of an on-lot septic system ordinance, see appendix 2.

- As population increases, public water supplies come under increased demand and the construction of new buildings may impinge on public groundwater supplies. Similarly, a need for new groundwater sources may occur. To protect groundwater supples, communities are turning to wellhead protection ordinances. New York City has embarked on an ambitious cooperative effort with upstate communities and landowners to protect the city's drinking water supply (see chapter 10).
- Stormwater runoff can cause soil erosion; damage to neighboring properties; siltation in rivers, lakes, and streams; and pollution from impervious surfaces such as roads and parking lots. A stormwater management ordinance can ensure that new development is properly sited to minimize runoff and employs retention basins and grass and woodland buffer strips to slow runoff and increase groundwater recharge.
- State and local governments need to be aware of the link between land uses and water quality. They may need to adopt and implement water quality standards that anticipate the impact of development. In some fringe areas, especially in the West, protecting water quantity is an important economic as well as environmental issue. A reliable water supply along with water rights can sometimes mean the difference between wasteland and developable land. The depletion of groundwater can reduce the livability of a property or a community. Also, a shortage of water can mean insufficient fire protection, a concern especially in forested areas.

"We're hitting some limits [to growth] right now [in Greater Atlanta], because we're making decisions about how much water can be taken out of the Chattahoochee," remarked Alan Hallum of the Georgia Environmental Protection Division. "We need to start thinking more seriously about conserving and re-using water."[29]

Competition over water supplies will intensify in the future. Agriculture is the leading user of water, but as more people move to the fringe, they compete for groundwater and push to develop public groundwater and surface water supplies on or near farmland.

Water planning, like land-use planning, is an essential component of a truly comprehensive plan. Too often, water issues have been left up to individual landowners, utilities, or even the federal government. Water must be recognized as a vital resource for sustainable community and regional growth and development.

State and local governments should ensure that adequate, long-term water supplies are available—from either private or public sources—before new developments are approved. In addition, state grants, such as in Maryland, can be helpful to develop and protect public drinking water supplies.

Wildlife

State and local governments need to do a better job of planning for and protecting entire ecosystems, not just bits of open space or woods. Developers and local and state governments need to work together to incorporate blocks and buffers of natural areas into communities and then link them through wildlife corridors. The Habitat Conservation Plans discussed in chapter 6 seem to provide a workable model.

Coordination of State Agencies and Local Governments

Several state agencies have programs and policies that directly affect local land use. The departments of transportation, commerce, housing and community affairs, natural resources, and agriculture have important yet sometimes conflicting interests. For example, the department of agriculture may be charged with protecting agricultural land, while the department of transportation is proposing to build a bypass through fringe farmland. To resolve such conflicts, governors in Pennsylvania and Vermont have issued executive orders requiring their departments of agriculture to review all state agency projects that would involve the conversion of prime and important farmlands. This sort of review can improve the design of projects by minimizing impacts, suggesting alternatives, and avoiding costly mistakes.

State agencies have a long history of not coordinating their plans with local governments. This is especially important when the state is proposing a development with a region-wide impact, such as the construction of a major new road or the purchase of several hundred acres of parkland. The state of Vermont in its Act 200 of 1988 addressed this problem by requiring that "state agencies that have programs or take actions affecting land use . . . engage in a continuing planning process to assure those programs are consistent with [state] goals . . . and compatible with regional and approved municipal plans."[30] Although municipal and regional plans have proceeded halfheartedly, seventeen state agencies have adopted plans. In Oregon, the Department of Land Conservation and Development, which oversees the state land-use program, also has reviewed the plans of other state agencies for consistency with statewide goals and local plans.

If taxpayers are to receive more efficient and better-targeted state investments in infrastructure and the protection of natural resources, state agencies will have to improve their cooperation with local governments. The state agencies may be able to bring a regional perspective to economic development and environmental quality that individual local governments lack. A local government's authority stops at its borders (or a couple of miles beyond in the case of extraterritorial jurisdiction). Watersheds, for example, usually extend across the boundaries of several local governments. In 1991, the state of New York created the Hudson River Valley Greenway Communities Council to promote cooperative, regional, economic and environmental planning in a ten-county area from Yonkers to Albany.

Political Will to Tame Sprawl

It is easy to complain about a land-use system that nurtures sprawl. But sprawl occurs as part of an ill-informed and not always scrupulous political and planning system. In many cases, sprawl happens because of a lack of political will on the part of local elected officials to oppose it.

Commenting on post-Olympic metro Atlanta, Olympic organizer A. D. Frazier said, "But now I don't see a unifying vision, nor do I see any incentive for anyone to create one."[31] Meanwhile, metro Atlanta's air quality, transportation, racial segregation, and sprawl problems continue.

To many politicians, growth means prosperity, and prosperity means reelection. Not a few local politicians also have real estate holdings or business interests that would profit from more people moving into the community. Such conflicts of interest are not often recognized by the voting public. Finally, few politicians like to take risks and support innovative growth management programs, especially if they cost money.

Yet it is the voters who elect the politicians. If a large, vocal, and voting growth management constituency can be formed, politicians will have to deliver growth management programs or else face defeat. Unfortunately, in most places, growth management is not a well-articulated issue. Voters are more concerned about taxes and want to see immediate results, and politicians have been slow to explain that growth management can keep a better grip on property taxes than continued sprawl.

In most states, growth management rarely plays into political races for statewide offices. Proponents of growth management need to recognize that they have to become involved in the political process, however repugnant the thought. Grassroots activism and organizing interest groups can translate into positive change. Lobbying may seem a dirty practice to some, but a letter, phone call, e-mail, or fax to elected officials can attract attention and generate momentum for growth management. The keys are to have a thick skin and not give up. Compromises may have to be made, as is common in politics. But concerned, dedicated citizens can be the source of political will.

Summary

State and local governments have done much to encourage sprawl and the growth of the rural-urban fringe. Pro-growth strategies have consciously or unconsciously held sway. New and improved road networks have helped to open up formerly hard-to-reach places and have brought them into the metropolitan sphere of influence. The pursuit of expanding the local property tax base has led to fiscal zoning and overzoning for large residential lots and commercial and industrial space.

Perhaps even more detrimental to managing growth are those counties and communities that think they are achieving balanced growth but in reality are using weak land-use planning techniques. The development densities allowed on farmland encourage the creation of rural estates that consume more land than necessary, not the retention of productive farms.

Water quality and water quantity issues are becoming more acute. Better regulation of on-site septic systems and wells is a clear need. The joining of water planning and land-use planning is essential for sustainable community and regional development.

State agencies need to improve their coordination of projects so as not to work at cross-purposes. Also, state agencies need to coordinate their plans with local and regional plans to achieve more efficient provision of infrastructure and protection of natural resources and environmental quality.

Chapter 8 examines several programs and planning techniques that local and state governments can use to manage growth in the fringe more effectively.

CHAPTER 8

Blending Regulations and Incentives to Manage Fringe Growth

> Responsible growth means avoiding sprawl. Responsible growth means helping communities in their efforts to maintain vital downtowns.
>
> —*Vermont Governor Howard Dean*

> This is good politics; it was something people were looking for—a significant change in development patterns. . . . Sprawl is a disease eating away at the heart of America.
>
> —*Maryland Governor Parris Glendening, on Smart Growth legislation*

How can state and local governments improve the management of land and development? What incentives are needed to encourage developers to build good projects in the right places? And what incentives and regulations can maintain open spaces? Can a balance between growth and land conservation be sustained in the long run?

The search for remedies to land-use conflicts in the fringe has long frustrated planners, environmentalists, developers, politicians, and the public. To date, successes have been modest. Successful growth management programs combine a variety of techniques in a coordinated package. These techniques fall in two main types: the "carrots," which encourage good development, and the "sticks," which regulate development. In the fringe, the tendency so far has been to attempt to limit development than to accommodate growth within and adjacent to existing settlements. Communities have more often reacted to development proposals than proactively set forth regulations to discourage development in the wrong locations.

Government taxation, spending, and regulations influence the land market either to encourage development or to control, shape, or discourage it. Yet there is no guarantee that a government program will result in better land use than letting the private developers build what they want where they want. Successful growth management programs take time and require competent and adequate staff and a commitment from politicians, the building community, and the general public.

In adopting a set of growth management techniques, local and state governments need to undertake two kinds of planning efforts. The first is remedial planning and development for those cities, suburbs, and fringe places that have already been poorly designed and are in need of a makeover. The second is proactive planning to identify where fringe development should go and can be serviced, and where it should not go or only at very low densities.

Bottom-Up or Top-Down Planning or a Combination of the Two

Chapters 6 and 7 explored the federal, state, and local government policies and actions that promote sprawl in the fringe. Although federal programs exert powerful influences on local land use, the actual land-use planning decisions are made by local governments. Local governments have control over zoning and most subdivision regulations. A state government does not have the power to impose zoning, but some state governments have enacted subdivision regulations. For example, Colorado allows thirty-five-acre subdivisions without local government review.

A frequent debate in growth management is whether more effective results occur from top-down or bottom-up planning. Or whether some combination of the two is best.

Local governments are creations of state government. The state decides what powers local governments can exercise. In a top-down approach, the state sets the standards and guidelines for local governments to follow. Table 8.1 lists ten states with growth management acts. Oregon, for example, legally requires all 236 cities and 36 counties to adopt comprehensive plans that incorporate nineteen statewide planning goals—from farmland protection (Goal 3) to affordable housing (Goal 10). Vermont's Act 200 calls for state agencies to coordinate their plans with regional and municipal comprehensive plans; and in turn regional and municipal plans should generally be consistent. Oregon mandated local plans that had to be reviewed and "acknowledged" by the state Department of Land Conservation and Development. By contrast, Vermont has made planning voluntary but has added financial inducements for municipalities that plan in accordance with thirty-two state goals. In both states, local governments have complained about a loss of local control, but in Oregon, the results have been fairly good. More land has been zoned for industrial development, and the farm economy has continued to grow, thanks in part to extensive agricultural zoning.

Maryland is implementing a concurrency or adequate facilities policy, which means that state infrastructure dollars will be available only in places where development is planned. Ron Kreitner, Maryland state planning director, explains that the state government does not have "an open-ended obligation, regardless of where you choose to build a house or open a business, to be there to build roads, schools, and sewers."[1]

One example of collaborative state and local planning has been the urban growth-boundary process in Oregon. The state land-use law

Table 8.1 Ten States with Growth Management Acts

State	*Year Begun*	*Local Planning*	*State Planning*
Hawaii	1961	mandatory	state land-use plan
Vermont	1970, 1988	voluntary	state and regional review of developments of regional impact; state agency plans; statewide goals
Florida	1972, 1985	mandatory	state review of local plans; state review of developments of regional impact
Oregon	1973	mandatory	state review of local plans; statewide goals
Maine	1985	mandatory but much weakened	state review of local plans
Rhode Island	1988, 1991	mandatory	state review of local plans; statewide goals
Georgia	1989	voluntary for local, mandatory for regional	guidelines for local plans; state review of developments of regional impact
New Jersey	1986, 1992	voluntary	state land-use plan with statewide goals; state review of local plans
Washington	1990	mandatory	state review of local plans; statewide goals
Maryland	1992, 1997	mandatory	state review of local plans; infrastructure priorities; land preservation
Minnesota	1997	voluntary	state review of local plans; statewide goals

requires each city to work with the surrounding county to identify an area adjacent to the city within which there is enough buildable land for the next twenty years and beyond which urban-type services, especially public sewer and water, will not be extended. The growth boundary takes effect in the form of a legal agreement between the city and county. The state plays a role first in approving the locally devised growth boundaries and then in reviewing proposed expansions or contractions of the boundaries.

Ideally, there should be a planning partnership between state and local governments. At a minimum, a state should work with local governments to draft a land-use policy plan that:

1. says it is a goal of the state to reduce sprawl;
2. recommends a Governor's Executive Order to minimize sprawl through the targeted expenditure of state funds (state agencies should be asked to review whether their projects would contribute to or mitigate sprawl and to coordinate their plans and projects with other agencies and local government plans);
3. spells out guidelines for local and county comprehensive plans and *implementing ordinances* (guidelines should require citizen involvement and periodic updating of plans and ordinances, as well as promote sustainable development practices, affordable housing, environmental protection, and economic fairness among communities);
4. establishes a concurrency policy so that new development requiring state funds could not proceed until the necessary services (sewer, water, roads, and schools) were in place; and
5. makes planning grants available to counties and municipalities (for example, the state of Oregon has made millions in local planning grants to implement the goals of its state land-use plan; the state of Vermont has made a few million in grants for the drafting of regional and local plans; and more modestly, but still important, in 1995 New York appropriated $300,000 for county farmland protection planning grants). State planning grants can help solve the problem of unfunded mandates on local governments, as well as create incentives for local planning.

To make local planning stick, there may be a need for periodic review by a state agency and enforcement of the planning process and implementing ordinances. Also, monitoring by a nonprofit group, such as the 1,000 Friends organizations that have sprung up in several states, can be helpful to keep the planning process on track and in the public eye. But perhaps most important is the continued support of state officials and legislatures for planning and cooperation between the state and local governments.

Top-down planning can provide helpful direction, technical assistance, and planning grants to local governments. That is particularly the case when developments of regional impact are proposed. Vermont, through Act 250 (1970), and Florida, since 1972, have used a "permit development" system for reviewing large developments. A state agency reviews the application, which it may approve or reject. More often, an application is approved with conditions. The idea is that the state has adequate staff and financial resources to review large projects that an individual municipality does not. In addition, both Vermont and Florida identified critical areas of state concern (mostly coastal lands in Florida and lands over the 2,500-foot level in Vermont).

State-level planning runs the risk of being bureaucratic and out of touch with local conditions and needs. Oregon has tried to overcome this problem by having field representatives of the Department of Land Conservation and Development living and working in different parts of the state. A state one-size-fits-all planning approach for cities, towns, and counties will not work, especially in a large and diverse state. Some flexibility for local implementation within the framework of statewide goals can make local governments and residents more accepting of the planning process.

State-level planning can also evolve to meet changing conditions. For example, the State of Florida added a compact development requirement for local plans in order to promote in-fill development. A year later, in 1994, Florida devised an antisprawl law to control commercial highway strip development.

Bottom-up planning by itself is vulnerable to spill-over development from neighboring jurisdictions, conflict of interest by local politicians, bullying by large developers, population growth that exceeds the capacity of public services, an absence of affordable housing ordinances, a lack of adequate planning staff, and public apathy. For instance:

- In the early 1960s, IBM built a large plant in Essex Junction, Vermont, and within a few years became the largest private employer in the state. Essex Junction enjoyed a windfall in property tax revenues, while neighboring townships experienced rapid residential growth and infrastructure demands to house IBM workers and educate their children.
- Local politicians in fringe communities often have significant

real estate holdings; voting on developments that could eventually benefit themselves is not uncommon.

- In the mid-1990s Wal-Mart was initially denied permission to build a 200,000-square-foot superstore in Ephrata Township, Lancaster County, Pennsylvania. The company threatened to take the township to court. The township soon capitulated and granted Wal-Mart permission to build the superstore.
- New Jersey communities did not adopt affordable housing ordinances until they were compelled to by the state supreme court.[2]
- Planners in many fringe communities are so preoccupied with reviewing development proposals that they have no time for drafting long-range comprehensive plans.
- There are many fringe communities whose comprehensive plans and zoning ordinances are out of date, but residents are not lobbying the politicians to pay to update them.

In putting together a growth management system, local governments need to:

1. emphasize citizen involvement to reach a consensus on growth management (A true bottom-up approach depends on the participation of a wide array of citizens and interest groups. That way, those people become stakeholders in the growth management effort and will be willing to work and spend money to make it succeed.);
2. consider the cost of management and the necessary staff, compared to the community's financial ability (The more sophisticated the techniques, the more staff that will be needed and more highly trained they will be need to be. Also, if the local government decides to purchase land or interests in land (development rights), the community or county residents will be asked to make a substantial financial commitment.);
3. consider the legal aspects of different growth management techniques (Check what your state's enabling legislation allows. Don't be afraid to seek legal opinions from your state attorney general's office. A bit of homework can protect the community or county from costly legal battles. Bear in mind that municipal and county attorneys are often not well versed in land-use law and tend to be conservative when reviewing new growth management techniques. You should also consult with

your state chapter of the American Planning Association for advice.

4. consider which techniques are needed to put together an effective growth management package (It is always wise for a local government to examine how different growth management techniques have worked in other communities or counties. Learning from the experience of others can save both time and money.);
5. consider how state and federal regulations influence local growth management plans and programs;
6. consider the political acceptability of different growth management techniques (Often the timing has to be right to gain the support of voters who will back politicians to implement growth management programs. Growth management is a political process. Even the best growth management system can be swept away through the election of different local officials. Politicians need to feel the support of their constituents before they will adopt new growth management programs. This does not mean that there can be no controversy, but no politician wants to take an unpopular stand and be voted out of office.);
7. consider what neighboring communities or counties are doing about growth management (Look for opportunities to cooperate on regional planning and zoning. For example, in San Luis Obispo County, California, County Commissioner Ruth Brackett said, "Each city and town relies on the county to preserve green spaces and belts that separate places and preserve community identity."[3]
8. be sure to involve the development community (The development community often feels threatened at any mention of growth management. An honest discussion of what the local government expects from the development community and vice versa can result in a reasonable compromise. Such compromise is more likely in a balanced-growth community than in a no- or slow-growth community.);
9. match community goals with the appropriate growth management techniques (For example, a goal to curb sprawl might be met by an intergovernmental agreement, extraterritorial planning and zoning powers, or a growth boundary.);
10. blend growth management techniques into a coherent system (For example, several townships in Lancaster County, Pennsyl-

vania, use a combination of growth boundaries to accommodate development in designated growth areas with adequate public services, and agricultural zoning to protect the farmland base and limit nonfarm development to a very low density.);

A combination of state and local planning efforts can help everyone see how the local planning programs and development projects fit together in a regional mosaic of land-use, environmental, economic, housing, and transportation patterns. This combination can serve as the foundation for regional planning and property tax sharing programs that guide how the region can look and function in the future.

Finding the Right Regulations, Spending Programs, and Incentives

No one set of growth management techniques fits every community, county, or state. But it is useful for elected officials, planners, developers, and concerned citizens to have a knowledge of the growth management tools and how they can work. Table 8.2 lists the many spending programs, regulations, and incentives that state and local governments employ or could implement to manage growth in fringe areas, and examines their pros and cons.

The subject of regulations conjures up visions of government run rampant. No one enjoys winding through a maze of rules or unwinding red tape. But regulations can be useful in encouraging good behavior and discouraging negative results. The following issue often arises: Is the cost of complying with the regulation worth the results? Government officials need to be sensitive to the impacts of regulations on developers, businesses, landowners, and private citizens. On the other hand, government regulations must have a public purpose: to protect the public's health, safety, or welfare.

Spending programs and tax incentives have the power to influence not only the location, timing, and amount of development, but also where development will not occur (see box 8.1). Incentives and some spending programs are discretionary rather than mandatory. Governments should periodically evaluate the effects of those programs and incentives against specific goals (see "Benchmarking," box 3.5).

Guiding Development: The Right Development in the Right Location

Sustainable development is the logical goal of growth management. Development should be the appropriate type, on a reasonable scale

Table 8.2 The Pros and Cons of Growth Management Techniques Used in the Fringe

Development Guidelines

Technique	*Purpose*	*Pros*	*Cons*
Municipal or county comprehensive plan	To set a vision and to guide development based on population projections and future land-use needs.	Legal basis for zoning and other regulations. List goals and objectives to work toward. Basis for deciding what type of development goes where.	Not legally binding by themselves. Often ignored in day-to-day planning decisions. May not have a regional vision.
State planning requirements (mandated or advisory)	To require local governments to adopt comprehensive plans and to establish guidelines and standards for development and land protection.	Encourages growth management and efficient development. Planning grants and assistance from state helpful.	May have a "one size fits all" approach. Possible local resistance to state role. Fear of loss of local control.
Joint planning and joint zoning ordinances for regional planning	To foster regional cooperation on growth management. Most often used between a city and a county.	Greater control over the location of development. More efficient provision of public services.	May be difficult to set up and administer. Joint zoning ordinance needed to make joint plan work.
Intermunicipal agreements	To coordinate growth management efforts between local governments.	Can be used to share public services or create urban growth boundaries.	Voluntary. Agreements may be difficult to reach and maintain. Not as strong as joint planning and zoning.
Annexation policies	State laws that spell out how a municipality can incorporate county land into the municipality.	Cities without suburbs. Better coordination of phased growth with availability of public services. Result in less dependence on wells and on-site septic systems.	Often lead to battles between county losing land and city gaining land. May cause premature development.

(*continues*)

Table 8.2 (continued)

Technique	*Purpose*	*Pros*	*Cons*
Extraterritorial planning and zoning	State-granted power to cities to control the development of county land at the edge of cities.	A start for regional planning cooperation between city and county. Phasing development, limiting sprawl.	Potential source of friction between city and county. Some county residents under city planning control.
Capital improvements programs	To plan for the location, expense, and timing of major infrastructure construction and repair.	Better financial management, more careful locating of growth.	Rarely used by smaller communities. Need to be linked to zoning to be effective.
Concurrency or adequate facilities policies	To ensure that adequate infrastructure is in place before a development is built. To create phased development.	Slow down the pace of development. Minimize leapfrog patterns. Put more of the infrastructure cost on the developer.	Developers may fear they will lead to moratoria on infrastructure and delay their projects.
Urban growth boundaries, village growth boundaries	To set a limit on the extension of urban-type services such as public sewer and water, while identifying enough buildable land for 10–20 years.	Encourage more compact and cheaper-to-service development. Limit sprawl.	Need to have restrictive zoning outside boundaries. Need policies on phased growth within boundaries. Can be changed like zoning. If boundaries are too tight, can raise the cost of land.
Growth rate caps	To set a limit on the percentage rate of annual growth in the municipality.	Foster phased, fiscally affordable development.	Can raise the cost of land and housing. Monitoring headache.
Housing caps	To limit the number of houses built each year while the local government works to provide the needed sewerage, water, roads,etc.	Allow for phased development. Legally supported.[1]	Temporary solutions to rapid growth situations. May drive up the price of housing.
Moratoria	To temporarily halt new	Protect the public health. Phased	May drive up housing costs.

on sewer and water hookups	construction while sewer and water services are upgraded or expanded.	development. Stop premature development.	Slow economic development. Length of moratoria uncertain.

Zoning Ordinances

Technique	*Purpose*	*Pros*	*Cons*
Agricultural zoning	To separate farming activities from conflicting nonfarm land uses. To protect a critical mass of farms and farmland.	Can help protect an agricultural industry. Reduce farmer versus nonfarmer complaints. Maintains open space and wildlife habitat.	Requires large contiguous blocks of farmland. Requires large-lot zoning (40 acres or more) to discourage nonfarm buyers. Farmers may oppose. Farmers not compensated for land-use restrictions. Zoning can be changed.
Forestry zoning	To protect a critical mass of commercial timberland. To separate forestry operations from conflicting nonforestry land uses.	Can help protect a forestry industry. Maintains open space and wildlife habitat.	Requires large contiguous blocks of quality timberland. Requires large-lot zoning (80 acres or more) to discourage nonforestry buyers. Forest industry may oppose. Forest owners not compensated for restrictions. Zoning can change.
Conservation zoning	To protect sensitive lands. May take the form of large-lot zoning or an overlay zone. For example, floodplain overlay is a health and safety issue.	Can help protect wildlife habitat, wetlands, and floodplains. Maintains open space.	May be hard to prove that an economic use of the property remains. May require a large minimum lot size (10 or more acres). Landowners may oppose, not compensated for land-use restrictions. Zoning can be changed.
Steep-slope zoning	To prohibit construction on steep slopes. To protect health and safety.	Reduces soil erosion, mud slides, storm-water runoff, and septic runoff.	Limits where landowner can build. No compensation. Zoning can be changed.

(*continues*)

Table 8.2 (continued)

Technique	*Purpose*	*Pros*	*Cons*
Rural residential zone	To provide an area for nonfarm and nonforest housing in the countryside. Usually will have a 3- to 5-acre minimum lot size.	Can accommodate demand for rural lifestyle without interfering with commercial farm and forestry operations.	Must be located away from farm and forestry operations. Large minimum lot-size favors higher-income buyers. Relies on wells and on-site septic systems.
Maximum lot sizes	To set a limit on the size of residential lots. Often used with agricultural and forestry zones	Encourage greater density, less development of farm and forestlands.	Lots must be large enough to use with wells and on-site septic systems.
Open-space zoning or cluster zoning	To concentrate buildings on part of a property while maintaining a significant amount of open space. Sometimes used to allow developers a bonus of more buildings on a site.	Sensitive site-specific develop ment. Conserves open space, wildlife habitat. May avoid takings challenge. Less costly to develop than suburban-style housing.	Overuse can cause clustered sprawl. If density is too high, can lead to sewer and water problems.
On-site septic ordinances	To ensure proper installation and maintenance of on-site septic systems. To protect water quality and health.	Can reduce sewage disposal and water quality problems. Promote sustainable use of septic systems.	Monitoring may be time consuming and expensive. Ordinances may be unpopular with on-site septic owners.
Performance zoning	To regulate the impacts of development through standards on noise, view, water. Does not require separation into zones by land uses.	Can produce more flexible development design and mix of uses.	May be difficult to set standards and administer.
Historic district ordinances	To protect groups of historic buildings. To set standards for	Maintain community identity. Tourism potential. Encourage	May limit developers' options.

	changes to buildings and demolition approvals.	reuse of older buildings.	

Property Aquisitions

Technique	*Purpose*	*Pros*	*Cons*
Fee-simple purchases	To acquire property for public use, e.g. parkland.	Give public control over the use of the property. Can stop development of property.	Can be expensive. Public support for purchase may be hard to obtain.
Advance acquisition, land banking	Government purchases land before it is ready to be developed. Government can resell with restrictions, e.g., a conservation easement with limited development.	Better control over timing and type of development. Discourages land speculation and leapfrog development.	Uncertain how long government will hold land. Can be expensive, politically controversial.
Purchases of development rights	To provide stronger and longer protection than zoning for farmland, forests, and natural areas. To provide compensation for landowners.	Remove development potential from resource lands. Can help maintain a critical mass of resource lands. Voluntary. Property remains in private hands.	Potentially expensive. May only create islands of protected land.
Transfers of development rights	To send development potential from resource lands to designated growth areas.	Private developers pay for them. Growth better concentrated. Part of a community-wide growth management approach.	Difficult to agree on sending and receiving areas. Public TDR bank may be needed. Require careful planning and highly trained staff.
Developer exactions and dedications	To require developers to provide parks, streets, and even school space in return for development approval.	Place greater cost of servicing development on the developer than on the public.	Opposition from developers. Require more staff review. Raise the cost of development.

(continues)

Table 8.2 (continued)

Technique	*Purpose*	*Pros*	*Cons*
Impact fees	One-time payments from a developer to cover the cost of providing new services (police, parks, roads, etc.) for new development.	Place more of the cost of servicing new development on the developer.	Raise the cost of development. Must be linked to actually paying for new services. Setting fees somewhat a hit-or-miss process.
Private land trusts, (501(c)(3) nonprofit organizations	Can acquire property in fee-simple or purchase conservation easements. Can accept gifts of land and money and conservation easements. Trusts aim to protect natural areas, farm and forestlands. Sometimes are involved in limited developments.	Can coordinate efforts with public agencies. Can work with private landowners who are suspicious of government.	May lack financial resources and adequate staff. May create islands of protected land.

Incentives

Technique	*Purpose*	*Pros*	*Cons*
Preferential property taxation	To encourage owners of farm and forestlands to keep their lands in those uses. To encourage the maintenance of historic properties.	Encourages keeping land open. Helps the finances of farm and forestry businesses. Maintains historic properties.	May be used by land speculators. Eligibility rules often loose. Significant cost over time.
Agricultural districts	To encourage farmers to keep their land in farm use. Some districts include preferential	Tax breaks help farm finances. Protection from eminent domain means greater sense of stability.	Voluntary. Farmers near built-up areas often do not participate. Need to be combined with agricultural

	property taxation, exemption from sewer assessments, greater protection from eminent domain.		zoning to be effective over time.
Right-to-farm law	To give farmers protection from nuisance suits for standard farming practices.	Strengthen the legal position of farming in regard to nonfarm neighbors.	May not discourage the filing of nuisance suits. Largely untested.
Density bonuses for sensitive design	To encourage sensitive site design that maintains significant open space.	Maintain open space and rural character.	May rely too much on wells and on-site septic systems. If too many houses allowed, conservation value limited.

Other Development Controls

Technique	*Purpose*	*Pros*	*Cons*
Subdivision regulations	To ensure safe and consistent creation of new lots with adequate services.	Promote orderly development. A standard process for development and legal transfer of land.	May be too rigid, resulting in "cookie cutter" lots.
Special assessments	To place the cost of certain public facilities, such as the extension of public sewer or water service, on the landowners in a specific area.	Link those who benefit from the infrastructure to the costs. Entire community does not have to pay.	May cause the premature conversion of farmland if public sewer or water run into the countryside.
Design standards	To ensure that new development blends in rather than clashes with existing buildings and landscape.	Maintain the quality appearance of the community. Show a caring attitude. Helpful for tourism and attracting quality development.	May raise development costs. May require more staff for design reviews.
Land conversion tax	To discourage the development of certain lands, e.g., farmland,	Slows rate of growth. Funds preservation efforts.	Revenue raised only if land developed. Tax may not be high enough to

(*continues*)

Table 8.2 (continued)

Technique	*Purpose*	*Pros*	*Cons*
Land conversion tax (*continued*)	and to raise revenue for land preservation.		discourage growth in rapid growth area. More likely used at state level.
Environmental impact assessments	To assess the likely effects of development on water, air, and land resources. To look at alternative sites for proposed development.	Identify potential problems before a project is built so project can be withdrawn or altered. Help ensure environmental soundness of projects that pass assessment.	Increase the cost of development. Can be used as a delaying tactic by NIMBYs.
Regional tax base sharing	To make all communities in the region share some property tax revenues based on ability to pay.	Reduces the use of fiscal zoning to attract ratables. Helps finances of older suburbs and inner city.	Difficult to achieve region-wide cooperation.
Regional fair share	To set standards to ensure that all communities accept a share of regional growth and affordable housing.	Spreads growth evenly. Makes for more units of affordable housing.	Supersedes local control. Local resistance.
Fiscal impact analysis	To estimate public costs and public revenues from a proposed development. In particular, to estimate the impact on community property taxes.	Helps officials decide whether to approve a development, set impact fees, or impose conditions on developers to mitigate negative impacts.	Different methods can be used, giving different results. Fairly sophisticated. Zoning and other regulations may supersede.
The courts	To decide arguments between landowners, between landowners and governments, and between governments.	Time-tested institutions. Provide resolution of disputes.	Rulings somewhat uncertain. Expensive.

1. See *Golden v. Planning Board of Town of Ramapo, 1972*, New York Appeals Court; *Construction Industry Association of Sonoma County v. Petaluma*, 522F.2nd 897, Ninth Circuit Court, 1975, certiorari denied 424 U.S. 934 (1976); and *Mark Schenk v. City of Hudson, Ohio,* Sixth Circuit Court of Appeals, 1997.

Box 8.2 Avoiding Sprawl by Avoiding Spending on Highways

Johnson County, Kansas, is a prosperous, fast-growing suburb on the west side of Kansas City. In 1988, the county commissioners proposed an outer beltway, optimistically called the 21st Century Parkway. But in 1996, the commissioners voted against the same highway. The change was brought about by a grassroots coalition of activists, environmental groups, and concerned citizens. After many public forums and letters to the editor, city councils near the proposed road turned against it. Then the *Kansas City Star* voiced its opposition. The county commissioners got the message. Greater Kansas City is already one of the most decentralized metro regions in the nation. But activist Diane Stewart commented, "People don't want Kansas City to be known as 'Los Angeles of the Prairie.'"[4]

for the community, and in the right location. Fringe communities that are pursuing balanced-growth or no- or slow-growth strategies must be careful to avoid scattered development in the countryside, for example. Such development can conflict with farm and forest operations and spur the conversion of farms and forestlands into housing subdivisions and commercial strips.

Two techniques for accommodating development are urban or village growth boundaries and rural residential zones. A growth boundary (discussed more fully in chapter 9) contains sufficient land and urban services to support the expansion of a city or village for twenty years. If properly drawn and enforced, such a boundary can promote more compact development that is cheaper and easier to service, and reduce sprawl by keeping urban services from stretching into the countryside. A growth boundary can work together with efforts to clean up brownfields and encourage in-fill development.

For a growth boundary to function effectively, the land outside the boundary must be zoned for low-density development. Otherwise, development will simply leapfrog over the boundary line and continue to sprawl. In Oregon, for instance, most of the land outside of the boundaries is zoned for farm or forest uses at minimum lot sizes ranging from 10 acres in secondary farm zones to 320 acres in the rangeland of Deschutes County in eastern Oregon.

Balanced-growth communities and even pro-growth communities may want to examine the creation of rural residential zones. These areas of three- to five-acre minimum lot sizes should consist of lower-quality soils and should be located away from commercial farm and forest territory. Rural residential zones can provide an opportunity for people who want a "rural lifestyle," with a few farm animals, a garden, and perhaps a horse. The large lot sizes should be adequate to support wells and on-site septic systems, because they would be difficult and expensive to sewer. Also, large lot properties are more likely to generate enough property taxes to cover the cost of the public services they use.

The Quality and Design of Development

Chapter 5 presented several design strategies for new development that local governments can pursue to strengthen communities and protect the countryside. In cities and towns, flexible zoning ordinances that allow a mix of land uses—especially commercial and residential—would enable developers to build more compact, creative, and pedestrian-oriented projects. That would reduce the need for new development to sprawl out into the countryside. Also, a state policy requiring state agencies to locate offices in downtowns would help curb sprawl.

The preservation of historic structures and landscapes can also add to good design and a pleasing environment. For example, state income and property tax incentives and state grants for the adaptive reuse of historic structures can encourage reinvestment in downtowns. Historic structures and landscapes not only provide an appealing setting, they also can serve as the basis of a tourist industry.[5]

Maintaining a human scale of development is also important. The city of Mequon, Wisconsin, just north of Milwaukee, limits the size of commercial buildings to no more than 20,000 square feet, slightly under half an acre.[6] By comparison, the typical Wal-Mart store covers over 200,000 square feet. Because their size violates the local zoning ordinance, big box retailers and huge supermarkets are discouraged from locating in Mequon.

Appealing city and town environments are essential if urban growth boundary strategies are to be successful. If households prefer to settle in the fringe countryside, sprawl will continue. But if attractive, affordable living conditions are created and maintained within the growth boundaries, then hopefully most households will locate there. In short, local governments will have to work closely with developers to bring about good, functional design.

If the village or small city is to be the design model for accommodating development in the fringe, then the state government can create incentives for businesses to locate in the downtowns rather than outside of town in a big mall or a commercial strip.

A growth boundary approach can work if the size, type, and location of development in the fringe countryside is tightly controlled. Most new development should be occurring within the growth boundaries. Zoning and subdivision ordinances that allow the countryside to be carved into large residential lots and commercial strips only serve to promote sprawl and hasten the decline of cities and towns.

In his 1997 inaugural address, Governor Howard Dean of Vermont outlined a package of incentives to stimulate downtown development. First, communities would draft downtown development plans to be reviewed and approved by the state agency of Commerce and Community Development. In an approved downtown district, developers would be eligible to receive:

- income tax credits of 5 to 25 percent for refurbishing historic and older buildings;
- reduced state permit fees, grants, low-interest loans, and a sales tax exemption on construction materials;
- liability protection for developers who redevelop buildings with environmental hazards; and
- help in meeting government requirements.

A final piece of the program would place a heavy charge on developers who build superstores outside the downtown. This would discourage such stores from being built and draining retail sales from downtowns, or else would generate funds to pay for the four downtown incentives.

The price tag of Governor Dean's downtown boosting proposals is uncertain. But it represents a bold attempt to intervene in the real estate market to offset the federal tax incentives that encourage new development on greenfields rather than the reuse of older buildings downtown. In the spring of 1997, the Vermont House of Representatives passed a bill based on Governor Dean's proposal, but the Senate failed to take action.

Blending protection of the countryside with limited development can sustain the economic development attractiveness of the fringe. Once sprawl takes over, a community simply becomes Anywhere, USA, and loses competitive advantage. The industries tied to the information economy have considerable flexibility in where they choose to locate. Business owners want an attractive environment for themselves and their workers.

Influencing the Amount, Type, and Density of Development

State and local spending on infrastructure and open space affect the appearance, location, amount, and rate of development in the community. Sewers, water lines and treatment facilities, roads, and schools are all major growth-inducing public investments. A state concurrency policy, such as in Florida, or an adequate public facilities ordinance, such as in Ramapo, New York, can help ensure that development does not occur until there is a public ability to pay for new services, a clear demand for those services, and, finally, the necessary infrastructure. That way, public service demands do not swamp taxpayers or cause rapid and premature development. Also, new development projects are more likely to be compact and adjacent to existing built-up areas.

The New Jersey state plan includes a comprehensive urban, suburban, and rural policy on infrastructure spending:

> The essential element of Statewide Policies for Infrastructure Investment is to provide infrastructure and related services more efficiently by restoring systems in distressed areas, maintaining existing infrastructure investments, creating more compact settlement patterns . . . and timing and sequencing the maintenance of capital facilities service levels with development throughout the state.

An urban growth boundary (see chapter 9) can limit the extension of public services—especially growth-inducing sewer and water lines—and so discourage sprawl.

Infrastructure planning by state and local governments coordinated with local zoning provides greater certainty for private developers about where development is desired and will be adequately serviced. Cutting through regulatory red tape can also increase development potential. A good example of this is provided by Pennsylvania's brownfields redevelopment law, which set statewide cleanup standards and offered landowners and developers immunity from liabilty for previous contamination. Since 1995, more than 100 brownfield sites, mainly in urban areas, have been rehabilitated.[7] The brownfields law encourages developers to look to already developed sites rather than rush to greenfields in the fringe.

A recent infrastructure challenge in the fringe countryside has been the need to control the siting of telecommunications towers brought on by the boom in cellular phones (see appendix 3).

Privately owned open space needs to be seen as a form of infrastructure. In addition, public expenditures on open space can help control public service costs. For example, in Buckingham Township, Pennsylvania, not far from Philadelphia, voters approved a $4 million bond issue in 1995 to buy development rights to farmland. The compelling reason for the program was a need to control the number of students to educate and so avoid having to build expensive new schools. According to Bucks County planner Rich Harvey, "The underlying theme is it costs more to build a school than preserve the land."[8]

Similarly, government land purchases for parks and natural areas protect important open space, but reduce the supply of developable land in the community.

Land-use controls will tend to drive up land prices and the cost of housing in the fringe. In many parts of the United States, fringe real estate is already more expensive than some urban and suburban properties. While some fringe communities want to minimize growth, others recognize a need to accept a fair share of housing—particularly affordable housing. An affordable housing requirement says that if a development has a certain number of dwelling units, a certain percentage of the units must be affordable to low- and middle-income families. In Montgomery County, Maryland, for example, in every residential development of fifty or more dwelling units, 10 percent of the units must be affordable housing.

Managing the Public Service Costs of Development

High-end housing, retail outlets, and office space have become desirable sources of property taxes. Zoning codes often require large, expensive lots for home sites so that new housing will produce adequate tax revenues to pay for the necessary public services. Also, the zoning of arterial highways for commercial strip development is common.

As development occurs, longer-term residents often complain about rising property tax bills to pay for services demanded by newcomers. Impact fees, developer exactions, and dedications are ways of making developers pay for public services that new developments will need. In turn, developers will attempt to pass along the cost of these fees and regulations to the new home buyers, and they will usually succeed.

The property tax has long been considered a regressive tax, falling more heavily on low-income people than on middle- and upper-income people. State tax revenues come mainly from state income taxes, which are progressive, and sales taxes, which are regressive. Tax reform that allows a local income tax could result in reduced reliance on the local property tax. In turn, communities would not have to pursue fiscal zoning by requiring large housing lots and designating an overabundance of land along highways for commercial development.

A good place to start in controlling the public service costs of development is to do a cost-of-community-services study. This study can show how much different land uses contribute in property taxes and how much they demand in public services. Several of these studies have been performed with the help of the American Farmland Trust.[9] They demonstrate that farmland pays more in property taxes than it demands in services, as has been mentioned, and residential development on average demands more in services than it pays in taxes. In 1994, the town of Dunn in Dane County, Wisconsin, estimated that while residential development was costing taxpayers $1.06 in services for every $1.00 paid in property taxes, farm and parkland were costing only $.18 for each $1.00 paid.[10] Two years later, Dunn became the first municipality in Wisconsin to tax itself for buying development rights to farmland.

It is not unreasonable for citizens to review estimates of the full public service costs and benefits of new development. A fiscal impact statement—similar to an environmental impact statement—would help local residents understand the effects of proposed development projects on the community's financial resources. This information is especially helpful:

- if the community or county negotiates with developers for exactions and dedications of land;
- in setting realistic impact fees;
- in reviewing large residential developments;
- in reviewing large commercial or industrial projects, particularly when the owners want to negotiate property tax agreements; and
- in gaining public support for land preservation and park acquisition.

Although property owners are generally opposed to property tax increases, these taxpayers basically have two choices: (1) to continue to help subsidize sprawl and development; or (2) to have tax revenues spent on preserving land from development. Neither choice necessarily means that taxes will go down, though in the long run one would expect the land preservation option to produce tax savings. The choice is between a pro-growth strategy and a balanced- or slow-growth approach.

Environmental Impacts

New buildings and population growth can change the environmental quality of a community or report region. These impacts will affect air, land, and water resources. Several states require an environmental impact statement for any development project that will have a significant impact on the environment. The statement describes the type and extent of projected impacts, how the local government or developer will address them, and alternative project designs. California even requires an environmental impact report when amendements to a local comprehensive plan make major changes in planned land uses. The value of impact statements is that they make local governments think carefully about development. For instance, local governments have little control over air quality standards, except that more development means more cars generating air pollution.

Possible negative impacts on land quality come from building on steep slopes, natural hazards such as mud slides, soil erosion from construction and poor farming or forestry practices, and sanitary landfills. A steep-slope ordinance can discourage the construction of buildings on steep slopes (see appendix 4 for a sample ordinance). Natural hazards should be identified as part of the comprehensive planning process and mapped, ideally on a GIS system. Soil erosion presents a more difficult problem. Your county conservation district staff can draft soil and water conservation plans for farmers, but monitoring compliance with the plans is often spotty. Construction sites near waterways may need to be monitored as well.

Few issues stir up emotions like the siting of a regional landfill. Such a facility takes up several acres and can send off a pungent smell over a wide area. Also, local residents resent having to take someone else's garbage. A regional landfill is a good example of a LULU (Large Unwanted Land Use). The state often enters into the location decision-making process. The rural-urban fringe is somewhat vulnerable to new landfill sites because of the proximity to major trash generators in the suburbs and central city and because transportation costs are an important factor. The alternatives to landfills are incinerators and recycling. Incinerators produce some air pollution, and recycling does not recycle all trash.

Although local governments do not set water quality standards, they can take steps to protect water quality and quantity. As discussed previously, a large amount of the new development in fringe communities relies on wells for drinking water and on-site septic systems for sewage disposal.

In 1971, Maine required municipalities to zone within 250 feet of rivers and bodies of water.[11] As part of the Oregon Land Use Program, a Willamette River Greenway was created, with a mandatory hundred-foot buffer of open space along most of its banks. In the 1990s, water management districts in Florida have been buying up acreage along rivers and conservation easements on farmland to keep the land open and reduce runoff into waterways. The Kentucky State Health Department requires a minimum of ten acres for the use of septic tanks.[12]

A 1995 Massachusetts law known as Title 5 requires a property owner to have the on-site septic system inspected by a professional engineer before the property can be sold or the house expanded. If the engineer discovers deficiencies in the system, the system must be repaired or replaced at the seller's expense before the expansion or sale of the property can go through. In the first two years of the law, about fifty-four hundred polluting septic systems were detected. Repairs typically averaged from $6,000 to $10,000.[13]

Landowner Incentives

Regulation alone will not achieve successful growth management in the long run. Landowners need to see that it is in their financial interest to keep their land open. Community residents need to recognize the value of open land, not just for its aesthetic benefits but for the fiscal advantages as well.

There are two voluntary ways that governments can encourage landowners to hold on to their land. The first is through preferential property taxation, taxing land at its use-value rather than at its highest and best use for development (for a discussion of preferental property taxation, see chapter 10). Second, governments can purchase development rights (conservation easements) from landowners and restrict the land to farm, forestry, and open space uses.

Fifteen states and dozens of county and municipal governments operate purchase-of-development-rights (PDR) programs to preserve farmland (see tables 8.3 and 8.4). State programs began with Maryland in 1977 and have spread throughout the Northeast. In the 1990s, new programs became active in the important farming states of California and Michigan. Some state PDR programs operate in cooperation with county or township programs. This is the case in Maryland, Pennsylvania, and New Jersey. As part of Maryland's Rural Legacy Program, Governor Parris Glendening pushed for and won $90 million over five years to purchase development rights to farmland "so farmers can keep their investment in the land."[14] In addition, the state of Maryland exempts the sale of a preserved farm from the .5 percent real estate transfer tax.

In the 1990s, Pennsylvania counties have authorized an average of over $5 million a year to match $21 million in state farmland preservation funds. East Amwell Township, New Jersey, has put up $1.2 million to match $6.5 million in state funds and preserve over sixteen hundred acres. The requirement of local matching funds makes the local government take a stake in the PDR effort and gives it control over which parcels of farmland are preserved.

Some local governments are using the transfer of development rights (TDR) to enable development potential to be transferred from

Table 8.3 Purchase of Development Rights by State, May 1998

State	*Year PDR Begun*	*Acres/Farms Preserved*	*Funds Authorized/Spent*
California	1995	940/4	$3.2/$3.2 million
Colorado	1994	1,878/3	$3.4/.6 million
Connecticut	1978	25,658/170	$80.2/$75.6 million
Delaware	1995	16,107/66	$32/$18 million
Kentucky	1994	0/0	$1.6/$0 million
Maine	1990	540/3	$.5/$.5 million
Maryland	1977	139,828/968	$166.9/$156.9 million
Massachusetts	1977	40,040/441	$115/$96.2 million
Michigan	1997	540/4	$16/$2 million
New Hampshire	1979	11,732/57	$11.4/$11.4 million
New Jersey	1983	43,294/278	$195/$129 million
New York	1997	1,600/8	$35/$3.7 million
Pennsylvania	1989	117,934/927	$217/$204.1 million
Rhode Island	1982	2,529/31	$13.7/$13.2 million
Vermont	1987	69,693/202	$38.3/$34.8 million
Total		472,213/3,162	$929.2/$749.2 million

Source: American Farmland Trust, Fact Sheet Status of State PACE Programs, March, 1998, Deborah Bowers, *Farmland Preservation Report* (unpublished data).

Table 8.4 County and Municipal Purchase-of-Development-Rights Programs, May 1998.

Locality	*Acres Preserved*	*Active Program?*	*Main Funding Source*
Marin County, CA	25,504	Yes	State bond
Monterey, CA	3,785	Yes	State bond
Solano County, CA	6,000	Yes	State bond
Sonoma County, CA	25,146	Yes	Sales tax
City of Boulder, CO	1,904	Yes	Sales tax
Peninsula Township, MI	3,200	Yes	Property tax
Forsyth County, NC	1,236	No	Property tax
Suffolk County, NY	6,081	Yes	Local bond
City of Virginia Beach, VA	3,995	Yes	Property tax
King County, WA	12,731	Yes	Local bond
Buckingham Township, PA	239	Yes	Local bond
Pittsford Township, NY	100	Yes	Local bond
Total	89,921		

Source: American Farmland Trust, Fact Sheet Status of State PACE Programs, March, 1998, Deborah Bowers, *Farmland Preservation Report* (unpublished data).

rural preservation areas to developing areas. Although the aim with TDRs is for private developers to purchase the TDRs and use them in growth areas, some governments have set up TDR banks to buy and sell TDRs and keep both land preservation and development active. The sale of TDRs by a landowner is voluntary; however, the landowner's property may have stiff zoning restrictions that tightly limit development. The sale of TDRs provides the rural landowner with financial compensation for keeping the land undeveloped (see chapter 10).

Summary

Growth management emerges from a set of government spending, taxation, and regulatory programs. The relative success of different remedies and solutions will vary among fringe communities. Part of the success will depend on the strategy that the community is pursuing: pro-growth, balanced-growth, or no- or slow-growth. State governments can adopt policies and grant programs to encourage or require thorough, thoughtful comprehensive planning by counties and communities. The state framework can provide direction and planning grants to help communities to accommodate growth, protect natural resources, and avoid spillovers from one community to the next. Chapter 9 explores how local governments can cooperate to pursue regional solutions in managing growth.

CHAPTER 9

Regional Planning: Making the City, Suburb, and Fringe Connection

> Only if life is perceived as pleasant and affordable by the real human beings living farther in, will there be any hope of relieving pressure on the land farthest out.
>
> —*Joel Garreau,* Edge City

> The ultimate need for regional solutions becomes more obvious every day, and the movement to create them keeps getting stronger.
>
> —*Alan Ehrenhalt,* Governing *magazine*

The fringe, suburbs, and central city must recognize that they are allies in managing the location of development. This is the necessary first step if regional planning and the coordination of land use, transportation systems, and other infrastructure are to have a chance. The older suburbs, as ably demonstrated by Myron Orfield in his book *Metropolitics,* have a stake as large as that of the central city. In Orfield's experience, the newer, expanding, and wealthier suburbs have tended to withstand regional planning and tax base sharing. But today's prosperous suburbs could easily be tomorrow's older, stagnant suburbs if development pushes farther out and turns fringe areas and beyond into new suburbs. For example, America has over thirty-five thousand shopping malls, but already sprawling development patterns have left behind four thousand "dead malls," according to Constance Beaumont of the National Trust.[1]

A Regional Vision for Land Use

In order for regional planning to take shape, the public, politicians, developers, and planners must transform abstract land-use planning concepts into real, visual, and tangible examples. People must be shown how regional planning is in their financial interests and can provide a good quality of life.

First, careful, effective planning can help a region hold on to its competitive edge in the national and international economy. Better transportation, better management of public finances, and a quality environment in which to live and work will enhance the ability of the region to attract investment and provide jobs.

Regional planning holds the promise of greater effectiveness in creating greenbelts for open space, recreation trails and parks, and the protection of natural areas. Regional governments might have more spending power than individual cities and counties and be able to purchase more land for public parks and more conservation easements to protect valuable farmland and natural lands.[2]

Second, fragmented governments and a lack of predictability in development projects are wasteful and hamper economic growth. Local politicians are perhaps the greatest impediment to regional planning because they would have to give up some of their power. Ironically, it is in the long-term interest of the *residents* of towns, small cities, and suburbs to pursue a more economically competitive strategy that a regional approach offers. Tax savings will probably occur from consolidating government units, special districts, and authorities. This will help achieve economies of scale in public services and avoid the duplication of services from one municipality to the next.

Developers need to see that the days of playing off one community against another to extract property tax breaks are over. That would be one result of regional tax base sharing. Developers have met stiffening resistance to their construction projects in the fringe. A regional approach to land-use planning can:

- designate land for development and protect open space using the urban growth boundary (UGB) and village growth boundary (VGB) concepts;
- simplify regulations (is your project inside or outside a growth boundary?);
- give more predictable outcomes (if you build inside a growth boundary, it is easier, cheaper, and quicker than if you try to build outside a growth boundary).

As an example of the last point, in Oregon, the local government must respond to a developer's proposed project within 120 days if the project is slated to go inside an urban growth boundary. This avoids costly and unnecessary regulatory delays. Inside growth boundaries it will be easier to meet state guidelines, such as concurrency requirements; and inside UGBs land is zoned for development—the developer doesn't have to fight a long and costly rezoning battle to change the zoning from agriculture to residential or commercial use. The NIMBY forces are likely to be less vocal if the type and size of development for land inside growth boundaries has already been agreed upon. Environmentalists should support developers for proposing projects that would not eat up farmland and rural open space. The only downside for the development community is that both small and large developers will have a harder time carving up the countryside if it is zoned for low-density housing and limited commercial development.

Land-use policy in the rural-urban fringe is an integral part of addressing urban problems. As long as the fringe areas continue to welcome corporate office parks, along with the residential and commercial development they generate, our older suburbs and inner cities will continue to rot at their cores. And farmland, forestland, and natural areas will continue to be paved over.

The majority of techniques discussed in chapter 8 are designed for small, incremental changes in managing growth. If these techniques can be coordinated into a regional growth management system, then major changes can occur in a relatively short time. Growth boundaries, which have been used for over thirty years around Lexington, Kentucky, and Lincoln, Nebraska, have the potential to serve as the centerpiece for managing regional growth and controlling sprawl over the long run.

Growth Boundaries

The key land-use planning technique to effect major change in managing growth is the urban growth boundary, along with its variant, the

Box 9.1 Advocacy Groups Working for Metropolitan Regional Planning

America's oldest regional planning organization is the Regional Plan Association, formed in the 1920s. The association has produced three regional plans for the Greater New York metro area: in 1929, 1961, and, most recently, 1995. The 1995 plan emphasized five components for the future growth of the region: (1) mobility—improved rail and highway service; (2) centered development—to attract half of all job growth into existing downtowns; (3) greenspace protection—to protect eleven regional open areas for watersheds, farming, and natural areas; (4) improving the region's workforce—increase high-technology education, improve education funding, and link the private sector with educational institutions to raise the competitive edge of the region; and (5) improving government in the

(continued)

Box 9.1 (*continued*)

region through better coordination of spending and state-level growth management.[3]

A more widespread effort has arisen from 1,000 Friends of Oregon, a private, nonprofit, land-use watchdog group formed in 1975 to help implement the Oregon Land Use Act of 1973. The 1,000 Friends approach has featured tackling key legal cases, reviewing public plans and development decisions, and undertaking land-use studies. 1,000 Friends has staunchly supported urban growth boundaries to contain sprawl along with farm and forest zoning to maintain a working rural landscape.

The success of 1,000 Friends of Oregon has sparked similar 1,000 Friends organizations in Florida, Hawaii, Iowa, Maryland, Massachusetts, Minnesota, New Mexico, and Wisconsin. Pennsylvania, being slightly more ambitious, formed 10,000 Friends of Pennsylvania; that group has pushed for statewide legislation that would expressly allow the creation of urban growth boundaries and place greater planning power in the hands of counties. The 1,000 Friends organizations in Florida and Hawaii have helped to implement the statewide planning programs in their respective states.

The Greenbelt Alliance dates back to 1958 and was orginally concerned with maintaining open space in the San Francisco Bay Area. Recently, the Greenbelt Alliance has worked for regional planning and urban growth boundaries (see the Sonoma County case study in chapter 11).

The Land Stewardship Project, based in Minnesota, has successfully sponsored legislation to exempt metropolitan agriculture from sewer assessments and to create a pilot purchase-of-development-rights program in the rural-urban fringe of the Twin Cities metro region.

Over twenty state and regional organizations are members of the National Growth Management Leadership Project based in Portland, Oregon. Led by Henry Richmond, cofounder of 1,000 Friends of Oregon, the project has a goal of creating a national land-use policy institute to promote regional planning, urban revitalization, growth boundaries, and rural land protection.

village growth boundary. Growth boundaries are nothing more than an attempt to bring common sense to the development process. They encourage compact, cheaper-to-service development; they separate communities from merging into one another; and they are flexible enough to expand over time and in appropriate directions as additional land is needed. Because public sewer and water will not be extended beyond growth boundaries, developers have a strong incentive to look inside the boundaries for development land rather than search for greenfield sites in the countryside. The growth boundary approach dovetails with programs to clean up and reuse brownfields and to promote in-fill building projects. In the meantime, sprawl is kept to a minimum.

Planner-architect Jonathan Barnett has gone so far as to advocate that urban growth boundaries become a national planning policy, with federal grants to states for drafting boundaries:

> Restricting growth at the urban fringe and making improvements in bypassed parts of the older city are interdependent policies. Growth restraints at the fringe make bypassed areas a more significant alternative, but only if a decisive effort makes new investment possible.[4]

As good as growth boundaries sound, they alone are not a panacea. If the countryside beyond the growth boundaries is zoned for one-acre house lots and commercial strips, then a considerable amount of development will leap over the boundaries and settle in the country. This will result in a continued carpet of sprawl, which will eventually defeat the purpose of the growth boundaries. In short, growth bound-

Photo 9.1 A road serves as an urban growth boundary to separate houses and farmland.

aries can function well only if the majority of growth winds up within the boundaries.

A study of the performance of four growth boundaries in Oregon found that in Greater Portland between 1985 and 1989, only 5 percent of new homes were located outside of the Portland Metropolitan Service District. In the east-central community of Bend, 57 percent of new homes were built outside of the growth boundary; Brookings, on the southwest coast, had 37 percent of its new growth outside its UGB, and 24 percent of new homes were built beyond the growth boundary of the southern city of Medford.

So far, one obvious drawback to growth boundaries is that the pattern and style of development within the boundaries often continues to be spread out and auto-dependent. As one magazine commented: "Even Portland has its share of suburban eyesores—cement-block strip malls, rows of fast-food restaurants, and banal split-level homes marching up hillsides denuded of trees."[5] Also, houses on five- to ten-acre lots have been built on land just outside of Portland's growth boundary, which eventually could hinder orderly expansion of the boundary.

The real long-term threat to the growth boundary approach is a large increase in population: If the boundary has to expand dramatically to accommodate sharply rising numbers of people, then sprawl will occur. For example, an additional 1.1 million people are expected to live within the growth boundary of metro Portland by the year 2040. At first, another nine thousand acres was proposed for inclusion inside the boundary to accommodate this jump in population; but in 1997, only forty-five hundred acres were added to the developable area within the boundary. Even so, Portland's Metro 2040 plan envisions 2.5 million people living on four hundred square miles, compared to Greater Denver's current 2 million people already sprawled across five hundred square miles.[6]

A growth boundary may lead to higher housing prices within the boundary. This fact, pointed out by journalist Alan Ehrenhalt, means that a growth boundary may involve a conscious trade-off between, on the one hand, conserving open space and public services and achieving investment in the core city downtown and, on the other, higher home prices (see the discussion of Boulder, Colorado, in box 4.5).[7]

A growth boundary will by no means accommodate all of the new development in a region. In Lancaster County, Pennsylvania, between 1991 and 1995, nearly three-quarters of all new dwelling units were located within twenty-six proposed or adopted urban and village growth boundaries. However, new rural residences on large lots consumed more land than the residential development within the growth boundaries.[8] Had the majority of new dwellings been built outside of the growth boundaries, there would have been a greater loss of farmland, more pressure on roads and groundwater supplies, and a scattering of more people throughout the countryside.

A growth boundary must be able to provide for an orderly expansion of public infrastructure: roads, sewer and water facilities, and schools. A shortage of infrastructure will mean that development will go elsewhere, probably outside the boundary. An uneven provision of public services may skew the direction in which the growth boundary expands over time.

How Urban and Village Growth Boundaries Work

In *The New Heartland*, John Herbers expressed doubts about whether cities and towns could remain physically separated. He saw that dispersed settlement patterns were filling in open areas between fringe communities, making it increasingly difficult to tell where one community ended and another began. As development continued, towns, villages, and small cities were losing any sense of identity and distinctiveness.

Perhaps the effort to retain clearly separated communities does sound like trying to turn back the clock. But consider the alternatives: (1) a re-creation of vast, monotonous suburbs farther out on the metropolitan frontier; or (2) clustered sprawl, in which a hodgepodge of houses and commercial pods are interlaced with bits of open space to retain "rural character." This is the newer, less dense type of suburb.

There are five main purposes to setting growth boundaries:

1. To promote compact development, which is cheaper for taxpayers and governments to service. There is less need for new roads, sewer and water facilities, schools, and fire and police stations.

2. To discourage land speculation that results in the premature development of the countryside and creates leapfrogging development patterns that are difficult and expensive to service. Developers generally hold land for less than ten years. A growth boundary should have a twenty-year horizon and should be reviewed every few years and adjusted as needed. But adjustments should fine-tune the boundary, not greatly expand it. The boundary will help to reduce land speculation at the outside edge and thus keep the countryside undeveloped until needed.

3. To create a process for phasing development as land is needed to expand the growth boundaries.

4. To conserve farmland, forestland, natural areas, and open space by limiting sprawl.
5. To keep distinct communities from merging into a mass of development in which it is impossible to tell where one community ends and another begins.

In addition, growth boundaries can help encourage the redevelopment of older neighborhoods and promote investment within the growth boundary. Existing home and business investments are better protected, because it is less likely that neighborhoods will be abandoned if most of the new growth can be contained within the boundary. Also, a more streamlined review and approval process for new developments within the boundary can spur reinvestment. More compact development makes mass transit more feasible, and, along with the reduction in sprawl, there will be savings from energy conservation.

Steps in Creating a Growth Boundary

State legislation that allows local governments to create growth boundaries strengthens their legal basis and encourages their use. For example, all cities and counties in Oregon are legally required to draft and officially adopt growth boundaries. Vermont permits the formation of growth boundaries in Act 200 of 1987, and the state of Washington encourages them in its 1990 state growth management act: "To prevent sprawl by defining urban growth areas and providing open space and low-density rural development at the perimeter of urban areas;" and "To prohibit development that requires or encourages urbanization of lands not designated for urban uses in the comprehensive plan."

But growth boundaries may come to life without such specific state legislation. Lexington, Kentucky, and adjacent Fayette County have had a growth boundary since 1958. In most states, intergovernmental agreements between local governments can put growth boundaries into practice. Many local governments have designated urban service areas and sewer service areas that effectively function like growth boundaries. Florida's state concurrency policy means that developers cannot build new projects unless adequate public facilities are already in place.

Local governments should reach a growth boundary agreement only after completing four studies:

1. An estimate of population growth of the city and county over the next twenty years, usually based on past trends. The popu-

Box 9.2 State Programs That Require or Encourage Growth Boundaries

California: Allows local governments to create LAFCOS (Local Agency Formation Commissions) to settle annexation disputes and to discourage the premature extension of urban services into the countryside. State law does not expressly allow for growth boundaries; individual communities can create them through a referendum or by vote of the city council.

Florida: The 1985 Growth Management Act requires that urban services (sewer, water, and roads) be in place before development can occur. This policy of concurrency has resulted in local governments setting urban service limits that act as short-term growth boundaries to accommodate urban development.

Maryland: The 1997 Smart Growth bill allows the cities and counties to set growth boundaries with state review. State infrastructure spending will go within the growth areas.

New Jersey: Growth centers were identified as part of the 1992 state land-use plan.

Oregon: The 1973 state land-use act requires the 36 counties and 236 municipalities to agree on urban growth boundaries with state review.

Vermont: The growth centers concept was recommended in 1988's Act 200.

Washington: Growth boundaries were encouraged in the 1990 state land-use act.

lation estimates help to identify the amount of land needed for new development of housing, commercial, industrial, and public spaces and buildings. These are the kinds of population projections and estimates of land needs made in a community or county comprehensive plan.

2. An inventory of existing public facilities (sewer, water, roads, schools, parks), their capacity, and projected needs. The projected needs should reflect any concurrency and adequate public facilities requirements. The estimates of future infrastructure should reflect anticipated development densities and realistic costs and financial ability to pay for new and upgraded public services.

3. An estimate of the amount of buildable land needed for the next twenty years. This estimate should include a study of available land, topography, and different types of land uses (housing, commercial, industrial, and parks and other public uses) that will be needed. In addition, development densities should be estimated and any physical or political barriers to the expansion of the growth boundary identified.

4. A detailed map showing the growth boundary and the area to be included inside the boundary (see figure 9.1). A geographic information system can generate maps based on specific parcels. The GIS system, with soils, slope, water and sewer, and road coverages, can identify development limitations to certain tracts as well as positive development features. The GIS system can produce maps with appropriate growth boundaries, such as roads and waterways. This avoids as much as possible situations where part of a property is within a growth boundary and part is outside. This GIS approach was used by Lancaster County, Pennsylvania, in successfully negotiating with townships and boroughs over the location of twenty growth boundaries.

The Growth Boundary Agreement

The growth boundary agreement should consist of three parts: (1) a recognition of the findings of the four background studies above; (2) amendments to city and county (or city and township) comprehensive plans and zoning maps to make consonant the agreed upon location of the growth boundary; and (3) procedures for reviewing and changing the growth boundary.

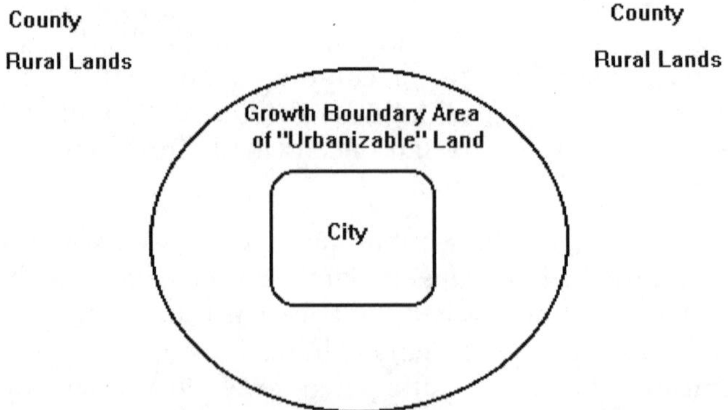

Figure 9.1 Growth Boundary Example.

As part of the agreement, the city and county (or city and township) should state that urban services, especially public sewer and water lines, will not be extended beyond the growth boundary—though the boundary itself may change over time.[9]

The county or township should agree to implement low-density agricultural, forestry, or conservation zoning on lands outside of the growth boundary. This will protect not only farm and forest lands but also water supplies, wildlife habitat, and sensitive rural lands.[10] Low-density zoning outside the growth boundary can ensure that large residential and commercial developments do not simply leapfrog over the growth boundary, or that hobby farms and ranchettes do not overrun the agricultural area.

Box 9.3 Maryland's Smart Growth and Rural Legacy Programs

In 1997, Governor Parris Glendening and the Maryland legislature enacted a groundbreaking effort to curb sprawl, encourage investment within growth centers, and protect the countryside. Under the Smart Growth bill, the state of Maryland is requiring counties and incorporated cities and towns to identify growth boundaries. These "Priority Funding Areas" of developed and developing places will be reviewed for approval by the Maryland Office of State Planning. Inside the growth boundaries, state funds will be invested in the schools, roads, and sewer and water facilities that support development. If development occurs outside of the growth areas on land with less than 3.5 dwelling units per acre, the state will not furnish money for infrastructure. Instead, the private developers or the counties must pay for the necessary services, except that industrially zoned lands were exempted from sewer and water requirements. State office buildings, economic development funds, housing loans, and industrial development financing will be targeted within growth areas.

To enhance the antisprawl purpose of the growth centers, the Rural Legacy Program will provide $90 million over five years for the purchase of land and conservation easements. The state of Maryland will make Rural Legacy grants to local governments and private land trusts to acquire land and conservation easements in locally determined areas.

Maryland has recognized that state infrastructure dollars can greatly help to curb sprawl by influencing the location and amount of development. The state has made a conscious choice to try to maintain distinct communities by investing state dollars in and next to built-up places. At the same time, landowners in the countryside can receive state funds by preserving their land through the sale of conservation easements.

Obstacles to Creating Growth Boundaries

There are nine major obstacles that local governments must overcome in order to implement effective growth boundaries.

- Lack of state enabling legislation
- Difficulty in reaching cooperation among local governments
- Need for good information on population and land-use needs
- Opposition from landowners outside of proposed or potential boundaries
- Opposition from developers
- Opposition from people living inside the growth boundary
- Lack of public education and communication by planners and politicians
- Existing development patterns
- Timing

First, it is easier to form growth boundaries if there is specific state enabling legislation that allows or requires local governments to work together to identify and manage boundaries. Pennsylvania does not have specific enabling legislation, but boroughs (villages) and townships in Lancaster County have reached agreement on boundaries by resolution. In other states, intermunicipal agreements or joint planning and zoning districts may be adequate to create growth boundaries (see appendix 5). Vermont and New Jersey encourage growth centers but have not required municipalities to establish growth boundaries. So even if enabling legislation for growth boundaries were available, there is no guarantee that local governments would use them.

State enabling legislation can also instruct state agencies to coordinate their investments and projects to be consistent with local growth boundaries. One of the main purposes of growth boundaries is to concentrate public and private investment within the boundaries and next to or in cities and villages. The placing of state office buildings and the targeting of highway improvements within growth boundaries can help to limit sprawl and add economic strength to the core cities and villages.

Second, getting local governments to cooperate on growth boundaries can be difficult. A city may not want to grow much, but a neighboring county is hungry for economic development, or vice versa. A city can use its extraterritorial powers to designate a growth area, but the county could allow a large amount of residential and commercial development in the hinterlands, which would defeat the city's growth boundary effort. The large number of cities and villages makes creating several growth boundaries difficult.

Third, local governments need good information on projected population growth and land-use needs in order to establish realistic growth boundaries. A growth boundary should include within its borders enough buildable land to accommodate development needs over the next ten to twenty years. This long-term supply of land avoids artificial shortages that could drive up land prices. On the other hand, the growth boundary should not be drawn so loosely as to designate too much land for development and create sprawl, which in turn would squander any potential savings on public service costs. If there is too little land, land prices could be bid up, driving up the cost of housing and other development. Some places have included a "market factor" of 10 to 15 percent additional land. This extra land ensures that land supplies are not constrained if growth occurs more rapidly than expected. On the other hand, an extra 10 to 15 percent of buildable land can encourage development to occur more rapidly. A growth boundary should be reviewed by the participating governments every three to five years to see if adjustments to the boundary are needed and where land might be added or removed.

Fourth, opposition can arise from landowners outside of proposed boundaries. Some landowners may be counting on the expansion of nearby cities and villages to reach them, thereby increasing the value of their property. Access to public sewer and water lines can mean a windfall profit in the sale of land for development. Meanwhile, public health requirements for the testing of well water and the construction and maintenance of on-site septic systems are likely to become more strict; this would limit the development potential of land outside of growth boundaries.

Fifth, developers may oppose the growth boundary concept out of a fear that the supply of buildable land will be limited and will curtail their business. At a minimum, a growth boundary approach suggests an attempt at achieving balanced growth. But a no- or slow-growth community could use a growth boundary as a way to tightly restrict the amount of new development. So far, developers have argued that they build what people want and what local ordinances require, and they have made good money. A growth boundary, on the one hand, sets aside land for development; on the other, it reduces the development potential of land outside the boundary. Over time, will this create a shortage of building sites?

Although growth boundaries have been in place only since 1993 in

Lancaster County, Pennsylvania, the development community played an important role in making them happen. Scott Jackson, then executive vice president of the county Building Industry Association, stated the view of his organization: "As long as there are places where we can logically extend our business, we have no qualms."[11] Buildable land has been set aside within twenty growth boundaries, and developers have supported the program. From 1994 to 1997, Wal-Mart proposed the construction of six superstores in the county. Although only three stores have been approved so far, all six sites were located within an existing or proposed growth boundary.

Sixth, the designation of a growth boundary does not include how the land inside the boundary is to be developed. In many ways, the creation of a quality living and working environment within the boundary may be the biggest challenge over time. Within the Portland, Oregon, boundary, development densities have increased to accommodate more multifamily housing. There are other communities within the boundary that planners want to "densify" or "upzone" to allow more dwelling units per acre. For example, citizens in the mainly single-family residential community of Oak Grove have protested plans by the Metro government to quadruple the residential density. In its 2040 plan, Metro has set a goal of an average of fifteen units per acre for new housing, up from the current five units per acre. The difficult choices facing any region are how densely to develop within the growth boundary and when and how much to expand the boundary to accommodate new growth.

Seventh, a growth boundary is a new concept for the public and most politicians to understand. A concerted public education effort would be needed before growth boundaries become an accepted practice. As Rutgers University planning professor Robert Burchell notes, "Sprawl has been bought into big-time by the American public, and it will be a very difficult trend to alter."[12]

By contrast, the head of one of Portland, Oregon's largest banks declared, "Everybody in the Portland business community buys into growth management."[13]

Eighth, a growth boundary sounds like a common sense way to achieve balanced growth. Yet planners, politicians, and the public must be realistic about the existing land-use patterns in their vicinity. Where waves of residential and commercial sprawl have already spilled beyond city or village limits, and where there is substantial fragmentation of the countryside into house lots, a growth boundary approach will be difficult to implement. It will not be obvious where to draw the growth boundary, and even if a boundary is drawn, it may be impossible to keep large numbers of people from settling in the countryside.

A final obstacle is the timing of when to create the growth boundary. If a county or township is looking at drawing a growth boundary to curb sprawl, it is better to draw the boundary sooner than later. The stronger the expectations landowners and developers have about developing rural land, the more vigorously they will resist growth boundaries. Estimating population growth and land-use needs and mapping out growth areas require careful study. But it is more important to put a functioning boundary in place and then adjust it as needed than to worry about getting it exactly right. Planning is an inexact science, and, accordingly, growth boundaries are flexible, allowing for correcting mistakes and meeting changing conditions.

Administering the Growth Boundary

Once local governments agree on a growth boundary, they have to administer it. Managing the growth boundary has three connected parts:

- When and where to change the location of the boundary
- How to phase in development inside the boundary
- How to limit development in the countryside so that sprawl doesn't just vault over the boundary

When and Where to Expand a Growth Boundary

A growth boundary is designed to be flexible over time. During a periodic review, every three to five years, cooperating governments can decide whether to change the location of the boundary. Changes may add or delete land from the growth boundary and may involve small acreages or thousands of acres. In proposing changes to the boundary, governments should recognize that a major purpose of the boundary is to provide a degree of certainty about where development should or should not go. Big changes should not be needed if the original boundary was drawn carefully. Furthermore, adding large areas within the boundary can simply promote sprawl and the loss of open space. Governments should be prepared to provide services to any areas brought within the growth boundary.

The metropolitan area of Portland, Oregon, has had a growth boundary since 1979. But between 1979 and 1997, the metro population increased by a staggering 700,000 people. By the year 2020, another 700,000 residents are expected. In the meantime, housing costs in the Portland area have risen to levels topped only by San

Francisco for lack of affordability. In October 1997, the Portland Metro Council voted to increase the growth boundary by forty-five hundred acres. But the growth boundary may need to expand by as much as eighteen thousand acres by 2020 to accommodate the new growth.

The Portland example suggests that with rapid and sustained population growth, a growth boundary may only limit the pace of sprawl, not contain it.

Phased Development

Phased development is a way to promote orderly and cost-efficient growth. The idea behind phased development is to build on open land only when necessary and then only on open land that is adjacent to existing development. Oregon State Planning Goal 11 requires local governments to draft public facilities plans to ensure that land inside growth boundaries will be developed at urban densities. If a community wants to curb urban and suburban sprawl and encourage new development within growth boundaries, new development must be attractive and affordable. For example, Oregon's Goal 10 makes local governments provide housing for all income levels.

The phased development approach can fit nicely with "neotraditional" and "New Urbanism" designs, which feature neighborhoods, town centers, a mix of land uses, public transit, and pedestrian access to shops, schools, and recreation. Houses often have zero lot lines (no setbacks) and are set close to the sidewalk; they also include porches and balconies to promote social interaction and liven up streets. Compact development of four to twelve dwelling units per acre can make use of existing infrastructure, recycle older buildings, and fill in open lots that have been fragmented through leapfrog development. Developers can mix houses and shops so people do not have to get in a car and drive to do their shopping. The compact development also makes possible mass transit and transit-oriented development. The result is considerable energy and transportation cost savings, as well as improved air quality.

An important benefit of urban growth boundaries is that they compel local governments to plan together. They can help to avoid much of the squabbles over annexation of county land by cities, as discussed in chapter 7. A city and a county can undertake a joint comprehensive plan to identify areas of the county that should be protected and where the city should grow. This sort of forethought and cooperation will conserve the countryside and save taxpayers millions of dollars in infrastructure costs over the long run.

Box 9.4 New Jersey's Growth-Center Approach

New Jersey, "the Garden State," is one of the nation's most urbanized states. In the New Jersey State Plan of 1992, the Office of State Planning worked with counties and municipalities to designate more than six hundred population centers, ranging from large cities such as Newark and Trenton to small hamlets of a few hundred people. Although the state plan makes compliance by local governments voluntary, municipalities are encouraged to draw development boundaries around the centers to show the area that can be developed over the next twenty years. Within the centers, pedestrian-oriented development with a mix of houses, offices, and stores will be promoted. Outside the boundaries, limited rural-oriented development will be allowed.

Within the growth centers, municipalities plan for their fair share of affordable housing and have the housing plan certified by the Council on Affordable Housing.

The New Jersey Office of State Planning has pursued an extensive cross-acceptance process involving local governments, concerned citizens, and interest groups. The Planning Office has reviewed thirty-five local plans for consistency with the state plan. Another round of reviews will occur in 1999. The overall result is gradually moving toward a vertical integration of planning policy from townships, counties, and state agencies. Says state planning commission member Michelle Byers, "Over time the state plan will become the master plan guidance document it's supposed to be. It will be used more and more by towns that want to be protected from lawsuits."[14]

A 1992 study by Rutgers University estimated that the growth center strategy of the state plan would save New Jersey taxpayers $1.3 billion in infrastructure costs and $400 million in annual operating costs over twenty years. The study also estimated that development would cover an additional 78,000 acres of farmland under the state plan, but without the plan, 108,000 acres would be consumed by the year 2010.[15]

Already New Jersey voters have spoken with their pocketbooks about keeping the countryside open. In the 1990s, New Jersey voters passed four referendums to approve over $200 million in bonds for purchasing development rights to farmland, and over 43,000 acres have been preserved. So much for a taxpayer revolt.

Limiting Development in the Countryside

A growth-boundary strategy will be successful only if a large majority of new development is located within the boundary. This means that new development in the countryside must be kept to a low density. In fringe places where farming, ranching, or forestry is still viable and an important part of the local economy, growth boundaries will have a better chance of working. But if the countryside has already been carved up into hundreds of house lots, ranchettes, and farmettes and commercial or industrial strips along highways, a growth boundary will have to be very large to encompass this development. In that case, the growth boundary could limit future sprawl but would contain a considerable amount of sprawl and potential in-fill development within its borders.

In metro areas, it makes little sense to place a growth boundary around the core city, which is already surrounded by suburbs. The boundaries will have to be placed on the periphery of the suburbs and edge cities to phase their growth. In some of these situations, growth boundaries will act primarily as *community separators*, keeping some land open between communities for at least several more years.

Oregon legislators recognized the connection between growth boundaries and the countryside in the 1973 land-use law. While cities and counties were required to agree on urban growth boundaries, the counties were also given the task of zoning rural lands not needed or committed to urban uses for exclusive farm use or timber conservation. Until the rise of the "silicon forest" in the 1990s, Oregon's two main industries were farming and forestry, and they are still the second- and third-leading industries. As of 1998, about 16 million acres of farm and ranch lands have been zoned for exclusive farm use,[16] and another 9 million acres for timber conservation. Oregon also pioneered the use of rural residential zones with three- to five-acre minimum lot sizes. In the Willamette Valley alone, over 250,000 acres have been designated for rural residential development.

Following the Oregon approach, townships in Lancaster County, Pennsylvania, have agreed on twenty growth boundaries and have zoned 320,000 acres (slightly over half the county) for agriculture, mostly at a density of one building lot of no more than two acres for every twenty-five owned. Two potential threats to Lancaster's growth boundaries are: (1) a large amount of rural residential land zoned for one-acre lots; and (2) the extension of water and sewer lines beyond growth boundaries to service existing developments with failing septic systems.

Should Growth Boundaries Be Permanent?

Growth boundaries provide greater certainty for the location of desired development and desired conservation. A valid question is: How flexible should a growth boundary be over time? Should it be allowed to increase in every direction?

A permanent boundary around a city or village does not necessarily restrict the right of free travel as long as the city or village does not impose a population cap. *Nonetheless, the idea of a permanent growth boundary suggests that there is an optimal size to a city or town.*

Otherwise, the density of housing within the boundary must increase. Oregon homebuilders lobbyist John Chandler points out that "the strongest advocates for keeping the [Portland] UGB where it is are builders who have bet on high density."[17]

In spearheading the effort to adopt a growth boundary called the green line, San Jose, California, Mayor Susan Hammer said, "My intent is to lock in a permanent green line around the City of San Jose. I think we have a responsibility to protect our hillsides and protect some open space for future generations."[18] Still, the green line will be reviewed every ten years and could be changed. Meanwhile, San Jose contains 835,000 inhabitants and stretches across 174 square miles. This is the largest city in America so far to choose the growth boundary technique.

Gussie McRobert, mayor of Gresham, Oregon, a Portland suburb, is an opponent of expanding the Metro growth boundary. "Every time you move out another ring in the circle," she argues, "something inside the circle dies."[19]

Lancaster County, Pennsylvania, has pioneered the use of purchase-of-development-rights to farmland to reinforce sections of urban growth boundaries (see figure 9.2). Because the purchase-of-development-rights is a voluntary program between landowners and the

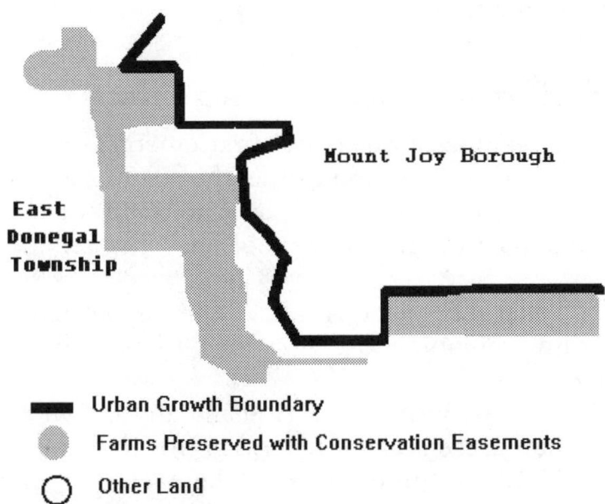

Figure 9.2 Farms Preserved by Conservation Easements Create a Growth Boundary in Lancaster County, Pennsylvania.

county, there is no violation of the takings issue of the Fifth Amendment. The county buys development rights in perpetuity and restricts the use of the land to farming and open space.

Figure 9.2 illustrates the preserved farmland along the growth boundary of the borough of Mount Joy. Technically, it is legal to extend utilities, such as public sewer and water lines, across a preserved farm. But the land to the left of the preserved farms is zoned for agriculture at one building lot of no more than two acres for each twenty-five acres owned. This means that if that land is not rezoned to high-density residential, commercial, or industrial use, it will not pay to run utilities out into the countryside. Mount Joy borough is not completely surrounded by preserved farms. It can expand to the east over time.

The farmers behind the line of preserved farms have a reasonable assurance that major developments will not be coming their way for a long time. Some scattered residences may crop up in the countryside, but generally the number of nonfarm neighbors will be kept to a minimum. This reduces the likelihood of conflicts between farmers and nonfarmers.

Growth boundaries are a creation of government; they are created by the political process, and they can be removed by the political process. The Oregon Land Use Act has survived three referenda to abolish it. But like most things in politics, a change in leadership or party in power can reverse previous policies and programs. Nonetheless, growth boundaries imply a greater sense of stability if not permanence. That is a dramatic change in mindset from the standard planning-for-development attitude that has pervaded American land-use planning in this century.

Regional Government and Planning Efforts

The concept of regional government first emerged with the help of federal funding in the 1960s. Over time, the need for better coordination of local government services for sewage, solid waste, transportation, parks and recreation, and schools has pointed to a regional approach.

In 1962, the Federal Highway Aid Act required metro areas to establish metropolitan planning organizations to plan for region-wide transportation.

In 1966, the U.S. Department of Housing and Urban Development required all urban areas seeking federal grants to form metro region planning organizations (different from the MPOs). Today, there are more than three hundred of those metros. The metros initially insured that there would not be competing grant proposals from different jurisdictions within a metro region. But some metros have grown into much more than grant administrators. They have taken over some infrastructure planning functions, drafting comprehensive plans, and encouraging local planning.

Most states have regional planning agencies (also known as councils of government), started with the help of federal funds, that provide technical assistance to counties and municipalities. These agencies, however, have virtually no political base or clout. They are not elected by the public, and their decisions are advisory, not legally binding. Since the early 1980s, federal funding for regional planning agencies has fallen off substantially.

With some exceptions, the implementation of regional plans has so far proven difficult. Most regional planning agencies lack a political base, and hence the plans they draft are frequently ignored. The reality of the fringe, as Joseph Doherty pointed out nearly two decades ago, is that a plethora of small, inadequate town and county governments are left to wrestle with development problems that are simply too big to handle:

> Who's to plan, who's to set the property tax? Who's to write and approve a meaningful capital budget appropriate to the territory? The answer today is that this job is relegated to a thousand or more elected officials and their technicians struggling away in a hundred or more local general purpose and special district government offices, all of them hampered by too few resources, too much confusion, and too little power.[20]

Regional governments are still in the experimental stage, but they are starting to combine the planning functions of the regional planning agencies with the capital spending aspects of the metropolitan governments. Portland, Oregon's Metro and the Twin Cities' Met Council are the nation's leading examples. The big breakthroughs are the election of regional government, as has occurred in Portland, and the merger of a core city with a surrounding county.

Urbanist David Rusk has identified three ways in which core cities can evolve into regional governments:

1. By annexation
2. Through mergers with counties
3. Through local government cooperation and coordination

To Rusk, the main purposes of regional government are: (1) to disperse the concentration of poor and minority inhabitants from the inner city throughout the region; (2) to provide affordable low- and moderate-income housing throughout the region; and (3) to redistribute property tax revenues from wealthier to less wealthy communities. He makes a persuasive case that improving economic opportunity and social integration will result in a region with "balance, diversity, and stability."[21]

For growth management, Rusk advocates a regional comprehensive plan, an urban growth boundary, adequate facilities requirements, and transportation planning. Even so, regional growth management does not stand out as a high priority to Rusk, compared to alleviating urban poverty. Perhaps the biggest challenge to forming regional governments or cooperative agreements among municipalities is that many communities are afraid of losing some of their authority.

Annexation of county land has been especially popular in the Sun Belt, with cities in the South and West accounting for the large majority of annexations over the past fifty years. According to Rusk, annexation allows a core city to capture tax base and well-to-do residents that otherwise would be separated in suburban enclaves.

For example, according to growth management expert Douglas Porter, Lincoln, Nebraska, used aggressive annexation to capture nearly 95 percent of the population growth in Lancaster County in the 1980s.[22] Across the nation, income levels over time are higher in cities that annex than in cities that do not annex territory. Also, the "elastic" cities have a more even racial mix.[23]

The downside to the annexation approach is that it can create huge sprawling cities such as Phoenix and Houston. Even though Rusk does advocate urban growth boundaries, that technique seems contrary to the aggressive annexation that he champions.

The merging of city and county governments into a single unit is rare. But mergers can reduce the fragmentation of political power and the separation of economic strength between the core city and the suburbs. The three best examples are Nashville and Davidson County, Tennessee; Jacksonville and Duval County, Florida; and Indianapolis and Marion County, Indiana. Both Nashville and Jacksonville are economic success stories, but their percentage of regional population has steadily declined as new growth has occurred in outlying metro counties. Unigov, created in 1969 by the Indiana legislature to meld Indianapolis with Marion County, has won high praise for economic growth and greater efficiency in providing services.[24]

Instead of expanding its boundaries or forming a city-county government, a core city can work with suburban municipalities and counties to coordinate planning, housing, transportation, and even regional sharing of property tax revenue. Both of the Metro governments of Greater Portland, Oregon, and Minnesota's Twin Cities region contain elements of this description.

In 1967, the Minnesota legislature created the Metropolitan Council of the Twin Cities for the Greater Minneapolis–St. Paul metropolis. Initially, the council focused on regional transportation planning and solid waste disposal. Over time, it has drafted comprehensive plans to guide the growth of the seven-county region, including the areas of housing, sewage, transportation, solid waste, water, recreation, and farmland protection. In addition, the 187 municipalities have had to submit comprehensive plans to the council to ensure that their plans are consistent with the council's regional plan. In 1980 the concept of a Metropolitan Urban Service Area (MUSA) was approved by the legislature. The MUSA line, like a growth boundary, determines the limit of urbanizable land and urban-type services such as public sewer and water. The MUSA line has not been aggressively defended, however. For example, there were seventy-eight boundary changes between 1987 and 1991, which added eighteen thousand acres within the MUSA line.[25] Perhaps part of the reason for granting so many changes was that the Met Council is not elected by the voters but appointed by the governor.

The Twin Cities Fiscal Disparities Plan, enacted by the Minnesota legislature in 1971, was the nation's first and so far only example of regional tax base sharing. The law applies to 187 municipalities in the Twin Cities metro area and requires them to place 40 percent of the increases in commercial and residential property assessments into a regional pool. The tax revenues are then redistributed according to population and the ratio of a municipality's per capita property value to the metro-wide per capita property value. In 1995, the regional tax pool amounted to $241 million. Of the 187 municipalities, 47 were net contributors and 140 net gainers.[26]

In 1979, the voters of Greater Portland, Oregon, established the nation's first elected regional government, named Metro, which covers an area of 234,000 acres in three counties and twenty-four municipalities. In the same year, Greater Portland drew a growth boundary called the Metropolitan Service District. The elected seven-member Metro council and its elected executive director have planning control over the expansion of the boundary line.

In 1995, Metro completed a comprehensive plan to guide growth to the year 2040. The population of the metro region is expected to increase by 1.1 million over that time. Also in 1995, voters in the Metro area approved a $135 million bond issue to buy parkland, natural areas, and open space to help maintain the quality of life. But already, Portland had experienced growing pains in its attempt to

Table 9.1 County-City Growth Boundaries

County	*Cities*
Alameda County, CA	Pleasanton
Santa Clara County, CA	Cupertino, Morgan Hill, San Jose
Sonoma County, CA	Healdsburg, Santa Rosa, Sebastopol
Boulder County, CO	Boulder
Larimer County, CO	Fort Collins
Sarasota County, FL	Sarasota, Venice
Fayette County, KY	Lexington
Seven County Twin Cities Region, MN	Minneapolis–St. Paul
Durham County, NC	Durham
Virginia Beach, VA	Virginia Beach
Clark County, WA	Vancouver
King County, WA	Seattle
Spokane County, WA	Spokane
Thurston County, WA	Lacey, Olympia, and Tumwater

curb sprawl. Between 1979 and 1997, its growth boundary expanded by about 1 percent, while the population soared by more than a quarter of a million. The Portland area had been cited by the National Association of Homebuilders as having the second most expensive housing in America, after San Francisco.[27] In response, in October of 1997, Metro decided to redraw the boundary, adding forty-five hundred acres for up to thirty thousand units of urban-density housing. But Greater Portland could easily face an increase of hundreds of thousands of people by the year 2020.

To succeed in the long run, a regional government must be elected and must have power over major public infrastructure such as transportation systems, solid waste disposal, sewer and water systems, and the financing of schools and governments through regional tax base sharing. Regional government also needs to review proposed private developments with region-wide impacts. Such a regional government may prove unwieldly around enormous metro areas such as New York, Los Angeles, Chicago, and Houston. But the successes of smaller metro regions like Portland and the Twin Cities point the way to the future. The popularity of county-city growth boundaries (see table 9.1) is spreading across the nation.

Summary

Urban growth boundaries, urban service areas, and village growth boundaries hold considerable promise as tools to organize the location of urban-type development. These boundaries can be effective in controlling the location of infrastructure, limiting costly sprawl, and helping to protect greenbelts of farmland and open space around cities and suburbs. Growth boundaries can be successful if development within the boundaries is done efficiently, affordably, and tastefully. At the same time, land outside the boundaries must be zoned for low-density development to avoid residential and large commercial developments leaping over the boundaries and continuing the march of sprawl and disinvestment in population centers.

Governments in metropolitan areas will have to reinvent themselves in order to be more effective and efficient. The growth boundary process ties together regional land-use planning, capital improvements programs, economic development, and phased growth to combat sprawl. Regional planning between city and county or village and township is the sort of cooperation that is rapidly becoming a necessity. Regional metropolitan governments with, at a minimum, jurisdiction over planning and transportation promise to be the wave of the future.

CHAPTER 10

Managing Growth in the Fringe Countryside

When everybody's moving out to the countryside, there's no longer a countryside, and the kind of life that forces people to drive everywhere is the kind of life that does the greatest damage to the environment.

—*Tom Hylton, author of* Save Our Land, Save Our Towns

. . . A sensible person can no longer believe in the rightness of turning huge expanses of farmland, forest, desert, and other rural landscapes into additional suburbs.

—*Philip Langdon,* A Better Place to Live

Chapter 9 emphasizes growth boundaries to manage the growth of urban and suburban areas in the fringe, but because much of the development in the fringe is occurring outside of established cities and towns, it is important to examine how the countryside can remain an open and working landscape. Growth boundaries ultimately will fail if a major share of growth and development can simply jump over the boundary lines and spread throughout the hinterlands.

Land Tenure and Land Ownership Patterns

Before devising and implementing land-use controls in the fringe countryside, local governments should examine the land tenure and land ownership patterns. Land tenure defines who owns or rents the land and why. In fringe areas, land tenure and ownership patterns have been undergoing major changes for several years. A good way to track the change in the pattern of land ownership is through a parcel-specific GIS program—that is, to look at where tracts of land are being subdivided into smaller parcels that suggest new or impending residential or commercial development. But finding out who owns the land and why would require an extensive search of deeds or a company that would publish a plat book of landowners, the parcels they own, and the acreage of the parcels.

In most fringe areas, the most noteworthy changes in land ownership have been:

- the breakup of larger tracts into smaller parcels;
- the rise in the number of newcomers owning land; and
- the decline in landownership by natural resource users and the increase in residential and recreational land consumers and land speculators.

In short, the motivations of fringe landowners have generally changed from using land for farm and forest production to using land for a residence, a business, or an investment. Newcomers want to protect their few acres of paradise. Speculators profit from the continuing influx of newcomers who need housing and want to start businesses. Large, long-term landowners are tempted to sell farm and forest lands for development and often do. For example, an acre of good farmland might sell for $2,000 to $5,000 an acre for farming. But as a building lot, that acre might fetch $40,000 or more.

One indication of the strong demand for fringe land is the increase in the number of hobby farms nationwide. These farms cover less than fifty acres and generate under $10,000 a year in sales. Hobby farms fragment the land base, drive land prices above what a commercial farmer is willing to pay, and entice commercial farmers to sell out. Some states even make the creation of hobby farms attractive through subdivision laws that exempt large lots from a thorough review.[1]

Land speculators have played a significant role in transforming the fringe countryside into residential and commercial properties. Speculators seek to earn quick profits through the purchase and resale of land. They generally spend little money on improving the land and sell the property within five years. Speculators hope to gain an "unearned increment" by purchasing land that will increase in value, often benefiting from public investment in roads and nearby private development.

Speculators are often criticized for causing premature development and parcellation of the land base. On the other hand, speculators may hold land off the market while they wait for the land to "ripen" as demand increases. But the withholding of land can result in awkward development patterns in the fringe, where leapfrog and scattered "buckshot" development produce a sprawling jumble of open space and development.

The presence of speculators and the potential for capital gains have caught the attention of many fringe landowners. An often cited study of fringe land markets found that "a substantial number [of landowners] would sell immediately if a good offer were forthcoming."[2] This behavior serves only to speed the transition of open land to residential and commercial uses. Such a transition, however, is a cumulative process that changes the landscape over several years. In their study of rural land markets, Robert Healy and James Short found that "the expectation that agricultural land will be put to urban or other developed use is usually reflected in the land's price years before a single building is constructed."[3]

Landowner expectations of capital gains have a way of being translated into political pressure against tighter land-use controls. People with the mentality of it's-my-land-I-can-do-what-I-want-with-it rarely recognize that government has no obligation to guarantee a landowner's capital gain; the government's only obligation is to guarantee the landowner a right to an economic use of the property.

How to Limit Development in the Countryside

Many fringe conflicts over land use involve farmland. That is because farmland often has the most level and best-drained soils, which are ideal for home and business sites. But good-quality farmland is a limited resource in the metropolitan fringe. Approximately 16 percent of the nation's prime farmland is located within metropolitan areas. That land produces about one-quarter of the nation's food. Counties adjacent to metropolitan counties contain another fifth of the nation's prime farm ground and produce around one-third of total farm output. About 372 of the nation's 640 leading agricultural counties are either within or adjacent to major metropolitan areas.

Five trends have been defining the structure of American agriculture over the past twenty-five years. First, the number of farms has been steadily declining to about 2 million. Second, large farms have been getting bigger, to the point where the top 200,000 farms produce about 40 percent of the nation's output. Third, the number of medium-size family farms grossing from $40,000 to $250,000 a year has been shrinking. Fourth, small part-time farms earning less than $40,000 a year (and most of them grossing less than $10,000 a year) have increased and now make up more than half of the nation's farms. And fifth, the number of acres in farm use have been declining. Economists, planners, and interest groups disagree on the rate of loss of farmland, but between several hundred thousand acres and a million acres a year is plausible.

From a national perspective, the loss of farmland to other uses is not yet a threat to America's overall food supply. But the conversion of farmland to residential, commercial, and industrial development in fringe areas can have a sharply negative impact on the local farm economy.

Already, some of the best farming areas in the nation are threatened by urban sprawl. According to the American Farmland Trust, the Central Valley of California, where most of the nation's fruits and vegetables are grown, will lose more than 1 million acres of farmland to urban sprawl by the year 2040.[4] South Florida, home to major citrus groves, is under heavy development pressure because of the estimated ten thousand people a week who move to the Sunshine State. Even the Midwest breadbasket is experiencing growth pains. In its 1996 study *Farming on the Edge*, the American Farmland Trust cited metropolitan parts of Wisconsin, Illinois, Ohio, and Minnesota as among the top ten most endangered farming areas in the nation.[5]

Farmers on the edge of many metro regions have been feeling the squeeze of higher property taxes, more nonfarm neighbors, and higher land prices, which make expansion costly if not impossible. Urbanites settle outside of central cities in part because they enjoy the open space and bucolic environment farming provides. As more people

Box 10.1 Stanislaus County, California, Feels the Pressure

Stanislaus County, California, is both a metropolitan county and one of the nation's leading agricultural counties. In 1996, county farmers produced $1.2 *billion* in food and fiber. But this San Joaquin Valley county is also one of California's fastest-growing counties. In the 1980s, the county's population grew by over 100,000 and at a rate of 39 percent, compared to 26 percent statewide.

Between 1982 and 1992, Stanislaus County lost forty-seven thousand acres of farmland to development, and the conversion pressure on the county's remaining farms and farmland is sure to intensify. By the year 2020, the county is expected to have over 700,000 people, up from 412,000 in 1994. Part of the influx comes from the Greater San Francisco Bay Area, eighty miles away, where high housing prices have been forcing workers to seek homes farther inland.

Although the county employs agricultural zoning with a forty-acre minimum lot size, annexations by cities will continue to consume farmland.

relocate to the rural-urban fringe, they drive up property taxes and the price of land, isolate tracts of farmland, and hasten the decline of local farming. When land prices rise and the land base is fragmented, it becomes increasingly difficult for a farmer to expand and function efficiently. Also, more development and more people moving in usually means that farmers see increased incidents of vandalism to crops and livestock.

Some farmers who see themselves in the path of development will reduce investment in their farms as they wait to sell their land for development. These farmers may be looking to sell their land and buy a farm in a less congested area, or they may be hoping to sell their land for a high price to set up a retirement fund. The more farmers in an area that leave farming, the harder they make it on the remaining farmers to survive. Farm support businesses have fewer customers and are more likely to shut down. The farther farmers have to travel for feed, seed, fertilizer, machinery, and marketing services, the more difficult farming becomes.

Some fringe farmers have adapted successfully to the influx of newcomers. Having more consumers close at hand can boost the profitability of labor-intensive agriculture such as the raising of fruits, vegetables, and nursery stock. Greater job opportunities off the farm in nearby suburbs offer a way to supplement farm income. In the fringe, many traditional livestock farms (dairy, hogs, and chickens) and grain farms have given way to horses, specialty crops, and horticulture. Farm sizes tend to be considerably smaller than in truly rural areas because of high land costs.

Because of the greater value of most fringe land for development than for farming, the free market alone may not be able to maintain an adequate amount of farmland or farming operations necessary to sustain farm-support businesses. In fact, much of the new construction of houses, shopping centers, and corporate office parks occurs on what was previously farmland. As a result, farmland protection methods are frequently the primary means local governments use to try to manage growth in the fringe countryside.

Farmland protection efforts are usually aimed at open-space preservation rather than maintaining agriculture as an economically viable industry. Table 10.1 shows that only two of the leading counties in purchasing development rights to farmland—Lancaster, Pennsylvania, and Sonoma, California—have strong agricultural industries.

Preferential Taxation of Farmland

Because the federal government has provided little direction in planning for farmland protection, the task has largely fallen to state and

Table 10.1 Metro Counties Leading in Farmland Preserved for Agriculture, 1997, and Value of Farm Production, 1992

County	*Acres Preserved Through Purchase or Transfer of Development Rights*[1]	*Value of Farm Output*[2]
Montgomery County, MD	45,775	$27.7 million
Lancaster, PA	25,735	$680.6 million
Marin County, CA	25,504	$42.1 million
Harford County, MD	22,500	$28.7 million
Sonoma, CA	21,162	$280.8 million
Howard County, MD	18,949	$18.9 million
Baltimore, MD	12,383	$40.6 million
Burlington, NJ	9,506	$64.5 million

Source: *Farmland Preservation Report*, June 1997.
Note: The value of farm output is estimated by the U.S. Department of Agriculture. A number of counties have taken issue with the USDA figures because they include only the value of farm output, not the total economic value of the agricultural industry, such as the machinery, hardware, feed mills, transportation, and processing businesses.
1. *Farmland Preservation Report*, June 1997.
2. 1992 Census of Agriculture.

local governments.[6] The most common state program is the use of preferential property tax assessment to reduce the property tax burden on farmers to encourage them to remain in operation. Every state offers some form of preferential assessment, usually either a simple tax break without penalty if the land is converted to a nonfarm use, or a tax break combined with a "rollback" penalty (a recapture of the tax break) if the land is converted. Some states, towns, and counties have entered into contracts withlandowners whereby the landowner agrees not to develop the land for a certain period of time in return for a tax break. A few states have even made tax benefits contingent on the land being zoned for agriculture and on the farmer adopting soil conservation practices.

Most state laws require local governments to conduct a new assessment of property value every five years or so. Property is typically assessed for tax purposes at its "highest and best use," or development potential. In growing communities the value of the highest and best use of land (e.g., for building sites) can skyrocket within five years. Hence, use-value taxation of farmland provides some protection against a soaring tax bill based on highest and best use. Even so, the tax rate may have to rise to pay for additional public services demanded by the growing population.

Property tax breaks for agricultural land have not been very effective in retaining land for farm use in fringe areas. The tax breaks are woefully small compared to the large sums that developers are prepared to offer. And there has been some abuse of farm property tax breaks by land speculators who use the reduced taxes to subsidize the holding of land until it ripens for nonfarm development. Similarly, because a farmer's land is also a retirement account, the tax break enables the farmer to hold the land longer and eventually sell the farm for top dollar, which often means for development. As a result, farmers in fringe areas are reluctant to enter agreements that limit their options to sell land. In addition, preferential assessment for farmland may cause the property tax burden to shift from farmland owners—even wealthy hobby farm owners—to owners of nonfarm property. Local tax revenues may decline, prompting a search for more intensive development to bolster tax receipts.

Agricultural Zoning

The most widely used technique for farmland protection in the fringe is agricultural zoning. The strength of agricultural zoning is that it can help keep conflicting farm and nonfarm land uses separate and prevent the fragmentation of the farmland base into parcels too small to farm. There are several types of agricultural zoning. These vary according to: (1) the uses allowed in the zone—exclusive or nonexclusive farm use; (2) the minimum farm size allowed, such as a fifty-acre minimum lot size; (3) the number of nonfarm dwellings allowed, such as one building lot per twenty-five acres; and (4) the size of setbacks or buffer areas between farms and non-farm properties.

Many fringe counties and communities view agricultural zoning as a means of preserving open space, rather than maintaining a viable agricultural sector in the local economy. This is especially the case in pro-growth communities that consider farmland as a holding area for future suburban growth, where farms appear as "vacant land" on the current land-use map and as residential developments on the future land-use map. The farms are then zoned "Agricultural-Residential" or "Agricultural Holding" as if farms and houses are compatible or farmers will continue to farm their land until the local government says its okay to put up houses as the final crop. Pro-growth communities typically employ minimum lot sizes under twenty acres, which means that many nonfarm residences and hobby farms are allowed in the agricultural zone.

But only where minimum lot sizes are large enough to discourage intrusions by low-density residential development and hobby farmers can commercial agriculture be protected from the parcellation of the land base and land prices that far exceed the agricultural value.

Large-lot agricultural zoning may also result in more land being taken up by residences than necessary. For example, if a buyer purchases the minimum lot size in an agricultural zone, then the local jurisdiction will usually grant a building permit. Also, sliding-scale agricultural zoning, which allows a single half- to two-acre lot to be created for every so many acres, can lead to a proliferation of nonfarm residences. For example, sliding-scale zoning usually permits one subdivision of parcels of two to twenty-five acres, which have very limited farming value. Where there are many of these smaller parcels in an agricultural zone, the potential for nonfarm development poses a threat to nearby commercial farming operations.

Agricultural zoning has an uneven history in fringe areas. It is often criticized for its impermanence because even the most carefully prepared zoning maps and ordinances may be subject to variances, zoning amendments, rezonings to nonfarm uses, and special exceptions. Zoning decisions are usually made by politically vulnerable local governments, and agricultural zoning is likely to change in the face of development pressures. Moreover, zoning decisions are made on a case-by-case basis. As a consequence, the cumulative effect of these individual decisions may not be fully recognized. Also the lack of coordination among townships or counties can easily frustrate comprehensive regional agricultural zoning.

The management of agricultural zones may therefore be crucial to the long-term viability of farming in a county or region. If some farmers sell out because of incompatible development in the neighborhood, the remaining farmers are likely to experience both greater difficulty in retaining farm support businesses and increased conflicts with the growing numbers of nonfarm neighbors.

A Note on Agricultural Zoning versus Cluster Zoning

Politicians and planners in fringe communities have racked their brains about how to keep the countryside open. Large areas of the fringe are still in farm use; however, farming requires long hours, hard work, and a substantial investment and often offers a low return. The average age of American farmers is around fifty-four years. Many farmers do not have children who want to farm. And the cost to get into farming is high, running into the hundreds of thousands of dollars.

Perhaps in an ideal world, farmers would earn enough from farming that they would not be tempted to sell land for development. But with the typical value of farmland at a few thousand dollars an acre and the value of that land as house lots at tens of thousands an acre, the temptation is great.

Farmers often have most of their net worth tied up in their land.

The challenge they face is how to get some of that value out of the land and still have enough land left to farm profitably. Although a public purchase-of-development-rights program or a sale or donation of easements to a private land trust may be attractive for some farmers, many farmers resist placing any restrictions on their land.

The question for both the local government and the farmers becomes: How much nonfarm development can take place in the countryside before the farmers decide they can't farm any more? Agricultural zoning that features either large minimum lot size or area-based allocation (such as one building lot of no more than two acres for each twenty-five acres owned) attempts to allow some development but not too much.

Cluster zoning, also known as open-space zoning, has been promoted as a way to allow nonfarm development in farming areas. The idea is to allow part of the farm to be developed while the remaining portion is maintained for farming and open space. The problem with cluster zoning is that most places that use it allow a fairly high density of one dwelling per two acres or one to three or five acres. At those densities, the result is likely to be clustered sprawl. Moreover, the remaining farmland will probably be used for low-value crops such as hay because animal agriculture with its manure smells is not very compatible with nonfarm neighbors and their kids and dogs.

A further problem is that clustered development works best with public sewer and water facilities. Putting several houses close together with individual on-site septic systems and wells is a recipe for health problems. Time and again, failing septic systems have required the extension of public sewer and water lines, which has opened up wide areas of farmland to development.

A final issue with cluster zoning is that many people who move to the countryside do not want to live close to others. They want their own place and their own space of a few acres. The state of Oregon came up with a novel way to handle the demand for rural residences. Oregon counties have designated "rural residential zones" on lower-quality land located away from commercial farming areas. In the rural residential zones, densities are set at three- to five-acre minimum lot sizes—generally enough land to support on-site septic systems and wells.

The California Farm Bureau has come out against cluster development in farming areas as "ill-conceived land use planning at its worst." According to Farm Bureau attorney David Guy, "Mixing housing and agriculture just doesn't work."[7]

Baltimore County, Maryland, planners have taken a dim view of the results of their cluster ordinance, which allows clustering at a density of one dwelling per five acres on land adjacent to an agricultural zone, as long as the development covers no more than 30 percent of the site and leaves at least 70 percent open. In 1996, a developer proposed putting thirty-four houses on 1-acre lots amid a 173-acre tract but next to a 200-acre cattle operation. The working farm was also preserved for agriculture with a taxpayer-purchased conservation easement. The farmer has complained that he would not be able to remain in farming because of the increased liability insurance he would have to carry, not to mention the complaints of neighbors about flies and manure smells.

In response to the controversy over the cluster zoning ordinance, Baltimore County Planning Director Pat Keller said, "Without a doubt we will change it. It's been nothing short of a disaster."[8]

Agricultural Districts

Agricultural districts have been employed as a compromise between preferential assessment and agricultural zoning. They were first formed in New York State in 1971 and have since been adopted in fourteen other states. Typically, farmers may voluntarily create a district of at least five hundred acres in return for property tax benefits and exemption from nuisance laws that would restrict normal farming practices. Also, there are usually controls on the extension of public sewer and water lines and roads into the district. But no penalties are levied if a farmer withdraws land from the district.

Although the formation of agricultural districts has been popular in rural areas, few districts have been formed within a twenty-five-mile radius of major cities. Farmland owners in the fringe face increased pressure to sell out for development as the amount of developed land increases. Owners anticipate an eventual conversion of their land to nonfarm uses and hence do not initiate farm districts or enroll their land.

Right-to-Farm Laws

At least forty-seven states have enacted right-to-farm laws to provide farmers with protection against nuisance suits for standard farming practices. The existence of such laws is especially important in fringe areas where newcomers have been influential in having nuisance ordinances passed and in pressing nuisance suits against farmers to limit their operating practices. Right-to-farm laws do not exempt farmers from state and federal laws relating to pollution and safety. They do, however, serve to underscore the legitimacy of farm uses, even the primacy of farm uses above other land uses that may develop in the vicinity.

Conflicts between farmers and nonfarmers are likely to intensify in fringe areas, and increasingly the burden will be on farmers, rather than nonfarmers, to be good neighbors. New large livestock operations will face setback requirements of up to a half a mile from the nearest residence.[9] Despite the existence of right-to-farm laws, some fringe communities will pass nuisance ordinances that restrict normal farming practices to certain hours of the day. One such example occurred in Illinois, where a farmer was jailed for violating an ordinance that restricted when he could operate machinery.[10] The more regulations placed on farmers, the more difficult it becomes for farmers to earn a decent living. And the more attractive it becomes to sell the land for development.

Purchase of Development Rights

Many farmers are skeptical of agricultural zoning because it restricts the use of their land without compensation. A farmer's land is not only a source of livelihood but an insurance policy and a retirement fund, as well. Thus, the farmer often has only two choices: either to keep farming and hope to pass along the farm to heirs (or another farmer) or try to sell out for development.

The purchase of development rights (legally known as conservation easements) by a government or land trust offers farmers a middle ground between those two choices. The sale of development rights provides the farmer with compensation for not selling the land for development and gives the farmer needed cash liquidity. Most farmers use the money to buy down debt, reinvest in the farm, or set up a retirement fund. A farmer can sell development rights in return for cash (or cash and income tax benefits in a bargain sale) and still own the land, which can be used for farming or as open space. Once preserved, the land can be sold or passed on to heirs, though the restrictions spelled out in the deed of easement will apply to subsequent landowners.

The value of the development rights is determined by an appraisal, based on comparable sales of farms that have retained their development rights, to determine a market value, and sales of farms that have sold their development rights, to determine a restricted agricultural value. The difference between the market value and the restricted agricultural value is the value of the development rights (see boxes 10.2 and 10.3). A government or private land trust may offer a cash payment equal to the full appraised value of the development rights or a bargain sale of part cash and part income tax deduction (see box 10.3).

Twenty-five years ago, the purchase of development rights by state and local governments to restrict the use of privately owned land might have seemed "radical" or "left leaning." Such a practice—in

Box 10.2 Sale-of-Development-Rights Example for a 250-Acre Farm

	$750,000	Appraised Fair Market Value
	$500,000	Appraised Value Restricted to Farming or Open Space
	$250,000	Appraised Easement Value and Cash Paid
Subtract	$170,000	Landowner's Basis in Farm (the cost of the land and buildings plus improvements minus depreciation)
	$80,000	Taxable Capital Gain

Gains Tax Due (at 20% federal and 5% state) = $20,000
Net Return on Sale of Development Rights = $230,000

Box 10.3 Bargain-Sale-of-Development-Rights Example for a 250-Acre Farm

$750,000	Appraised Fair Market Value
$500,000	Appraised Value Restricted to Farming or Open Space
$250,000	Appraised Easement Value
$200,000	Bargain Sale Cash Price
$50,000	Donation
$170,000	Landowner's Basis in Farm
$136,000	Deductible Basis (80% of $170,000)
$64,000	Taxable Capital Gain
$50,000	Donation Deduction*
$14,000	Taxable Capital Gain

Gains Tax Due (at 20% federal and 5% state) = $3,500
Net Return on Sale of Development Rights = $196,500

* The landowner may use the donation to deduct up to 30% of Adjusted Gross Income in the year of the sale and for up to five future years. The example simplifies the assumption that the full donation value will be deducted over time, not in the first year.

effect, buying an interest in a farm—might have appeared foolhardy or doomed to failure. But in the late 1990s, over 150 local governments and 15 states were actively purchasing development rights to farmland, mainly in the rural-urban fringe where farmland is most threatened (see table 10.2). In the 1996 Farm Bill, the U.S. Congress joined the effort by authorizing $35 million in grants to state and local governments for the purchase of development rights to farmland.

Although purchase-of-development-rights (PDR) programs are likely to remain controversial because of the sizable costs involved, they offer a more permanent solution than zoning and provide private landowners with compensation in return for giving up the right to put houses, malls, and factories on their land. PDR programs also avoid the Fifth Amendment takings challenge that can hamper zoning. The purchase of development rights is a voluntary process entered into by a landowner and a government agency in a legally binding contract.

The two main strengths of a PDR program are that it scores high in fairness to landowners who participate and provides substantial per-

Table 10.2 The Purchase of Development Rights, June 1997

A Sample of Metropolitan Counties	*Farmland Acres Preserved*	*Total Farmland in Acres*	*Percent of County in Farms*	*Average Cost Per Acre, 1996*	*Value of Farm Products*
Lancaster, PA	25,735	388,368	64	$1,400	$680 million
Harford, MD	22,500	97,312	35	$2,426	$28 million
Sonoma, CA	21,162	550,000	54	$1,458	$281 million
Baltimore, MD	12,383	83,232	22	$4,049	$40 million
Worcester, MA	11,841	114,805	12	$2,097	$49 million
York, PA	11,139	252,052	44	$1,368	$120 million
Burlington, NJ	9,506	97,186	19	$4,495	$64 million
Kent, DE	9,233	197,375	52	$858	$111 million
Chester, PA	8,439	176,643	37	$4,060	$282 million
Suffolk, NY	7,641	35,353	6	$6,627	$133 million
New London, CT	6,252	65,987	16	$2,500	$97 million
Nonmetro Adjacent Counties	*Farmland Acres Preserved*	*Land in Farms*	*Percent in Farms*	*Average Cost Per Acre, 1996*	*Value of Farm Products*
Carroll, MD	26,543	157,505	55	$1,817	$66 million
Marin, CA	25,504	165,000	62	$666	$42 million
Caroline, MD	19,198	126,981	62	$534	$85 million
Addison, VT	17,896	209,677	43	$700	$93 million
Franklin, VT	14,661	203,503	50	$700	$94 million
Adams, PA	5,860	172,366	37	$1,531	$123 million

Source: *Farmland Preservation Report*, June 1997.

manence in farmland preservation. The landowner is compensated for development restrictions, and the land generally cannot be developed except for farming.

A purchase-of-development-rights program makes sense if contiguous parcels of land can be preserved to create blocks of several hundred acres or more. The large preserved blocks help to keep development at a distance, and the larger the blocks, the more likely that the farm-support businesses will keep going. On the other hand, if only a few scattered farms are preserved, they can act as magnets for developers who look to build houses next to the preserved farms and market the houses for their views of preserved farmland. The more houses that locate next to the preserved farms, the more conflicts between farming operations and nonfarm residents are likely to occur.

Also, the costs of a PDR program must be reasonable, or else it is probably not the proper tool or the right land to preserve. In some fringe areas with heavy suburban pressure, farmers have sold development rights for more than $10,000 an acre.[11] At those prices, rather little farmland will be saved, probably not enough to enable the farm support businesses to remain profitable. The preserved farmland will likely become "islands" of open land in a suburban landscape. In Maryland and Pennsylvania, a landowner may apply to buy back the development rights—at the appreciated value of those rights—if, at any time after twenty-five years, the farm becomes surrounded by development and it is simply not possible to farm the property.

The Transfer of Development Rights

The transfer of development rights (TDR) is the moving of development potential from one parcel of land to another, unlike the purchase of development rights in which the right to develop is retired. The number of development rights that can be transferred depends on the how many development-rights "credits" the government allocates and how much development potential the government allows in growth areas.

A local government creates a market in development rights through the comprehensive planning process. The local government first identifies and maps areas for preservation. These are called the "sending" areas. The local government then issues development-rights credits to landowners in the sending areas. Next, the government identifies and maps "receiving" areas and requires that developers who wish to build at increased densities in the receiving areas first purchase a certain number of development-rights credits from the landowners in the sending areas. For example, in Montgomery County, Maryland, a suburban area north of Washington, D.C., that has operated a TDR program since 1982, the county created a sending area of agricultural land first by down-zoning ninety thousand acres from one dwelling per five acres to one dwelling unit per twenty-five acres. Then, one transferable development-rights credit was issued for every five acres in the sending area. The county also identified receiving areas in which a developer could build an extra unit per acre by purchasing one transferable development right.

While the purchase of development rights has enjoyed greater popularity, several counties and municipalities in fringe areas have adopted transfer-of-development-rights programs to protect farm and forestlands, scenic areas, and wetlands (see table 10.3). In the process, residential development is channeled into growth areas. Local governments have found TDRs attractive for four main reasons:

1. They want to increase density in growth areas to make full use of public sewers, water systems, and other facilities. The increased density also works in tandem with accommodating a fair share of affordable housing.
2. In many cases, private developers will pay landowners directly for the TDRs, so that public money may not be needed to complete a transfer. This means a TDR program can be cheaper to taxpayers than a PDR program.
3. Landowners receive compensation for restrictions placed on their land, thus avoiding the takings issue of the Fifth Amendment.[12]
4. Over time, a local government can preserve a significant amount of land and at the same time channel new development into growth areas. This can help the local government achieve a balanced-growth strategy.

Table 10.3 Examples of Active TDR Programs, January 1998

Location and Date Begun	*Acres Preserved*	*Number of Transfers*	*Estimated Cost*	*Type of Zone*
Calvert County, MD, 1977	7,700	450	$9 million	Single
Manheim Township, Lancaster County, PA, 1991	212	3	$.9 million	Dual
Montgomery County, MD, 1982	38,250	5,000	$60 million	Dual
Buckingham Township, Montgomery County, PA, 1995	280	3	$2 million	Single

Source: American Farmland Trust.

The prices of development rights are determined by developers' bids and landowners' asking prices, just as in a private market. Initial TDR prices in Montgomery County were about $600 an acre, but more recently they have averaged between $10,000 and $12,000 an acre.[13]

The sale of TDRs provides compensation to landowners in the sending areas in exchange for the development restrictions placed on the area. In turn, the sale of TDRs helps to keep land prices attractive to agricultural uses. Montgomery County has protected thirty-four acres of farmland through over five thousand TDR transactions.

The transfer of development rights works best in towns and counties where resource lands are clearly separated from existing development and properties planned for development. This enables the creation of distinct sending and receiving zones. Also, an active real estate market and a growing population ensure that developers will be willing to purchase TDRs in order to build more intensively in the receiving areas. A public TDR bank can help set a floor price for TDRs, which compels developers to make competitive offers. The TDR bank provides landowners with a buyer for TDRs if economic conditions are slow or developers make no offers. The public TDR bank can eventually sell TDRs to developers.

There are two major variations in the types of TDR programs (for a model TDR ordinance, see appendix 6). Mandatory TDRs feature dual zones: the down-zoning of a sending area to low-density farm or forest uses and the designation of a separate receiving area. Landowners then sell development rights as a way to receive compensation for the down-zoning.

Voluntary TDRs involve a single zone that acts as both the sending and receiving area. In the single zone, landowners have the choice between developing some or all of their land according to a fairly permissive zoning of two- to five-acre lots or selling some or all of the development rights. Calvert County, Maryland, in the Washington, D.C., metro area, began with one TDR per acre and considered transfers on a case-by-case basis. Typically, landowners would develop some land and sell off some TDRs. This was leading to a rather large number of rural residences amid farming areas and woodlands.

In 1993, Calvert County created something of a hybrid TDR program with dual zones for sending areas and receiving areas, but landowners in the sending area may develop their property by clustering development on 20 percent of the site.

Transfers within a single zone are more of a limited development technique, preserving some open space fairly near to development. This is more of a suburban cluster development technique than a farm or forest preservation approach.

With both mandatory and voluntary zoning, keeping track of how many TDRs remain with which parcels is important. When all the TDRs are transferred from a property in the sending area, a permanent conservation easement is placed on the deed, restricting development to agricultural and open-space uses. But a landowner need not sell all of the TDRs. Some can be retained to develop the land in the sending area at the allowed zoning density.

In sum, mandatory TDR programs have dual zones and depend on down-zoning in the sending area and bonus zoning in the receiving area to create landowner incentives to sell TDRs and developer incentives to buy TDRs. Voluntary TDR programs occur within a single zone and on a permit basis; receiving areas are not closely defined. For example, in San Luis Obispo County, California, TDRs are used to retire substandard lots in antiquated subdivisions by transferring the development credit to a buildable lot. The advantage of the voluntary approach appears to be greater political acceptance, but the land development patterns will be more scattered than in a mandatory program.

The transfer of development rights has not enjoyed as much popularity as the purchase of development rights because of the difficulty in establishing well-defined sending and receiving areas. In receiving areas, residents may oppose having the density of development increase. Also, developers may not perceive a real benefit in purchasing TDRs if they feel they can make money by building according to the existing zoning in the receiving areas. Landowners may be reluctant to have their property placed in a sending area because of the uncertainty of the market value of their TDRs. Both Manheim Township in Pennsylvania and Montgomery County, Maryland, have established a TDR bank in which the local government will purchase TDRs from landowners at a set price. This price puts a floor under TDR values and keeps the TDR market active in the event of a building recession. The local governments can sell the TDRs to developers at some future date.

A further problem with TDRs is that they are based on the number of acres owned and not necessarily on location, soil quality, and access to public services. Montgomery County adopted a purchase-of-development-rights program in addition to the TDR program in order to supplement the land preservation effort. But with either a single-zone or dual-zone TDR program, the landowners need not sell off all of their TDRs. Many landowners in Montgomery County have sold off some TDRs and retained the right to build one dwelling per twenty-five acres, which the zoning allows. In such instances, the TDR program acts as a form of compensable zoning. The landowners who were down-zoned from one dwelling per five acres to one dwelling per twenty-five acres received one TDR for every five acres. This for example would allow the owner of one hundred acres to sell off sixteen TDRs and keep four to develop the property at one dwelling per twenty-five acres.

Finally, a TDR program may be ineffective if the counties and municipalities do not devote the time or expertise to do the necessary community-wide planning. An effective TDR program requires certainty about where development will happen and where it will not. For example, Manheim Township, Pennsylvania, has its sending area outside its urban growth boundary and the receiving areas inside the growth boundary. The TDR program administrators should be able to determine from the start how much development can occur and even what it could look like; that is, will it be conventional housing, or will it be neotraditional housing?

A Farmland Protection Package

Farmland protection makes sense only if agriculture is a profitable business. As author and farmer Victor Davis Hanson warns, "You have to make money in farming; it is no longer a way of life."[14] Wise community leaders will recognize that farming is a business that provides aesthetic, environmental, and fiscal benefits. Once farming leaves a community, it is nearly impossible to bring it back in a big way. Even small truck farms and horse operations will not keep as much land open as large dairy, grain, and cattle enterprises. Many communities and states are realizing that no single technique can address the number and complexity of pressures on farmland and farm operations. Rather, a package of farmland protection and preservation techniques is needed to encourage farmers to stay in farming. For example, agricultural zoning may be used to restrict development, while at the same time preferential property taxation keeps farm property taxes down and right-to-farm laws protect the farmer's normal farming practices. In 1995, Montgomery County adopted a 100 percent abatement on county property taxes on lands under a perpetual conservation easement. This created an incentive for landowners to preserve their land because the county in effect said that property taxes would not become a heavy burden on owners of preserved land.

Zoning and growth boundaries, discussed in chapter 9, are mandatory protection techniques. But most protection techniques are voluntary, such as PDR, TDR, agricultural districts, and preferential property taxation. Combining zoning with PDR or TDR and agricultural districts and preferential taxation can provide medium- to long-term protection that is financially attractive to farmers.

An important action that most local governments overlook is agricultural economic development. Farming is an industry, and more jobs are created in processing and transporting farm products than on the farm. Local farmers' markets and zoning that allows side businesses on farms can go far toward keeping farmers in business and keeping land open.

Forestland Protection

Forestry, more than any other private land use, demands a willingness to act for the future. In the words of the Roman orator Cicero, "He plants trees to benefit another generation." Many of the decisions affecting future timber production must be made years in advance and require a long-term investment in land, equipment, and management. Commercial timber takes between twenty-five and one hundred years to reach maturity. Because of this long time before harvest and because timberland usually sells for under a thousand dollars per acre, forestland is especially vulnerable to price competition for other land uses. Local land values rise as forestland is subdivided below commercially viable sizes and purchased for residential and recreational uses. A proliferation of small tracts often prohibits the construction of roads needed for timber management and harvest. The likelihood increases of spillovers from such forest practices—noise, herbicides, pesticides, and slashburn—onto nearby residences. And the more people living in or near the forest, the greater the risk of forest fires.

People are attracted by the privacy of the woods. Your neighbors can't see you through the trees, and your house is harder to find off main roads.

But the creation of small forestland parcels suggests that a large amount of forestland may not be available for future timber production. As more forestland is converted to house sites, a critical mass of available timber may be lost; and timber harvesting then becomes uneconomical. Mills close and commercial timber production vanishes from the area.

As population increases, some metro-fringe communities have enacted ordinances banning the clear-cutting of timber or logging altogether.[15] But more contentious is the struggle between forest landowners and neighbors over whether logging should occur even with government approval. One such controversy over logging pitted neighbors against each other in the Alpine Valley of east-central Sonoma County, California. Landowner Robert Harper filed a timber harvest plan with the California Department of Forestry to selectively cut twenty-seven acres of Douglas fir. Several neighbors threatened to go to court over the proposed logging, citing loss of privacy with fewer trees, threats to drinking water supplies and wildlife habitat, and increased flood damage.[16] This kind of conflict over the metro-fringe forest seems likely to continue, if not escalate.

Commercial forestland is concentrated in the Pacific Northwest, northern Maine, and the Southeast. Both commercial and noncommercial forestlands in fringe areas are especially vulnerable to conversion. Because of the length of time involved in timber stock reaching maturity, forestlands are vulnerable to changes in timber prices, price competition from more intensive land uses, and annual property taxes based on the market value of the land and timber rather than the use for forestry. Even major forest products companies have real estate subsidiaries to develop timberlands for nonforestry uses. As forestland is subdivided and sold for nonforestry uses, local land values rise and increase the opportunity cost of holding land for timber production. The forestland then is typically split up into small parcels of under fifty acres. Owners of these parcels have little incentive to spend time and energy becoming informed about forest management. In fringe areas it is common for owners of small forest parcels to use their timber resources primarily for firewood to heat their homes.

A few states have adopted special zoning ordinances to protect forestlands. Oregon employs timber conservation zones for forestlands capable of producing fifty or more cubic feet per acre per year of Douglas fir, the main commercial species. Minimum lot sizes in fringe areas range from forty to eighty acres per dwelling. Also forest landowners in those zones may apply for use-value property taxation, though harvested forestlands must be restocked for use-value assessment to continue. The tax break must be repaid if the land is sold for a nonforest use. In addition, forest landowners are exempt from nuisance ordinances that would limit standard forestry practices.

Some counties in California have created Timber Production Zones (TPZs) designating lands exclusively for timber production. Landowners receive property tax reductions in return for signing a binding agreement to keep the land in forest use. A landowner may petition the county to remove land from the TPZ, but permission may be granted only after a public review; even then the landowner must keep the land in forest use for another ten years. One researcher commented:

> Zoning land as TPZ helps control the influence of urban pressure on increasing land values. Land use is restricted, and speculative pressures are dampened because the zone runs for ten years. Available evidence shows that lands zoned at TPZ sell for less than lands not so zoned. This is some indication that with TPZ, land can be acquired at a price related to its ability to grow timber.[17]

Protecting Natural Areas and Critical Environmental Resources

In addition to productive resource lands, fringe areas contain important natural features such as wetlands, floodplains, unique flora and fauna habitats, and geological formations. Fringe communities have generally been lax about the protection of natural areas. These areas are usually privately owned, and public restrictions are often spotty because the public health, safety, and welfare values of these natural resources have been taken for granted or undervalued. The value of environmentally sensitive areas has only just begun to be understood and recognized by a large audience. Wetlands, for instance, provide a buffer against flooding, act as groundwater recharge areas and water filtration systems, and provide wildlife breeding grounds.

Development patterns should respond to the carrying capacity of a site. As explained previously, carrying capacity is the ability of a site to support development without undue adverse environmental impacts or risk to the development.

The most common means of protecting environmentally sensitive areas in the fringe is through zoning. Sensitive-area zoning restrictions include: (1) limitations on the types of land uses permitted—for example, commercial uses might be banned in a floodplain or the filling of wetlands might be prohibited; (2) the use of large minimum lot sizes and restrictions on the location of buildings; (3) performance standards that express the maximum acceptable level of disturbance to natural areas; and (4) cluster zoning to concentrate development on a portion of a property to preserve open space and minimize the environmental impact. Cluster zoning often means that a developer will have to redesign a project, but the economic value may be enhanced because of the improved amenities.

Capital improvements programs, involving the location of new roads and sewer and water lines, can be effective in directing development away from environmentally sensitive areas. Unfortunately, few communities below ten thousand inhabitants use capital improvements programs, and the scattered development patterns typically found in fringe areas make them difficult and expensive to implement.

In many parts of the rural-urban fringe, patches of green space are held hostage by nearby development. These bits of field and forest are often too small or rough for farming and do not have enough timber to sustain a forestry operation. These open spaces can provide areas for recreation and buffers between neighboring properties.

Attempts to zone land for low-density "conservation" have met with little success. The two cases in which conservation zoning has given some valuable protection are: (1) as an overlay zone for floodplains to limit building in flood-prone areas; and (2) as a steep slope ordinance (see appendix 3) to discourage development on hillsides. In these cases, conservation zoning has the clear purpose of protecting health and safety.

But, for the most part, strict conservation zoning may allow very little economic use of the property. A wildlife habitat zone of one dwelling per fifty acres that does not allow farming or forestry would probably not withstand legal challenges. On the other hand, a conservation zone that allowed one dwelling for every five acres might do little to protect wildlife habitat. For a government agency or a private land trust to buy the development rights to conservation land or buy the land outright for a wildlife refuge might be the best conservation solution.

Greenways, Trails, and Open Space

Greenways and trails have gained widespread public support as methods to link suburbs and cities with the nearby countryside. Many states and communities have authorized large amounts of money to buy land to create greenways. Greenways along watercourses help filter runoff before it reaches the water. In 1997 Jefferson County, Alabama, dedicated $30 million over ten years to purchase property along stream corridors to reduce nonpoint pollution and improve water quality. Oregon, through its state land-use process, established the Willamette River Greenway; in rural areas, no new development is allowed within one hundred feet of the river. The greenway has been credited with significantly improving the water quality of the Willamette.

Greenways also provide wildlife habitat, and when there is public access, recreation activities, such as boating, canoeing, swimming, and fishing. Greenways often incorporate paths for hiking, walking, and jogging. Trails may be dirt paths, of crushed rock, or even paved. People can travel along on foot, bicycle, or rollerblades. Greenways and trails can attract tourists as well and so create a local industry. Moreover, greenways can be a good first step to get counties to undertake water planning and recreation plans.

Abandoned railroad corridors often contain the only open space available for making trails. Rails-to-trails projects are also often the cheapest way to develop trails. The conversion of abandoned railroad beds into trails has given a major boost to tourism and recreation. There are some seven hundred rails-to-trails projects in operation nationwide. The nonprofit Rails-to-Trails Conservancy promotes the reuse of rail beds. The ISTEA plans drafted by several metropolitan planning organizations include rails-to-trails and rails-with-trails (trails alongside active railways) as nonmotorized connections to the intermodal transportation network. For example, Metro Portland's 2040 plan advocates a network of bicycle trails connecting to mass transit lines.

Open-space projects include greenways, natural areas, and parklands. Since the late 1980s, most states and several local governments, often with voter approval, have substantially increased expenditures for buying up open space as it has become more scarce. For instance, California took a huge step in 1988 when voters approved $776 million in bonds to protect natural areas, farmland, and Pacific coastline. In 1990, Florida passed a $3 billion ten-year bond for land conservation. In 1992, a citizens' initiative in Colorado earmarked $35 million a year in state lottery proceeds for the Colorado Open Space program to purchase parkland, natural areas, wildlife habitat, and conservation easements to farm and ranch lands. Pennsylvania's Key '93 program to purchase parkland and natural areas was launched with $50 million and receives about $10 million a year from the state real estate transfer tax. In 1996, Portland, Oregon, voters passed a regional $135 million park and open-space bond.

On the edge of Philadelphia, Chester County, set in motion a regional effort for land preservation with the approval of a $50 million bond program in 1989. In 1990, Chester County's western neighbor, Lancaster County, sold $10 million in bonds for farmland and open space preservation. In 1994, Montgomery County, north of Chester County, approved a $100 million open-space bond program, and Bucks County followed with a $59 million open-space bond program in 1996. (The Bucks County program is expected to leverage an additional $56 million in state and municipal funds over ten years.) The substantial sums of money approved for land preservation are a clear indication that maintaining open space and environmental quality is a high priority among fringe residents, and they are willing to pay for it. Local politicians who fear tax revolts should take notice.

Chester County is the second-leading agricultural county in Pennsylvania but lies within thirty miles of Philadelphia, the nation's fourth largest city. Growth pressures have been intense and sprawl a problem. In the 1980s, the county was losing farmland to development at a rate of one hundred acres a day. In 1989, the county commissioners appointed a citizen task force to study growth issues. The task force recommended a $50 million bond issue to purchase parks, natural areas, and development rights to farmland.

When the bond issue was put before the voters that fall, they overwhelmingly approved a nonbinding referendum for the $50 million. Emboldened by the strong outcome, the county commissioners then formally approved the sale of the bonds. The cost of the bond program was estimated at $35 per year per household over twenty years.

The bond money has enabled the county and local governments to leverage another $42 million in government and private funds. The county offered townships a 50 percent match up to $250,000 for park acquisition, but first the townships had to map out their open space and identify parcels for acquisition. A total of more than twelve thousand acres were purchased and preserved with the money. "Everybody thought we got good value for the money,"[18] says Peter Hausmann, a commercial real estate developer who led the referendum effort.

Since spending the bond money, the Chester County commissioners have included $5 million in their annual budget for open-space projects. That kind of political momentum will not soon diminish.

Hausmann contends that open-space protection is an investment in infrastructure and economic development. He predicts that as the baby-boom generation ages and retires, they will travel. Tourism and recreation will be growth industries. On the other hand, he argues, a quality environment creates jobs. Most new jobs are being formed by small companies, not large corporations. With the ongoing communications revolution and the global economy, companies and their workers have greater choices about where to set up business and live.

Land Trusts: Private Action and Public-Private Partnerships

Land trusts have gained increasing popularity in recent years as a means for preserving agricultural land and natural areas in the fringe. A land trust is a private nonprofit organization that has qualified as a charitable organization under Section 501(c)(3) of the Internal Revenue Code. A land trust may receive donations of property, conservation easements (development rights), or money. Donations may qualify as tax deductions (see box 10.4). A land trust may also purchase property and conservation easements.

Land trusts hold considerable promise, either operating alone or in tandem with government agencies, for preserving natural areas and farmland in fringe areas. By the end of 1997, there were more than fourteen hundred land trusts nationwide.

For example, the Vermont Land Trust, has acquired over 600 easements on more than 147,000 acres of farmland, forestland, and natural areas since 1974. It often works closely with the Vermont Housing and Conservation Board, a state agency, in a public-private partnership to preserve farmland.

At the national level, The Nature Conservancy has protected nearly 7 million acres of natural lands. Also, the Land Trust Alliance serves

Box 10.4 Donation of Conservation Easement Example for 100 Acres of Natural Area: Open Land, Forest, and Wetland

$600,000	Appraised Fair Market Value
$340,000	Appraised Value Restricts to Open Space and Wildlife Habitat
$260,000	Appraised Conservation Easement Value

Landowner's Adjusted Gross Income = $100,000
$30,000 × 6 = maximum one-year deduction over six years*
(assuming a constant income of $100,000 a year) = $180,000
(The landowner cannot use $80,000 of the $260,000 donation, and it is lost.)

Total tax savings = about $50,000

* 30% of Adjusted Gross Income is the maximum deduction for one year, but the landowner can spread the donation out over six years. Depending on income, however, the landowner may not be able to use the entire donation as an income tax deduction.

as an information clearinghouse for land trusts and sponsors an annual national conference (see "Contacts" at the back of the book).

Many landowners have a deep and abiding love for their land and do not wish to see it developed into shopping malls and housing subdivisions. But many landowners also distrust government. Land trusts can and do play a useful role both in working with landowners to preserve land and as intermediaries between landowners and government agencies who share a common interest in keeping the land intact. Of special importance is the fact that when land trusts hold a conservation easement, they also have a responsibility to monitor the property and enforce the terms of the easement. This sort of monitoring is often lacking in public land-use planning.

Local governments are increasingly calling upon land trusts to participate in land-use planning efforts. Land trusts often have a good understanding of the extent of sensitive lands and wildlife habitat in a region and the need to protect large blocks to maintain ecosystems.

Another role for land trusts is to hold conservation easements on lands that are left open as parts of residential developments. In building limited developments, developers are looking to retain some open space that will add to the amenities of the projects. There is some evidence that home buyers are willing to pay more for residences with protected open space.[19]

Henry Richmond, executive director of the National Growth Management Leadership Project, applauds the increase in land trusts but warns that they are not able to protect land at a rate anywhere close to the rate at which open land is being converted to development.[20] While the private role is important and growing, a government role is also necessary to guide the overall land-use planning and growth management process in the fringe.

Regional Water Planning

Most large cities obtain a major portion of their water supplies from sources many miles away. San Francisco has the Hetch Hetchy Reservoir in the Sierra Nevadas. Boston draws from the Quabbin Reservoir seventy miles to the west. Phoenix has purchased "water ranches" to suck up the underlying groundwater and takes a share of the distant Colorado River. Los Angeles also takes part of the Colorado River and pumps water in from the Owens Valley over 200 miles away.

In the arid West, an adequate water supply is the big concern; access to water brings value to land as the 1974 movie *Chinatown* brilliantly illustrated in the case of Los Angeles. In the East where rainfall is plentiful, water quality poses a greater challenge.

As fringe areas spread out, they are entering watersheds that feed the nation's leading cities and suburbs. The development of fringe land not only competes for water supplies with the far-off cities and suburbs, it also brings a serious pollution threat. The pollution comes partly from sewage treatment plants that expel wastewater into rivers and streams. Failing on-site septic systems, whose locations and numbers are difficult to identify, leak sewage into groundwater and sometimes directly into waterways. Fertilizers and pesticides from lawns and runoff from pavement make their way into water supplies. And farm sources such as cattle defecating in streams, manure and chemical fertilizers washing off fields, and soil erosion contribute to water pollution.

As the fringe becomes more developed, the water supply and quality problems intensify. Farms and ranches become developed in housing, commercial strips, and parking lots; more impervious surface means more runoff because less soil is exposed to absorb rainfall. More on-site septic systems are installed, and more sewage treatment plants are built to service the increased population.

Just as the ISTEA program has begun to join metro area transportation and land-use planning, so regional water planning must be linked with land-use planning. One such effort already under way is New York City's attempt to protect its water supplies in nineteen reservoirs in the Catskill Mountains, in the Delaware Valley, and east of the Hudson River. The U.S. Environmental Protection Agency told New York City that it had to either build a plant to filter its drinking water or clean up the water at the source by the year 2002. The filtration plant would cost an estimated $5 billion and another $300 million a year in operating expenses.[21]

In January of 1997, the city of New York embarked on an ambitious plan to coordinate efforts with metro fringe counties and towns and pay about $1 billion to protect land near reservoirs from encroaching development, improve farming practices, repair sewage treatment plants, and track down polluters.

The watershed that supplies 9 million New Yorkers with drinking water covers about two thousand square miles in eight counties. As of 1997, the city owned under 4 percent of the land in the watershed.[22] Meanwhile, most of the privately held land near the reservoirs is subject to only minimal zoning restrictions. The city plans to protect more than 300,000 acres through outright purchase or buying development rights by the year 2002 at a cost of up to $260 million. The protected land is intended to form a buffer zone around the reservoirs and along waterways. But clearly not all the land will be protected. The city cannot purchase land with any buildings on it or any wetlands under twelve acres, or ban the construction of impervious surfaces on land beyond one hundred feet of major streams.

Over $200 million is earmarked for upgrading sewage treatment plants. As much as $35 million is being spent to improve the manure management practices of dairy farmers so that bacteria such as giardia, crytpospiridium, and E. coli do not enter the streams and end up in reservoirs.[23] Environmental assessments of farms will be conducted, then whole farm plans drafted with landowner input to control pesticides, herbicides, pathogens, and soil erosion. As a gesture of good will, the city is giving roughly $72 million to communities in the watershed for economic development and local infrastructure projects. The city has allocated $14 million for replacing failing on-site septic systems but has to find them first. However, the city has a watershed police force to hunt for polluters!

Summary

The fringe countryside presents major growth management challenges because of the large area and the competing demands for land. While suburbs are often concerned with maintaining some open space in their communities, many fringe areas still have viable farms and forestry operations that are worth protecting. Natural areas and wildlife habitat can help to buffer those working landscapes.

At the same time, the countryside can be joined with fringe settlements, suburbs, and even cities through a network of greenways and trails. These corridors can provide recreation activities as well as protection for water quality and wildlife habitat.Finally, core cities and suburbs are increasingly dependent on fringe areas for water supplies. Careful land-use planning will be needed to protect water quality and quantity over the long run.

CHAPTER 11

Growth Management Case Studies: Common Problems, Different Solutions

We know how to grow more efficiently. But to get to that point will probably cause some pain.

—*Evan Richert, Maine State Planning Director*

The cliché is that we have to grow, or we go backward. Well, California proves the fallacy of that. Our big upsurge in population came from people who left California because they were so dissatisfied with growth there. . . . But now the same thing is going to happen here.

—*Jim Nelms, former mayor of Brighton, Colorado*

The following case studies illustrate how different places are accommodating growth and change in fringe areas. Some places are enjoying more success than others. Some are trying harder to manage growth. But residents in all of these places recognize that growth pressures will not dissipate any time soon. Growth management will be necessary for years to come.

Albuquerque, New Mexico, and Larimer County, Colorado: Responding to the Population Boom in the Intermountain West

Since the early 1980s, the states of the intermountain West—Utah, Colorado, Nevada, Idaho, New Mexico, and Arizona—have experienced a tidal wave of population growth. In the 1980s, each state grew by more than 14 percent, with Arizona in front at 35 percent.[1] In the 1990s, the pace of growth increased in many parts of the intermountain West. According to writer and consultant Jeff Gersh, from 1990 to 1995 thirty-nine counties in the region grew by 20 to 65 percent. Two million people have moved to the Rockies during that time, and about a third have settled in those thirty-nine counties.[2] Between 1990 and 1995, Colorado was the nation's fifth fastest-growing state growing by fifty thousand more people than during the entire decade of the eighties.[3]

The reasons behind this boom are many: (1) Californians migrating to the intermountain states; (2) an influx of retirees, especially in Arizona; (3) job opportunities, particularly in high-tech industries in Utah (Corel-WordPerfect), Idaho (Micron), Colorado (Hewlett-Packard), Arizona (Motorola), and New Mexico (Intel); (4) the lure of the West with its interesting mix of cowboy, Indian, and Hispanic cultures; and (5) spectacular scenery and skiing, hiking, biking, climbing, and rafting opportunities in the mountains, rivers, and wide-open spaces.

Some of the population boom has been absorbed in fringe areas. The chance to have a "ranchette" to go home to in the evening is very attractive. The metro areas of the West have been largely shaped by the automobile; they are more spread out than eastern metro areas, and the core city is less dominant. And traditionally, there have been few land-use controls.

Albuquerque, New Mexico, and Larimer County, Colorado, are two of the West's leading examples of efforts to control sprawl. Both places are projected to grow dramatically over the next twenty-five years. Because neither New Mexico nor Colorado has statewide land-use planning goals and guidelines, the local governments have been left to grapple with planning for development and conservation.

Albuquerque: A City without Suburbs?

Albuquerque, the Hot Air Balloon Capital of the World, has grown rapidly since 1980, when the city contained 333,000 people. By 1990, the population had risen to 385,000; by 1997, 410,000. Estimates project 454,000 residents in the year 2002. What is remarkable about Albuquerque is that the city's percentage of the Bernalillo County population has held steady at around 80 percent, and the city contained over 80 percent of the region's tax base in 1990.[4]

The reason? Over the past forty years, the amount of land within the Albuquerque city limits has nearly tripled through annexations. As a result, the problem of urbanites fleeing to the suburbs and beyond to the fringe is much less pronounced. Interestingly, the racial makeup of Albuquerque and of its environs is about the same: 3 percent black, 35 percent Hispanic, and 62 percent white in the city and 3 percent black, 37 percent Hispanic, and 60 percent white in the outskirts. Clearly, white flight has not been a problem.

In his 1993 book *Cities without Suburbs*, former Albuquerque mayor David Rusk explains the city's strategy of expanding the city limits to include areas that would otherwise become suburbs. Rusk argues that "the iron rule of urban sprawl is 'Today's winners become tomorrow's losers,'" meaning that suburbs that capture a region's wealth today will be overtaken by newer, more remote suburbs in the future.[5] Rusk goes on to show that as Albuquerque grew by swallowing up would-be suburbs, problems of inequality of incomes and public services have been much lower compared with those of East Coast cities and their suburbs. "The real city is now the whole metropolitan area," Rusk explains.[6]

The act of adding new lands onto a city is virtually unheard of in the Northeast. Not surprisingly, that is also the part of the United States with some of the most fragmented local governments and the most disjointed and racially segregated development patterns, thanks in part to fiscal zoning by local officials hungry for property tax revenues. The separation of wealthy suburbs from poor inner cities has done little to promote racial harmony, equitable school districts, adequate public facilities, and economic opportunity.

Albuquerque now covers about 150 square miles, with a density of not quite three thousand people per square mile. This density is low compared to that of East Coast cities; and it is half as dense as the expected density of 6,250 people per square mile in Greater Portland, Oregon, in the year 2040. But despite its elastic boundaries, Albuquerque has a density three times greater than that of Houston. Perhaps Albuquerque comes close to resembling Frank Lloyd Wright's Broadacre City, discussed in chapter 2. But Jane Holtz Kay, author of *Asphalt Nation*, dismisses Albuquerque as "that sprawling noncity."[7] Nonetheless between 1976 and 1996, Albuquerque spent $44 million to purchase twenty-two thousand acres of scenic mountain and volcano lands,[8] and in 1997, Albuquerque voters approved a $12.8 million bond issue for acquiring additional open land and parks.[9]

Still, the challenges of fringe growth and suburban sprawl are present. There is in effect a race between the consolidation of Albuquerque by increasing its size and the forces that would fragment the metro area. Albuquerque and Bernalillo County have had a joint comprehensive plan since the 1970s. But the metro area outside of Albuquerque consists of 250,000 people spread across four counties, seventeen municipalities, and nine Indian tribal governments. This region extends for up to a one-hour drive from the city, encompassing an area considerably larger than the city itself.

The land-use patterns in the outer metro region feature the separation of houses from work and shopping. This translates into dependence on the automobile and the greater expense of more roads and the extension of sewer and water lines. A proposed freeway that would cut through Petroglyph National Monument west of Albuquerque has raised a debate over suburban sprawl. Air pollution is a problem, especially on winter mornings, when inversions trap warmer, dirtier air underneath a layer of cold air. Water supplies are tenuous.

Water poses a very real limit to growth in the Southwest. In 1997, Albuquerque began to rely mainly on the Rio Grande River for its municipal supply. The city will abandon a regional aquifer by the year 2004. Per-person water consumption will have to decline from 250 gallons a day to 175 gallons to balance the reduction in supply. If water conservation efforts are successful, Albuquerque should be able to sustain a population of 700,000, which it is expected to reach by the year 2060.[10] But Albuquerque faces limits on what it can withdraw from the Rio Grande. Both Texas and Mexico also have claims on the river through water treaties.

Most open space in the outer fringe exists as islands in a sea of development. Many communities lack discernible edges, and it is impossible to tell where one community ends and another begins. Hobby farms and ranchettes dominate the agriculture in Bernalillo County. Although the county had 415,000 acres defined as agricultural land in 1992, agricultural products were valued at only $22 million. Four hundred of the county's five hundred farms and ranches were less than fifty acres in size, and most of those produced less than $2,500 a year in agricultural products. Only thirty-three farms and ranches had annual sales of over $25,000.

So although Albuquerque has maintained its population, economic base, and stature as a city in its region, those achievements may not be enough to discourage the overall growth in the size of the region, or enough to promote coordinated planning among local governments for transportation, air and water quality, and the location of new development. As a result, haphazard fringe growth is likely to continue, though probably not as much as in other places because of rugged terrain, limited water supplies, and Albuquerque's appetite for annexing land.

Fort Collins and Larimer County, Colorado

Colorado has experienced one of the fastest growth rates of any state in the 1990s. Between 1990 and 1996, its population increased by 16 percent,[11] and the Front Range along the eastern slope of the Rockies added 320,000 residents. Another 1 million people are expected in the Front Range by the year 2020.[12] The Rockies have drawn new residents with scenic open spaces, recreational opportunities, fairly clean air and water, and jobs. At the same time, the well-known impacts of growth have surfaced: houses and offices pushing into the rangeland, bringing traffic congestion, noise, and air pollution. The state of Colorado has nurtured residential sprawl in the countryside since Senate Bill 35 of 1972 allowed the creation of thirty-five-acre subdivisions by right. As a result, in the 1990s, Colorado has been losing ranch land at a rate of ninety thousand acres a year.[13]

Larimer County, at the northern end of the Front Range, and its county seat, Fort Collins, provide a good example of a small but burgeoning metropolitan area that is struggling to manage growth. Larimer County covers 2,640 square miles of north-central Colorado. Over half of the county is federal land, mostly the Roosevelt National Forest and the spectacular Rocky Mountain National Park. In 1996, 210,000 people were living in Larimer County, with 60,000 on unincorporated county lands. The majority of people reside in Fort Collins and Loveland, and only about one mile of open land separates the two cities. Larimer County and Weld County to the east make up the Fort Collins metropolitan statistical area. See figure 11.1.

Fort Collins, the county seat, has 101,000 inhabitants. The main public employer is Colorado State University, and the main private employer is Hewlett-Packard. Fort Collins sits on the Front Range, fifty-five miles north of Boulder, and is part of a two-hundred-mile development corridor that stretches along Interstate 25 from Pueblo, Colorado, north through Denver to the Wyoming border. One of the impacts of the recent growth has been greater levels of air pollution from automobiles, trucks, and wood-burning stoves that becomes trapped during winter inversions. The cold air coming off the Rockies seals in the warmer air below, so smoke and exhaust cannot readily escape.

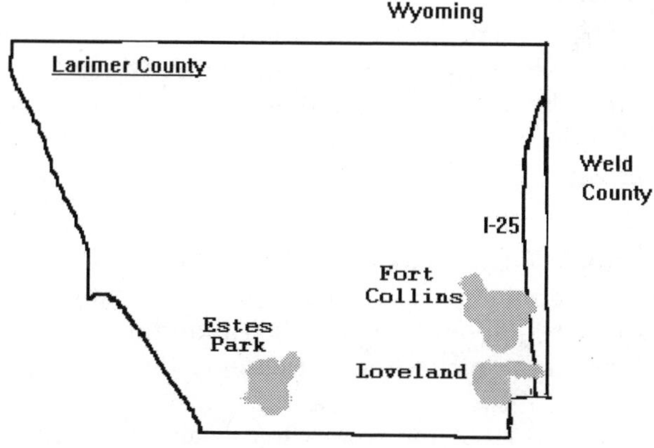

Figure 11.1 Larimer County, Colorado.

Until 1970, Fort Collins was a fairly quiet college town. Between 1970 and 1980, however, it annexed county land and grew from 43,337 to 65,092 inhabitants, a 50 percent jump. Meanwhile, Larimer County added two-thirds more residents to reach nearly 150,000. In the 1980s, the population of Fort Collins increased by another 22,000.

Over the past twenty-five years, Larimer County has added population at a rate of about 3.5 percent a year. If that rate continues, in twenty-five years the county will have 432,000 residents. The Larimer County Transportation Plan projects 316,000 people, and the state of Colorado, 294,000.[14]

Where will these new inhabitants live and work? Former county commissioner Janet Duvall summarizes the county's planning dilemma:

> Based on current zoning, over 60,000 new housing units could potentially be built outside city limits. With 2.65 people living in the average rural home, that's like adding another town larger than Fort Collins in the county on top of the growth taking place inside all existing cities. If Larimer County totally built out according to current zoning, most of us would not want to live here because our quality of life would be lost. At the same time, landowner expectations have been built on this zoning that has been in place for over 30 years.[15]

To complicate matters, residential development within the urban growth areas is not planned for high density. According to the county planning staff:

> New or proposed lots within the urban growth areas average .9 acres in size, while lots outside the growth areas average 3.3 acres. The average lot size within urban growth areas is considerably larger than the 12,000 square feet that is generally considered the largest average urban lot. Continued development of these large lots in the urban growth areas would lead to higher service costs and require expansion of the urban growth area.[16]

About one-third of Larimer County is agricultural land, with cattle ranching the main enterprise. Of the county's twelve hundred farms and ranches in 1992, about half were less than fifty acres. Only one-sixth of all farms and ranches registered more than $25,000 a year in gross sales.

Between 1987 and 1992, the county lost nearly thirty-five thousand acres of farm and ranch land. Nonetheless, it has a very respectable

$95 million-a-year agricultural industry. One reason for the loss of farm and ranch land is that the state of Colorado exempts new lots of thirty-five or more acres from subdivision review.

In response, Larimer County appointed a committee to recommend alternatives to thirty-five-acre lots. The committee agreed upon a clustering of residential development in rural areas. The cluster density would not change any existing zoning, which varies from one dwelling for every 2.29 acres to one dwelling per 10 acres. A maximum of 20 percent of a site could be developed, but at least 80 percent would have to remain as open space. Although clustering is not required by the county, by the end of 1997 there were twenty rural cluster projects in the works.

At the current rural residential densities, on a 100-acre site there could be from ten to forty dwellings on 20 acres with 80 acres left open. A development of forty dwellings on 20 acres is a suburban pod-type of subdivision. The danger with that approach is that it could easily lead to clustered sprawl.

By contrast, neighboring Weld County uses a tough standard of a 160-acre minimum lot size to protect land in its agricultural zone.

Many residents of Fort Collins and Larimer County have a strong desire to protect the remaining open landscape, and they recognize that region-wide cooperation is necessary. For several years, Larimer County has explored creating a transfer-of-development-rights program to protect critical natural areas and the buffer lands between Fort Collins and Loveland. As yet no receiving areas have been identified, but county planners have recommended that those areas have adequate public services and facilities.

In 1995, county voters passed an eight-year 1/4-cent sales tax to raise funds for an open-space preservation program. In 1996, the sales tax—known as the Help Preserve Open Spaces tax—brought in $5.4 million. A total of $12.5 million was committed to projects, with $3.4 million leveraged from Colorado's Great Outdoors Colorado program. Open lands eligible for preservation include ranch land, natural lands, wildlife habitat, parks and trails, and large open spaces, which have been identified through county plans. The Poudre–Big Thompson Rivers Legacy Project, the major project so far, will protect over eight thousand acres of land stretching from the foothills to Greeley. Partners in the project include municipalities, Great Outdoors Colorado, land trusts, and private individuals.

The county commissioners have hired staff for the Open Lands program and have appointed an Open Lands Advisory Board to help with long-term efforts to protect open space. Said county commissioner Jim Disney, "Everyone living here today appreciates the Larimer County Open Lands Program. But the people of future generations will benefit the most. They'll look back and say, 'We're really glad that the people of Larimer County voted to preserve open space back in 1995.'"[17]

Intergovernmental agreements have been a hallmark of Larimer County's growth management style. In the 1970s, Larimer County and the cities of Loveland and Fort Collins jointly agreed to establish urban service areas. Since 1980, urban growth areas have been set around Fort Collins and Loveland. One purpose of the growth areas has been to keep Fort Collins and Loveland as separate communities, even though they are only about a mile apart. These cities, with the help of the county identified Cooperative Planning Areas and Community, influence areas to promote orderly, phased growth (see figure 11.2). In 1994, the county and the town of Berthoud signed an intergovernmental agreement that established an urban growth boundary around the town. In 1997, Larimer County and the town of Estes Park approved an intergovernmental agreement to set up a joint planning commission for the Estes Valley, gateway to Rocky Mountain National Park.

The county adopted a master plan in 1988 that soon became inadequate to deal with the steady growth. In 1997, the county approved a new master plan, based on the concepts of *consistency* (between county and local plans), *concurrency* (requiring that adequate public facilities be in place before the expansion of urban areas occurs), *cooperation* (between county and local governments through intergovernmental agreements), and *compatibility* of (new development with existing development and natural systems through environmen-

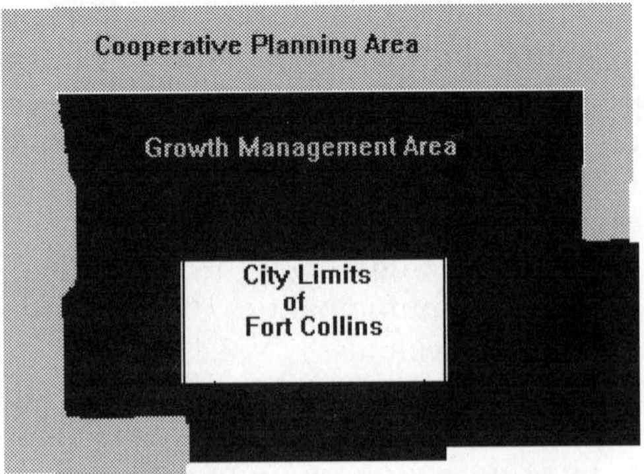

Figure 11.2 Growth Management Areas Around the City of Fort Collins, Colorado.

tal review and performance standards). The thrust of the new master plan is to influence the timing, location, and quality of new development.

Larimer County has emphasized cooperative planning between the county government and local governments. The use of growth boundaries to contain urban sprawl, the designation of Cooperative Planning Areas and Community Influence Areas adjacent to growth boundaries of Fort Collins and Loveland, and the expenditure of public funds to preserve key rural properties are laudable steps. However, Larimer County is poised to experience substantial growth of at least eighty thousand people over the next twenty-five years. And many of the newcomers will be tempted to settle in the countryside. The creation of thirty-five-acre lots to avoid subdivision review and the widespread application of rural residential zoning with a cluster requirement may not discourage many people from moving to the countryside and ultimately may defeat the purpose of the growth boundaries. Long-time Colorado planning consultant Bill Lamont believes that the sprawl of the Front Range will not be contained "unless we have a statewide growth management measure."[18]

The Twin Cities: A Tale of Two Counties on the Fringe

The seven-county Twin Cities metropolitan area is the economic powerhouse of Minnesota, as well as home to nearly half of the state's 4.6 million people. The Minneapolis and St. Paul region has grown steadily, thanks both to the strong economy and to the absence of mountains or large bodies of water that could impede sprawl. Even the harsh winters with sub-zero temperatures and a biting wind chill have not proven much of a deterrent.

An elaborate network of highways has helped the Twin Cities metro area become the third least-dense metropolitan area, with only Atlanta and Kansas City averaging fewer people per square mile. But accommodating growth in a sprawling pattern requires large amounts of land. Between 1970 and 1984, the population of the Twin Cities metro area increased by 9.7 percent, but the percentage of land used for urban purposes grew by 25 percent. By the late 1990s, the Greater Twin Cities was the fastest-growing region between the upper Midwest and the East Coast.

Between 1990 and 2020, the population of the metro area is expected to grow by more than 650,000 people. And many others will be tempted to locate just beyond the metro area into adjacent fringe communities.

The Twin Cities metro area was one of the first regions in the nation to appoint a regional council in the 1960s. But thirty years later, that

Metropolitan Council is not yet elected by metro voters. Meanwhile, its annual budget has grown to over half a billion dollars, and it has authority over solid waste, transportation, and some land-use planning.

Yet this power has not enabled the council to effectively control sprawl. According to planning expert John DeGrove, the Metropolitan Council "has seen its efforts to grow responsibly undermined by its inability to influence what happens beyond the borders of its seven-county region, and by significant limitations on its ability to effectively manage urban patterns inside the Council's boundary."[19] Within the Metropolitan Urban Service Area line, Met Council planners concede that most of the growth has been in the form of uncoordinated urban sprawl.

Chisago County is located in the northeast corner of the Minneapolis–St. Paul metropolitan area but does not fall within the reach of the Met Council (see figure 11.3). Chisago was home to 37,000 inhabitants in 1995, nearly 12,000 more than in 1980. State projections had pegged the county to grow to only 32,460 inhabitants by the year 2000. The main cities are Center City, Chisago City, Forest Lake, and North Branch.

Between 1982 and 1992, Chisago County lost 19 percent of its farmland. In 1992, the county still had 138,000 acres of farmland, accounting for slightly over half of the land in the county. But farming produced only $23.7 million worth of farm products. Cattle, corn, soybeans, and hogs were the leading farm enterprises.

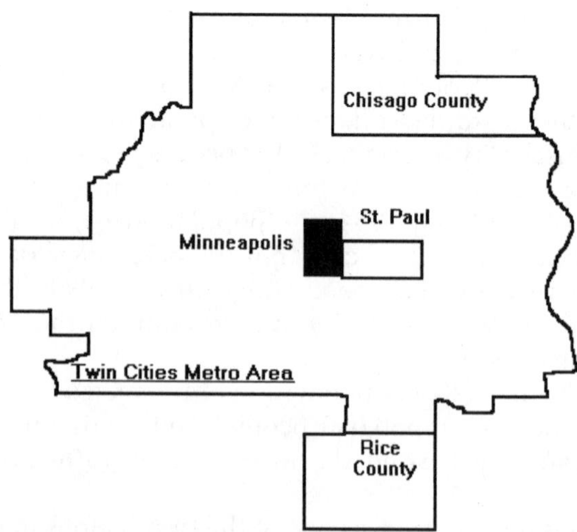

Figure 11.3 Chisago County and Rice County, Minnesota.

Rice County lies just outside the southern edge of the metro area but within a forty-five-minute commute to the Twin Cities along Interstate 35. The main cities are Northfield, home to Carleton College, and Faribault, the county seat. The county is a mosaic of small towns, forests, prairies, small lakes, wetlands, and agricultural fields. There were fifty-two thousand people living in Rice County in 1995, with 65 percent of the population in cities and 35 percent in the countryside. The population grew by only six thousand between 1980 and 1990, but by 1994 the county's population already had exceeded the projections for 2000.

In 1992, there were 227,000 acres of farmland in Rice County, reflecting a loss of 51,000 acres since 1969. Farms cover nearly three-quarters of the county, and the county farmers produce $88 million in gross sales. Hogs, dairy, cattle, corn, and soybeans were the leading enterprises. Rice County also contains one of the last remnants of the Big Woods, once a 3,400-square-mile stretch of oak, maple, and basswood forest, mixed with wetlands and prairie. Only a few thousand acres remain, but they provide a high-quality breeding ground for migratory forest songbirds. The Cannon River Watershed Partnership, the Minnesota Department of Natural Resources, the Nature Conservancy, and Friends of the Big Woods are working together to protect the Big Woods and to encourage reforestation on nearby properties.

In 1993, the Minnesota State Demographer's Office predicted that between 1990 and 2020, Rice County would be the fastest-growing nonmetro county in the state. Between 1990 and 1995, the county population increased by 5.5 percent, somewhat ahead of its predicted growth rate. Already, scattered rural residential development is fragmenting woodlots and farm fields. Between 1984 and 1994, 540 rural residences were built, nine out of ten not related to farming. Conflicts between farmers and nonfarm neighbors are on the increase. Of particular concern is the possibility of large animal feedlots that would generate large amounts of manure and odors. In the early 1990s, the county enacted an ordinance limiting the size of feedlots to 750 animal units, with a cow or steer counting as one unit and a hog as .75 unit. A variance could allow a maximum of 1,500 animal units.

The county's 1992 comprehensive plan emphasizes protecting prime agricultural lands because of their importance to the local economy, and protecting environmentally sensitive areas while providing for development.

The county zoning adopted in 1992 allows one dwelling per quarter-quarter section in the agricultural district. This looks like one house per forty acres but is somewhat different. A house may be built on a forty-acre lot, or one dwelling may be built on a five-acre piece subdivided from a forty-acre lot; but then no house can be built on that remaining thirty-five acres. While there has been some controversy about whether the five-acre lots have spurred the construction of rural residences, most residents are pleased with the agricultural zoning.

"I think the zoning density limit is working fine in preserving farmland," said county commissioner Milt Plaisance. "Being a rural county, we should support agriculture. If we don't, we'll just become a suburb area of the Twin Cities."[20]

Added county commissioner Heather Robbins, "Development is best within cities where there are municipal sewer and water services."[21]

Said realtor Paul Bedker, "Whether good or bad, Rice County's density restriction is working to preserve the rural charm that makes the county so attractive. All you have to do is drive up around Lakeville and Prior Lake and see how the many rural housing developments turn the countryside into an urban-like atmosphere far from the pastoral setting this county has so far retained."[22]

Economically, Chisago County is more closely tied to the Twin Cities region than Rice County is. In 1992, Chisago merchants enjoyed only half the retail sales of Rice County merchants; that implies that Chisago shoppers buy more goods outside the county in the Greater Twin Cities.

Both Rice and Chisago have large areas of farmland and open space. Perhaps the biggest difference is the zoning in rural areas. Chisago County employs a five-acre minimum lot size, while Rice mostly uses a forty-acre minimum lot size in its farming district. Most Chisago County landowners do not see much future in farming and so the county commissioners are allowing them to sell off large house lots so that: (1) the landowners can reap enough from the sale of land to amass a comfortable retirement nest egg; and (2) the buyers of the lots will construct high-value homes that will generate sufficient property taxes to pay for public services. The two drawbacks to this approach are the risk of groundwater pollution if the new houses use on-site septic systems in areas with a high water table, and the displeasing visual effect of dozens of large, suburban-style homes seemingly dropped at random throughout the countryside.

In 1997, the Minnesota legislature appropriated $500,000 for a Green Corridor Project aimed at preserving up to ten thousand acres in Chisago County and neighboring Washington County. That seed money could be important for preserving farms and open lands close to the St. Croix River in eastern Chisago County. But in the long run, county funds and additional state funding for land preservation will be needed.

Rice County, by virtue of its stronger farm economy, has a more wide open and unspoiled appearance than Chisago County. Many of the new rural residences have been built in the woods. Rice County citizens have discussed a variety of land protection tools and development options, including the transfer of development rights, cluster development, the purchase of development rights, and the donation of conservation easements to land trusts. Still, the zoning regulations on rural land will continue to be crucial, as will the interest of farmers to remain in farming.

Chittenden County, Vermont: Where Planning Is Not Quite Planning

In 1993, the National Trust for Historic Preservation placed the entire state of Vermont on its list of America's Most Endangered Historic Places. Trust President Richard Moe charged that "sprawl was, and still is, testing the state's commitment to the preservation of its cohesive small towns and countryside."[23] This challenge is most acute in Chittenden County, which contains over one-fifth of Vermont's population. Chittenden County stretches west from Mount Mansfield—the highest point in the state at 4,200 feet—over twenty miles to the broad blue waters of Lake Champlain, America's largest body of fresh water after the Great Lakes (see figure 11.4). In between, the Champlain Valley has a varied topography of gently rolling land interspersed with hillocks. Parts of Chittenden County suggest the classic New England landscape of tidy villages surrounded by working farms and forests. Not surprisingly, the Green Index has rated Vermont along with Hawaii as enjoying the best environmental conditions among the fifty states.[24]

A popular joke says that the best thing about Chittenden County is that it's so close to Vermont. The county stands out as Vermont's most populous county, with 141,000 people in 1997, an increase of 22 percent from 1980. A 1991 population projection by the Chittenden County Regional Planning Commission estimated that there would be 175,000 residents by 2010.[25] Chittenden and neighboring Franklin County (population 43,000) make up Vermont's only metropolitan region.

County residents verify John Herbers's observation that Vermonters are second only to North Carolinians in "living all over everywhere."[26] Burlington, Vermont's largest city, has only 40,000 people, while the virtually centerless town of Colchester with 16,000 inhabitants is the state's third largest community.

Like the rest of New England, Chittenden County has no county government outside of the court system. The government structure

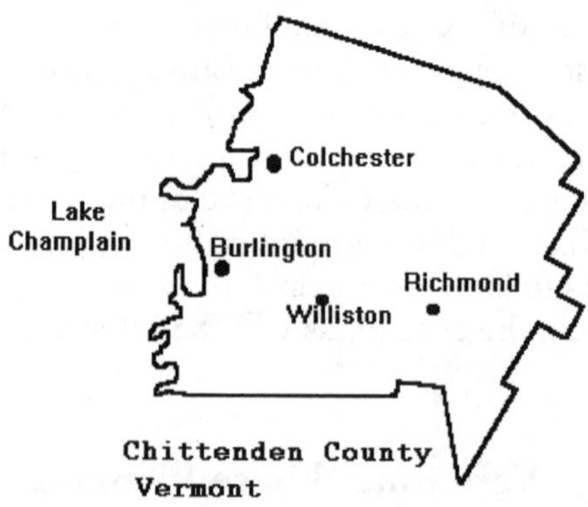

Figure 11.4 Chittenden County, Vermont.

consists of fourteen towns (as townships are called in New England) and three cites: Burlington, South Burlington, and Winooski. Each municipality has control over the planning and zoning of its own turf.

Vermont's approach to growth management has been shaped by two laws: Act 250 of 1970 and Act 200 of 1988. Act 250 established a permit development process by which developers who propose to build residential projects of ten or more dwellings, develop commercial projects of more than one acre, create ten or more lots, or build on land over twenty-five hundred feet above sea level first have to apply for a permit. The permit applications are reviewed by district environmental commissions, which consist of appointed lay people with hired staff. The proposed projects are judged according to ten criteria ranging from impact on government services to air and water quality and loss of farmland. The decision of a district commission may be appealed to the quasi-judicial State Environmental Board, and from there to the Vermont Supreme Court.

Over 95 percent of all Act 250 applications have been approved, most with conditions attached, though the conditions often are not effectively enforced. The effect of Act 250 has been to promote quality development, not create a regional planning system or a growth management program. The Act 250 process does not involve a comprehensive assessment of the cumulative impact of development over time, nor does it directly address where development should or should not go. For example, in 1988, a proposed circumferential highway sweeping a wide arc through the center of Chittenden County was granted an Act 250 permit. Critics complained that the ability of the road to foster further development did not receive close scrutiny.

Many Vermonters have recognized that Act 250 is not a substitute for planning. In 1988, the legislature passed Act 200, which set up incentives and grants for coordinated township and regional planning consistent with state agency plans. Act 200 recommended that new development occur within designated growth centers, and state agency plans reflect that strategy. But most municipal and regional plans have been vague about where growth centers are located and what a growth center means. The Chittenden County Regional Planning Commission has identified eighteen growth centers in the county but has no authority to direct growth to those centers.

The missing link in Vermont's approach to planning is strict zoning on lands outside of cities and villages. Most of the rural land in Chittenden County is zoned for two-acre lots. Moreover, the state subdivision regulations exempt lots of over ten acres, so that owners who build a house on such lots do not have to do a perc test or install a certain kind of septic system. As a result, significant amounts of the Vermont countryside have been parcelled into lots of between ten and twenty acres.[27] From 1982 to 1992, Chittenden County lost nearly 32,000 acres of farmland to other uses—an area of fifty square miles.[28] The rate of farmland loss, almost 30 percent in ten years, was one of the fastest in the nation. Only one-quarter of Chittenden County was in farm use in 1992, producing a mere $21.3 million in farm output. "You'll continue to see fewer farms," says Patrice Wright, owner of a 579-acre dairy farm in Williston, Vermont, "because of traffic, development, and a general unneighborliness of the people who are choosing to move in."[29]

Since 1987, the state of Vermont has operated a purchase-of-development-rights program to preserve farmland. In addition, the Vermont Land Trust has been very active in land preservation. As of 1997, however, there were fewer than 4,500 acres of preserved land in Chittenden County.

Perhaps no struggle encapsulates the controversy over growth and development in Chittenden County as much as the decades-long efforts to build major shopping outlets east of Burlington. The proposed developments have challenged the future of Burlington's downtown business district and have raised concerns about traffic congestion and sprawl into the countryside. On the other hand, broadening the local tax base and the rights of property owners to develop their land have added to the debate.

The center of this development controversy is Taft Corners, created by the intersection of US Route 2 and Vermont 2A in the town of Williston, about eight miles east of Burlington. Williston was traditionally an agricultural settlement, but by the end of the sixties it had good access to Interstate 89 and was rapidly becoming a bedroom community for workers at the IBM plant in nearby Essex Junction. In the mid-1970s, the Pyramid Corporation proposed to construct a mall at Taft Corners on open field. The mall would have contained more square feet of retail space than the entire central business district of downtown Burlington. The city challenged Pyramid through the Act 250 process and then took the developer to court to stop the mall and won.

In the early 1990s, a new commercial proposal surfaced for Taft Corners: Wal-Mart. The 107,000-square-foot store was approved by the town selectmen and then tied up in the Act 250 process for two years. Finally, Wal-Mart and the local developer agreed to make $3 million worth of traffic improvements, and the project received the green light. Today, the Wal-Mart has been joined at Taft Corners by Home Depot, Toys 'R Us, and other stores. In late 1997, another Taft Corners development—this one 550,000 square feet of mixed-use commercial and residential space—was approved under the Act 250 process.[30]

The eruption of development in Williston caused the *Burlington Free Press* to ask whether Williston was Vermont's first emerging edge city.[31] Later, the *Free Press* lamented that "the last thing Chittenden County needs is more stores, more cars, and more retail overbuilding."[32] The criteria used by Joel Garreau in defining an edge city are 5 million square feet of office space and 600,000 square feet of retail space. By 1997, Williston boasted over 440,000 square feet of office space and over 400,000 square feet of retail space. If the pending mixed-use development goes through, Williston will more than meet the retail space criterion for an edge city. In the words of planning professor John Mullin, "Taft Corners is already Anywhere, U.S.A."[33]

From 1990 to 1996, Williston's population boomed by 35 percent, the fastest rate of any community in Vermont.[34] The increase of 1,715 residents exceeded the increase of any other community in Chittenden County.

Ironically, once the Wal-Mart was built, the pro-growth Williston selectmen were voted out of office, replaced by a slow-growth faction. Steve Bradish, a Wal-Mart opponent and a newly appointed member of the Williston Planning Commission, summed up the town's experience with Taft Corners: "No one was thinking about big box retail, but about 90 to 95 percent of what was approved in some parts of Taft Corners was not intended by the town plan."[35]

By contrast, in 1997, a proposed Wal-Mart in neighboring Franklin County was stopped through the Act 250 process and the Vermont Supreme Court. The State Environmental Board, as if learning from the Williston struggle, ruled that the benefits of a Wal-Mart outside of the city of St. Albans would do more harm than good to the city's downtown.

The one notable exception to Chittenden County's sprawl is the town of Richmond (population 4,030) on the county's eastern edge.

While the neighboring town of Williston wooed, battled, and finally got a Wal-Mart, Richmond quietly went about changing its zoning ordinance. The new ordinance, passed in 1996, discourages big-box retail outlets like Wal-Mart and restricts highway strip development. At the same time, mixed-use development is promoted in the town center. Richmond has also debated adopting a growth boundary to ensure that new growth is concentrated near the existing village. The private, nonprofit Richmond Land Trust is looking to preserve rural lands outside the village center. In short, Richmond is trying to maintain its character as a New England village.

The lack of a county comprehensive planning and zoning process is painfully evident in Chittenden County. In addition to large superstores, retail strip development is posing a threat to traditional downtowns and small town character. At the same time, a huge manufacturing plant that would employ up to two thousand workers is under construction in another fringe community in the county. A sixteen-mile circumferential highway is being built, arcing from the north to the center of the county. As of 1998, only six miles had been completed, at a cost of $69 million; the remaining section will cost an estimated $80 million.[36]

Although Act 200 called for the coordination of local plans and a regional plan, the planning effort "has withered from a lack of funding and political support."[37] Moreover, lamented one newspaper editorial, "When will we plan like we mean it? Local leaders haven't created zoning laws which direct growth in the manner their community wants."[38] Instead, town zoning allows considerable development and is not coordinated from town to town.

An observer from central Vermont, attorney Josh Fitzhugh, has suggested that the time has come for Chittenden County to form a county government:

> A strong Chittenden County government, elected by county residents and funded by a state-collected income tax on people who work there, could help considerably in addressing regional problems like police protection, transportation difficulties, open space requirements and recreation needs. Existing regional groups could be consolidated and, in my opinion, better managed.[39]

Clearly, Chittenden County needs to take more coordinated steps toward managing growth. In 1997, sprawl critic James Howard Kunstler took a tour of the county and remarked that development favored cars more than people and was mostly devoid of civic life. He summed up his observations by saying: "What's new in Chittenden

County is that you've made either the conscious or the inadvertent decision to develop this county just like Los Angeles."[40]

Sonoma County, California

Sonoma County extends northwest from the northern edge of the San Francisco Bay, between Marin County to the west and Napa County to the east. (See figure 11.5.) The topography features a Pacific coastal headlands, a plain along the San Francisco Bay, long narrow valleys, and steep ridgelines. The climate is Mediterranean, warm and fairly dry. Though not quite as famous as neighboring Napa County, Sonoma County is a major wine-producing region and tourist destination.

According to the Census Bureau, Sonoma County had 414,000 people in 1995, an increase of 38 percent over 1980. The main cities are Petaluma, Sonoma, Santa Rosa, and Rohnert Park.

Beginning in the 1970s, Marin County designated new development for the Highway 101 corridor running along the county's eastern boundary and then up into Sonoma County. West of the development corridor, Marin created an agricultural zoning district with a sixty-acre minimum lot size and added a successful purchase-of-development-rights program in the 1980s. Marin's Pacific coastline is under federal control—the Point Reyes National Seashore and the Golden Gate National Recreation Area—and development is tightly controlled.

The success of Marin's planning efforts had the result of pushing development coming out of San Francisco north and east into Sonoma County. In 1995, Greenbelt Alliance, a nonprofit land-use group

Figure 11.5 Sonoma County, California.

based in San Francisco, estimated that over 100,000 acres of Sonoma County were at risk from urban sprawl.[41]

Farms and ranch lands cover just over half of Sonoma County. The more than 500,000 acres of agricultural land generate over $340 million a year in gross sales, with wine, grapes, cattle, and chickens the leading products. The Sonoma County General Plan, adopted in 1989, included several area plans with zoning ranging from one dwelling per 10 acres in vineyard areas to one dwelling per 160 acres on ranch lands. This uneven zoning makes "it nearly impossible to gauge how zoning will affect the county's [farmland] preservation goals," according to one source.[42]

In 1990, the voters of Sonoma County approved a .25 percent local sales tax to raise revenue to purchase development rights to farmland and open space. The tax will disappear after twenty years. So far, it is generating about $10 million a year, and more than 22,000 acres have been permanently preserved. Part of the county strategy is to preserve land to keep communities separate and distinct. "The general goal is 100,000 acres [of preserved land]. We could achieve that in 15 years,"[43] says David Hansen, manager of the county's purchase-of-development-rights program.

The Sonoma Local Agency Formation Commission (LAFCO), which has authority over annexations of county land by cities, has formally opposed the annexing of land that separates communities.

In 1996, three Sonoma County communities—Healdsburg, Santa Rosa, and Sebastopol—voted by convincing margins to adopt twenty-year urban growth boundaries. In Healdsburg, 71 percent of the voters supported the growth boundary, 59 percent in Santa Rosa, and two-thirds in Sebastopol. This was the first time in the nation that growth boundaries had been formed through a direct vote of the populace.

Since the vote endorsing the growth boundaries, other cities in Sonoma County and throughout California have been looking into adopting their own boundaries. And the action to create boundaries has spread to other cities in the San Francisco Bay Area. In Santa Clara County, the city councils of Cupertino, Morgan Hill, and San Jose each voted to create growth boundaries. Voters in Novato in Marin County adopted a growth boundary in 1997. The city of Windsor in Sonoma County kept the momentum going by voting in favor of a boundary early in 1998.

The Greenbelt Alliance played an instrumental role in waging the ballot campaign in Sonoma County. Beginning with roundtable discussions in 1990, the alliance pursued a strategy of involving the private sector in the planning process. It helped to forge a coalition of downtown businesspeople and the United Wine Growers in the countryside. Opposition to growth boundaries came from Sonoma Alliance, a building industry organization, and the Sonoma County Farm Bureau. But the downtown merchants did not want to lose business to sprawling commercial strips; and the wine growers did not want to have sprawl encroaching on their operations or detracting from the beautiful scenery of the grape-producing valleys.

Explained Greenbelt Alliance Executive Director Jim Sayer:

> Urban Growth Boundaries create a win-win situation for everyone. Farmers avoid suburban encroachment, developers know precisely where they can build, taxpayers know their hard-earned dollars won't be paying for extravagant service extensions, and the public knows where their community stops and where the countryside begins.[44]

Christa Shaw, the Greenbelt Alliance coordinator in Sonoma County, added:

> We need to focus now on using the land within the boundaries efficiently. . . . There is a strong push under way to find creative alternatives, especially in Santa Rosa, where there is a movement to revitalize the downtown. In that area, we need to build housing for people in all walks of life so that we will have a real community that works.[45]

The residents of Sonoma County are opting for slower growth that will be more compact. Annexations will be limited and public services more concentrated in existing settlements. Putting growth issues to a public vote may even set a national precedent.

Summary

These case studies illustrate a variety of efforts to manage the impacts of development and the inevitable increase in metro-fringe population. What is the wise course of action? In each case, public officials and private citizens have tried to tailor solutions that fit their particular circumstances and political realities.

The case studies share the problems of population growth, scattered rural residences, and dwindling farmland. Those places with a strong farming economy—Larimer County, Rice County, and Sonoma County—seem better positioned to manage growth, though farmland protection is much stronger in Rice and Sonoma counties. Where agriculture is weak—Bernadillo, Chisago, and Chittenden counties—

farmland protection efforts are also weak and low-density sprawl a real threat.

A common solution that emerges is the use of government regulations to encourage more compact development. Albuquerque has aggressively expanded its territory to encompass would-be suburbs. While Albuquerque is not compact compared to older eastern cities, it is to other western cities such as Phoenix and Houston. Moreover, Albuquerque has avoided most of the social and political problems of fragmented local governments that have produced well-to-do suburbs and large ghettos in central cities.

Larimer and Sonoma counties are implementing growth boundaries to limit sprawl and to keep their cities distinct from one another. By contrast, the Metropolitan Council of the Twin Cities has drawn the MUSA line, but most of Chisago County is as yet outside the boundary. The county has not embraced growth boundaries for its own cities and villages. A few villages in Chittenden County are taking their first steps to become growth centers, but permissive zoning in the countryside remains a hindrance.

Regional government, discussed in chapter 9, appears to be happening in Albuquerque simply by the shear size of the city. The Metropolitan Council of the Greater Twin Cities, following Portland's Metro example, may soon be elected rather than appointed. Fort Collins and Larimer County have entered into joint land-use planning, featuring a growth boundary. Chittenden County has a regional planning commission that is appointed; otherwise, there is no county government (except the court system). This lack of regional authority makes for uncoordinated planning, despite the best intentions of Vermont's planning law, Act 200. The Act 250 development review process injects a state role in regional planning, though in reaction to proposed developments rather than a proactive comprehensive planning approach.

But regional approaches to managing growth can benefit from state guidelines, such as in Oregon, and targeted state infrastructure funding, such as is emerging in Maryland.

The search for and implementation of effective public policy solutions to sprawl is a constant job. What works for a number of years may eventually become inadequate. It will be to the advantage of growing fringe counties and communities to stay abreast of growth management efforts in other parts of the nation.

A common thread in these case studies is a sense of urgency. Public officials know that more people and development are coming their way. How to manage that growth will be high on the public agenda for a long time. None of the case studies exhibits a strongly pro-growth stance. But growth is not strongly discouraged, either. The balanced-growth option still has time to work, but a different conclusion may be drawn in the year 2020 if:

1. the 1990s predictions of large population increases are accurate or underestimate actual population growth;
2. there has been a significant decline in air or water quality or water supplies;
3. growth management programs are unable to create compact development or limit sprawl in the countryside; or
4. the cost to the taxpayers of supporting new development is a heavy burden.

For these reasons, the time to make growth management work is now. Otherwise, truly draconian measures to limit growth may be needed in the future.

CHAPTER 12

The Promised Land: The Future of the Fringe

> Most national discussions of our discontents pay little attention to the impact of sprawl on the way we live, on the time and money spent commuting, on the cost of building new water systems, roads and schools to accommodate new development.
>
> —*E.J. Dionne, Jr.,* The Washington Post

> We no longer live under the illusion that growth equals progress.
>
> —*Linda Peters, Board of Commissioners, Washington County, Oregon*

Many fringe communities today are at a crossroads. In the past decade, scattered development and a surge of newcomers have brought new challenges to managing growth. There has been a loss of optimism about the landscape. The wide open spaces are disappearing under houses and asphalt. Residents of the fringe worry about what might happen to neighboring fields and forests. There is a lack of faith, noted by critic James Howard Kunstler, that anyone can build something that will add rather than detract from the community.

Some fringe communities are headed on a course of no-return to suburbia. In those places, the promised land of a semirural life in the metro fringe was only a fleeting illusion. Other communities want to resist the monotony and density of suburbia as much as possible. But in their resistance, communities become split between residents who want to absorb growth and those who favor putting up barriers to new development. The dilemma comes down to the reality that even the most desirable growth creates pressure for expanding housing, stores, businesses, schools, and roads. And adding new public services and upgrading old facilities cost money.

A community that wants more effective growth controls should realize that it cannot successfully manage growth by itself. Intermunicipal cooperation on the location of development, infrastructure, and land conservation is necessary, and a state role can be helpful.

Collisions between cities and the countryside will continue to happen, just as cars will continue to smash into each other. Drivers have collision insurance to pay for the damages. In the metro fringe, the insurance company is the taxpayer, who foots the bill for new infrastructure or to buy land or development rights to keep land open. But just as with cars, measures need to be taken to avoid collisions. The first step is slowing down the pace of development. If population growth or housing starts exceed a certain rate, then the brakes should be applied. Second, separating areas where growth should occur from areas that should remain open gives order to the landscape. Accommodating development where there are or could be adequate public facilities makes sense. It may sound easy for governments to make sprawl development more expensive and legally difficult, but keeping the countryside open presents a complex task when traditional rural industries of farming, ranching, and forestry are in retreat and the demand for large house lots and commercial strips remains strong.

The collision between the city and the countryside is not only a cultural clash between different people and different ways of earning a living. It is also a struggle between more people and less land. In recent years, there has been an increasing awareness among those who live in the fringe about the threat of suburbanization—the strip malls, large housing subdivisions, rising property taxes, greater traffic congestion, and loss of open space and rural and small-town ambiance. The more those fringe places are threatened, the more precious they become.

Planners argue for more compact development that consumes less land. But homeowners in the fringe have shown a strong preference for large house lots located away from established settlements. A fundamental change in consumer tastes and attitudes will be needed to make compact development the land-use pattern of choice. Planners, governments, developer groups, and concerned citizens will need to join in an educational effort to demonstrate that compact development is better for the environment, more cost-efficient for taxpayers and local governments, and at least as profitable for developers.

Future Growth Management Challenges in the Fringe

Metropolitan areas will keep expanding, barring a cataclysm in the oil markets or a sudden reversal of the trend of adding a new American every fourteen seconds. More metro-adjacent counties will become classified as metropolitan counties. Both fringe communities and those rural communities in the path of the spreading metropolitan regions should ask themselves:

- How fast will metro regions expand?
- Where will they expand?
- At what density and in what development style will they grow?
- Who will pay for the expanding communities and how much will it cost?

Current fringe communities and communities brought within the fringe will respond differently to change according to the three strategies of pro-growth, balanced-growth, and no- or slow-growth. Predicting what changes will occur and when is a bit like fortune telling. But several ongoing trends will probably continue to alter the way we live and work and where we live and work:

- Technology, especially the car and telecommunications.
- Public investment in roads for greater mobility.
- Affluence. A growing economy produces job opportunities and higher incomes; people can afford a long commute.
- Preferences for a more rural lifestyle featuring space and a more natural environment than the city or suburb provides.
- Population growth.

Advances in technology have had a profound influence on American settlement patterns in the twentieth century. The train, car, truck, and plane have made transportation and mobility fairly cheap and easy. Cheap and plentiful energy has been the driving force behind the decentralization of urban settlement into the fringe. The price and availability of energy will remain a big and uncertain factor affecting where people choose to live. According to the U.S. General Accounting Office, America imported 53 percent of its oil needs in 1997 and is expected to import 60 percent of its oil in 2015. The price of oil in 1997 averaged just under $20 a barrel. If oil remains inexpensive and plentiful, the settlement of the fringe will march on, pushing farther into the hinterlands. Or, if reliable natural gas–powered vehicles or electric vehicles can be mass produced cost-effectively, the fringe will grow.

New technologies are a key source of economic growth because they create new industries and increase worker productivity.

Increased output per worker means that the worker is worth more and should receive a higher rate of pay. The United States has been the world leader in the burgeoning information economy. The telecommunications and computer industries have transformed the American economy and the way we work. Increasingly, these new technologies are changing the way we live. A recent book on telecommunications dared to announce in its title the "death of distance."[1] Where we live is becoming less and less relevant for employment. Increasingly, people can choose a pleasant environment to live in that may or may not be close to where their paycheck comes from.

Telecommunications, in the words of the Office of Technological Assessment, are "facilitating an ever more spatially dispersed economy, which in turn is causing metropolitan areas to become larger, more dispersed, and less densely populated."[2] This "telesprawl" will be a challenge for decades to come.

The telecommunications revolution will compel communities to compete based on the quality of life they provide. Fringe communities will enjoy at least an initial advantage over core metro cities, edge cities, and older suburbs. The natural environment of open spaces and a human scale of development are two major attractions that most fringe places still have.

New road construction will be necessary to provide access to more distant areas of the expanding fringe. New roads will geometrically increase the commuting shed of fringe dwellers as well as enable businesses and households to settle farther from suburbs and the urban core.

Rising affluence has been one of the key ingredients in the settlement of the fringe. Continued affluence means that more people will be able to afford to live far from work and commute long distances. A related factor is the cost of housing in the fringe. If home prices and rentals in the fringe exceed those in urban or suburban areas, people will have an incentive to leave or avoid residing in the fringe.

Americans are showing a preference for environmental quality and a more rural lifestyle. An important question is whether fringe areas can continue to provide those qualities of open space, clean air and water, and low crime rates that attracted people in the past. An increase in population means greater pressure on public services, natural environments, and productive resource lands. For example, water quantity and water quality in some areas have been strained because of increased demands, and ultimately the extent of these supplies will act as a limit to growth.

Air pollution in metropolitan regions presents a serious challenge to environmental quality. Vehicle miles traveled continue to increase, resulting in greater gasoline consumption despite the improvement in the energy efficiency of cars and trucks over the past twenty years. Highway funds are slated to be withheld for projects that would increase air pollution levels above federal standards. Several metropolitan areas face the prospect of stifling themselves through a combination of air pollution and traffic congestion. The traffic congestion is made worse by the fact that people have been moving to homes and jobs away from the inner cities and suburbs and increasing their dependence on the automobile.

The ability of local governments to provide adequate public services for growing populations will be a major challenge for fringe communities. Given the cuts in federal spending for local communities in the 1990s, local governments will be increasingly forced to rely upon themselves to pay for new and upgraded services. If public service costs in fringe areas rise sharply, pulling up property taxes, then these areas may lose some of their attraction.

The increase in metro population documented in the case studies in chapter 11 and long-range population projections strongly suggest that fringe areas will be faced with accommodating large numbers of new residents in the coming decades. Some central cities have lost population, while the amount of developed land has increased because of people relocating to the fringe. For example, between 1970 and 1990, central Philadelphia lost 3 percent of its population while the amount of developed land in the metro region jumped by 32 percent.[3] Over that same period, the nation's population has grown by nearly 50 million people. With that kind of increase, cities and suburbs have had to push outward. But there is certain to be controversy over how many people the fringe can support before the quality of life declines.

The questions arise: Is development the problem? Or population growth? Or both? The United States has no policy on population. By the year 2050, there are expected to be 393 million Americans, an increase of 131 million above the 1995 figure of 262 million.[4] These additional people will require new places to live, work, shop, learn, and play. Even if development were to occur in creative and conserving ways, the strain on air, water, and land resources will be great. Recent development trends have been less dense, more land consuming, and more auto dependent. *If these trends continue, sprawl will cover perhaps 50 percent more land by the middle of the twenty-first century than is developed today.*

The Need for Land-Use Reform

The fringe presents the most challenging planning tasks in America today, and it will probably continue to be a prime growth region well into the twenty-first century. The fringe areas of the Sun Belt—Arizona, California, Florida, Texas, and the Southeast—will experience significant development pressures in the coming years. As one example, Maricopa County, home to Phoenix, is projected to grow by 1.6 million people from 1996 to 2020.[5] Most of these states and metro regions are ill prepared for the onslaught of population. As the number of people increases on a finite amount of fringe land, the need to plan for the location, type, scale, and timing of development will become more than evident. But that may become evident only after considerable sprawl and environmental damage have already occurred.

Land-use reform must occur along with the modernizing of planning laws, political restructuring, local tax reform, and a reorientation of public spending programs.

The American Planning Association has undertaken a Growing Smart program to work with states to update their planning and zoning enabling laws. Most of these laws were cobbled together in the 1920s and 1930s before there was much experience with planning and zoning. In updating their laws, states need to include language allowing county and municipal governments to use a wide array of growth management techniques, including growth boundaries, regional tax sharing, impact fees, purchase and transfer of development rights, low-density zoning in the countryside, the creation of new towns, and land banking.

There are several ways to help manage the growth of the fringe, though most of them have been applied sporadically, rather than in a unified package. (See box 12.1.) But for solutions to work, there will need to be dramatic changes in the attitude of Americans toward land, community, and the regions in which they live. Land is not only an asset in a portfolio; it is a piece of a community. While landowners have the right to develop their land, the density and type of development may legally be limited by community land-use policies. Communities and regions should recognize they are under no obligation to allow excessive development or development in the wrong place just to fill the bank accounts of a few landowners. Moreover, cities can be good places to live. Exploring urban life in Britain in 1997, *The Economist* magazine found, for example, that:

> The idea that urban living is a second-best choice is not one that strikes a chord with growing numbers of people under 40. Nor any longer with many of those much older for whom the bright lights (and public transport) of cities are attractive. With so much happening downtown, who wants to live in the sticks?[6]

Box 12.1 Solutions for Managing Growth in the Fringe

1. Compact cities and towns can be created through the use of growth boundaries.
2. Mass transit and transit-oriented development can promote energy-efficient development and less auto dependence within growth boundaries.
3. The protection and preservation of farmland, forestland, and natural areas discourages sprawl and encourages compact development.
4. Regional planning for transportation, sewer service, water supplies, economic development, property tax sharing, and land use can result in more efficient government services and better balanced metropolitan areas.
5. States and local governments need the legal ability to manage population growth.
6. Politicians must have the political will to be responsible for managing growth both in their communities and over a region. This includes a commitment to undertake planning and enact regulations and growth management spending programs.
7. The building community must design innovative, attractive, and compact developments. These must include affordable housing.
8. It is essential for governments and private interest groups to educate the public about the financial and environmental benefits of growth management.

In the 1990s, regional planning has emerged as a hot topic. Many people recognize that there are too many units of local government, most of which are anachronisms left over from the seventeenth, eighteenth, and nineteenth centuries. Utility authorities and special districts are strange concoctions of the twentieth century and only add to the confusion of who is providing local services. The concept of "local control" has been given sacred treatment, mainly in deference to local politicians. But the scale of mega-mall developments and sprawling residential subdivisions, water supply and quality, and the large numbers of mobile Americans pose overwhelming challenges to local control. The traffic and school impacts of a development in one municipality can easily spill over onto a neighboring municipality. One of the purposes of planning is to achieve some kind of control over the type and direction of growth. With so many units of government doing their own planning, conflicts are bound to arise and in many cases frustrate local planning.

The many municipal, township, and even county governments that make up a region must either consolidate politically into a regional government or else closely coordinate their planning for transportation, solid waste, water, air quality, wildlife habitat, farmland protection, and economic development. All of these elements are tied together by land-use planning. The bottom line is that if metropolitan regions do not improve their government structure, the cost of government services will be higher than necessary, which will place the entire region in a less competitive position in the global economy.

Compact cities and towns through growth boundaries should be planned to accommodate development in a cost-effective way and minimize sprawl. This will require regional planning for transportation, sewer service, water supplies, economic development, property tax sharing, and land use. Portland's Metro provides the nation's leading example. Within the growth boundaries, government investment in mass transit can spark private investment in transit-oriented development to absorb population increases, decrease auto dependence, reduce traffic congestion, and improve air quality. In-fill development and the reclamation of brownfield industrial sites will be important. But innovative, attractive, and compact development design by the building community is crucial for providing good living conditions within the growth boundaries. New residential development must include affordable housing.

A working rural landscape offers the best opportunity to support compact development from outside the growth boundaries and to minimize sprawl. Beyond the growth boundaries, the protection and preservation of farmland, ranch land, forestland, and natural areas must be implemented to discourage sprawl from leapfrogging over the boundaries and throughout the countryside. Perhaps the single most effective remedy would be to ban or severely limit on-site sewage disposal systems. These systems, which have a normal life of only twenty-five years and require at least two acres to operate safely, are the main culprit behind the low-density residential sprawl in the fringe and frequently contribute to groundwater pollution.

If fringe communities are unsuccessful in protecting or preserving their rural lands, then large amounts of open land will be developed. This development will probably include a few large residential and commercial projects, but more likely the nickel-and-dime small projects will continue to nibble away at fields and forests. Less open space means a less attractive environment, a less diverse economy, and the spread of thickening sprawl.

Educating the public about the financial and environmental benefits of growth management is necessary to overturn the conventional wisdom that any growth is good. Taxpayers need to understand that growth management can keep their taxes from rising to subsidize sprawl. The air quality, water quality, and open-space benefits from growth management can provide powerful arguments not just for maintaining a good quality of life, but also as assets in economic development efforts. Businesses both large and small select locations because of the local quality of life. Business owners want to live and raise families in safe, attractive, and comfortable surroundings.

Ultimately, counties, cities, towns, and regions may not succeed in managing growth in the long run unless they have the legal ability to limit increases in population.

The relative success of different regulations and spending programs will vary among fringe communities. The differences will depend to a large degree on how well local communities draft comprehensive plans and implement them through zoning, subdivision regulations, capital improvements plans, and other techniques to guide the location, timing, density, and types of development. Drastic short-term remedies, such as moratoria on sewer hookups or limits on the number of building permits issued in a year, or requirements that adequate infrastructure be in place before a building permit is issued, will likely become more popular in the years ahead. But sometimes those remedies are no more than attempts by fringe dwellers to close the door on newcomers.

The potential unifying process for more effective growth management is a public-private planning partnership. Planning is based on optimism about the future and is about solving problems. But in the metropolitan fringe, land-use and infrastructure planning by governments will have to change. Simply put, governments will have to become more efficient in land-use planning and will have to work more closely with private developers. Governments will have to spend funds for infrastructure and land conservation more carefully and with more justification. Private developers will have to produce environmentally sensitive and pedestrian-friendly projects, and creative designs should be encouraged and rewarded. The public will become less tolerant about allowing a few landowners to cash in big while other residents pick up the tab for the services that new developments require. In other words, *new developments will have to be in the right place and pay their way.*

Government intervention in the land market will be necessary in order to protect the public health, safety, and welfare over such issues as water quality, solid and toxic waste disposal, transportation, affordable housing, and open space. The challenge will be how to make the government role less bureaucratic and more responsive to the needs and desires of constituents. Although there is certain to be stiff resistance to planning, given the potential fortunes to be made in real estate development, local land-use controls will increase in sophistication, often within the framework of state goals and regulations. Also, citizen involvement in the comprehensive planning process and in the review of proposed developments will be crucial in helping to shape the future of the community.

An Observation on Community

Throughout this book, the term *community* has been used to describe the geographic and political boundaries in which people live. But the concept of community has changed dramatically since the beginning of the twentieth century. It used to be that you knew your neighbors, you worshipped together, your children went to school together, and you worked in the same city or town. Sometimes this closeness was stifling, but in times of emergency, there was support.

A community is supposed to be the building block of our democratic system. We should feel free to travel about the community and participate in community life. But today, gated communities are "the fastest growing residential segment in the nation."[7] More than 125,000 private homeowners' associations have assumed some of the features of private governments. In 1989, an estimated 40 million Americans belonged to these associations and were bound by the covenants, conditions, and restrictions that apply to everything from quiet hours to what color you can paint your house.[8] Residents have agreed to such limitations on personal freedom in exchange for private security, recreation, and protection of property values.

In a sense, the homeowners' associations provide more cohesion than the typical seminomadic suburban and fringe communities. There, whether in stand-alone subdivisions of a few dozen homes or single residences on large lots, people move in and out constantly. We don't know how long we will stay in a community. We care about our homes in large part because of the amount of money we have invested in them. We think about the value of our homes in case we decide to move and we need to sell them.

Socially, we have more in common with our fellow workers than with our neighbors. Most of us live in one community and work in another. We communicate as much by phone, fax, e-mail, and the cyberspace of the Internet as we do face to face. A growing number of cities and counties are putting up home pages on the worldwide web, however, and the information on those home pages can help to provide citizens with government services and keep them apprised of community news and events.

Still, a sense of regional identity and purpose may prove impossible to create in large metropolitan areas such as New York, Chicago, and Los Angeles. Individual communities may be fortunate to bring about local loyalty, but the connections between communities forty miles away from each other are not likely to be strong.

Community should engender a sense of belonging, a sense of connection, a sense of place, and a caring attitude. Newcomers bear the disadvantage of having no local history or roots. Long-time residents face the challenge of whether to share their community. And all the while regional forces are influencing—some would say bombarding—the community from the outside.

Planning should provide a forum for community residents and members of a region. It is too easy for people to feel overwhelmed and powerless. The democratic process (which is ultimately what the American style of planning reflects) is predicated on the ideals that one person can make a difference and that people can unite to compel change. Managing change is the essence of planning and getting things done. Deciding what is to be done, how, and when in a community or a region is a constant struggle that cannot be taken for granted.

Sustainable Development: What Everyone Wants

The goal of growth management in the rural-urban fringe should be: "development that meets the needs of the present without compromising the ability of future generations to meet their own needs."[9] Put in slightly different terms, sustainable development should enable long-term economic growth and social harmony without sacrificing environmental quality. That is a laudable goal. How to achieve it presents a recurring challenge, not just in fringe communities but throughout metro regions, the nation, and around the world.

The sustainable development principles for land use in the fringe include:

- Compact, transit-oriented development
- Mixed-use development that emphasizes walking and biking within and adjacent to existing cities and towns
- In-fill development and the reuse of brownfield sites
- Urban and village growth boundaries to separate growth areas from the countryside and to reinforce the sense of place
- Greenways—linear paths and corridors—to connect cities and towns to the countryside and to each other

- Low-density zoning in the countryside to discourage sprawl
- Purchase and transfer of development rights, along with preferential property taxation, to encourage rural landowners to keep their land open

Tremendous natural and financial resources have gone into the development of the fringe. Can America afford an ever-expanding fringe with long commutes, greater extensions of roads and sewer and water facilities, coupled with disinvestment in the infrastructure of core cities and older suburbs?

True sustainable development can occur only if communities work together within a regional framework to undertake the strategic planning of land use, infrastructure, and economic development resources.

Ideally, a mix of farms, forests, natural areas, and residential, commercial, and industrial uses could result in working rural-type landscapes with urban-type employment opportunities. But to achieve that balance, houses, malls, and offices will have to be largely confined to existing town and village areas, leaving the countryside mostly open.

For some places to remain sustainable, others might have to absorb an extra amount of growth. Ironically, no- and slow-growth communities probably have the best chance for achieving sustainable development if they carefully manage it.

Balanced-growth communities may face a long-run "death by halves." That is, the first twenty-year comprehensive plan envisions the development of only half of the planning area, and the zoning ordinance then carries out that scenario. Twenty years later, the next comprehensive plan and zoning ordinance permit the development of half of the remaining open space. In time, virtually all of the open space is gone, and the balance between development and open space has vanished.

Simple, magical solutions are tantalizing in a complex world. The American democratic system of checks and balances engenders mostly gradual governmental change, even in the face of rapid growth. Yet occasionally a bold new direction takes hold, usually in the wake of a crisis. The Chinese character for "crisis" has a double meaning: danger and opportunity. The danger to many fringe areas is that they will be transformed into mundane, bedroom-community suburbs. A more acute danger threatens the auto-dependent and oil-dependent lifestyle of the fringe: high oil prices and scarce oil supplies. A final danger is that the fringe will serve as a refuge from core cities and expanding suburbs. The growth of the fringe diverts local, state, and national attention from the plight of core cities.

The opportunities for growth management in the fringe are encouraging but need to be seized on quickly. Core cities, suburbs, edge cities, counties, and municipal governments will need to cooperate more closely. Regional metropolitan planning for infrastructure and land use will be essential. If regional planning fails, the financial, social, and environmental costs to America will be enormous.

APPENDIX 1

A Warning About Living in the Rural-Urban Fringe

The following advice for people thinking of buying land in the rural part of a metropolitan region was adapted from "The Code of the West," drafted by John Clarke, county commissioner of Larimer County, Colorado.

Introduction

It is important for you to know that life in the country is different from life in the city. County governments are not able to provide the same level of service that city governments provide. To that end, we are providing you with the following information to help you make an educated and informed decision about whether to purchase rural land.

Access

The fact that you can drive to your property does not necessarily guarantee that you, your guests, and emergency service vehicles can achieve the same level of access at all times.

1.1 Emergency response times (sheriff, fire, medical care) cannot be guaranteed. Under some extreme conditions, you may find that emergency response is very slow and expensive.

1.2 There can be problems with the legal aspects of access, especially if you gain access across property belonging to others. It is wise to obtain legal advice and understand the easements that may be necessary.

1.3 You may experience problems with the maintenance and cost of maintenance of your road. Some rural properties are served by public roads and some by private roads. Some roads are maintained by the county or municipality and some by private road associations. Make sure you know what type of maintenance to expect and who will provide that maintenance.

1.4 If your road is unpaved, it is highly unlikely that the county or municipality will pave it in the foreseeable future. Unpaved roads generate dust and are often slippery when wet.

1.5 Extreme weather conditions can destroy roads. It is wise to determine whether your road was properly constructed.

1.6 School buses travel only on maintained county or municipal roads that have been designated as school bus routes by the school district.

1.7 Many large construction vehicles cannot negotiate small, narrow roads. If you plan to build, it is prudent to check out construction access.

1.8 It may be more expensive and time consuming to build a rural residence due to utility delivery fees and the time required for inspectors to reach your site.

Utility Services

Water, sewer, electric, telephone, gas, and trash removal may be unavailable or may not operate at urban standards. Repairs can often take much longer than in cities and towns.

2.1 If sewer service is available to your property, it may be expensive to hook into the system. It also may be expensive to maintain the system.

2.2 If sewer service is not available, you will need to use an approved septic system or other treatment process. The type of soil available for a leach field will be very important in determining the cost and kind of system you should use. Have the system checked by a reliable sanitation firm and ask for assistance from the county health department or municipal building code officer.

2.3 If you have access to a public or private supply of treated domestic water, the tap fees can be expensive. You may also find that your monthly cost of service can be costly compared to a municipal system.

2.4 If you do not have access to a supply of treated domestic water, you will have to locate your own water supply. The most common method is to drill a well. Permits for wells are granted by the county or state engineer's office. The cost of drilling and pumping can be considerable. The quality and quantity of well water can vary considerably from place to place and from season to season.

2.5 Permits from the county or state engineer's office may restrict the use of water to only the home.

2.6 It is important to determine the proximity to electrical power. It can be very expensive to extend power lines.

2.7 It may be necessary to cross property owned by others in order to extend electricity service to your property. It is important to make sure that the proper easements are in place.

2.8 If you are purchasing land with the plan to build at a future date, there is a possibility that electrical lines (or sewer and water lines) may not be large enough to accommodate you if others connect during the time you wait to build.

2.9 Power outages can occur in outlying areas with more frequency than in more developed areas. A loss of electrical power can also interrupt your supply of water from a well.

2.10 Trash removal can be much more expensive in a rural area than in a city. It is illegal to create your own trash dump, even on your own land. It is good to know the cost for trash removal. In some cases, your only option may be to haul your trash to the landfill yourself. Recycling may be more difficult because pickup may not be widely available.

The Property

3.1 Not all lots are buildable. You must check with the county or municipal planning department to find out if you can build on a certain tract of land.

3.2 Easements may require you to allow the construction of roads, power lines, water lines, and sewer lines across your land. Easements should show up as part of a title search.

3.3 Some property owners do not own the mineral rights under their property. Owners of mineral rights have the ability to change the surface of the property in order to extract minerals. It is very important to know what minerals may be located under the land and who owns them.

3.4 You may be provided with a plat map of your property, but unless the land has recently been surveyed and pins placed by a licensed surveyor, you cannot assume that the plat map is accurate.

3.5 Fences that separate properties are often misaligned with the actual property boundaries. A survey of the property is the only way to confirm the location of your property lines.

3.6 Many subdivisions and planned unit developments have covenants that limit the use of property.

3.7 Homeowners' associations are required to take care of common roads, open space, etc. A dysfunctional homeowners' association or poor covenants can cause problems for you and even involve you in expensive litigation.

3.8 The properties surrounding your land will probably not remain as they are indefinitely. You can check with the municipal or county planning office to find out how the properties are zoned and to see what future developments may be in the planning stages. *The view from your property may change.*

3.9 It is important to make sure that any water rights you purchase with the land will provide enough water.

Mother Nature

Residents of the country usually experience more problems when the weather and earth turn unfriendly.

4.1 The physical characteristics of your property can be positive and negative. Trees are a wonderful amenity but can also involve your home in a forest fire. If you start a forest fire, you are responsible for paying the cost of extinguishing the fire.

4.2 Steep slopes can slide in unusually wet weather. Large rocks can also roll down steep slopes and present a great danger to people and property.

4.3 Expansive soils can buckle concrete foundations and twist steel I-beams. You can find out about the soil conditions on your property by having a soil test performed.

4.4 The topography of the land can tell you where storm water will go.

4.5 Spring runoff can cause a very small creek to become a major river. You can check floodplain maps at the county planning office.

4.6 Nature can provide you with some wonderful neighbors. But in general, it is best to enjoy wildlife from a distance and know that not handling your pets and trash properly could cause problems for you and the wildlife.

Agriculture

5.1 Farmers often work around the clock, especially during planting and harvest time. It is possible that adjoining agricultural activities will disturb your peace and quiet.

5.2 Land preparation and other farm activities can cause dust, especially during dry and windy weather.

5.3 Farmers typically use chemical fertilizers, pesticides, and herbicides in growing crops. You may be sensitive to these substances.

5.4 Animals and their manure can cause objectionable odors.

5.5 If you choose to live among farms and ranches, do not expect the county or municipal government to intervene in the normal day-to-day operations of your agribusiness neighbors. The state has "right to farm" legislation that protects farmers and ranchers from nuisance and liability lawsuits.

There may be other issues you wish to explore before deciding to move to the countryside. It is not our intent to dissuade you, only to inform you.

APPENDIX 2

Sample On-Lot Septic System Ordinance

This sample ordinance was adapted from the Lancaster County, Pennsylvania, Water Supply Plan, published in 1997 by the county planning commission. It is intended to serve as a source of ideas for communities that are looking to promote the safe location and use of on-lot septic systems.

Section 1. Planning Policies for On-Lot Sewage Disposal Systems (OLDS).

All developers within the (county or municipality) shall design sewage disposal systems in accordance with the planning policies set forth in this section. The developer shall include with any subdivision or land development plan a written explanation of the procedures used in determining the sewage disposal facilities proposed for the development. A similar explanation shall be required if the developer is seeking a permit to install, repair, alter, or modify an OLDS.

1. The (county or municipality) allows the use of OLDS outside of the present and future public sewer service area but only where feasible and economical. Developments shall promote the conservation of groundwater resources. At a minimum, the developer shall address the following (county or municipal) policies:

   a. Establish OLDS and community sewage disposal system ownership and maintenance responsibilities with the individual lot owner, homeowners' association, condominium unit owners' association, or the developer.

   b. Provide water conservation and waste-flow reduction by the use of water-saving devices and other state-of-the-art water conservation methods for all new construction and the replacement of any components of existing structures.

c. Recycle wastewater by relying on OLDS for groundwater recharge through subsurface disposal of treated water.

d. Restrict elevated sand mound systems.

e. Restrict subsurface community sewage disposal systems to solving sewage-related problems of existing structures.

2. The developer may consider and evaluate a community sewage system outside of current and future designated publicly sewered areas only when individual OLDS are not feasible. The (county or municipal) approved individual wastewater treatment systems are septic tanks, aerobic treatment units, spray irrigation systems, and, if no other method is feasible, individual stream discharge systems. These methods may be used with the effluent treatment and disposal methods outlined below:

   a. For a site suitable for a conventional subsurface absorption system, according to state standards, the following systems may be used: a septic or aerobic tank with an absorption area (standard trench, seepage bed, subsurface sand filter, or elevated sand mounds).

   b. For a site not suitable for a conventional subsurface absorption system, a conventional spray irrigation or individual stream discharge system may be used, in accordance with state standards.

   c. The developer shall evaluate alternate systems if there are inadequate soils or other concerns on the site that prevent the use of conventional septic systems. These systems shall use technology that has proven successful. The design of the alternate system shall be approved in accordance with state agency regulations.

Section 2. <u>Sewage Testing Required for All Proposed Lots.</u>

An applicant shall present evidence that each existing lot or lot to be created contains a suitable location for the installation of an initial OLDS, except when existing or proposed lots are to be served by a community sewage system. All tests required by state agencies and this ordinance for the location of an OLDS to confirm the suitability of the location shall be performed in accordance with state standards.

Section 3. Replacement Location for On-lot Sewage Disposal Systems Required.

A replacement location for an OLDS shall be required for all existing or proposed lots that are not serviced or proposed for service by a community sewage system operated by a government agency, and for which a valid OLDS permit has not been issued. The replacement location shall comply with all state regulations concerning OLDS, with the terms of this ordinance, and with any other (county or municipal) ordinances.

Section 4. Identification of Replacement Location.

An applicant for an OLDS permit shall demonstrate that a suitable area exists on the lot(s) or on each proposed lot for an initial OLDS and for the replacement location. All tests required by state agencies and this ordinance for the location of an OLDS shall be performed as approved by the state agencies. The designation of open land for the replacement location without testing shall not constitute compliance with the requirements of this section.

1. The developer shall identify the location of the initial OLDS and the replacement location on the plot plans and diagrams submitted as a part of the OLDS permit application.
2. If the developer is applying for a subdivision or land development approval, the developer shall include a note on the plans stating that no improvements shall be constructed upon the replacement location, and the deed to each lot created under the subdivision or land development shall contain language reflecting this limitation. The planting of trees, shrubs, or other plant matter is allowed upon the replacement location.
3. Any revisions to a permit or plan affecting a replacement location that has been previously approved shall be approved by the elected (county or municipal) body or its representative.

Section 5. Relief from Requirement of Designation of Replacement Location.

If any lot held in single and separate ownership as of the effective date of this ordinance shall not contain land suitable for a replacement location, the applicant for a zoning permit or an OLDS installation permit may request an exception to the requirement of providing a replacement location. The applicant shall present credible evidence that the lot was held in single and separate ownership on the effective date of this ordinance, the size of the lot, the inability of the applicant to acquire adjacent land or the unsuitability of adjacent land, and a test conducted to determine that the lot is not suitable to provide a replacement location.

Section 6. Environmental Impact Assessment.

The applicant for a subdivision or land development plan shall present to the (county or municipality) data sufficient to determine the impact of the proposed development on the environment. The applicant shall submit the following information:

1. A location map showing the entire tract and its relation to the surrounding area, drawn at a scale of one thousand (1,000) feet to the inch.
2. A plan of the entire tract with the information required by this section at a scale of between ten (10) feet to the inch and one hundred (100) feet to the inch.
3. Types of soils, based on the U.S. Department of Agriculture Soil Survey for the county.
4. Identification of all wells within a one-quarter-mile radius.
5. Geology information adequate to determine whether the area proposed for the use of OLDS is conducive to groundwater contamination.
6. Sufficient elevations and/or contours to determine the slope and natural drainage of the land. Contours shall be shown at intervals of five (5) feet.
7. The location of all existing floodplains, wetlands, watercourses, railroads, areas of subsidence, wooded areas, bridges, culverts, and other significant natural features on the tract and within two hundred (200) feet of the tract.
8. The location of all roads, adjoining tracts, and buildings within two hundred (200) feet of the tract.
9. Plans for the treatment and disposal of sewage and for the provision of a domestic water supply. The plan shall show a 100-foot well arc.
10. The location and number of residential and nonresidential lots, lot sizes, and the number and type of dwelling units.
11. Information on geological hazards such as flooding, subsidence, and land slides within and adjacent to the tract.

12. A detailed description of the methods for storm-water management, including calculations for storm-water runoff, and an erosion and sedimentation plan.
13. Proposed utilities, including water lines or wells, storm sewers, electric and gas, indicating the size or capacity of each.

Section 7. Permit Required for All Lots.

The landowner and any contractor performing work upon an OLDS shall obtain a permit from the (county or municipality) in accordance with this ordinance prior to the installation, alteration, repair, or replacement of any OLDS. This requirement shall apply to all lots within the (county or municipality) regardless of the size of the lot and regardless of the relationship of the person seeking to install the OLDS for the property owner. Section 4 of this ordinance regarding a suitable replacement location shall apply unless the county or municipality grants a waiver or unless the permit is requested to repair a malfunction of an existing OLDS.

1. The holder of a permit and the contractor performing the work shall notify the (county or municipality) at least three working days before commencing installation, repair, or alteration of the OLDS so that one or more inspections in addition to the final inspection may be scheduled and performed by the (county or municipality).
2. Any OLDS permit providing for the installation or repair of a septic tank shall require that the septic tank contain septic solid retainers as specified by the state regulations.
3. If construction or installation of the OLDS and of any building or structure for which such OLDs is to be installed has not commenced within two (2) years after the issuance of the OLDS permit, the permit shall expire. The landowner and contractor shall obtain a new permit prior to commencement of the installation, repair, replacement, or alteration of the OLDS.

Section 8. Proper Operation and Maintenance of OLDS Required.

All persons who own or occupy a lot upon which an OLDS is installed shall properly use and maintain such OLDS. Proper maintenance of an OLDS shall include, at a minimum:

1. Retention of a septage hauler to inspect the OLDS at least once

every three (3) years, beginning from the date of this ordinance, and removal of septage whenever the inspection demonstrates that the treatment tank is filled with solids (sludge and/or scum) in excess of 25% of the liquid depth of the tank. It is the responsibility of the property owner to insure that septage is removed from the tank of the OLDs in accordance with the requirements of this section. No person other than a septage hauler shall be permitted to remove septage from the tank of an OLDS or to otherwise dispose of any septage or any other substance within an OLDS.

2. For OLDS installed after the effective date of the ordinance, the property owner must have an inspection and, if necessary, septage removed from the OLDS within three (3) years from the date of final inspection of the OLDS, or in the case of new construction, within three (3) years of the date of the issuance of the certificate of use and occupancy. The property owner shall continue to have inspections and, as necessary, septage removed from the OLDS within three (3) years from the date of the last inspection as long as the OLDS continues to be used for sewage disposal.

3. When the inspection of the septage hauler reveals that the inlet or outlet baffles are in a deteriorated condition, the property owner shall be responsible for replacing immediately the deteriorated baffles with sanitary tees. The septage hauler shall inform the property owner of the responsibility to replace the deteriorated baffles. The manifest submitted by the septage hauler shall expressly state the condition of the baffles, whether the septage hauler informed the landowner that the baffles should be replaced, and whether the septage hauler replaced the deteriorated baffles.

4. Maintenance of surface contouring and other measures to divert storm water away from treatment facilities and absorption areas to protect the absorption areas from physical damage.

5. Following any operating and maintenance recommendations of the manufacturer of the OLDS.

6. Discharging only domestic sanitary sewage into an OLDS. The following types of waste shall not be discharged into an OLDS:

    a. Industrial waste.

    b. Automobile oil, other nondomestic oil, grease, nonbiodegradable soaps, detergents, and or inert materials such as coffee grounds.

c. Toxic or hazardous substances or chemicals including but not limited to pesticides, disinfectants, acids, paints, paint thinners, herbicides, gasoline, and other solvents.

d. Surface water or groundwater, including water from roof or cellar drains, springs, basement sump pumps, and french drains.

e. Vehicle wash water.

f. Disposable products, such as diapers.

g. Beauty shop waste.

h. Abattoir or butcher shop waste.

Section 9. Reporting of Malfunctioning OLDS or Community Sewage System.

Any person who owns or occupies a lot upon which an OLDS or community sewage system is installed and any septage hauler pumping out or otherwise maintaining an OLDS or community system shall report any malfunctioning of such OLDS or community sewage system to the (county or municipality). Such report shall be made as soon as possible but in no case later than four (4) days after the discovery of the malfunction.

Section 10. Registration of Septage Haulers Required.

Each septage hauler who performs maintenance upon an OLDS or community sewage system within the (county or municipality) shall annually register with the county or municipality and pay a registration fee. No person other than a registered septage hauler shall be permitted to remove septage from or maintain any OLDS or community sewage system in the county or municipality.

Section 11. Reports Required.

Each septage hauler who performs maintenance upon an OLDS or community sewage system within the (county or municipality) shall file a manifest with the (county or municipality) for each OLDS or community sewage system serviced within three (3) weeks of the date of such maintenance.

Section 12. Proper Operation and Maintenance of Community Sewage Systems Required.

All persons who own a lot that is serviced by a community sewage system shall properly use the system. The owner of the community sewage system shall properly maintain the system. Proper maintenance of a community sewage system shall include at a minimum:

1. Inspection of the community sewage system by the county or municipality on a monthly basis.
2. Removal of septage or sludge and operation and maintenance in accordance with manufacturer specifications.
3. Maintenance of surface contouring and other measures to divert storm water away from treatment facilities and absorption areas.
4. Requiring that all users of the community sewage system discharge only domestic sanitary sewage into the system. The owner of the community sewage system shall inform all users of the community sewage system that the types of waste described in Section 9 of this ordinance shall not be permitted to be discharged.

Section 13. Penalties.

For each violation of the provisions of this ordinance, the following persons shall be liable on conviction thereof in a summary proceeding to pay a fine of not less than two hundred dollars ($200.00) and no more than six hundred dollars ($600.00) for each offense, together with the costs of prosecution: the owner, developer, agent or contractor performing construction or maintenance, repair, or alteration of an OLDS or community sewage system; the owner of the lot upon which such violation shall exist; and/or the owner, agent, lessee, or contractor or any other person who commits or assists in any such violation; or the owner of a lot upon which an OLDS or community sewage system is installed and who fails to maintain such OLDS or community sewage system. In default of payment of such fine, such person shall be liable to imprisonment for a period not exceeding thirty (30) days.

Section 14. Remedies.

In case any improvement is constructed or any lot maintained in violation of this ordinance, or any OLDS is installed, repaired, or altered prior to obtaining a permit as required by this ordinance, or any OLDS or community sewage system is not properly maintained or the malfunction of any OLDS or community sewage system is not reported to the (county or municipality), in addition to other remedies provided by law, the (county or municipality) may commence appropriate action or proceedings in equity to prevent such unlawful construction of improvements or such unlawful maintenance of such lot or the continued use of such OLDS or community sewage system.

Section 15. Declaration of Nuisance.

The following activities are hereby declared to be nuisances:

1. Construction of improvements on the replacement location. Such construction renders the replacement location useless and therefore jeopardizes the water quality of other natural resources of the (county or municipality). Such harm is a danger to the health, safety, and welfare of the residents of the (county or municipality) and is hereby declared to be a nuisance and abatable.
2. Installation or alteration of an OLDS without having obtained a permit as required by this ordinance, or if a permit was obtained in a manner that violates the terms of the permit.
3. Failure to maintain an OLDS or community sewage system as required by this ordinance.

Section 16. Waiver of Liability.

Nothing contained within this ordinance shall be interpreted as a guarantee or warranty to applicants or other (county or municipal) residents that systems installed under the provisions of this ordinance will function as intended. The (county or municipality) assumes no responsibility for the location and/or maintenance of OLDS within the (county or municipality).

Section 17. Appeals.

Appeals from any action of the (county or municipality) under this ordinance shall be made in writing to the governing body. The written appeal shall specify the precise action from which the appeal is taken and shall set forth in concise terms the reason for the appeal and any legal authorities supporting the appeal. If a hearing is requested in writing, the governing body shall conduct the hearing at a regular or special public meeting that occurs not less than fourteen (14) days after receipt of the written appeal. The governing body shall render a decision on the appeal in accordance with state law.

Section 18. Severability.

The provisions of this ordinance are severable, and if any section, sentence, clause, part, or provision hereof shall be held illegal, invalid, or unconstitutional by any court of competent jurisdiction, such decision of the court shall not affect or impair the remaining sections, sentences, clauses, parts, or provisions of this ordinance.

APPENDIX 3

Telecommunications Tower and Antenna Ordinance

The sample ordinance presented here borrows from several recent county and municipal telecommunications ordinances that were drafted to comply with the federal Telecommunications Act of 1996.

Purpose

To comply with the federal Telecommunications Act of 1996 and to address the siting and use of telecommunication towers and antennas on privately owned property and to allow the leasing of sites for telecommunications towers and antennas on county- or municipal-owned land. Leasing county- or municipal-owned property may encourage the location of towers in nonresidential areas and minimize the total number of towers throughout the community, encourage the joint use of new and existing tower sites, encourage the location of towers and antennas in places where any potential adverse impact on the community is minimized, and enhance the ability of providers of telecommunications services to provide such services to the community quickly, effectively, and efficiently.

Definitions

Alternative Antenna Support Structure: Human-made trees, clock towers, campaniles, freestanding steeples, and other alternative design support structures that camouflage or conceal antennas as architectural or natural features.

Tower: Any structure that is designed and constructed primarily for the purpose of supporting one or more antennas, including self-supporting lattice towers, guyed towers and monopoles but not alternative antenna support structures. Towers include, but are not limited to, radio and television transmission towers, microwave towers, common carrier towers, and cellular telephone towers.

Section 1. Antenna or Tower, Associated Structures (Radio, Television, Microwave Broadcasting, Etc.), and Antenna Alternative Support Structures to Exceed the District Height.

A. Allowable Districts: Nonresidential districts.

B. Standards:

1. Towers must be set back a distance equal to the height of the tower from any residential property line.
2. Towers shall be enclosed by security fencing of not less than six (6) feet in height and shall also be equipped with an appropriate anti-climbing device.
3. A minimum 10-foot-wide landscape strip shall be required around the facility boundary outside of any fence or wall upon approval by (county or municipality). The property shall also comply with all buffer and landscape strips of the underlying zoning.
4. Height shall not exceed 300 feet from grade for towers or 150 feet for alternative antenna support structures.
5. The tower shall comply with the American National Standards Institute and shall be removed in case of abandonment.
6. Antennas and towers shall not have lights unless required by state or federal laws.

Section 2. Permits.

The applicant shall submit six (6) copies of the site plan for review by the planning commission. The planning commission shall review the site plan at a regularly scheduled public meeting or a special public meeting. The planning commission may consult with other county or municipal departments and/or retain outside consultants to assist in the review. The county or municipality shall issue a permit when a favorable review is reported.

Section 3. Leasing County or Municipal Property for the Location of Towers and Antennas.

A lease agreement between the county or municipality and a telecommunications provider shall make provision for the following:

1. The telecommunications provider shall construct, own, and maintain the tower at its own expense. The tower shall be a monopole design or an alternative tower structure, such as a human-made tree, clock tower, bell steeple, light pole, or similar alternative-design mounting structure that camouflages or conceals the presence of antennas or towers.
2. The lease agreement shall, consistent with Section 1 of this ordinance, provide for: (1) setbacks, (2) specified fencing, and (3) vegetative or other buffering.
3. Should the county or municipality determine that a tower site is desirable for co-location of third-party telecommunications providers, the lease agreement shall provide that any tower constructed by the telecommunications provider shall have space for multiple antennas.
4. The telecommunications provider shall pay a customary rent, which shall be recommended by the (county or municipal) staff. The rent payable by the telecommunications provider shall be increased when either an additional use or an additional antenna belonging to a third-party provider is added to the tower.
5. Prior to execution of any lease agreement, the telecommunications provider shall submit to the county or municipality: (1) a letter of intent to lease the applicable premises, and (2) a proposed preliminary site plan for the premises. The telecommunications provider shall, within sixty (60) days of execution of the lease agreement, provide to the (county or municipality) a proposed site plan and a survey of the leased premises. The (county or municipality) shall have thirty (30) days after receipt of the site plan and survey to approve or reject the site plan and survey.
6. The telecommunications provider shall be guaranteed appropriate ingress and egress for the life of the lease agreement. If a change in ingress or egress is necessary, the (county or municipality) where reasonably possible will avoid the relocation of

underground utilities that have been installed by the telecommunications provider.

7. The lease agreement shall provide for removal of the tower and accessory structures by the telecommunications provider at the close of the lease or in case of abandonment of the tower. The agreement shall further require that the lessee secure an environmental audit at the close of the final lease term, share the results with the (county or municipality), and remediate any hazardous waste or toxic substance contamination caused by the telecommunications provider, its assigns, subtenants, or licensees. The (county or municipality) may require a performance bond or other security for the purpose of securing the performance of the terms and conditions of the lease agreement.
8. The lease agreement shall not prevent the sale of the subject property by the (county or municipality), provided that any such sale shall be subject to the lease agreement.
9. The lease agreement shall provide for indemnification of the (county or municipality) for damages or claims, especially those resulting from the lessee's use or production of hazardous or toxic materials on the premises.
10. The lease agreement shall require the lessee to comply with all applicable federal, state, and local ordinances, regulations, and statutes and shall allow the (county or municipality) to review and approve all construction plans and specifications prior to construction of the tower.
11. The lease agreement shall require insurance, including but not limited to, coverage for public liability and property damage, in a form and amount satisfactory to the (county or municipality).
12. The (county or municipality) shall have the right to approve the assignment of the lease agreement to any third party, and shall further have the right to require a performance bond and indemnification from such third party. At a minimum, the (county or municipality) shall reserve the right to approve any additional use or antenna proposed to be located on the telecommunications tower.

Section 4. Leasing County-owned Buildings and Structures for the Location of Telecommunications Antennas.

1. The telecommunications provider shall pay a customary rent agreed upon by the provider and the (county or municipality).
2. The telecommunications provider shall be guaranteed appropriate access to the antenna for the life of the lease agreement. But the provider shall agree in advance to necessary changes in access (at no cost to the county or municipality) that may be later reasonably required by the (county or municipality).
3. The lease agreement shall provide for removal of the antenna and accessory structures by the telecommunications provider at the close of the lease or in the case of abandonment of the antenna.
4. The lease agreement shall not prevent the sale of the subject property by the (county or municipality), provided that any such sale shall be subject to the lease agreement.
5. The lease agreement shall provide that the (county or municipality) may reasonably require relocation of the antenna to another location on the building or structure, or relocation to a different county-owned building or structure, all at the lessee's own expense.
6. The lease agreement shall provide for indemnification of the (county or municipality).
7. The lease agreement shall require the lessee to comply with all applicable federal, state, and local ordinances, regulations, and statutes and shall allow the (county or municipality) to review and approve any plans and specifications prior to the installation of the antenna.
8. The lease agreement shall require insurance, including but not limited to, coverage for public liability and property damage, in a form and amount satisfactory to the (county or municipality).

APPENDIX 4

Model County or Municipal Steep-Slope Overlay Zone

This model overlay zone was adapted from the model zone of the Lancaster County, Pennsylvania, Planning Commission.

Section 1. Purpose

The intent of the Steep Slope Conservation District (SS) shall be to conserve and protect those areas having steep slopes from inappropriate development and excessive grading, as well as to permit and encourage the use of steep-slope areas for open space purposes. Consistent with the general purposes of the comprehensive plan and zoning ordinance, the Steep Slope Conservation District is intended to accomplish the following objectives:

1. To create an overlay zoning district, combined with other zoning requirements, with certain restrictions for steep-slope areas to promote the general health, safety, and welfare of the residents of the (county or municipality).
2. To prevent inappropriate development of steep-slope areas in order to avoid potential dangers to individuals, adjacent landowners, and property caused by erosion, stream siltation, accelerated seepage, soil failure leading to structural collapse or damage, and/or unsanitary conditions and associated hazards.
3. To minimize danger to public health and safety by promoting safe and sanitary drainage.
4. To permit only those uses that are compatible with the development of steep-slope areas and with the preservation of existing natural features, including vegetative cover, by restricting the grading of steep-slope areas.

5. To promote an ecological balance among those natural system elements (such as wildlife, vegetation, and aquatic life) that could be adversely affected by erosion, stream siltation, or soil failure caused by inappropriate development.
6. To prevent development that would cause excessive erosion and a resultant reduction in the water-carrying capacity of the watercourses that flow through or around the (county or municipality) with the consequences of increased flood crests and flood hazards within the (county or municipality) and to both upriver and downriver municipalities or counties.
7. To protect the (county or municipality) from inappropriate development of steep slope areas, which could adversely affect subsequent expenditures for public works and disaster relief and, thus, adversely affect the economic well-being of the (county or municipality).
8. To promote the provision of safe and reliable access ways, parking areas, and utility systems serving development on or around steep-slope areas, where more sensitive grading and siting is essential.
9. To assist in the implementation of pertinent state laws and regulations concerning erosion and sedimentation control practices.

Section 2. Definition of the Boundary of the Steep Slope Conservation District.

The Steep Slope Conservation District is defined and established as those areas having slopes of fifteen percent (15%) or greater as delineated on the attached map, which is hereby made part of this ordinance. Any portion of a lot that lies within those areas identified as having slopes equal to or greater than fifteen percent (15%) shall be considered to be in the Steep Slope Conservation District.

Section 3. Steep Slope Conservation District Overlay Concept.

The Steep Slope Conservation District shall be deemed to be an overlay on any zoning district(s) now or hereafter enacted to regulate the use of land in the (county or municipality).

1. The Steep Slope Conservation District shall have no effect on the permitted uses in the underlying zoning district, except

where those permitted uses conflict with the permitted uses of the Steep Slope Conservation District.

2. In those areas of the (county or municipality) where the Steep Slope Conservation District applies, the requirements of the Steep Slope Conservation District shall supersede the requirements of the underlying zoning district(s).

3. Should the zoning classification(s) of any parcel or any part thereof on which the Steep Slope Conservation District is an overlay be changed, as a result of legislative or administrative actions or judicial decision, such change(s) in classification shall have no effect on the boundaries of the Steep Slope Conservation District, unless an amendment to those boundaries was included as part of the proceedings from which the subsequent change(s) originated.

Section 4. Boundary Interpretation and Appeals Procedure.

An initial determination as to whether the Steep Slope Conservation District applies to a given parcel shall be made by the (county or municipal) zoning officer. Any party aggrieved by the decision of the zoning officer, either because of an interpretation of the exact location of the Steep Slope Conservation District boundary or because the criteria used in delineating the boundary are or have become incorrect because of changes due to natural or other causes, may appeal the decision to the zoning hearing board (zoning board of adjustment) as provided for in Article ______ of the (county or municipal) ordinance.

Section 5. Land Use and Development Regulations in the Steep Slope Conservation District.

In the Steep Slope Conservation District, the following land-use and development regulations shall apply:

1. On those lands having a slope of less than fifteen percent (15%), the land-use and development regulations of the Steep Slope Conservation District shall not apply. However, the use and development of such lands shall still be governed by the standards of the underlying zoning district(s) and minimum acreage requirements.

2. On those lands having a slope of greater than fifteen percent (15%), only those uses listed in Subsections (A) and (B) of this section shall be permitted. Furthermore, all applications for

permits for building or development allowed under Subsection (B) shall be accompanied by an erosion and sediment control plan. The plan shall comply with the erosion and sediment control practices set forth by the State of ________, as well as other recognized conservation practices.

3. In evaluating the proposed development plan, erosion and sedimentation control plan, and any additional information submitted by the applicant, the county commissioners (or municipal board of supervisors), (county or municipal) planning commission, (county or municipal) engineer, and, where appropriate, the zoning hearing board (zoning board of adjustment) shall consider the following factors:

   a. The percent of slope on the site.

   b. The extent of the existing vegetative cover on the site and proposed disturbance of the vegetative cover.

   c. The soil types and underlying geology of the site.

   d. The length or extent of the slope both on the site in question and on adjacent lands within two hundred (200) feet of the site.

   e. Evidence that the proposed development, any impervious ground cover, and disturbance to the land and vegetative cover will not cause excessive runoff and/or related environmental problems.

A. Conservation Uses Permitted Throughout the Steep Slope Conservation District.

The following uses shall be permitted in the Steep Slope Conservation District without the submission of an erosion and sedimentation control plan:

1. Wildlife sanctuary, game farm, or hunting preserve for the protection and propagation of wildlife, woodland preserve, arboretum, and passive recreation, including parks, but excluding enclosed structures.

2. The planting of trees and shrubbery, or reforestation in accordance with recognized soil conservation practices.

3. Recreational uses, with such activities as hiking, bicycle and bridle trails, camps, picnic areas, but excluding enclosed structures and excluding the riding or driving (either on trails or off

road) of motorcycles, all-terrain vehicles, or other motorized vehicles, except snowmobiles.

4. Agricultural uses, such as general farming, horticulture, truck farming, and wild crop harvesting, in accordance with recognized soil conservation practices.
5. Nonstructural accessory uses (except swimming pools, tennis courts, or sport courts) necessary for the operation and maintenance of the above permitted uses.
6. Front, side, and rear yards and required lot area in the underlying zoning district(s) provided such yards are not to be used for on-site sewage disposal systems or any use prohibited under Subsection (C) or that requires a special exception in accordance with Subsection (B).
7. Similar uses to those above that are in compliance with the intent of this section.

B. Uses Permitted by Special Exception.

The following uses shall be permitted by a special exception from the zoning hearing board (zoning board of adjustment) on the submission of an erosion and sedimentation plan and any other supporting evidence by the applicant:

1. Sealed public water supply wells with the approval of the county health department (or state department of environmental resources).
2. Water mains, sanitary or storm sewers and laterals, and impoundment basins with the approval of the (county or municipal) engineer and the county health department (or state department of environmental resources).
3. Underground utility transmission lines.

C. Prohibited Uses.

The following uses shall be prohibited within the boundaries of the Steep Slope Conservation District on lands having a slope of fifteen percent (15%) or more:

1. Freestanding enclosed structures, buildings, and retaining walls.
2. Roads, access driveways, and parking facilities.

3. The filling or removal of soil except when related to an activity approved by special exception, as set forth in Subsection (B) of this section.
4. Swimming pool, tennis court, and/or sport court.
5. Junkyards or other outdoor storage of vehicles and materials.
6. On-site sewage disposal systems.
7. Extraction of natural resources, burrow pits, and sanitary landfills.
8. Any other uses not specifically permitted under Subsection (A) or permitted by special exception under Subsection (B).

D. Application Procedure.

For any use of land in the Steep Slope Conservation District, excepting uses existing as of the date of the enactment of this ordinance, a written application for a Steep Slope Use Permit shall be filed with the (county or municipal) zoning officer, who shall make an initial determination on the application.

1. For a use other than those permitted in Subsection (A), an application seeking approval by special exception shall be forwarded to the zoning hearing board along with required studies or information and the findings of the zoning officer.
2. Any application for a special exception use under Subsection (B) shall be accompanied by a plan certified by a registered professional engineer. This plan shall show:

    a. The location of the proposed use with respect to the Steep Slope Conservation District boundaries and existing development within the property.

    b. The nature of the proposed use.

    c. The results of topographical surveys showing the contours of the property in two-foot (2-foot) intervals as well as typical tract cross-sections at a scale of not more than one hundred (100) feet and at a vertical and horizontal scale.

    d. Surface view of construction, grading, or fill elevations.

    e. Size, location, and arrangement of all proposed and existing structures on the site, as well as specifications for building construction and materials and storage of materials.

f. Location, elevation, and specification for water supply, sanitary facilities, and streets.

g. Soil types, existing vegetation, proposed changes to the existing topography and vegetative cover; the means of accommodating storm-water runoff; engineering and conservation techniques to be used to prevent erosion and alleviate environmental problems created by the proposed development activities.

E. Procedures for Consideration of a Special Exception.

All applications for approval by special exception shall be in writing and shall be considered in accordance with the provisions of Article _____ in the (county or municipal) zoning ordinance and with the following procedures:

1. The applicant shall request, at least forty-five (45) days prior to the public hearing, the review and recommendation of the (county or municipal) planning commission and shall present evidence that such review has been requested.
2. The applicant shall request the review and recommendations by the Natural Resources Conservation Service and the county conservation district, and other technical agencies such as appropriate watershed associations or other planning agencies, to assist in determining the environmental impact of the proposed use(s) at least forty-five (45) days prior to the public hearing and shall present evidence that such review has been requested.

APPENDIX 5

Model Intergovernmental Agreement Between a County and a City or Village

In the West, most of the South, and the midwestern states, cities and incorporated villages have extraterritorial powers to plan and zone for areas of county land up to two miles from the city or village. Cities and municipalities also have the power to annex county land to make the city or village larger. The purpose of an intergovernmental agreement is to promote more compact development at the edge of cities and villages, to allow for annexation only when necessary, and to minimize uncontrolled sprawl.

This model agreement was adapted from Will County, Illinois. A map of the area covered by the agreement would need to be attached to the agreement. This agreement can be changed to be between: (1) a county and more than one city or village; (2) townships in the northeastern states; or, (3) a township (or townships) and a village or city. It is advisable to check with a local attorney to confirm that your state's laws allow intergovernmental agreements and the form those agreements must take.

WHEREAS, the County and the City (or Village) are units of local government as defined by the Constitution of the State of _________; and

WHEREAS, the County and the City (or Village) are authorized to enter into intergovernmental agreements, specifically for joint planning and zoning; and

WHEREAS, the County and the City (or Village) have determined that it is in their mutual interests, and for the general welfare of the citizens of the County, the City (or Village), and the State of ___________ for the County and City (or Village) to join together in this agreement in order to assure the overall development pattern for the planning area in and around the City (or Village) of ______ in

________County (the geographic limits of which are described in Exhibit A attached hereto and made a part hereof) to promote compact and contiguous development, to protect agricultural lands, and to establish procedures for cooperation and coordination between the City (or Village) and the County on issues of planning and development management.

NOW THEREFORE, in consideration of the foregoing and of the mutual agreements and promises herein contained, the parties agree as follows:

Section 1. Definitions.

Planning area means the planning area of the City (or Village), located within _______ County, as determined by intergovernmental boundary agreements with neighboring municipalities, and shall refer to the area set forth in Exhibit.

Governmental unit means the county or a municipality that is a party to this agreement.

Section 2. Purpose.

The parties hereto, through their respective governing bodies, have investigated the facts necessary to determine the need for an intergovernmental planning agreement, and hereby find and declare:

1. That the proposed development of the planning area gives rise to problems concerning comprehensive land-use planning, agricultural protection, compact and contiguous growth, and development management and coordination.
2. That parties hereto individually and collectively are affected by said problems and any attempt to solve them. The welfare, prosperity, and enjoyment of the County and the City (or Village) will benefit from mutual actions and intergovernmental cooperation.
3. That it is the intention of the parties to cooperate with each other and to contract in the joint exercise of responsibility for the planning and management of the planning area.
4. That the County and the City (or Village) may seek to enter into agreements with state agencies or other units of local government to further the goals of this agreement; however, any such additional agreement shall not be binding on any governmental unit not a party thereto.

5. That it is also the intent of this agreement to provide procedures through which the County and City (or Village) may coordinate planning and zoning, share information on development impacts, and seek to avoid overloading public facilities, creating environmental damage, and fostering destructive intergovernmental competition.

Section 3. Compact and Contiguous Growth.

The County and City (or Village) agree to encourage phased development that proceeds outward from existing developed communities in a logical and orderly fashion. This shall be performed using all available means, including, but not limited to, comprehensive planning, zoning, subdivision regulations and development codes, and controlled extension of road and utility improvements. The County agrees to support the City (or Village) in its efforts to control non-agricultural development on lands located within the planning area.

Section 4. Future Planning Cooperation.

The City (or Village) agrees to consult the County when it considers any revision of the existing City (or Village) comprehensive plan, zoning ordinance, or capital improvements plan that would affect the planning area. The City (or Village) and County agree to review their comprehensive plans at regular intervals, not to exceed five years, to determine whether the planning area should be revised.

The County and City (or Village) agree to cooperate to study jointly and pursue solutions to development concerns, including but not limited to: comprehensive planning, development regulation, environmental and open-space protection, and transportation and utility service. Such efforts may, at the wish of both parties, include other government agencies or local governments.

Section 5. Governing Law.

This agreement shall be construed in accordance with the laws of the State of ____________.

____

County of ________
Date _____________

____

City or Village of ________
Date _____________

APPENDIX G

Model Transfer-of-Development-Rights Ordinance

The model transferable development rights ordinance presented here was based on ordinances used in Maryland counties and Pennsylvania townships, and allows for the transfer of development potential from agricultural lands. A transfer program could be used to transfer development potential from forestland or open land. To do that, the terms "farm," "agricultural land," and "agricultural zone" in the following model would have to be replaced with the name of the kind of land and zone designated in the sending (preservation) area.

Also, this ordinance does not expressly include a TDR bank in which the county or municipality would offer to purchase TDRs from landowners at a guaranteed price. Section 8 does allow public purchase of TDRs if the county or municipality were to create a TDR bank.

Finally, the model ordinance does not make the sale of TDRs mandatory for landowners. The sale of TDRs occurs strictly on a voluntary basis.

Section 1. Purpose.

In accordance with state law and Sections ____ of the (county or municipal) zoning ordinance, this section establishes procedures by which transferable development rights are granted, conveyed, applied, and recorded, in the preservation of the (county's or municipality's) valuable agricultural land and economy.

Section 2. Granting Transferable Development Rights Within the Sending Area.

Except as noted below, every parcel within the agricultural zone that, on the effective date of this ordinance, contains a farm (as defined herein) is granted one (1) transferable development right for each two (2) gross acres contained therein, excepting two (2) acres of the curtilage around an existing house. Should a farm that was not classified as part of the agricultural zone on the effective date of this ordinance be subsequently rezoned to the agricultural zone, that farm, too, will be granted one (1) transferable development right for each two (2) gross acres contained therein, excepting two (2) acres of the curtilage around an existing house, on the effective date of the rezoning.

Transferable development rights are *not* granted to:

1. tracts of land or portions thereof owned by or subject to easements (including, but not limited to, easements of roads, rights-of-way, railroads, electrical transmission lines, telephone lines, and water, sewer, gas or petroleum pipelines) in favor of governmental agencies, utilities, and nonprofit corporations; or
2. land restricted from development by covenant, easement, or deed restriction, unless and until such time as said covenant, easement, or restriction is dissolved or rescinded.

Section 3. Obligation of Landowner to Convey Transferable Development Rights.

The conveyance of transferable development rights occurs solely on a voluntary basis. Landowners are in no way compelled to convey their transferable development rights. If conveyances occur, they must be done according to Section 5 of this ordinance. Unconveyed transferable development rights may be transferred with land sold, donated, or bequeathed.

Section 4. Value of Transferable Development Rights.

The monetary value of transferable development rights is completely determined between buyer and seller.

Section 5. Process of Conveying a Transferable Development Right from the Sending Area.

Transferable development rights granted through Section 2 of this ordinance may be sold and/or donated to any party, subject to the following:

1. *Application Materials.* The transferor and transferee shall sub-

mit a signed application on a form developed by the (county or municipality). Along with the application form, the following shall be submitted:

a. A metes-and-bounds description of the property of the owner of the land from which the rights will be transferred and a plot plan or survey, showing total acreage of the owner's property, areas of land or portions thereof, subject to easements in favor of governmental agencies, utilities, and nonprofit corporations, land restricted against development by covenant, easement, or deed restriction and excepting two (2) acres of the curtilage around any existing house;

b. If a transfer of development rights involves less than the entire number of rights of a parcel, the portion of the parcel from which the development rights are transferred shall be clearly identified on a plan showing the whole parcel, accurate to one foot of error for every ten thousand feet. Such plan shall also include a notation of: (1) the number of development rights attributed to the entire parcel, (2) the number of development rights attributed to the identified portion of the parcel from which the development rights are to be transferred, and (3) the number of development rights that would remain available to the parcel after the proposed transfer;

c. A title search of the tract from which the transferable development rights will be conveyed sufficient to determine all owners of the tract and all lienholders;

d. A copy of the proposed Deed of Transferable Development Rights and a copy of the proposed agricultural conservation easement in accordance with Section 6 of this ordinance.

2. *Review, Endorsement, and Recording of Conveyance.*

a. Upon receiving a complete application, as required above, the zoning officer shall determine the number of transferable development rights that can be conveyed from the sending tract. The zoning officer shall also determine, with the advice of the (county or municipal) attorney and/or engineer, the sufficiency of: (1) the plan indicating the portion of the parcel to be restricted from future development if the development rights from less than the entire parcel are conveyed, (2) the agricultural conservation easement, and (3) the Deed of Transferable Development Rights. The zoning officer shall inform the transferor and transferee of the development rights of his/her determination in writing. Any appeals of the determination of the zoning officer shall be made in accordance with the provisions of Section ___ of this ordinance; and

b. Upon receipt of written approval by the zoning officer, as provided in Section 5.2.a., the transferor and transferee may present the (county or municipality) with the Deed of Transferable Development Rights for endorsement. The (county or municipality) shall not endorse the Deed of Transferable Development Rights until the (county or municipality) has received evidence that the agricultural conservation easement has been duly signed by all relevant parties and recorded with the county recorder of deeds.

Section 6. Conditions of the Agricultural Conservation Easement.

The owner conveying transferable development rights from the sending area shall perpetually restrict the use of the parcel, or portion thereof, from which transferable development rights are conveyed by an agricultural conservation easement. The agricultural conservation easement shall be in a form approved by the (county or municipal) attorney and shall restrict future use of the property to agricultural uses, any accessory agricultural uses, and open-space uses.

Any agricultural conservation easement shall designate the (county or municipality) as a third-party beneficiary of the restrictions imposed upon the transferor and his/her property. Such restrictions shall be enforceable by the (county or municipality) as such third-party beneficiary.

Land from which transferable development rights have been conveyed shall continue to be owned, subject to said restrictions, by the landowner, his/her heirs, executors, administrators, successors, and assigns.

If the development rights are to be conveyed from less than the entire parcel, the plan prepared in accordance with Section 5.1.b above shall be attached to and recorded with the agricultural conservation easement. All owners of the tracts from which transferable development rights are conveyed shall execute the agricultural conservation easement. All lienholders of the tract from which transferable development rights are conveyed shall execute a subordination agreement to the agricultural conservation easement. Such subordination agreement shall be recorded with the county recorder of deeds.

Section 7. The Use of Transferable Development Rights with Property Within the Receiving Area to Increase Permitted Density.

Transferable development rights may only be used to increase permitted density in the (county's or municipality's) designated receiving areas: R-1 Single Family Residential Zones. When the transferee has acquired transferable development rights for use within receiving areas, the following shall apply:

1. For each transferable development right that is approved for conveyance, the transferee is entitled an increase of one dwelling unit per acre, subject to a minimum lot size of 8,000 square feet.
2. *Application Materials.* Along with those materials required by Section 5, the transferee shall submit:
    a. A preliminary subdivision plan prepared in accordance with the (county or municipal) subdivision ordinance. The preliminary plan must indicate: (1) that transferable development rights are to be used, (2) the base density allowed for the site, (3) the proposed number and size of lots of the site, and (4) the number of transferable development rights to be applied to the site;

    b. An agreement of conveyance for the development rights between (1) the owner of the tract to which development rights have been granted, or the owner of development rights that have previously been severed from a tract in the sending area (as evidenced by a recorded Deed of Transferable Development Rights), and (2) the owner of the tract proposed to be developed with the transferred development rights. The agreement may be contingent upon approval of a final subdivision plan of the tract to which the transferable development rights are to be conveyed; and

    c. A title search of previously severed transferable development rights if the transferee proposes to use transferable development rights that were previously severed from a tract in the sending area.

3. *Review, Approval, and Recording of Transferable Development Rights Applied to Lands Within the Receiving Area.* In addition to

those procedures presented in Section 5.2, the following shall apply to proposed developments that rely on transferred development rights to increase permitted dwelling units per acre beyond that of the base permitted density: No final plan for any subdivision that utilizes transferable development rights shall be executed on behalf of the (county or municipality) until the (county or municipality) has been presented with a copy of the recorded Deed of Transferable Development Rights and a copy of the recorded agricultural conservation easement.

Section 8. Public Acquisition of Transferable Development Rights.

The (county or municipality) may purchase development rights and may accept ownership of transferable development rights through gift. Any such purchase or gift shall be accompanied by an agricultural conservation easement, as specified in Section 6 of this ordinance. The (county or municipality) may resell or retire any transferable development rights it has acquired.

Section 9. Reservation of (County or Municipal) Rights.

The (county or municipality) reserves the right to amend this ordinance in the future, and the (county or municipality) expressly reserves the right to change the manner in which the number of development rights shall be apportioned to a tract in the sending area, the manner in which development rights may be attached to land within the receiving area, the locations of the sending areas and the receiving areas, and the procedures by which development rights can be conveyed. The (county or municipality) further expressly reserves the right to terminate its transferable development rights program at any time. No landowner or owner of development rights shall have any claim against the (county or municipality) for damages resulting from a change in this ordinance relating to the regulations governing the apportionment, transfer, and use of development rights or the abolition of the transferable development rights program. If the transferable development rights program is abolished by the (county or municipality), no developer may attach development rights to any tract in the receiving area after the effective date of the ordinance abolishing the transferable development rights program unless an application in conformance with the provisions of Sections 5.1 and 7.2 was filed prior to the date of such ordinance.

Contacts

For general land-use planning information:
Cyburbia—Planning and Architecture Internet Resource Center (PAIRC)
http://www.arch.buffalo.edu/pairc

For information on Sprawl:
The Planning Commissioners Journal
Sprawl Resource Guide
http://www.plannersweb.com

For a subscription:
Planning Commissioners Journal
P.O. Box 4295
Burlington, VT 05406
Phone: (802) 864-9083
Fax: (802) 862-1882
A 1-year subscription is $45.

For information on the American Planning Association's Smart Growth program:
Stuart Meck
American Planning Association
122 S. Michigan Avenue, Suite 1600
Chicago, IL 60603
Phone: (312) 431-9100
Fax: (312) 431-9985

For information on computer imaging and kiosks:
The Land Information Access Association
322 Munson Avenue
Traverse City, MI 49696
(616) 929-3696
http://www.liaa.org

For information on urban growth boundaries and greenbelts:
Greenbelt Alliance
530 Bush Street, Suite 303
San Francisco, CA 94108
(415) 398-3730
http://www.greenbelt.org

For information on farmland protection:
Farmland Preservation Report
900 La Grange Road
Street, MD 21154
(410) 692-2708

American Farmland Trust
1920 N Street NW, Suite 400
Washington, DC 20036
(202) 659-5170
http://www.farmland.org

The American Farmland Trust also has field offices in California, Illinois, Massachusetts, Michigan, New York, and Ohio.

Farmland Information Library
http://www.farmlandinfo.org

The library contains a bibliography and abstracts of farmland protection topics, state statutes relating to farmland protection, and news and upcoming events.

For information about land trusts:
The Land Trust Alliance
1319 F Street NW
Washington, DC 20004
(202) 638-4725
http://www.lta.org

The alliance sponsors an annual Land Trust Rally, which features a wide range of presentations on land trust operations, land protection, and land stewardship. Highly recommended.

For information on protecting land for public use:
The Trust for Public Land
116 New Montgomery Street, 4th floor
San Francisco, CA 94105
Phone: (415) 495-4014
Fax: (415) 495-4103
http://www.tpl.org

For information on transportation issues:
Surface Transportation Policy Project
1400 16th Street NW, Suite 300
Washington, DC 20036
(202) 466-2636
http://www.transact.org/stpp.htm

For information on rails-to-trails projects:
The Rails-to-Trails Conservancy
1100 17th Street NW, 10th floor
Washington, DC 20036
Fax: (202) 466-3742
http://www.railtrails.org

For information on water quality:
Environmental Working Group
http://www.ewg.org
Click on *Where You Live* by state and county to find public and private water systems that have violated federal water pollution standards.

United States Environmental Protection Agency
http://www.epa.gov
EPA has information on clean air and water regulations, the brownfields program, and toxic waste cleanup. Also, EPA and the Urban Land Institute have set up a Smart Growth Network:
http://www.smartgrowt.org

For community design issues:
The Congress for the New Urbanism
(415) 495-2255

For information on sustainable development:
The Center for Livable Communities
1414 K Street, Suite 250
Sacramento, CA 95814
(916) 448-1198
http://www.lgc.org
The Center for Livable Communities is a nonprofit organization that assists local governments in California and other states. Center programs are aimed at expanding transportation alternatives, reducing infrastructure costs, creating more affordable housing, conserving farmland and natural resources, and restoring economic and social vitality.

Notes

Chapter 1

1. Quoted in Melody Simmons, "Cluster Zoning Portends Rural Clash of Lifestyles," *Baltimore Sun,* February 11, 1997.

2. Quoted on the cover of *Planning for Prosperity: Building Successful Communities in the Sierra Nevada* (Truckee, CA: Sierra Business Council, 1997).

3. Peter Gordon and Harry W. Richardson, "Are Compact Cities a Desirable Planning Goal?" *Journal of the American Planning Association* 63, no. 1 (1997): 100.

4. The Office of Management and the Budget has defined three types of metropolitan areas: metropolitan statistical areas (MSAs), consolidated metropolitan areas (CMSAs), and primary metropolitan statistical areas (PMSAs). As of June 1993, there were 250 MSAs and 18 CMSAs made up of 73 PMSAs. There is also a special category (NECMAs) for the New England states.

An MSA includes one city with 50,000 or more inhabitants, or has an urbanized area of at least 50,000 inhabitants and a total metropolitan population of at least 100,000 (75,000 in New England). The MSA first contains a county or counties with a central city. Outlying counties are included if they have an "urban" density and at least 2 percent of their population commutes to the central county (or counties). An MSA with more than 1 million people may be classified as a CMSA with component PMSAs. See *Statistical Abstract of the United States, 1995,* p. 960.

5. David Rusk cites the fact that "ten of America's 12 largest cities hit their population peaks in the 1950 census," as one indication of the shrinking importance of the central city in metropolitan regions. David Rusk, *Baltimore Unbound: A Strategy for Regional Renewal* (Baltimore: Abell Foundation, 1996).

6. Rutherford H. Platt, *Land Use and Society: Geography, Law, and Public Policy.* (Washington, DC: Island Press, 1996), p. 131.

7. Glenn Frankel and Stephen C. Fehr, "As the Economy Grows, the Trees Fall," *Washington Post,* March 23, 1997, p. A20, 21.

8. *Statistical Abstract of the United States, 1995,* p. 34.

9. Christopher B. Leinberger, "Metropolitan Development Trends of the Late 1990s: Social and Environmental Implications," in Diamond and Noonan, eds., *Land Use in America* (Washington, DC: Island Press, 1996), p. 220.

10. Christopher B. Leinberger, "Be Careful What You Wish For . . . , For You Will Surely Get It: The Need for a New Vision for Metropolitan Development," *Exchange: The Journal of the Land Trust Alliance,* (Spring 1998): 9.

11. Urban Land Institute, *The Case for Multifamily Housing* (Washington, DC: Urban Land Institute, 1991).

12. John Herbers, "Take Me Home, Country Roads," *Planning* (November 1987): 4.

13. Neal R. Peirce, *Citistates: How Urban America Can Prosper in a Competitive World* (Washington, DC: Seven Locks Press, 1993), p. 28.

14. Robert D. Yaro and Tony Hiss, *A Region at Risk: The Third Regional Plan for the New York–New Jersey–Connecticut Metropolitan Area* (Washington, DC: Island Press, 1996), p. 17.

15. U.S. Department of Commerce, Bureau of the Census, *Geographical Mobility, March 1995 to March 1996* (Washington, DC: U.S. Government Printing Office, 1997).

16. Herbers, "Take Me Home," p. 13.

17. Quoted in Fred D. Baldwin, "Lessons from Lancaster: Preserving Central Pennsylvania Farmland," *Central Pennsylvania's Apprise* (Harrisburg, PA: WITF-TV, September 1997), p. 26.

18. Peirce, *Citistates.*

19. This definition of edge cities comes from Joel Garreau, *Edge City: Life on the New Frontier* (Garden City, NY: Doubleday, 1992).

20. Herbers, "Take Me Home," p. 5.

21. H. James Brown, Robin S. Phillips, and Neil A. Roberts, "Land Markets at the Urban Fringe," *Journal of the American Planning Association,* 47, no. 1 (1981): 138.

22. "America's Cities: They Can Yet Be Resurrected," *The Economist,* (January 10, 1998): 18.

23. See Philip Langdon, *A Better Place to Live: Reshaping the American Suburb* (Amherst: University of Massachusetts Press, 1994).

24. U.S. Department of Commerce, Bureau of the Census, *Demographic State of the Nation* (Washington, DC: U.S. Government Prnting Office, 1997).

Chapter 2

1. Douglas Porter, *Managing Growth in America's Communities* (Washington, DC: Island Press, 1997), p. 176.

2. For a discussion of fringe areas added to metropolitan territory over the past forty years, see Alfred Nucci and Larry Long, "Spatial and Demographic Dynamics of Metropolitan and Nonmetropolitan Territory in the United States," revised version of a paper presented at the annual meeting of the Population Association of America, San Francisco, April 6, 1995. Forthcoming in *The International Journal of Population Geography.*

3. Robert Fishman, *Bourgeois Utopias: The Rise and Fall of Suburbia* (New York: Basic Books, 1987), p. 145.

4. See Kenneth T. Jackson, *Crabgrass Frontier: The Suburbanization of the United States* (New York: Oxford University Press, 1985), chapter 14.

5. Jackson, *Crabgrass Frontier,* p. 175.

6. Ibid., p. 162.

7. Quoted in Fishman, *Bourgeois Utopias,* p. x.

8. John Herbers, *The New Heartland: America's Flight Beyond the Suburbs and How It Is Changing Our Future* (New York: Times Books, 1986).

9. *The Economist,* July 26, 1997, p. 26.

10. Jane Holtz Kay, *Asphalt Nation: How the Automobile Took Over America, and How We Can Take It Back* (New York: Crown Publishers, Inc., 1997), p. 271.

11. Fishman, *Bourgeois Utopias,* p. x.

12. Ibid.

13. Quoted in Kay, *Asphalt Nation,* p. 216.

14. Fishman, *Bourgeois Utopias,* p. 182.

15. In his 1928 classic study of regional planning, *The New Exploration,* Benton MacKaye, a cofounder of the Regional Planning Association of America, discussed in detail the invasion of "indigenous" America by metropolitan America.

16. Quoted in Mark Luccarelli, *Lewis Mumford and the Ecological Region* (New York: Guilford Press, 1995), p. 30.

17. Ibid., p. 2.

18. Lewis Mumford, "The Natural History of Urbanization," in W.L. Thomas, ed., *Man's Role in Changing the Face of the Earth* (Chicago: University of Chicago Press, 1956). Quoted in Rutherford H. Platt, *Land Use and Society: Geography, Law, and Public Policy* (Washington, DC: Island Press, 1996), p. 395.

19. William H. Whyte, "Urban Sprawl," in *Exploding Metropolis* (Garden City, NY: Doubleday-Anchor, 1958).

20. The nation's largest mall, the Mall of America, located in Bloomington, Minnesota, outside of Minneapolis, is an eight-story mall. However, the majority of malls are more horizontal than vertical.

21. Jennifer Steinhauer, "On Long Island, the Mall as History Book," *New York Times,* December 21, 1997, Section 3, p. 1.

22. Ibid.

23. Herbers, *The New Heartland,* p. 3.

24. Ibid., p. 17.

25. James Howard Kunstler, *The Geography of Nowhere* (New York: Simon & Schuster, 1993), p. 147.

26. *New York Times,* May 24, 1998, Section 3, p. 2.

27. Jackson, *Crabgrass Frontier,* p. 203.

28. Bruce Lambert, "At 50, Levittown Contends with Legacy of Racial Bias," *New York Times,* December 28, 1997, p. 23.

29. Real Estate Research Corporation, *The Costs of Sprawl* a HUD research report, part 2 (Washington, DC: U.S. Government Printing Office, 1974), p. 18. All values are given in 1973 dollars in comparing six neighborhood types, ranging from high-density walk-up apartments to five-acre single-family homes in the fringe.

30. Kenneth T. Jackson, "100 Years of Being Really Big," *New York Times,* December 28, 1997, Section 4, p. 9.

31. Herbers, *The New Heartland,* p. 29.

32. For example, a 1985 Gallup Poll reported that 48 percent of respondents preferred to live in a rural area or a small town, and another 29 percent chose a small city of 10,000 to 100,000 inhabitants. Cited in Herbers, *The New Heartland,* p. 188.

33. Kay, *Asphalt Nation,* p. 14–15.

Chapter 3

1. Quoted in Dan Eggen and Peter Pae, "Anti-Development Forces Massing Along Home Front," *Washington Post,* December 14, 1997, p. A24.

2. Ibid., p. A23.

3. Henry Diamond and Patrick Noonan, *Land Use in America* (Washington, DC: Island Press, 1996), p. 35.

4. Eggen and Pae, "Anti-Development Forces," p. A24.

5. Georgia Public Television, "Will This Traffic Jam Ever End?" news release, October 20, 1997.

6. David Rusk, *Baltimore Unbound: A Strategy for Regional Renewal* (Baltimore: Abell Foundation, 1996), p. 94.

7. Ibid., p. 90.

8. Ann O'Hanlon "In Fauquier, Developers Fight Rural Past for a Say in the Future," *Washington Post,* May 5, 1996, p. B1.

9. Ibid.

10. Glenn Frankel and Peter Pae, "In Loudoun, Two Worlds," *Washington Post,* March 24, 1997, p. A1.

11. Ibid.

12. Ibid.

13. O'Hanlon, "In Fauquier."

14. Eggen and Pae, "Anti-Development Forces," p. A23.

15. Ibid.

16. Gary Mattson, "Small Community Governance: Some Impediments to Policy Making," in J.J. Gargan, ed., *Handbook of Local Government Administration* (New York: Marcel-Dekker, 1996), p. 323.

17. "Growing a New Atlanta," editorial, *Atlanta Journal-Constitution,* June 10, 1997, p. A26.

18. Ibid.

19. John J. Tarrant, *The End of Exurbia: Who Are Those People and Why Do They Want to Ruin Our Town?* (New York: Stein and Day, 1976), p. 203.

20. Lisa Scheid, "Development Taps Water Resources," *Reading* (Pennsylvania) *Eagle,* October 19, 1997, p. A20.

21. For example, see Stephen Fehr and Peter Pae, "Aging Septic Tanks Worry D.C. Suburbs: Failed Systems Threaten Bay and Region's Water Supply," *Washington Post,* May 18, 1997, pp. A1, A16.

22. Patrick O'Discroll, "Rural Areas Rustle Up Rules for City Slickers," *USA Today,* August 8, 1997, p. 4A.

23. Peter Pochna, "Standish: Manager Sees Solution in Use of Development Impact Fees," *Portland* (Maine) *Press Herald,* July 7, 1997.

24. Jonathan Barnett, *The Fractured Metropolis* (New York: HarperCollins, 1995), p. 7.

25. Jonathan Barnett, "Rebuilding America's Cities," *Architecture* (April 1995): 55–56.

26. H. James Brown, Robin S. Phillips, and Neil A. Roberts, "Land Markets at the Urban Fringe," *Journal of the American Planning Association* 47, no. 1 (1981): 134.

27. Quoted in Gail Rippey, "Suburban Dream Can Be a Nightmare," *Reading* (Pennsylvania) *Eagle,* September 7, 1997, p. A16.

28. Interview with Scott Standish, July 14, 1997.

Chapter 4

1. Peter Pochna and Clarke Canfield, "State Policies Fostering Suburban Sprawl," *Portland* (Maine) *Press Herald*. July 8, 1997.

2. Michael D. Shear and William Casey. "Just Saying 'Yes' to Developers," *Washington Post,* July 21, 1996, p. A1.

3. Ibid.

4. Ibid.

5. For a discussion of the Disney theme park proposal, see Richard Moe and Carter Wilkie, *Changing Places: Rebuilding Community in the Age of Sprawl* (New York: Henry Holt, 1997), chapter 1.

6. Shear and Casey, p. A1. In 1996, the property tax rate in Prince William County was $1.36 per $100 of assessed value.

7. Charles Johnson and Linda H. Smith, "When Urban Sprawl Chokes Agriculture," *Farm Journal* (March 1996): p. 27.

8. Ibid., p. 28.

9. Interview with Norman Greig, May 1, 1997.

10. Ibid.

11. Adapted from the New Jersey Office of State Planning, "The Resource Planning and Management Structure: The Fringe Planning Area." Trenton, NJ, May 13, 1996.

12. See David Dillon, 1994. "Fortress America," *Planning* 60, no. 6: 8–12.

13. Neal Peirce, "Boulder Controls Its Own Destiny," *Burlington* (Vermont) *Free Press,* May 31, 1989.

14. See Jonathan Harr, *A Civil Action* (New York: Vintage Books, 1995). This powerful story revolves around the pollution of groundwater in Woburn, Massachusetts.

15. Douglas Porter, *Managing Growth in America's Communities* (Washington, DC: Island Press, 1997), p. 67.

16. See Goal 10 of the Housing Goals of the Oregon Land Use Act: ORS 197.005–197.650; and two New Jersey Supreme Court cases, *Southern Burlington County NAACP v. Township of Mount Laurel* 336 A.2d 713 (1975) (known as Mount Laurel I); and *Southern Burlington County NAACP v. Township of Mount Laurel* 456 A.2d 390 (1983)(known as Mount Laurel II).

17. *Nollan v. California Coastal Commission,* 483 U.S. 825 (1987); *First English Evangelical Lutheran Church of Glendale v. The County of Los Angeles,* 482

U.S. 304 (1987); *Lucas v. South Carolina Coastal Council,* 112 S. Ct. 2886 (1992); *Dolan v. City of Tigard,* 114 S. Ct. 2309 (1994).

18. For example, in the *Appeal of Girsh,* the Pennsylvania Supreme Court ruled, "It is intolerable to allow one municipality (or many municipalities) to close its doors at the expense of surrounding communities and the central city" (263 A.2d, at 399)(1970).

19. Early New England towns restricted the right of outsiders to settle within their borders as a way to control growth. See Rutherford H. Platt, *Land Use and Society: Geography, Law, and Public Policy* (Washington, DC: Island Press, 1996), p. 124.

20. "California's Water: Want Some More?" *The Economist* (October 8, 1994): 31–32.

21. For example, Albuquerque has decided to stop pumping dwindling groundwater and rely on surface water for its water needs.

Chapter 5

1. Ann Scott Tyson, "Stemming Suburbia's Sprawl," *Christian Science Monitor,* January 9, 1998, p. 5.

2. Judith Corbett, "The Ahwahnee Principles: Toward More Liveable Communities," Local Government Commission, Sacramento, CA. Posted at Internet address http://www.lgc.org/clc/ahwnprin.html, 1997, p. 1.

3. Michael J. Major, "Containing Growth in the Pacific Northwest," *Urban Land* (March 1994): 16.

4. Peter Calthorpe, *The Next American Metropolis* (Princeton, NJ: Princeton Architectural Press, 1993), pp. 15, 35.

5. Quoted in Nancy Petersen, "A Modern Development Offers an Old-Time Aura," *Philadelphia Inquirer,* September 26, 1995.

6. James Howard Kunstler, *Home from Nowhere: Remaking Our Everyday World for the 21st Century* (New York: Simon & Schuster, 1996), p. 189.

7. Quoted in *Governing Magazine* (July 1997): 10.

8. F.J. Osborn, ed., *Ebenezer Howard's Garden Cities of Tomorrow* (Cambridge: MIT Press, 1965), p. 20.

9. *Federal Urban Growth and New Community Development Act of 1970,* Title VII, Section 701, 1970, p. 1.

10. Raymond J. Burby and Shirley F. Weiss. *New Communities U.S.A.* (Lexington, MA: D.C. Heath, 1976).

11. William Alonso, "The Mirage of New Towns," in Don N. Rothblatt, ed., *National Policy for Urban and Regional Development,* (Lexington, MA: Lexington Books, 1974), p. 243.

12. Michael Pollan, "Town-Building Is No Mickey Mouse Operation," *New York Times Magazine,* December 14, 1997, p. 62.

13. Quoted in Liz Atwood, "Va. County Shapes Growth to Save Land," *Baltimore Sun,* August 24, 1997, p. B2.

14. Ibid.

15. Jonathan Barnett, *The Fractured Metropolis* (New York: HarperCollins, 1995), p. 7.

16. Barnett, *Fractured Metropolis,* p. 48.

17. East Amwell Township Planning Board and Banisch Associates, *Draft, 2020 Vision: Planning for Farming in the Future of East Amwell*, East Amwell Township, New Jersey, 1997.

18. Reid Ewing, "Is Los Angeles–Style Sprawl Desirable?" *Journal of the American Planning Association* 63, no. 1 (1997): 110.

19. Barnett, *Fractured Metropolis*, p. 49.

Chapter 6

1. *The Economist* (June 28, 1997): p. 29. The figures are from a federal government report entitled "The State of the Cities."

2. Chris Lester and Jeffrey Spivak, "Buying Bigger Allows Better Housing Benefit Tax; Mortgage Policies Discourage Owners from Buying in Core," *The Kansas City Star*, December 19, 1995.

3. Deductible property taxes and mortgage interest will enable the homeowner to itemize deductions rather than use the standard deduction, which was $7,500 in 1997. By itemizing, the homeowner can also deduct any state and local income taxes, charitable donations, and certain medical expenses. In taking advantage of these additional deductions, the homeowner further lowers his or her overall tax burden. The example in box 6.1 is for a homeowner in the 28 percent income tax bracket. The income tax savings are lower for someone in the 15% bracket and higher for homeowners in the 31 percent and 39.6 percent brackets.

4. David Rusk, *Baltimore Unbound: A Strategy for Regional Renewal* (Baltimore: Abell Foundation, 1996), p. 74.

5. Phillip J. Longman, "Who Pays for Sprawl?" *U.S. News & World Report*, April 27, 1998, p. 23.

6. James Howard Kuntstler, *Home from Nowhere: Remaking Our Everyday World for the Twenty-first Century* (New York: Simon & Schuster, 1996), p. 69.

7. *Wall Street Journal*, April 24, 1997, p. B1.

8. Neal Peirce, "Maryland's Smart Growth Law: A National Model?" Washington Post Writers Group, Washington, D.C., April 20, 1997.

9. Jane Holtz Kay reports that "between World War II and the mid-1960s, the nation had spent a meager $1.5 billion for local public transportation, an average of $75 million a year, while doling out $51 billion a year to motor vehicles" *(Asphalt Nation*, New York: Crown, 1997, p. 254).

10. Federal Highway Administration, "Selected Highway Statistics and Charts, 1989," quoted in *Special Trends* (Washington, DC: Urban Land Institute, March 1991).

11. *Statistical Abstract of the United States, 1989*, quoted in Anthony Downs, "The Need for a New Vision for the Development of Large U.S. Metropolitan Areas," *The New Planner* 14, no. 4 (April 1990).

12. See "TRI-MET Strategic Plan (Discussion Draft)," April 1994, as cited in Internet document at http://www.pan.ci.seattle.wa.us/BUSINESS/DC/MOR/ilbsrsrc.htm, 1997, p. 3.

13. According to the American Association of State Highway and Trans-

portation Officials, cited in Ben Orsbon, "Reauthorization of ISTEA," *Small Town and Rural Planning Division Newsletter*, July 1997, p. 3.

14. Orsbon, "Reauthorization," p. 3. The state highway officials estimate that highways need $31 billion a year in federal funds just to maintain highways in their current condition, and $6 billion a year for mass transit.

15. *The Economist* (July 26, 1997): 88.

16. *The Economist* (August 2, 1997): 80.

17. See Marlow Vesterby, Ralph Heimlich, and Ken Krupa, *Urbanization of Rural Land in the United States* Report AER-673 (Washington, DC: U.S. Department of Agriculture, Economic Research Service, 1994).

18. Section 2031(c) of the Internal Revenue Code.

19. The law requires a donated conservation easement to reduce the value of the land by 30 percent to qualify for the 40 percent exclusion from the taxable estate. If the 30 percent reduction is not met, the law allows a 2 percent decrease in the 40 percent exclusion for every 1 percent below the 30 percent reduction in land value. For example, if land is worth $500,000 before the easement and $375,000 after the easement, the reduction in land value is 25 percent and the exclusion would be 30 percent of the remaining land value ($375,000), or $112,500.

20. If there is any debt on the farm or ranch land being inherited, the value of the debt must be subtracted from the value of the land under the conservation easement. For example, if the land has a value of $400,000 under the easement and the decedent had a $100,000 mortgage on the property, the value for computing the exemption is $300,000. At the 40 percent level, this would mean an estate exemption of $120,000 (rather than $160,000), or an estate tax saving in the 50 percent bracket of $60,000 (rather than $80,000).

21. Natural Resources Defense Council, *Amicus Journal* (Summer 1997): 38.

22. Marc Reisner, *Water Policy and Farmland Protection: A New Approach to Saving California's Best Agricultural Lands* (Washington, DC: American Farmland Trust, 1997).

23. Quoted in Tom Arrandale, "The Price of Potability," *Governing* (December 1997): 72.

24. Kay, *Asphalt Nation*, p. 110.

25. U.S. Environmental Protection Agency, Office of Air and Radiation, *1995 National Air Quality: Status and Trends, Summary* (Washington, DC: EPA, 1995), p. 1.

26. Quoted in the *Report of the Ohio Farmland Preservation Task Force*, Columbus, OH, June 1997, p. 30.

27. U.S. Environmental Protection Agency, *1995 National Air Quality*, p. 2.

28. For a list of violations of federal drinking water standards, see the Environmental Working Group's web site listed in the "Contacts" section following the appendices.

29. *The Economist* (June 28, 1997): 28.

30. Natural Resources Defense Council, *Amicus Journal* (Summer 1997): 38.

31. Public Law 91-190 (1969), 42 U.S.C. § 4331 *et seq.*

32. Longman, "Who Pays for Sprawl?" p. 23.

33. *The Economist* (August 2, 1997): 80.

34. "The Family Truck," *New York Times,* December 10, 1997, A28.

35. Ibid.

36. *The Economist* (January 10, 1998): 19.

37. Randy Kennedy, "From Harlem's Worst to the City's Star," *New York Times,* August 3, 1997, p. 29.

Chapter 7

1. Henry L. Diamond and Patrick F. Noonan, eds. *Land Use in America* (Washington, DC: Island Press, 1996), p. 6.

2. Alistair M. Hanna, *New York Land Opinion Survey* (White Plains, NY: Pace University Law School, 1993).

3. Philip Langdon, *A Better Place to Live* (New York: HarperCollins, 1995), p. 77.

4. Stuart Meck, "Rhode Island Gets It Right," *Planning* 63, no. 11 (1997): 13.

5. James Howard Kunstler, *Home from Nowhere* (New York: Simon & Schuster, 1996), p. 242.

6. Rutherford H. Platt, *Land Use and Society* (Washington, DC: Island Press, 1996), p. 119.

7. Financial advisors have been encouraging clients to buy as much house as they can to take full advantage of the mortgage interest and property tax deductions from federal income taxes. Also, a house has become an investment vehicle for building up equity as the mortgage is paid off. For these reasons, housing consumers have an incentive to purchase expensive houses on large lots, often called "McMansions."

8. Myron Orfield, *Metropolitics: A Regional Agenda for Community and Stability* (Washington, DC: Brookings Institution and Lincoln Institute of Land Policy, 1997), p. 5.

9. John T. Ewing, "Act 60 Will Allow Selective Growth," *Burlington* (Vermont) *Free Press,* November 14, 1997.

10. For example, a cost-of-community-services study conducted by the Land Stewardship Project in three Twin Cities fringe communities found that residential development in those communities was receiving 4 to 7 percent more in services than it generated in property taxes, and farmland used only fifty cents in services for every dollar paid in property taxes (Land Stewardship Project, "Why Minnesota Needs Community-Based Planning," White Bear Lake, Minnesota, 1997, p. 3). The town of Dunn, Wisconsin, just south of Madison, did a cost-of-community-services study in 1994, which concluded that residential development cost $1.06 in public services for every dollar it generated in taxes, while farmland cost only $.18 in services for every local tax dollar it paid in (Town of Dunn, "Cost of Community Services by Land Use," July 25, 1994).

11. Jane Holtz Kay, *Asphalt Nation* (New York: Crown, 1997), p. 124.

12. Mike Tidwell, "Highways Aren't the Ticket to Bigger, Better Cities," *Christian Science Monitor,* September 12, 1997, p. 18.

13. Quoted in "A Better Way," editorial, *Burlington* (Vermont) *Free Press,* September 15, 1997.

14. David Rusk, *Baltimore Unbound* (Baltimore: Abell Foundation, 1996), p. 32.

15. Peter Pae, "Towns in Loudoun Look to Annex Land," *Washington Post,* June 17, 1996, p. D1.

16. Quoted in Chris Lester and Jeffrey Spivak, "Divisions Threaten Kansas City Area, Expert Says, Author Kicks Off Yearlong Metro Development Forum," *Kansas City Star,* October 12, 1995.

17. Quoted in Terry Pindell, *A Good Place to Live: America's Last Migration* (New York: Henry Holt, 1996), p. 55.

18. Quoted in the *Report of the Ohio Farmland Preservation Task Force,* Columbus, Ohio, June 1997, p. 30.

19. Quoted in Lester and Spivak. "Divisions Threaten Kansas City Area."

20. James E. Frank, *The Cost of Alternative Development Patterns: A Review of the Literature* (Washington, DC: Urban Land Institute, 1989).

21. T.J. Becker, "Horizon: Business, Growth, and Change in Metro Atlanta: Gordon Looks North and South—Skeptically," *Atlanta Journal-Constitution,* March 17, 1998, p. E3.

22. Wendy Mellilo, "Builders Face School Fee for Crowding," *Washington Post,* December 5, 1996, p. M1.

23. Sam Hemingway, "Dean Slow to Grasp Sprawl Issue," *Burlington* (Vermont) *Free Press,* January 9, 1998, p. B1.

24. "Growing a New Atlanta," editorial, *Atlanta Journal-Constitution,* June 10, 1997, p. A26.

25. Maria Saporta, "Lessons from Denver: Atlanta Needs Unity; Urban, Suburban Leaders Shouldn't Wait for a Crisis," *Atlanta Journal-Constitution,* June 13, 1997, p. F3.

26. Peter J. Kent, "Fight Suburban Sprawl, Business Leaders Urged; Developers Should Take the Lead, Consultant Says,"*Atlanta Journal-Constitution,* August 7, 1997, p. J1.

27. Thomas L. Daniels and Mark B. Lapping. "Has the Vermont State Land Use Program Failed? An Analysis of Vermont's Act 250," *Journal of the American Planning Association* 50, no. 4 (1984): 502–508.

28. Land Stewardship Project, "Why Minnesota Needs Community-Based Planning," Land Stewardship Project, White Bear Lake, Minnesota, 1997, p. 2.

29. David Goldberg, "Horizon: City Without Limits: Regional Growing Pains," *Atlanta Journal-Constitution,* March 10, 1997, p. E5.

30. Vermont Statutes Annotated, title 3, 4020(a).

31. Goldberg, "Horizon: City Without Limits," p. E5.

Chapter 8

1. Quoted in Neal Peirce, "Maryland's Smart Growth Law: A National Model?" Washington Post Writers Group, Washington, D.C., April 20, 1997.

2. See *Southern Burlington County NAACP v. Township of Mount Laurel* 336

A.2d 713 (1975), and *Southern Burlington County NAACP v. Township of Mount Laurel* 456 A.2d 390 (1983).

3. Quoted in Terry Pindell, *A Good Place to Live* (New York: Henry Holt, 1996), p. 55.

4. Sierra Club, *The Planet* 3, no. 5 (June 1996): 1.

5. For a thorough discussion of state and local historic preservation ordinances and programs, see Constance Beaumont, *Smart States, Better Communities: How State Governments Can Help Citizens Preserve Their Communities* (Washington, DC: National Trust for Historic Preservation, 1996).

6. *The Economist* (August 13, 1994): 28.

7. "Reclaiming Brownfields," *Governing* (January 1998): 32.

8. Quoted in *Farmland Preservation Report* 6, no. 4 (February 1996): 2.

9. See American Farmland Trust, *Dutchess County: Cost of Community Services Study* (Washington, DC: American Farmland Trust, 1989); *Does Farmland Protection Pay: The Cost of Community Services in Three Massachusetts Towns* (Washington, DC: American Farmland Trust, 1992); and *Is Farmland Protection a Community Investment? How to Do a Cost of Community Services Study* (Washington, DC: American Farmland Trust, 1993).

10. Town of Dunn, Wisconsin, *Town of Dunn Cost of Community Services by Land Use,* 1994.

11. Tim Palmer, *America by Rivers* (Washington, DC: Island Press, 1996), p. 21.

12. Douglas R. Porter, *Managing Growth in America's Communities* (Washington, DC: Island Press, 1997), p. 73.

13. Mickey Baca, "A Massachusetts Law Squeezes Sellers," *New York Times,* August 17, 1997, p. 43.

14. Quoted in *Lancaster Farming* (weekly newspaper, Ephrata, Pennsylvania), August 2, 1997, p. 1.

Chapter 9

1. Personal communication, August 12, 1997.

2. Urban Land Institute, *The Costs of Alternative Development Patterns: A Review of the Literature* (Washington, DC: Urban Land Institute, 1992).

3. See Douglas R. Porter, *Managing Growth in America's Communities* (Washington, DC: Island Press, 1997), p. 241.

4. Jonathan Barnett, *The Fractured Metropolis,* (New York: HarperCollins, 1995), p. 160.

5. *The Economist* (August 9, 1997): 22.

6. Jeff Gersh, "Subdivide and Conquer," *Amicus Journal,* (Natural Resources Defense Council, Fall 1996): 22.

7. Alan Ehrenhalt, "The Great Wall of Portland," *Governing* (May 1997): 20–24.

8. Lancaster County Planning Commission, Lancaster, Pennsylvania, *Comprehensive Plan Progress Report, 1991–1995,* 1997.

9. In the early 1990s, in Lancaster County, Pennsylvania, a major sewer line was extended a mile beyond a proposed growth boundary before the boundary was finalized. The purpose of the sewer extension was to alleviate on-site

sewage disposal problems at a mobile home park. That was a valid health issue, but it would have been possible to limit the size of the sewer pipe to service only the mobile home park. Instead, the pipe was "oversized" to accommodate, and in fact encourage, future development in the countryside.

10. Researchers in the New York metro fringe suggest that low-density residential and commercial development can be just as devastating to wildlife as fairly dense, village-type development. Fragmenting land parcels, paving new roads and parking lots, and even planting large lawns all take a toll on wildlife. These findings support a growth boundary and open countryside strategy for wildlife protection. See Andrew C. Revkin, "When Swamp and Suburb Collide," *New York Times,* September 7, 1997, p. 46.

11. Quoted in the *Philadelphia Inquirer,* December 1, 1991, p. 6-B.

12. Peter Pochna and Clarke Canfield, "State Policies Fostering Suburban Sprawl," *Portland* (Maine) *Press Herald,* July 8, 1997.

13. Quoted in *The Economist* (October 26, 1991): 11.

14. Quoted in *Farmland Preservation Report* 8, no. 2 (November 1997), p. 2.

15. New Jersey Office of State Planning, "The Final Report of the Economic Impact Assessment of the New Jersey Interim State Plan," (Office of State Planning, Trenton, NJ, 1992); Robert W. Burchell, "Impact Assessment of the New Jersey Interim State Development and Redevelopment Plan," Rutgers University Center for Urban Policy Research, New Brunswick, NJ, 1992.

16. Despite Oregon's widespread use of agricultural zoning, there are nine ways that new dwellings can be allowed on farmland, according to the Oregon Department of Land Conservation and Development: (1) as "farm dwellings"; (2) as "nonfarm dwellings" in the nine Willamette Valley counties; (3) as "nonfarm dwellings" in the twenty-seven other counties; (4) for "farm help" (relatives of the farmer who live on the farm and help operate it); (5) on "lots of record"; (6) on hard-to-farm parcels of high-value farmland; (7) on small tracts of high-value farmland; 8) temporarily, during a medical hardship; and 9) to replace a dwelling.

17. Ehrenhalt, "The Great Wall of Portland," p. 22.

18. Daniel Sneider, "To Halt Sprawl, San Jose Draws Green Line in Sand," *Christian Science Monitor,* April 17, 1996.

19. Ehrenhalt, "The Great Wall of Portland," p. 22.

20. Joseph C. Doherty, "The Countrified City," *American Demographics* 2, no. 4 (1984): 7–8.

21. David Rusk, *Baltimore Unbound* (Baltimore: Abell Foundation, 1996), p. 91.

22. Douglas R. Porter, *Managing Growth in America's Communities* (Washington, DC: Island Press, 1997), p. 75.

23. See Rusk, *Baltimore Unbound,* p. 31.

24. See Rusk, *Baltimore Unbound,* pp. 41–44; and C. James Owen and York Willbern, *Governing Metropolitan Indianapolis: The Politics of Unigov* (Berkeley: University of California Press, 1985).

25. Myron Orfield, *Metropolitics: A Regional Agenda for Community and Stability* (Washington, DC: Brookings Institution; and Cambridge, MA: Lincoln Institute of Land Policy, 1997), p. 102.

26. Rusk, *Baltimore Unbound,* p. 69.

27. Timothy Egan, "Seattle and Portland in Struggle to Avert Another Paradise Lost," *New York Times,* November 1, 1997, p. A10.

Chapter 10

1. In Colorado, subdivisions of thirty-five or more acres are exempt from the subdivision review process. In Illinois, subdivisions of five or more acres are exempt from subdivision review. In Vermont, subdivisions of more than ten acres are exempt from Health Department subdivision regulations for perc tests and the siting and type of on-site septic system.

2. H. James Brown, Robin S. Phillips, and Neil A. Roberts, "Land Markets at the Urban Fringe," *Journal of the American Planning Association* 47, no. 1 (1981): 138.

3. Robert Healy and James L. Short, *The Market for Rural Land* (Washington, DC: Conservation Foundation, 1981), p. 2.

4. American Farmland Trust, *Alternatives for Future Urban Growth in California's Central Valley: The Bottom Line for Agriculture and Taxpayers* (Washington, DC: American Farmland Trust, 1995).

5. American Farmland Trust, *Farming on the Edge* (Washington, DC: American Farmland Trust, 1996).

6. For an in-depth discussion of farmland protection tools, see Tom Daniels and Deborah Bowers, *Holding Our Ground: Protecting America's Farms and Farmland* (Washington, DC: Island Press, 1997).

7. Quoted in "Farmland Protection Ruling Hailed," California Farm Bureau News Release, February 24, 1998.

8. Quoted in Melody Simmons, "Cluster Zoning Portends Rural Clash of Lifestyles," *Baltimore Sun,* February 11, 1997, p. 1B.

9. See, for example, the Illinois Livestock Management Facilities Act, chapter 510, paragraph 77/1 *et seq.,* 1996.

10. Daniels and Bowers, *Holding Our Ground,* p. 20.

11. For example, in Rhode Island, development rights were purchased on the 65-acre Panciera farm for $1 million in 1997 (*Providence Sunday Journal,* November 23, 1997, p. c-1). In the early 1990s, Montgomery County, Pennsylvania, just outside of Philadelphia, purchased development rights to two farms for $15,000 and $16,000 an acre. Neither farm is anywhere close to other farms. Elsewhere in Pennsylvania, Bucks County and Buckingham Township purchased development rights to a 240-acre farm for over $12,000 an acre in 1997.

12. The Montgomery County, Maryland, TDR program has withstood such a legal challenge in court. In 1997, the U.S. Supreme Court was asked to rule on Suitum v. Tahoe Regional Planning Agency (96-243) in which a landowner, Bernadine Suitum, claimed that the Tahoe Regional Planning Agency had "taken" her property by not allowing her to build on her land but instead gave her transferable development rights. Because Mrs. Suitum had not tried to sell the TDRs, the Supreme Court said that the case was not "ripe." To be on the safe side, a local government could allow a landowner the option of devel-

oping some land based on low-density zoning combined with TDRs. This, for example, is what Montgomery County, Maryland, has done.

13. Robert A. Johnston and Mary E. Madison, "From Landmarks to Landscapes: A Review of Current Practices in the Transfer of Development Rights," *Journal of the American Planning Association* 63, no. 3 (1997): 370.

14. Victor Davis Hanson, *Fields Without Dreams* (New York: Simon & Schuster, 1997), p. 95.

15. Andrew C. Revkin, "A Question of Green: Forests Versus Money," *New York Times,* November 17, 1997, p. B1.

16. Dylan Bennett, "Timber Wars," *Sonoma County* (California) *Independent,* November 13–19, 1997.

17. David A. Cromwell, "Strategies for Dealing with the Urban/Forest Interface: The Recent California Experience," in G.A. Bradley, ed., *Land Use and Forest Resources in a Changing Environment* (Seattle: Universiy of Washington Press, 1984), p. 158.

18. Remarks by Peter Hausmann to the Pennsylvania Farmland Preservation Association, Chambersburg, Pennsylvania, October 15, 1997.

19. Elizabeth Brabec, "On the Value of Open Spaces," *Scenic America Technical Bulletin* (Scenic America, Washington, D.C.) 1, no. 2 (1992).

20. Remarks at the American Planning Association Conference, San Diego, California, April 6, 1997.

21. Andrew C. Revkin, "Billion-Dollar Plan to Clean the City's Water at Its Source," *New York Times,* August 31, 1997, pp. 25, 27.

22. Revkin, "Billion-Dollar Plan," p. 25.

23. To give an idea of the danger of bacteria, in 1993 an outbreak of cryptosporidium in Milwaukee's drinking water made 400,000 people sick with cramps, vomiting, diarrhea, and fever.

Chapter 11

1. U.S. Bureau of the Census, *Statistical Abstract of the United States, 1996* (Washington, DC: U.S. Department of Commerce, 1996), p. 28.

2. Jeff Gersh, "Subdivide and Conquer," *E-Amicus* (Natural Resources Defense Council, Fall 1996): 2.

3. *Statistical Abstract of the United States, 1996,* p. 28.

4. This case study draws on data from Hy and Joan Rosner, *Albuquerque's Environmental Story: Toward a Sustainable Community,* 3rd edition (Albuquerque: Albuquerque Conservation Association, 1996). Also, the figure on tax base comes from David Rusk, *The Rusk Report: State Should Strengthen Planning,* newsletter, 1997.

5. Quoted in Jeff Kralowetz, "Rusk: Sprawl an Enemy of Prosperity," *York* (Pennsylvania) *Dispatch,* September 10, 1996, p. A5.

6. Quoted in Tom Hylton, *Save Our Lands, Save Our Towns* (Harrisburg, PA: Richly Beautiful Books, 1995), p. 117.

7. Jane Holtz Kay, *Asphalt Nation* (New York: Crown, 1997), p. 76.

8. David Rusk, *The Rusk Report: State Should Strengthen Planning,* 1997.

9. *Common Ground* (The Conservation Fund, November–December 1997): 6.

10. "To Support Growth, Albuquerque Will Shift Source for Water." *New*

York Times, May 25, 1997, p. 16. By contrast, Arizona now requires proof of a one-hundred-year water supply before it will approve a new development. Phoenix is expected to reach the limit of its present water supply within about ten years. See Timothy Egan, "Urban Sprawl Strains Western States," *New York Times,* December 29, 1996, p. 20.

11. *New York Times,* June 29, 1997, p. 20.

12. Michael E. Long, "Colorado's Front Range," *National Geographic* 190, no. 5 (November 1996): 87.

13. Tom Daniels and Deborah Bowers, *Holding Our Ground* (Washington, DC: Island Press, 1997), p. 1.

14. Larimer County Planning Division, "Partnership Land Use System—Issues and Options," Discussion Draft and Working Paper, Fort Collins, Colorado, April 1996, p. 5.

15. Janet Duvall, "Keeping the Good Life: Can We Protect Our Lifestyle in the Face of Growth and Change?" Larimer County Planning Division, Partnership Land Use System, Fort Collins, Colorado, 1996.

16. Larimer County Planning Division, "Partnership Land Use System," p. 3.

17. Larimer County Parks and Open Lands, *Open Lands Program, Annual Report 1996* (Fort Collins, CO: Larimer County Government, 1997).

18. Quoted in Kathleen McCormick, "Home, Home on the Ranchette," *Planning* 64, no. 2 (March 1998): 8.

19. John DeGrove, "Minnesota: The Key Ingredients," *Land Patterns* (White Bear Lake, MN: 1,000 Friends of Minnesota, Fall 1996), p. 2.

20. Pauline Schreiber, "Commissioners: Rural Areas Should Be Reserved for Farms," *Faribault* (Minnesota) *Daily News,* Profile '96, page 13G.

21. Ibid.

22. Pauline Schreiber, "Striking the Balance: Farms and Homes Vie for the Same Land," *Faribault* (Minnesota) *Daily News,* Profile '96, p. 10G.

23. Quoted in Kay, *Asphalt Nation,* p. 275.

24. Tim Palmer, *America by Rivers* (Washington, DC: Island Press, 1996), p. 21.

25. Chittenden County Regional Planning Commission, *Chittenden County Regional Plan,* Essex Junction, Vermont, 1991, p. 6.

26. John Herbers, *The New Heartland* (New York: Times Books, 1986), p. 49.

27. See Thomas L. Daniels and Mark B. Lapping, "Has Vermont's Land Use Control Program Failed?" *Journal of the American Planning Association* 50, no. 4: 502–507.

28. U.S. Department of Agriculture, *1992 Census of Agriculture* (Washington, DC: USDA, 1994).

29. Rachel Klein, "Development, Taxes, Debt Overwhelming, Farmers Say," *Burlington* (Vermont) *Free Press,* June 20, 1997, p. 1B

30. Matt Sutkoski, "Williston Mall Approval Ends 20-year Battle." *Burlington* (Vermont) *Free Press,* December 12, 1997, p. 1A.

31. Matt Sutkoski, "Williston: Vt.'s First Edge City?" *Burlington* (Vermont) *Free Press,* May 31, 1993, p. 1B.

32. "Here Come the Cannibals," *Burlington* (Vermont) *Free Press,* December 15, 1997, p. 4A.

33. Sutkoski, "Williston: Vt.'s First Edge City?" p. 4B.

34. Tamara Lush, "Williston's Population Booms," *Burlington* (Vermont) *Free Press,* December 8, 1997, p. 1A.

35. Shay Totten, "Bigger Boxes or Fewer Choices?" *Vermont Times,* October 22, 1997, p. 19.

36. Molly Walsh, "State Cool to Highway Bypasses," *Burlington Free Press,* September 10, 1997, p. A1.

37. "You Can't Buy Vermont Character at a Strip Mall." *Burlington* (Vermont) *Free Press,* May 8, 1997, p. 12A.

38. "Yield to Progress," *Vermont Times,* October 8, 1997, p. 8.

39. Josh Fitzhugh, "It's Time to Take Another Look at Counties," *Burlington* (Vermont) *Free Press,* January 12, 1997, p. A11.

40. Molly Walsh, "Postcard from the Edge," *Burlington* (Vermont) *Free Press,* August 24, 1997, p. 1E.

41. Greenbelt Alliance, "Sonoma County AT RISK Assessment," press release. San Francisco, April 10, 1995.

42. *Farmland Preservation Report* 6, no. 9 (July–August 1996): 2.

43. Quoted in *Farmland Preservation Report* 6, no. 9 (July–August 1996), p. 2.

44. Greenbelt Alliance, press release, San Francisco, October 8, 1997.

45. Quoted in Greg Cahill, "Voters Put Sprawl-Busting Measures to the Test," *Sonoma* (California) *Independent,* November 7–13, 1996.

Chapter 12

1. Frances Cairncross, *The Death of Distance: How the Communications Revolution Will Change Our Lives* (Boston: Harvard Business School Press, 1997).

2. Office of Technological Assessment, *The Technological Reshaping of Metropolitan America* (Washington, DC: U.S. Government Printing Office, 1995), p. 1.

3. Tom Hylton, *Save Our Land, Save Our Towns* (Harrisburg, PA: Richly Beautiful Books, 1995), p. 42.

4. U.S. Department of Commerce, Bureau of the Census. *Demographic State of the Nation* (Washington, DC: U.S. Government Printing Office, 1997).

5. Maricopa County, Arizona. *Agricultural White Paper: Farmland Preservation in Maricopa County: Political, Social and Economic Implications,* Phoenix, August 1996.

6. "The Music of the Metropolis: Britain's Cities Are Booming Thanks to a Reviving Economy and Changed Attitudes to Urban Living," *The Economist* (August 2, 1997): 44.

7. Jane Holtz Kay, *Asphalt Nation* (New York: Crown, 1997), p. 31.

8. Evan McKenzie, "Morning in Privatopia," *Dissent* (Spring 1989): 257.

9. World Commission on Environment and Development, quoted in *The Economist* (September 16, 1989): 77.

Bibliography

American Farmland Trust. *Dutchess County: Cost of Community Services Study*. Washington, DC: American Farmland Trust, 1989.

———. *Does Farmland Protection Pay: The Cost of Community Services in Three Massachusetts Towns*. Washington, DC: 1992.

———. *Is Farmland Protection a Community Investment? How to Do a Cost of Community Services Study*. Washington, DC: American Farmland Trust, 1993.

———. *Farming on the Edge*. Washington, DC: American Farmland Trust, 1996.

———. *Alternatives for Future Urban Growth in California's Central Valley: The Bottom Line for Agriculture and Taxpayers*. Washington, DC: 1995.

American Farmland Trust and Lake County, Ohio, Soil and Water Conservation District. *The Cost of Community Services in Madison Village and Township, Lake County, Ohio*. Washington, DC: American Farmland Trust, 1993.

Arendt, Randall. *Rural by Design*. Chicago: Planners Press, 1994.

Barlow, Raleigh. *Land Resource Economics*, third edition. Englewood Cliffs, NJ: Prentice-Hall, 1978.

Barnett, Jonathan. *The Fractured Metropolis: Improving the New City, Restoring the Old City, Reshaping the Region*. New York: HarperCollins, 1995.

Beaumont, Constance E. *How Superstore Sprawl Can Harm Communities and What Citizens Can Do About It*. Washington, DC: National Trust for Historic Preservation, 1994.

———. *Smart States, Better Communities*. Washington, DC: National Trust for Historic Preservation, 1996.

Bernick, Michael, and Robert Cervero. *Transit Villages in the 21st Century*. New York: McGraw-Hill, 1996.

Blakely, Edward J., and Mary Gail Snyder. *Fortress America: Gated Communities in the United States*. Washington, DC: Brookings Institution Press/Lincoln Institute, 1997.

Bowers, Deborah. *Farmland Preservation Report*. Street, MD: Bowers Publishing, 1996–1998.

Brower, David J., Candace Carraway, Thomas Pollard, and C. Luther Propst. *Managing Development in Small Towns*. Chicago: Planners Press, 1984.

Brown, H. James, Robin S. Phillips, and Neil A. Roberts. "Land Markets at the Urban Fringe." *Journal of the American Planning Association* 47, no. 1, pp. 131–145.

Burchell, Robert W., and David Listokin. *Land, Infrastructure, Housing Costs, and Fiscal Impacts Associated with Growth*. Cambridge, MA: Lincoln Institute of Land Policy, 1995.

Calthorpe, Peter. *The Next American Metropolis: Ecology, Community, and the American Dream*. New York: Simon & Schuster, 1993.

Clawson, Marion. *Suburban Land Conversion in the United States: An Economic and Governmental Process*. Baltimore: Johns Hopkins University Press (for Resources for the Future, Washington, DC), 1971.

Corser, Susan Ernst. *Preserving Rural Character Through Cluster Development*. Chicago: American Planning Association, Planners Advisory Service Memo, July 1994.

Cromartie, John, and Linda Swanson. *Defining Metropolitan Areas and the Rural-Urban Continuum*, Economic Research Service Report No. 9603. Washington, DC: U.S. Department of Agriculture, 1996.

Daniels, Thomas L. "Hobby Farming in America: Rural Development or Threat to Commercial Agriculture." *Journal of Rural Studies*. 2, no. 1 (1986): 31–40.

———. "Do Tax Breaks on Farmland Help Protect It from Conversion?" *Farmland Preservation Report*, Special Report, January 1991.

———. "The Purchase of Development Rights: Preserving Agricultural Land and Open Space." *Journal of the American Planning Association*. 57, no. 4 (1991): 421–431.

———. "Agricultural Zoning: Managing growth, Protecting Farms." *Zoning News*. Chicago: American Planning Association, August 1993.

———. "Where Does Cluster Zoning Fit in Farmland Protection?" *Journal of the American Planning Association* 63, no. 1 (1997): 129–137.

Daniels, Thomas L., John W. Keller, and Mark B. Lapping. *The Small Town Planning Handbook*, 2nd edition. Chicago: Planners Press, 1995.

Daniels, Thomas L., and Mark B. Lapping. "The Two Rural America Need More, Not Less Planning." *Journal of the American Planning Association* 62, no. 3 (1996): 285–288.

Daniels, Tom, and Deborah Bowers. *Holding Our Ground: Protecting America's Farms and Farmland*. Washington, DC: Island Press, 1997.

Diamond, Henry L., and Patrick F. Noonan, eds. *Land Use in America*. Washington, DC: Island Press, 1996.

Dillon, David. "Fortress America." *Planning* 60, no. 6: (1994) 8–12, (1994).

Doherty, Joseph C. "The Countrified City." *American Demographics* 2, no. 4: (1984) 7–8.

———. *Growth Management in Countrified Cities*. Alexandria, VA: Vert Milon Press, 1984.

Easley, V. Gail. *Staying Inside the Lines: Urban Growth Boundaries*, Planners Advisory Service Report No. 440. Chicago: American Planning Association, 1992.

Endicott, Eve, ed. *Land Conservation through Public-Private Partnerships*. Washington, DC: Island Press, 1994.

Etzioni, Amitai. *The Spirit of Community: Rights, Responsibilities, and Communitarian Agenda*. New York: Crown Publishers, 1993.

Fishman, Robert. *Bourgeois Utopias: The Rise and Fall of Suburbia*. New York: Basic Books, 1987.

Fulton, William. *The Reluctant Metropolis: The Politics of Urban Growth in Los Angeles*. Point Arena, CA: Solano Press Books, 1997.

Garreau, Joel. *Edge City: Life on the New Frontier*. New York: Doubleday, 1991.

Gottsegen, Amanda Jones. *Planning for Transfer of Development Rights: A Handbook for New Jersey Municipalities*. Mount Holly, NJ: Burlington County Board of Chosen Freeholders, 1992.

Healy, Robert, and James L. Short. *The Market for Rural Land*. Washington, DC: The Conservation Foundation, 1981.

Heenan, David A. *The New Corporate Frontier: The Big Move to Small Town, USA*. New York: McGraw-Hill, 1991.

Heimlich, Ralph E. "Metropolitan Agriculture: Farming in the City's Shadow." *Journal of the American Planning Association* 55, no. 4 (1989): 457–466.

———. *The New Heartland: America's Flight Beyond the Suburbs and How It Is Changing Our Future*. New York: Times Books, 1986.

Herbers, John. "Take Me Home, Country Road." *Planning* (November 1987).

Hiss, Tony. *The Experience of Place*. New York: Knopf, 1990.

Hylton, Thomas. *Save Our Land, Save Our Towns*. Harrisburg, PA: Richly Beautiful Books, 1995.

Jackson, Kenneth. *The Crabgrass Frontier: A History of Suburbanization in the United States*. New York: Columbia University Press, 1985.

Jacobs, Jane. *Cities and the Wealth of Nations*. New York: Vintage Books, 1987.

Johnston, Robert A., and Mary E. Madison. "From Landmarks to Landscapes: A Review of Current Practices in the Transfer of Development Rights." *Journal of the American Planning Association* 63, no. 3 (1997): 365–378.

Katz, Peter. *The New Urbanism: Toward an Architecture of Community*. New York: McGraw-Hill, 1994.

Kay, Jane Holtz. *Asphalt Nation: How the Automobile Took Over America, and How We Can Take It Back*. New York: Crown Publishers, 1997.

Kowinski, William Severini. *The Malling of America: An Inside Look at the Great Consumer Paradise*. New York: William Morrow, 1985.

Kunstler, James Howard. *The Geography of Nowhere: The Rise and Decline of America's Man-Made Landscape*. New York: Simon & Schuster, 1993.

———. *Home from Nowhere: Remaking Our Everyday World for the Twenty-first Century*. New York: Simon & Schuster, 1996.

Langdon, Philip. *A Better Place to Live: Reshaping the American Suburb*. Amherst: University of Massachusetts Press, 1994.

Lapping, Mark B., Thomas L. Daniels, and John W. Keller. *Rural Planning and Development in the United States*. New York: Guilford Publications, 1989.

Lapping, Mark B., George E. Penfold, and Susan Macpherson. "Right-to-Farm Laws: Do They Resolve Land Use Conflicts?" *Journal of Soil and Water Conservation* 26, no. 6 (1983): 465–467.

Le Courbusier. *The City of Tomorrow and Its Planning*. New York: Dover, 1987.

Leinberger, Christopher B., and Charles Lockwood. "How Business Is Reshaping America." *Atlantic Monthly* (October 1986).

Lewis, Peirce F. "The Galactic Metropolis." In *Beyond the Urban Fringe*, edited by Rutherford H. Platt and George Macinko. Minneapolis: University of Minnesota Press, 1983.

Lewis, Tom. *Divided Highways: Building the Interstate Highways, Transforming American Life*. New York: Viking, 1997.

Little, Charles. *Greenways for America*. Baltimore: Johns Hopkins University Press, 1990.

Lockeretz, William, ed. *Sustaining Agriculture Near Cities*. Ankeny, IA: Soil and Water Conservation Society, 1987.

Louv, Richard. *America II*. New York: Viking/Penguin, 1983.

Luccarelli, Mark. *Lewis Mumford and the Ecological Region*. New York: Guilford Press, 1995.

Moe, Richard, and Carter Wilkie. *Changing Places: Rebuilding Community in the Age of Sprawl*. New York: Henry Holt, 1997.

New Jersey Conservation Foundation, *Farmland Forum* Morristown, NJ: New Jersey Conservation Foundation, 1990–1996.

Orfield, Myron. *Metropolitics*. Washington, DC: The Brookings Institution and Lincoln Institute for Land Policy, 1997.

Palmer, Tim. *America by Rivers*. Washington, DC: Island Press, 1996.

Peirce, Neal R. *Citistates: How Urban America Can Prosper in a Competitive World*. Washington, DC: Seven Locks Press, 1993.

Platt, Rutherford H. *Land Use and Society: Geography, Law, and Public Policy*. Washington, DC: Island Press, 1996.

Pindell, Terry. *A Good Place to Live*. New York: Henry Holt, 1996.

Porter, Douglas R. *Managing Growth in America's Communities*. Washington, DC: Island Press, 1997.

Real Estate Research Corporation. *The Cost of Sprawl: Environmental and Economic Costs of Alternative Development Patterns at the Urban Fringe*. Washington, DC: U.S. Government Printing Office, 1974.

Rusk, David. *Cities Without Suburbs*. Washington, DC: The Woodrow Wilson Center Press, 1993.

———. *Baltimore Unbound: A Strategy for Regional Renewal*. Baltimore: The Abell Foundation, 1996.

Schiffman, Irving. *Alternative Techniques for Managing Growth*. Berkeley: Institute of Governmental Studies, University of California, 1989.

Spectorsky, Auguste C. *The Exurbanites*. Philadelphia: J.B. Liipincott, 1955.

Stilgoe, John. *Borderland: Origins of the American Suburb, 1820–1939*. New Haven: Yale University Press, 1988.

Stokes, Samuel, A. Elizabeth Watson, Timothy Keller, and Genevieve Keller. *Saving America's Countryside*. Baltimore: Johns Hopkins University Press, 1989.

Sutro, Suzanne. *Reinventing the Village*, Planners Advisory Service Report No. 430. Chicago: American Planning Association, 1990.

Urban Land Institute. *The Costs of Alternative Development Patterns: A Review of the Literature*. Washington, DC: Urban Land Institute, 1992.

U.S. Department of Commerce, Bureau of the Census. *1992 Census of Agriculture*. Washington, DC: U.S. Government Printing Office, 1994.

———. *Statistical Abstract of the United States, 1995*. Washington, DC: U.S. Government Printing Office, 1996.

U.S. Department of Commerce, Bureau of the Census. *Demographuc State of the Nation*. Washington, DC: U.S. Government Printing Office, 1997.

U.S. House of Representatives, Committee on Banking, Finance and Urban Affairs, Subcommittee on the City. *Compact Cities: Energy Saving Strategies for the Eighties*. Washington, DC: U.S. Government Printing Office, 1980.

Vaughan, Gerald F. *Land Use Planning in the Rural-Urban Fringe*, Extension Bulletin No. 157.Newark: University of Delaware Press, 1994.

Warner, Sam Bass, Jr. *Streetcar Suburbs: The Process of Growth in Boston, 1870–1900*. Cambridge, MA: Harvard University Press, 1962.

Whyte, William H. *The Last Landscape*. Garden City, NY: Doubleday, 1968.

Wolf, Peter M. *Land in America: Its Value, Use, and Control*. New York: Pantheon Books, 1981.

Wright, Frank Lloyd. *The Living City*. New York: Horizon Press, 1958.

Yaro, Robert D., Randall G. Arendt, Harry L. Dodson, and Elizabeth A. Brabec. *Dealing with Change in the Connecticut River Valley: A Design Manual for Conservation and Development*. Amherst: University of Massachusetts Center for Rural Massachusetts, 1988.

Yaro, Robert D., and Tony Hiss. *A Region at Risk: The Third Regional Plan for the New York–New Jersey–Connecticut Metropolitan Area*. Washington, DC: Island Press, 1996.

About the Author

Tom Daniels is professor of planning in the Department of Geography and Planning at the State University of New York at Albany. He was formerly the director of the Agricultural Preserve Board of Lancaster, Pennsylvania, where he managed a nationally recognized farmland preservation program. He holds a Ph.D. in agricultural economics and has taught rural and small town planning at Iowa State and Kansas State universities. He is a coauthor of *The Small Town Planning Handbook* (Chicago: Planners Press) and *Holding Our Ground: Protecting America's Farms and Farmland* (Washington, DC: Island Press).

Index

Island Press Board of Directors